HAL LEONARD UKULELE METHOD BOOK 1 PLUS CHORD FINDER

BY LIL' REV & CHAD JOHNSON

To access audio visit:
www.halleonard.com/mylibrary

Enter Code
1949-5506-4242-4957

ISBN 978-1-61780-457-1

7777 W. BLUEMOUND RD. P.O. BOX 13819 MILWAUKEE, WI 53213

In Australia Contact:
Hal Leonard Australia Pty. Ltd.
4 Lentara Court
Cheltenham, Victoria, 3192 Australia
Email: ausadmin@halleonard.com.au

Visit Hal Leonard Online at
www.halleonard.com

CONTENTS

PAGE

CHORD FINDER

INTRODUCTION TO THE UKULELE METHOD

Welcome to the Hal Leonard *Ukulele Method.* This method has been designed to help you accomplish your goal of becoming a proficient ukulele player. While there are many styles and techniques to learn from, this book will focus on individual note or melody playing.

Once you begin, you will find that the ukulele is a magical little instrument that always seems to attract a smile. It really has the power to make people happy. Whether it is the novelty of its size or its infectious rhythmic nature, you can expect that your endeavors to play the uke will result in a lot of toe-tapping, finger-snapping, hand-clapping, and plain old-fashioned singing along.

Over time, you will also find that the ukulele's potential extends far beyond the parameters of simple strumming to include fingerpicking, solo, lead and chord-melody playing, intricate strums, rolls, tremolo, slides, and a whole slew of rhythmic and novelty effects.

Practice may not always make perfect, but it sure helps to keep ya moving along. While it is important to work hard, please remember that music should first of all be fun! You don't have to practice for ten hours a day in order to improve. Rather, strive for more consistent practice over shorter periods of time. With diligence, soon you will master important techniques and concepts.

Good luck and happy strumming!

—Lil' Rev

Special Thanks to Jennifer Rupp, Will Branch, and Dennis Felber for technical assistance.

ABOUT THE AUTHOR

Lil' Rev is a Milwaukee, Wisconsin-based award-winning multi-instrumentalist, writer, and music historian. He tours the U.S. teaching and performing original and traditional folk, blues, ethnic, and old-time music.

To learn more about Lil' Rev's schedule, recordings, or programs, visit *www.lilrev.com*

ABOUT THE AUDIO

The audio accompanying this book contains recordings of select exercises and tunes within the lessons. Wherever you see an audio icon (🔊), play the corresponding track number. Your goal should be to learn the piece well enough to play along with the recorded uke. Many examples have both chords and melodies written out, so you can play one part while the recorded uke plays the other.

Recorded at Velvet Sky, Milwaukee, WI

Engineered by Scott Finch

Performed by Lil' Rev

A BRIEF HISTORY OF THE UKULELE

Most ukulele historians agree that the birth of the ukulele began in 1879, when Portuguese agricultural workers arrived in Honolulu aboard the English ship *Ravenscrag*. Many of these workers—like Augusto Dias, Manuel Nunes, Joao Fernandes, Joao Luiz Correa, and Jose do Espirito Santo—brought with them a remarkable ability to play the machete (a small guitar-like instrument with four cat-gut strings, the precursor to the uke). In turn, these workers also shared an intense passion for working with wood, and thus began a rich tradition of ukulele craftsmanship on the islands.

The year 1915 brought with it the Pan-Pacific International Exposition held in San Francisco. Here, the Hawaiian contingent and their beloved ukulele helped to spark its popular appeal amongst players and consumers alike. What followed were Hawaiian-themed songs and musicians, a sheet-music industry that regularly printed ukulele chord symbols on its music, uke-strumming Vaudeville entertainers, and mainland manufacturing companies like Martin, Gibson, Harmony, Lyon & Healy, and Epiphone all working overtime to meet the demand for quality ukes.

Some of the greatest players to emerge from this early era included Cliff Edwards (Ukulele Ike), Wendell Hall (The Red-Headed Uke Player), Johnny Marvin (Honey Duke), Roy Smeck, Frank Crumit, King Bennie Nawahi, Ukulele Bailey, and George Formby (in the UK).

While the depression years of the 1930s and the war years of the forties may have brought a temporary lapse of interest, uke hysteria began anew in the 1950s with the appearance of baritone uke player Arthur Godfrey, whose numerous television and radio appearances helped to put the ukulele back in the limelight. In the next decade, Tiny Tim's 1968 novelty cover of the Nick Lucas tune "Tiptoe Through the Tulips" made quite a splash, and it's safe to say it is still the best-known uke song amongst non-players in the U.S.

Today's ukulele revival is experiencing a groundswell of interest amongst both the young and old, while drawing from traditional and eclectic sources. There is a vitality to the current crop of professional players, all of whom treat the uke with a lot of historic respect while continuing to push the envelope in many new directions. We are just as likely to hear Canadian virtuoso James Hill play his incredible rendition of the "Super Mario Brothers" theme as we are to hear the young Hawaiian star Jake Shimabukuro play Paul Simon's "Mrs. Robinson," or for that matter, ukulele guru Jumpin' Jim Beloff croon the classic "Bye Bye Blackbird."

So ya see, once you learn the basics of picking and strumming, the sky is the limit... for the history is still being written!

Courtesy of David Garrick

Cliff Edwards: the Golden Voice of the 1920s and '30s.

From BBC Picture Archives/Redferns

George Formby: the Uke Star of the U.K.

Photo by Dick Barnatt/Redferns

Tiny Tim: broke into pop culture with his novelty cover of the Nick Lucas tune "Tip Toe Through the Tulips."

YOUR UKULELE

This book is designed for use with any type of soprano, concert, or tenor ukulele—whether they are wood-bodied, banjo-ukulele, or resonator-style ukuleles. You may use any of these models to study the music in this manual.

Wood-Bodied Ukulele

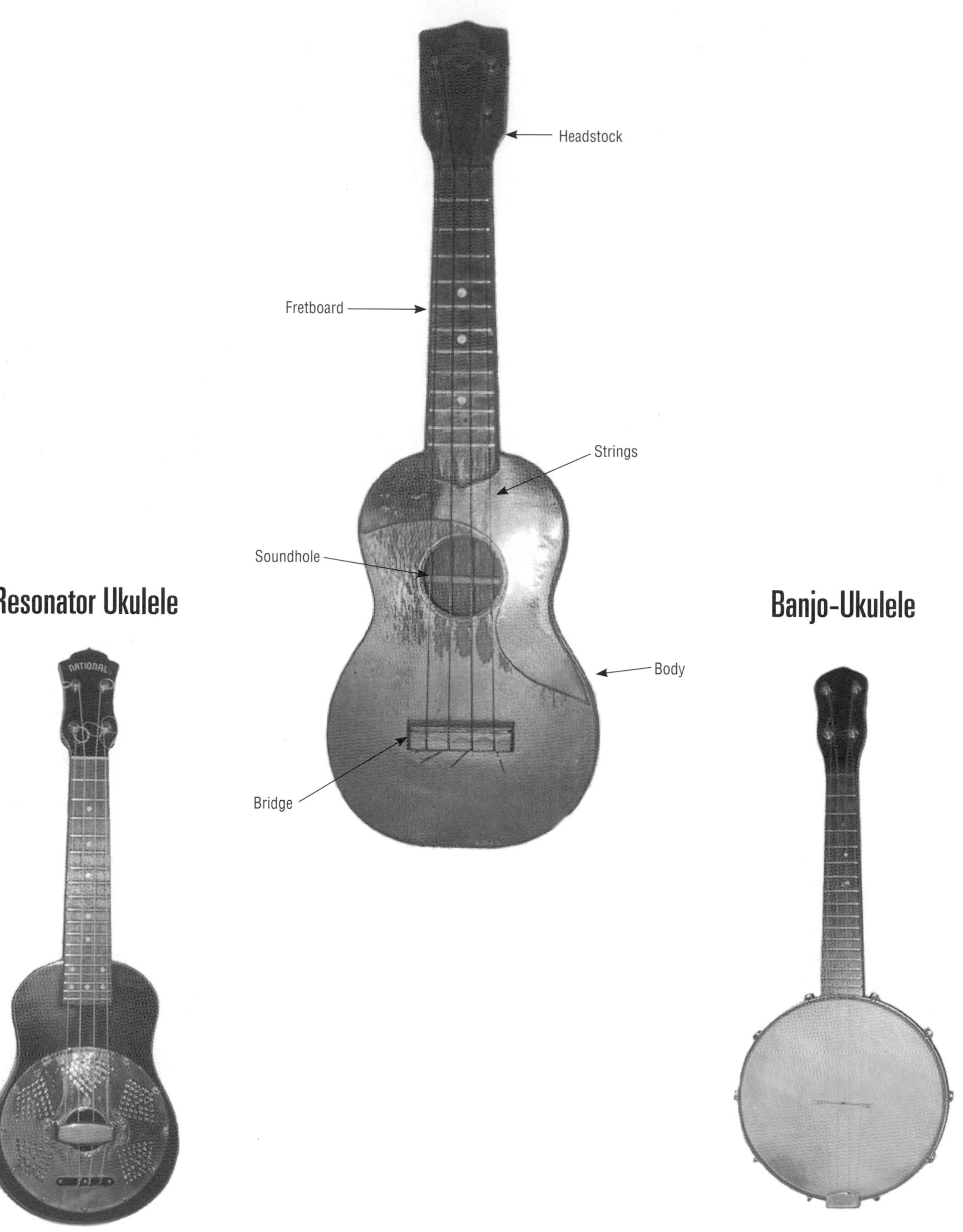

Resonator Ukulele

Banjo-Ukulele

PLAYING POSITION

There are many ways to hold your ukulele comfortably. Typically, you will be seated, but you may find it necessary to stand on occasion. See what works best for you.

The seated position allows you to rest the uke on your right leg. Or, apply a small amount of pressure with your right forearm to press the uke up against your right side rib cage.

The standing position takes a little more getting used to. You must apply a little more pressure with your right forearm to keep the uke in place.

Some folks like to use a strap to hold their uke in place.

THE RIGHT HAND

Once you are comfortable holding the uke, you will need to become familiar with the proper hand, thumb, and finger positions so that you will be able to pick and strum properly.

Hand

Hold your hand just slightly above the sound hole with your fingers extended over the fretboard.

Thumb

Place your thumb over the lower end of the fretboard for a gentle brush.

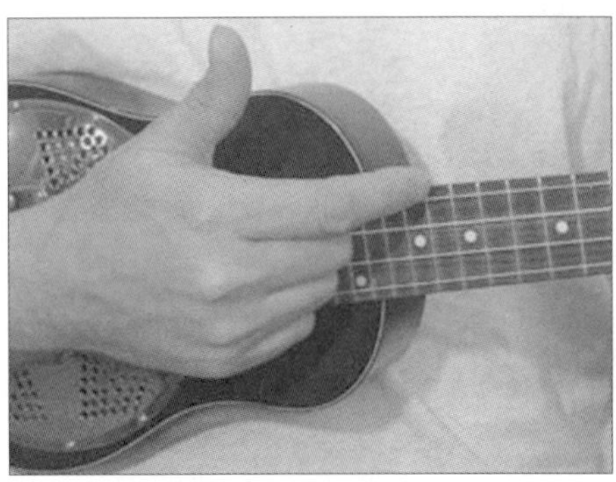

Finger

Slightly curl your right pointer finger inward and place it just above the tenth fret (you'll learn more about fret numbers soon).

TUNING

When you tune your ukulele, you will adjust the **pitch** (highness or lowness) of each individual string. When you tighten a string you will raise the pitch. When you loosen a string you will lower the pitch.

TUNING TO THE AUDIO

The strings on your uke are numbered 1 through 4, with string 4 being the one closest to your chest. This book uses the standard C tuning (the most common ukulele tuning), so your uke would be tuned as follows:

TRACK 1

Pitch:	G	C	E	A
String:	4	3	2	1

Listen to the correct pitch given on the audio track #1 and gently turn the tuning key until the sound of each string matches the sound on the audio.

TUNING WITH AN ELECTRONIC TUNER

An electronic tuner will "hear" whether or not your strings are in tune, allowing you to adjust them to the correct pitch. While I advocate learning how to tune by ear (being able to recognize and match the sound of a pitch without the help of a machine), an electronic tuner can be real handy when you are just starting out and have not yet developed the ability to recognize in-tune pitches. A tuner's accuracy and efficiency make it a useful tool.

TUNING BY EAR

Tune the G string (string 4) to a reliable source like a piano, tuning fork, or pitch pipe. Then tune the other strings to the following notes to create this musical phrase (as heard on track 1):

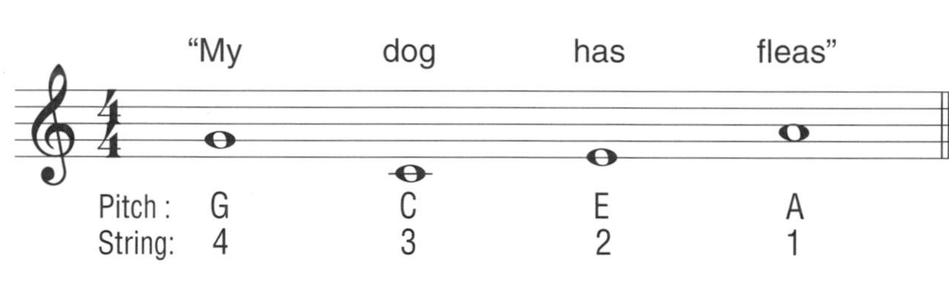

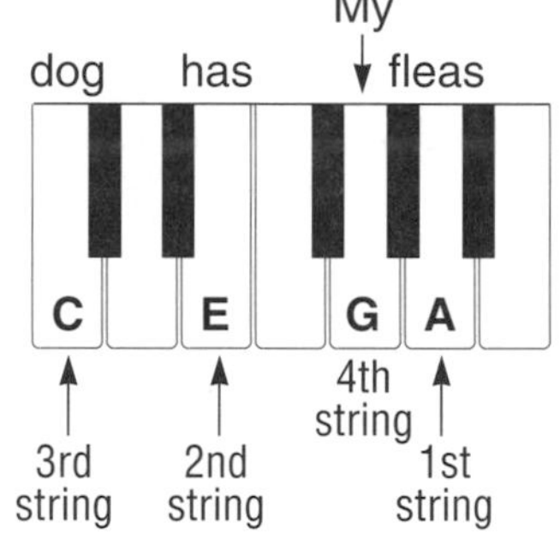

RELATIVE TUNING

Often, you may have to tune your instrument to itself when there is no other source available. To do this, follow these steps:

1. Assume the third string is tuned correctly to C.
2. Press down on the third string behind the fourth fret (E) and tune the second string until they sound alike.
3. Press down on the second string at the fifth fret (A) and tune the open first string to it.
4. Finally, press down on the second string above the third fret (G) and tune the fourth string to it.

When all of the strings are in tune, they will sound out the familiar musical phrase:

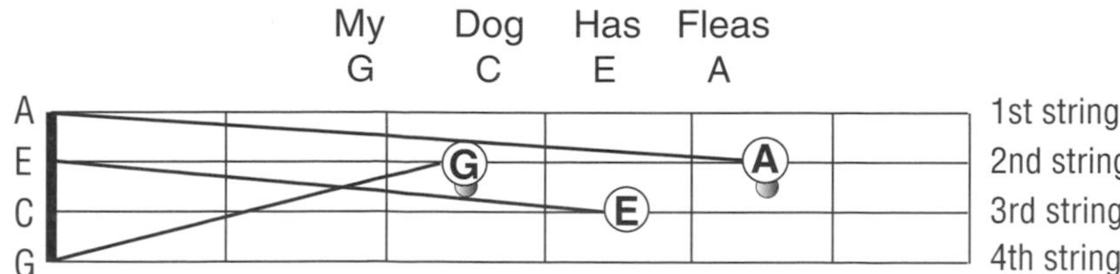

MUSICAL SYMBOLS

Music is written with notes on a **staff**. The staff has five lines and four spaces between the lines. Where a note is written on the staff determines its pitch (highness or lowness). At the beginning of the staff is a clef sign. Ukulele music is written in the treble clef.

Each line and space of the staff has a letter name. The **lines** are (from bottom to top) E–G–B–D–F, which you can remember as "Every Good Boy Does Fine." The **spaces** are (from bottom to top) F–A–C–E, which spells "face.

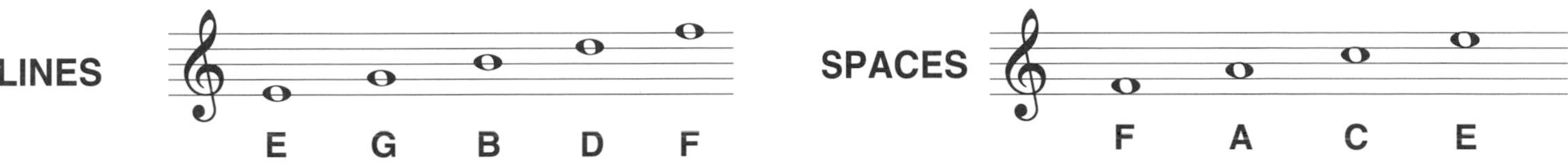

"The staff is divided into several parts by bar lines. The space between two bar lines is called a **measure** (also known as a "bar"). At the end of a piece of music a double bar is placed on the staff.

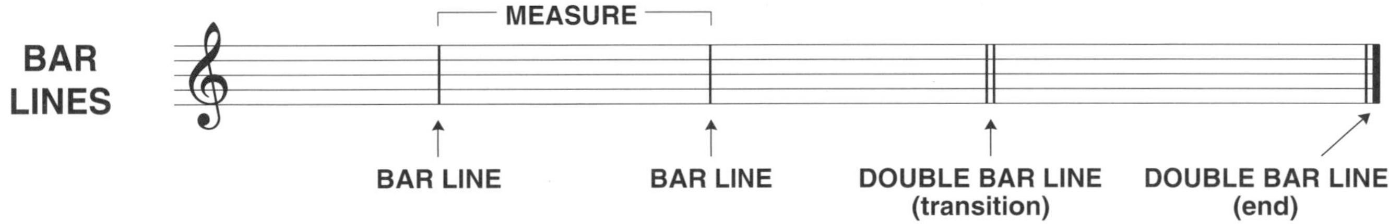

Each measure contains a group of **beats**. Beats are the steady pulse of music. You respond to the pulse or beat when you tap your foot.

The two numbers placed next to the clef sign are the **time signature**. The top number tells you how many beats are in one measure.

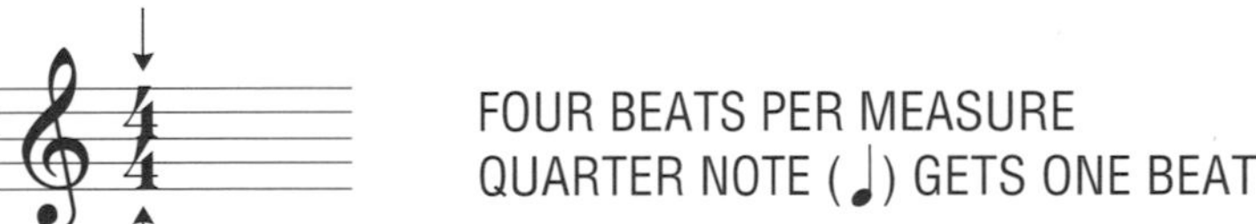

The bottom number of the time signature tells you what kind of note will receive one beat.

Notes indicate the length (number of counts) of a musical sound.

When different kinds of notes are placed on different lines or spaces, you will know the pitch of the note and how long to play the sound.

NOTES ON THE C STRING

We begin learning notes on the C string, or third string, because in C tuning, the fourth (G) string is usually not fingered except when making chords. However, many players (like Hawaii's legendary Ohta San) tune the G string low so that it can be used for melody playing.

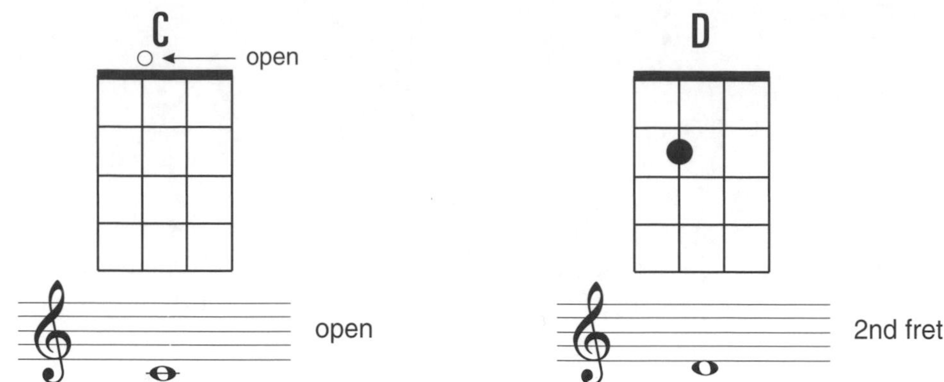

Play these whole notes using your thumb, and count "1–2–3–4."

Now try playing C and D using half notes. Count "1–2–3–4."

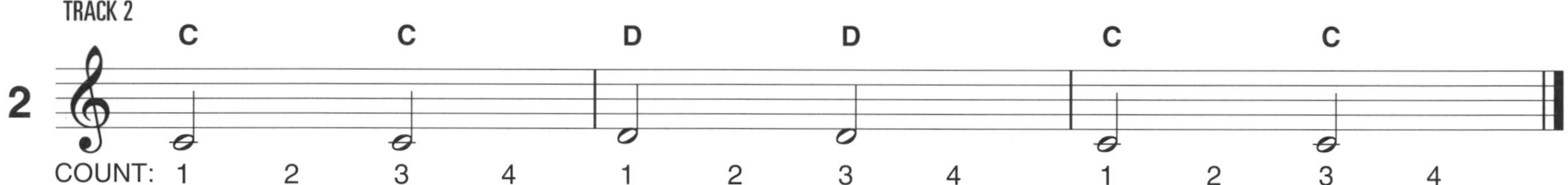

In **tablature** (or tab) notation, the horizontal lines represent strings. The numbers indicate which fret to play (0 = open). You'll always see the tab staff under the main staff.

Keep using your thumb, and count "1–2–3–4" while playing these quarter notes.

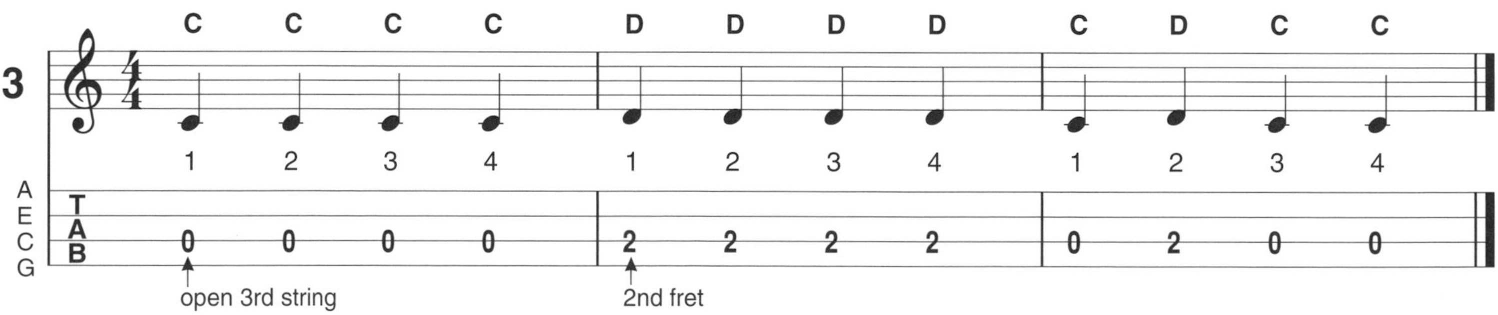

Let's mix it up a little more now!

NOTES ON THE E STRING

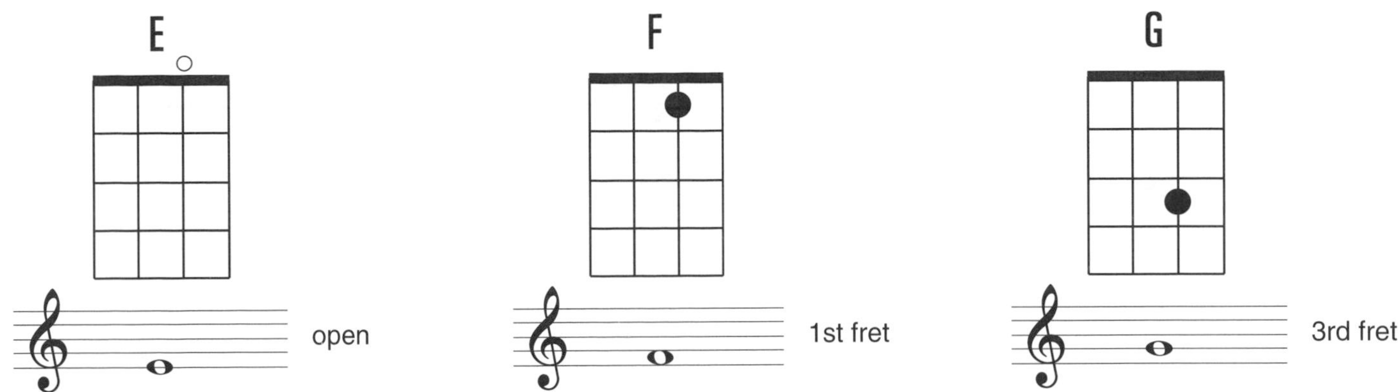

Count "1–2–3–4" as you did on the last exercise.

Each time you repeat these exercises, try picking up the speed without sacrificing accuracy.

Now let's mix it up again.

C AND E STRING REVIEW

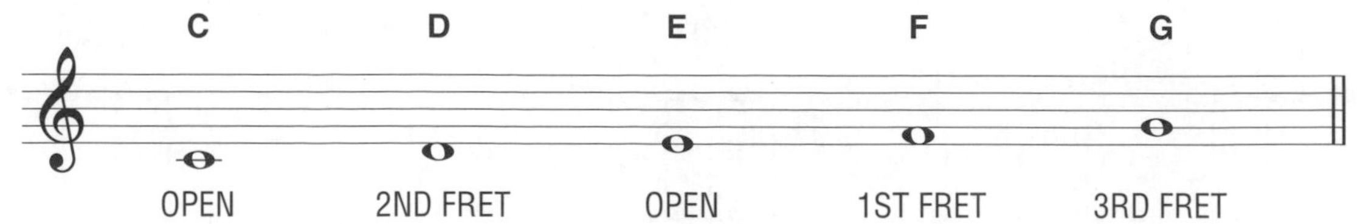

FRÉRE JACQUES
(Are You Sleeping?)

Children's Melody

8

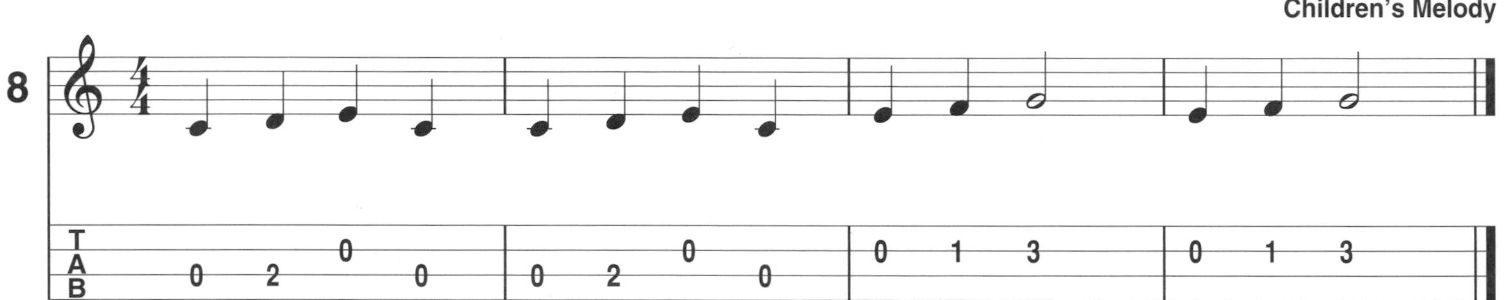

MARY HAD A LITTLE LAMB

TRACK 5

9

This American folk melody, like "Skip to My Lou," "Old Dan Tucker," and so many other "play party" tunes, has become an enduring classic. Just for fun, I have added a schnazzy little ending.

Gray chord symbols are used throughout this book to indicate the chords that back up your melody—they can be played by an instructor or another uke player.

GO TELL AUNT RHODY

TRACK 6

American Folk Song

10

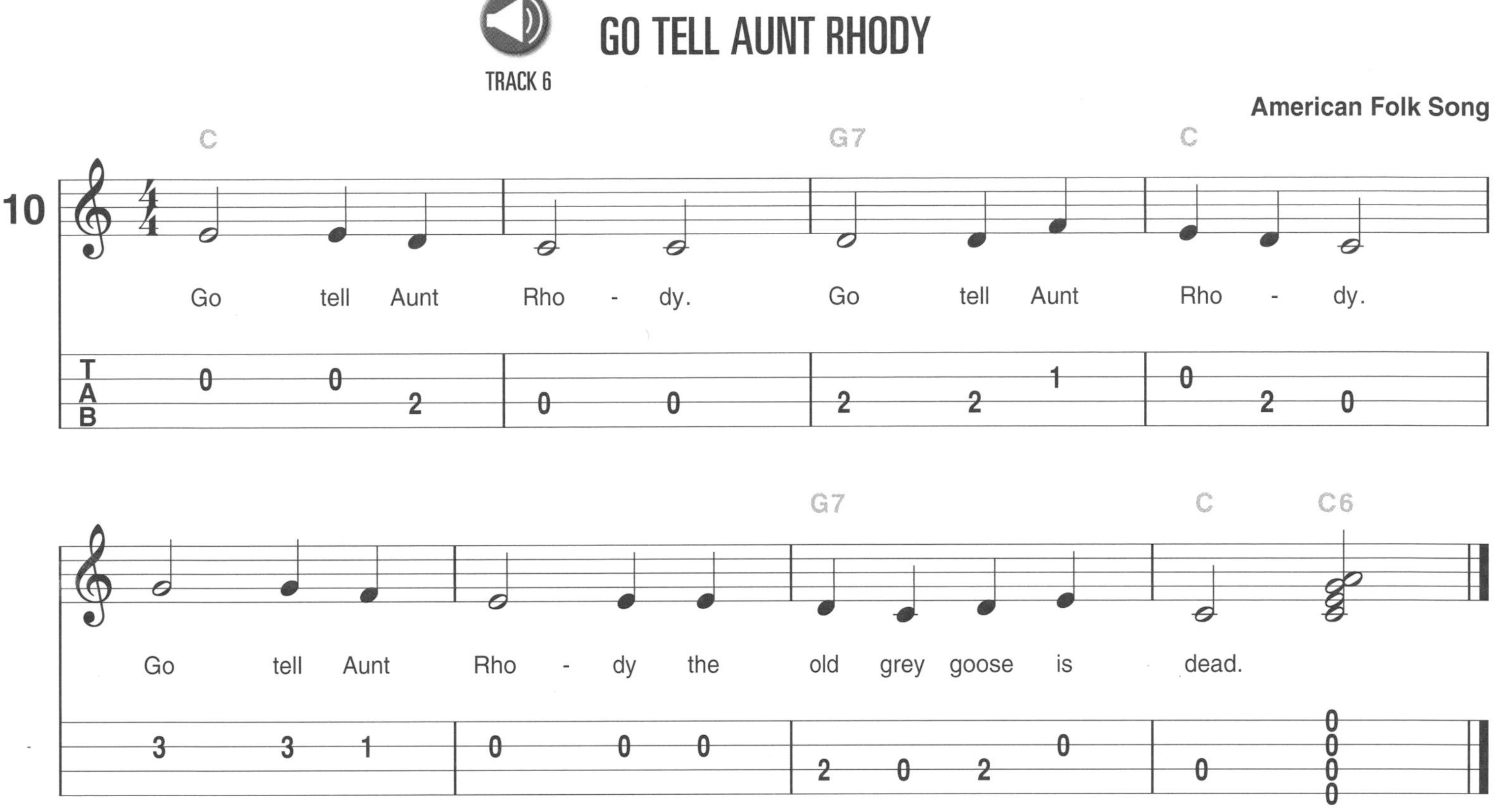

This classical uke arrangement will help you get familiar with many of the notes you've just learned while switching back and forth between the C and E strings.

ODE TO JOY

TRACK 7

Beethoven

11

NOTES ON THE A STRING

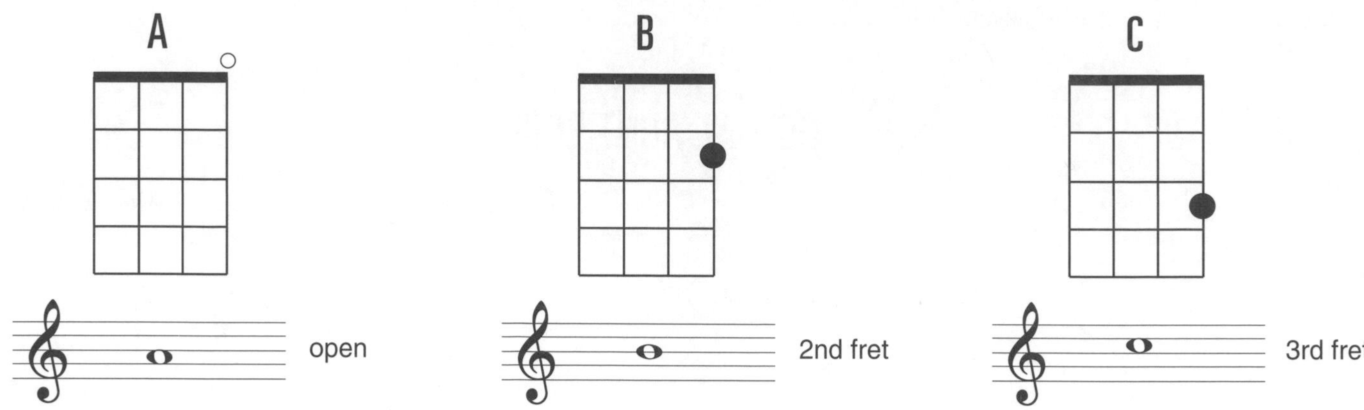

Count "1–2–3–4" as you did in the previous exercises.

TRACK 8

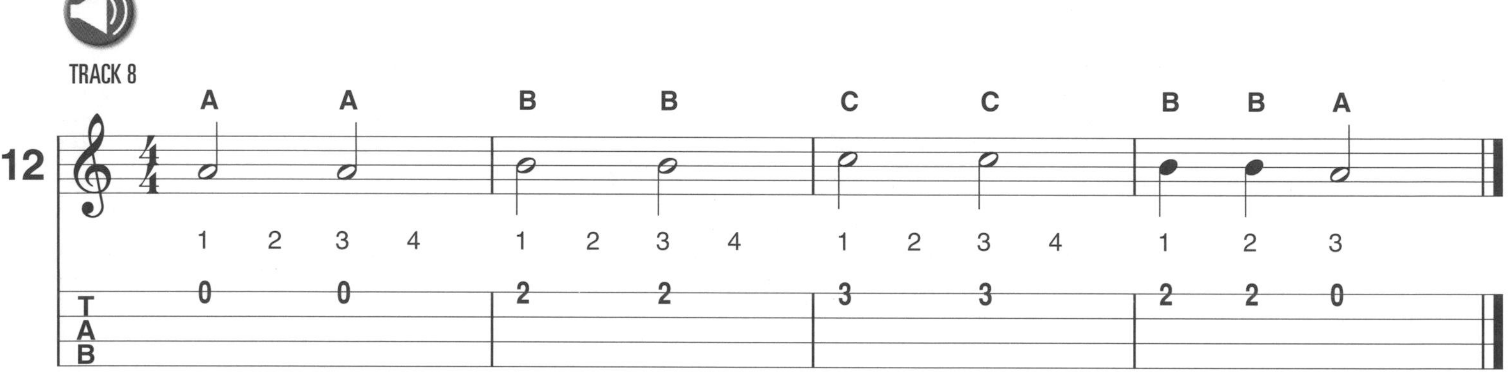

Try saying each note aloud as you play it.

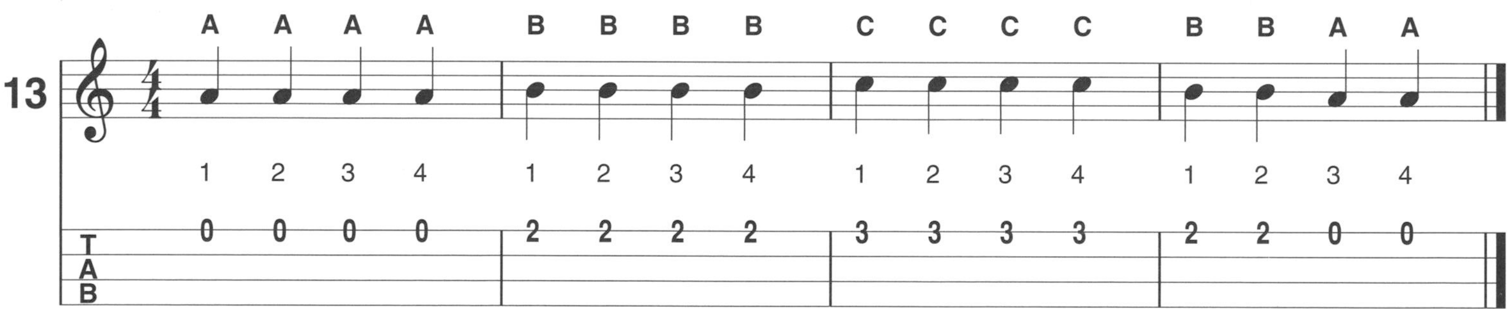

Now let's mix it up again.

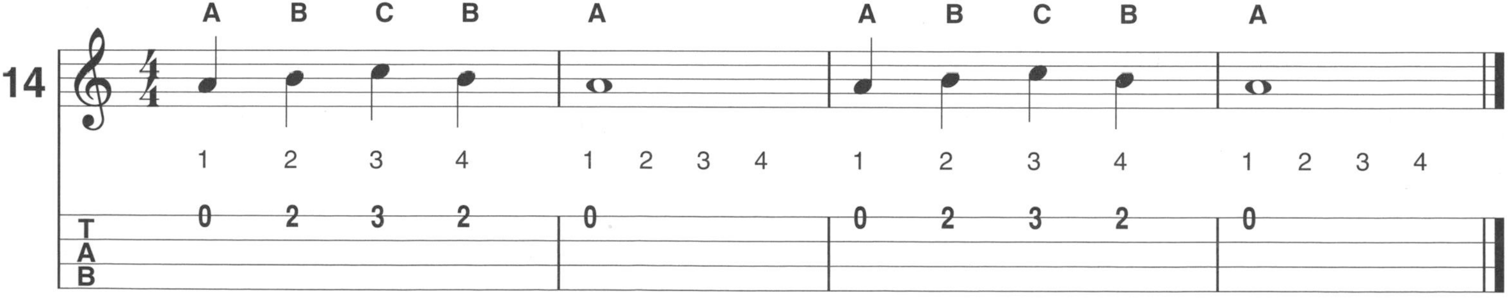

Now let's play a basic melody everyone knows using the notes we've learned on the C, E, and A strings. Observe the quarter notes and half notes, and play with your thumb.

TRACK 9

TWINKLE, TWINKLE LITTLE STAR

Children's Melody

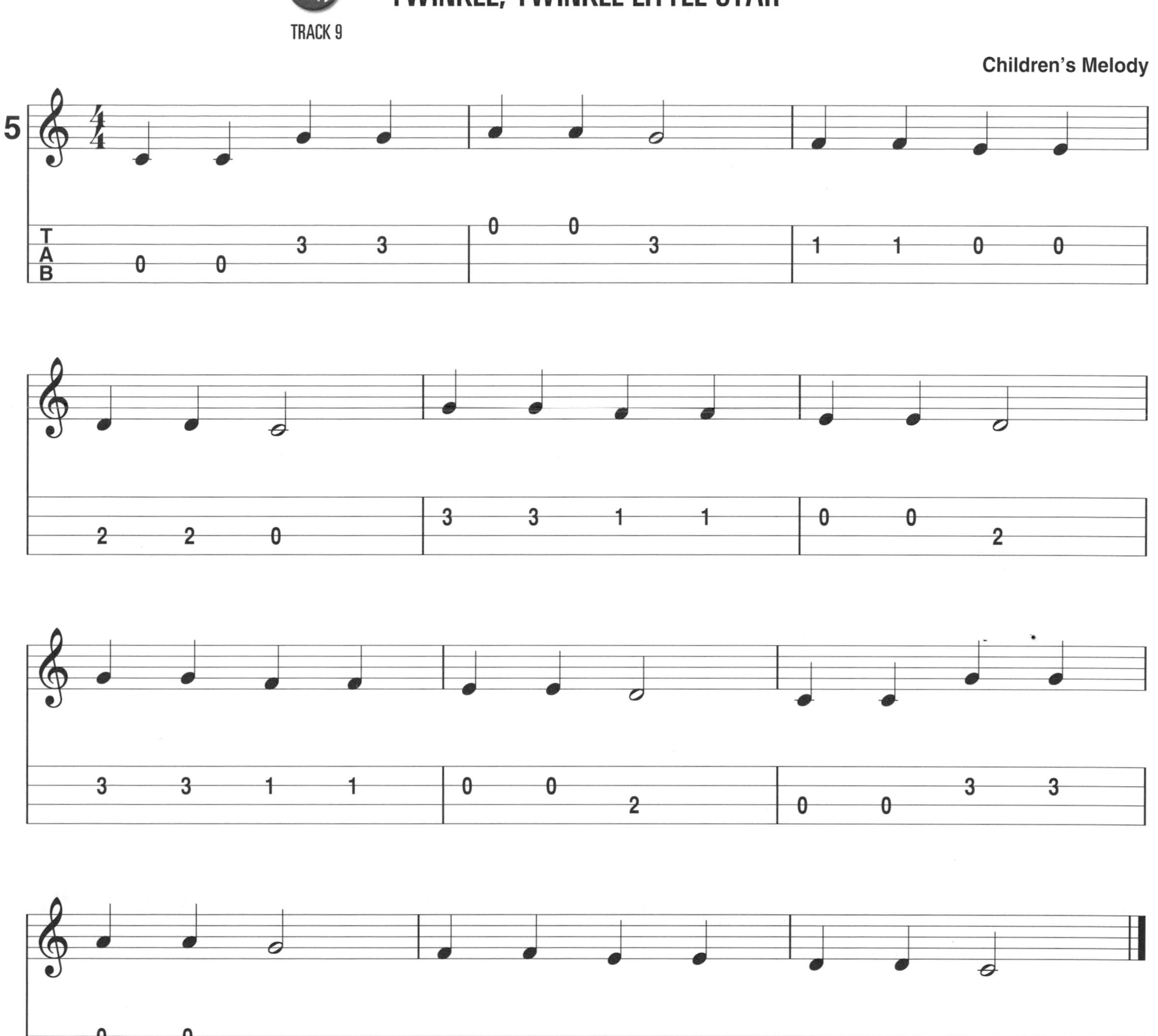

Great melodies never stray too far from our hearts. Often they inspire parodies, like the classic "Twinkle, Twinkle Little Star," which we also know as "Bah Bah Black Sheep" and "The Alphabet Song."

Little known and often neglected is the great body of work recorded in the 1920s and thirties by old-time country, blues, and jug bands. Their use of the ukulele demonstrates not only its percussive role, but also the full gamut of uke styling—from intricate strums, rolls, and fingerpicking to tremolo and single-string lead work—all, of course, complimented by scat singing, whistling, yodeling, and other vocal embellishments of the period. Some of these important bands were the Hillbillies, Fiddlin' Powers Family, Jimmie Rodgers, Memphis Jug Band, and DaCosta Woltz's Southern Broadcasters.

PICKUP NOTES

Sometimes a melody will begin before the first beat of the first measure. These notes are called **pickup notes** and they appear in a partial measure called the **pickup measure**. Always remember to count the missing beats before playing your first pickup note. When a song begins with pickup notes, the last measure will be short the exact number of beats used as pickups.

The pickup measure in this exercise has only one quarter note. Count "1–2–3–" silently before playing the quarter note on beat 4. Notice that the last measure is short by one beat to balance out the one-beat pickup note.

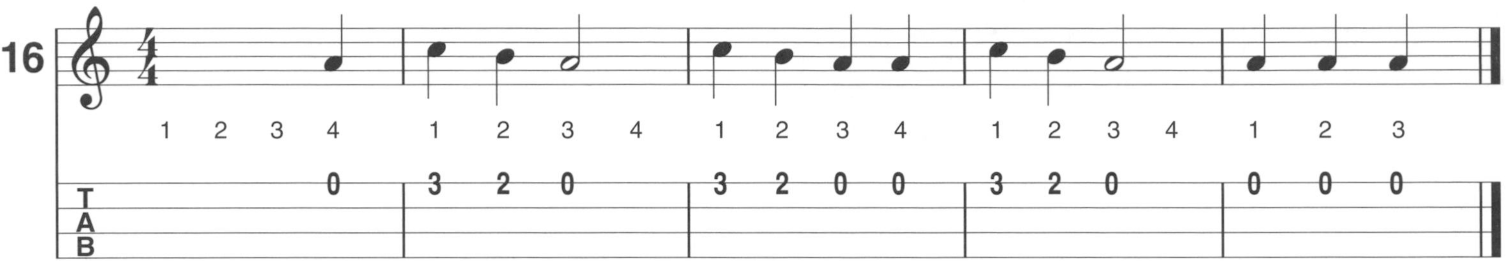

The following pickup measure has two quarter notes. Count "1–2–" silently before playing beats 3 and 4.

DOTTED NOTES

When you see a **dotted note**, hold that note 50% longer than you would normally hold it. For example, a dotted half note (𝅗𝅥.) lasts as long as a half note plus a quarter note. A dot adds half the value of the note.

Watch for the dotted half notes on this one.

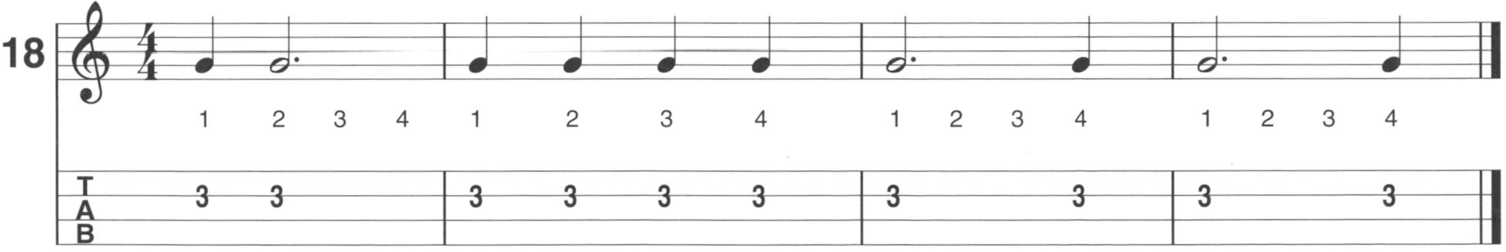

OH! SUSANNA

TRACK 10

Stephen C. Foster

19

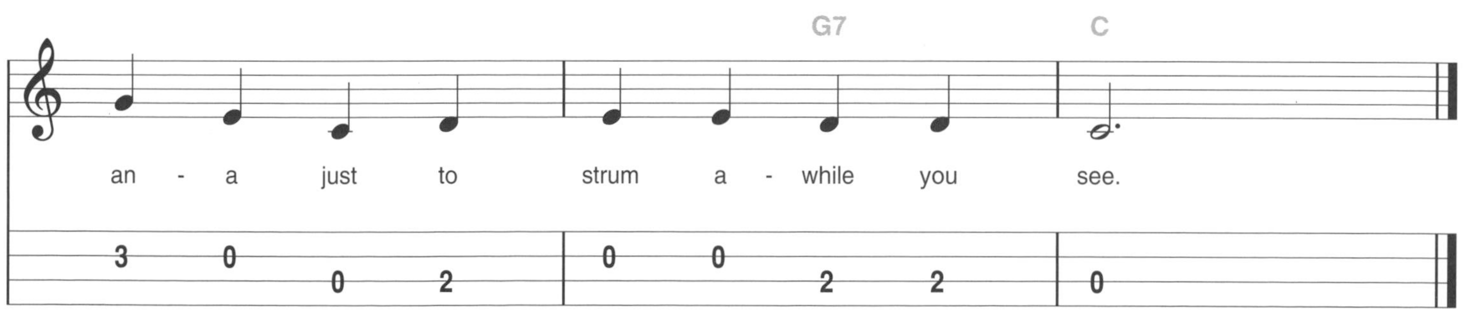

THE C MAJOR SCALE

PUTTIN' IT ALL TOGETHER

Begin by playing the scale in both directions, up and down. Use your thumb (or a felt-tip pick) and go slowly, gradually building up speed. While you are playing the scale, say the notes aloud as you pick them. When you can do this smoothly without breaking your rhythm, then you're ready to begin playing some more basic melodies.

TRACK 11

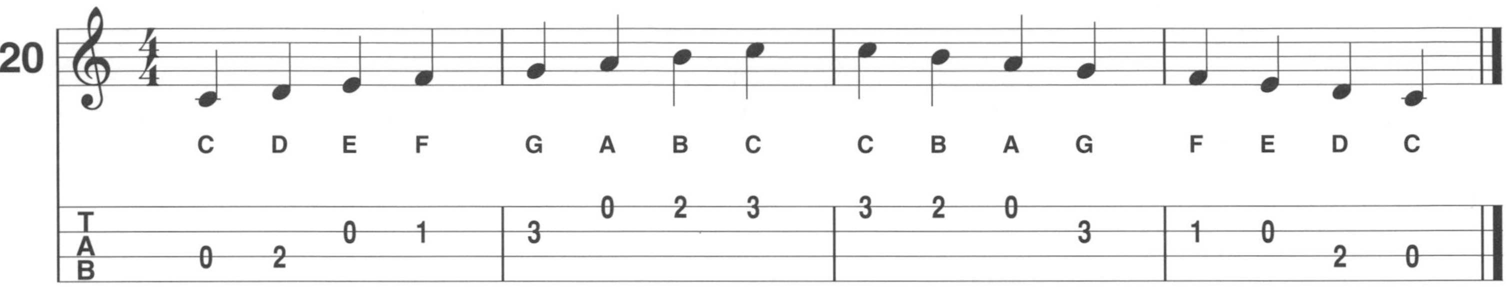

Try playing up and down the C scale, picking twice per note. Your goal is to sound smooth and even.

TRACK 12

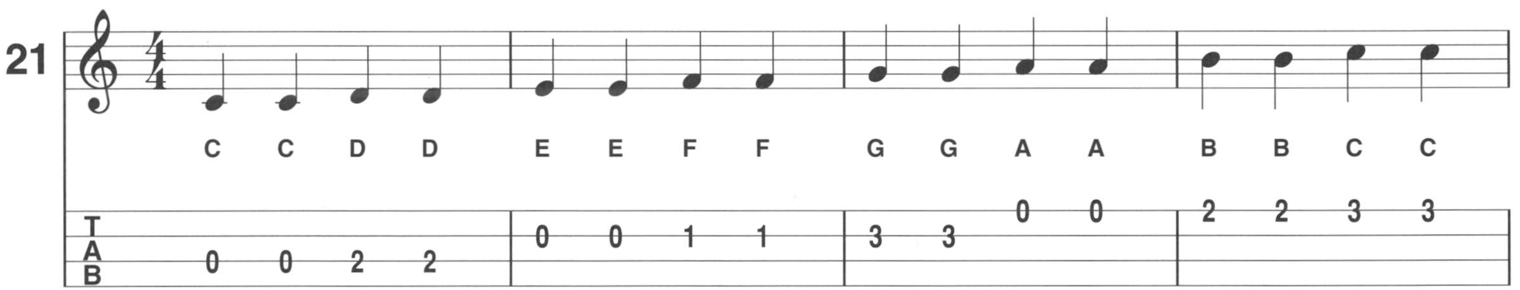

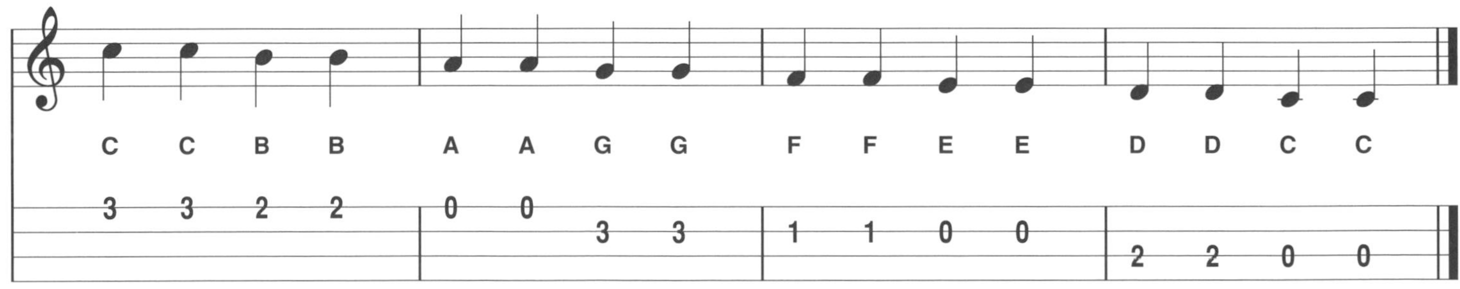

HIGH D AND HIGH E

You already know the fingering for low D and E. Higher versions (or **octaves**) of these notes exist along the A string. Here they are:

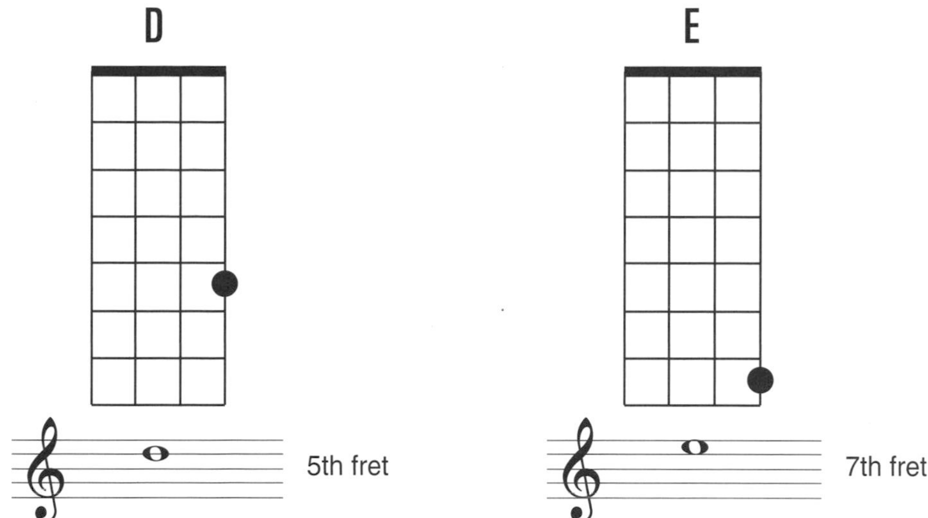

Try playing high D and high E using half notes. Count "1–2–3–4."

TRACK 13

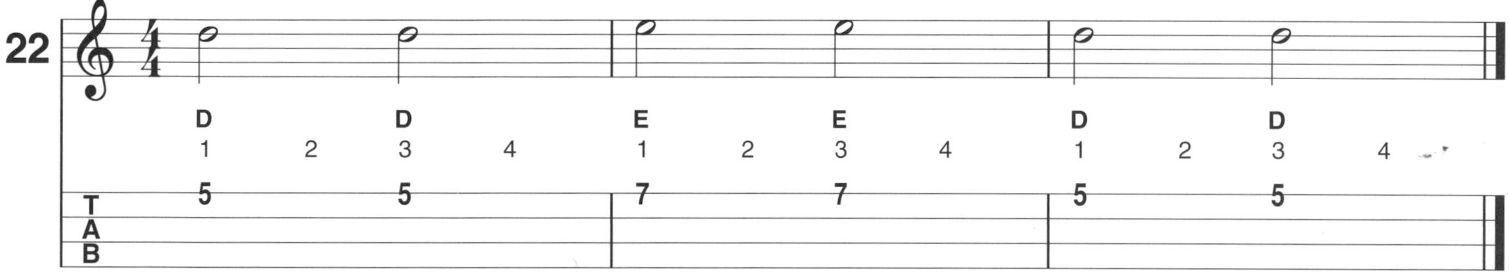

Remember, use your thumb and count while playing these quarter notes.

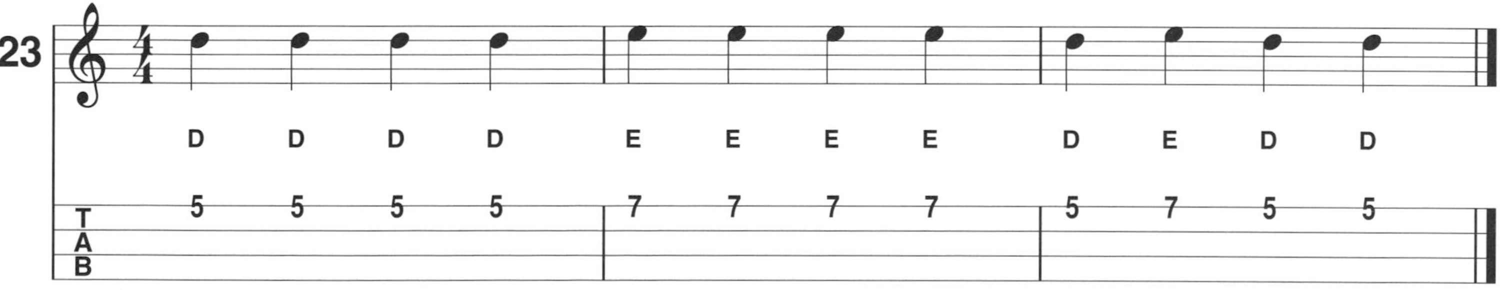

Let's mix it up a little more now!

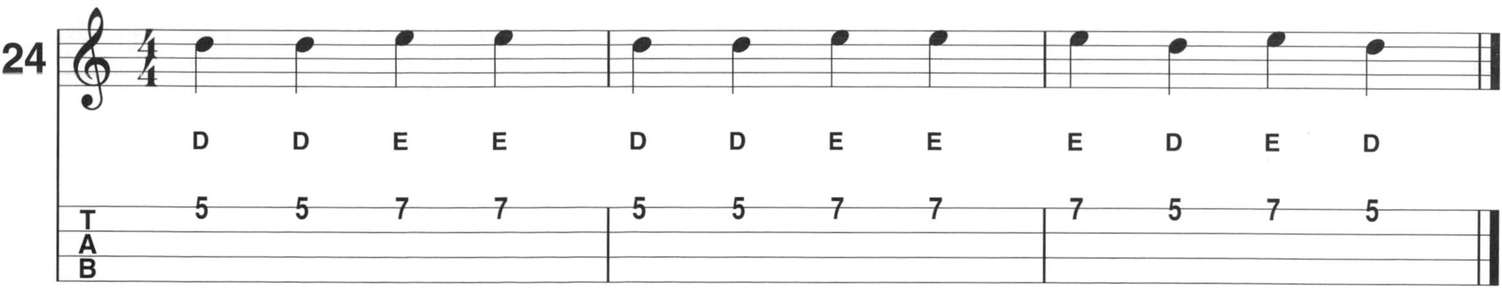

This lovely folk melody was known as "Aura Lee" until 1956, when Elvis Presley's rendition made it popular as "Love Me Tender."

TIES

This symbol (‿) is known as a **tie**. When you see two notes tied together (♩‿♩), even across measures, play them as a single note. In other words, you simply add the first note to the second and hold them out for the full duration of both notes.

In the twelfth measure of “Wildwood Flower,” the number (3) over the first two notes means that you should play these notes with the third (or ring) finger of your left hand. Watch for ties!

WILDWOOD FLOWER

TRACK 15

Traditional, Late 1800s

EIGHTH NOTES

We're about to encounter some tunes with **eighth notes**. Two eighth notes equal one quarter note in value.

1 quarter note ♩ = 2 eighth notes ♫

One eighth note is written with a flag (♪). Consecutive eighth notes are connected with a beam (♫).

To count eighth notes, say "and" in between the beats. In 4/4 time, there are eight eighth notes in a measure.

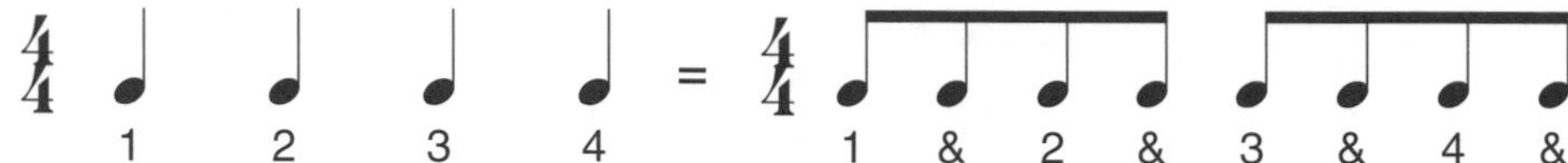

Try these eighth notes. Go slowly and evenly, and count "1 and 2 and 3 and 4 and."

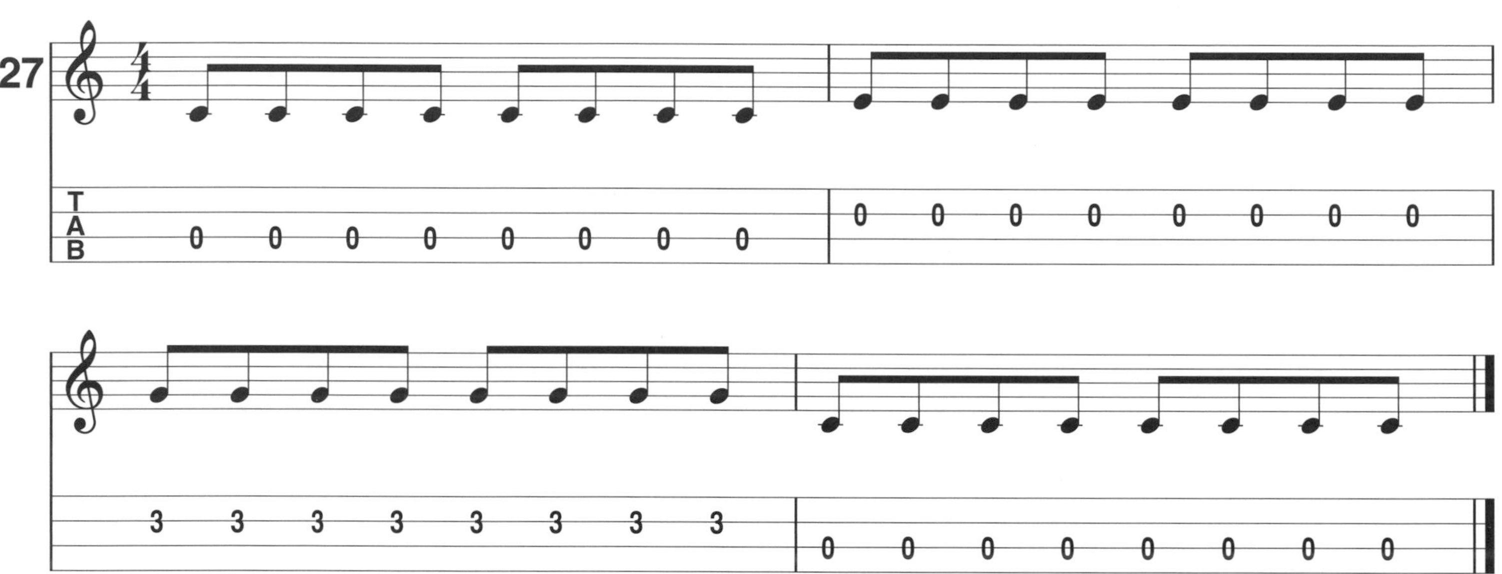

The next tune mixes quarter and eighth notes.

FRÉRE JACQUES
(Are You Sleeping?)

Children's Melody

First, play this melody using mostly quarter notes.

SHORTENING BREAD

TRACK 17

Southern Folk Song

Now, play the same melody using eighth notes. As always, play very slowly at first, then gradually work up to speed.

SHORTENING BREAD
Puttin' It All Together

TRACK 18

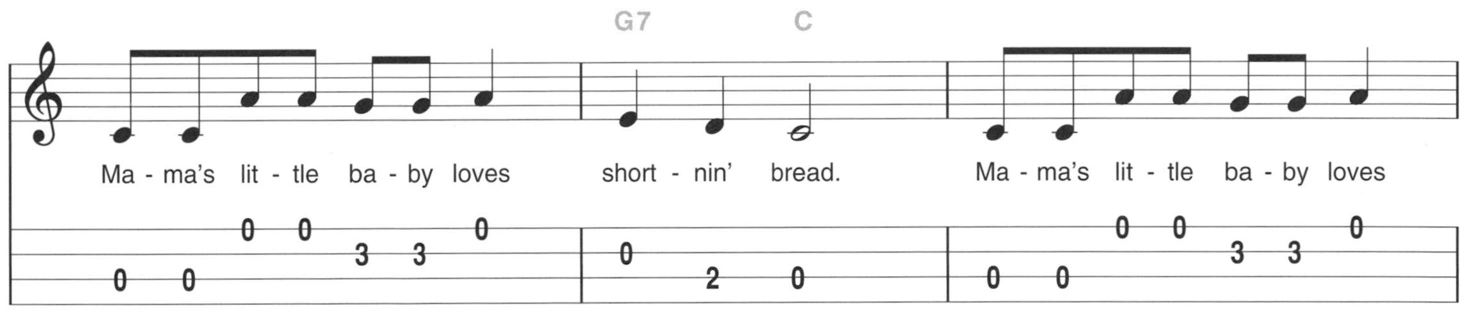

"The ukulele became the official instrument of the Islands when King Kalakaua took it up in 1886 and featured it for the first time with hula dancers."

–Acoustic Guitar and Other Fretted Instruments

TRACK 19

LITTLE BROWN JUG

31

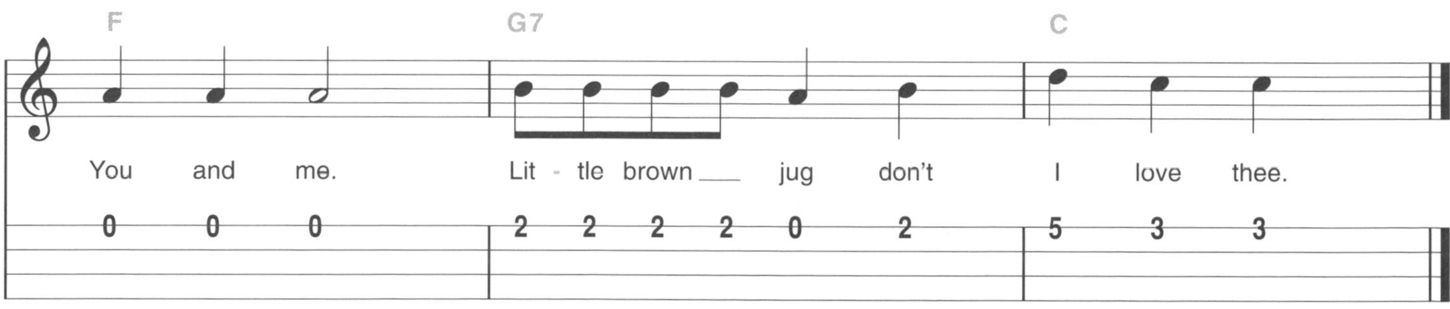

"The ukulele had this advantage: not even a trained musician could tell if you were really playing it or just monkeying around with it."—*Will Rogers*

PLAYING CHORDS

C Chord

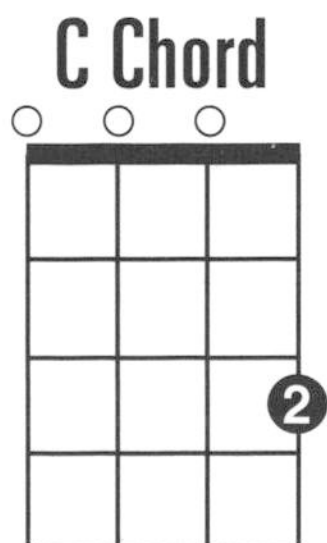

F Chord

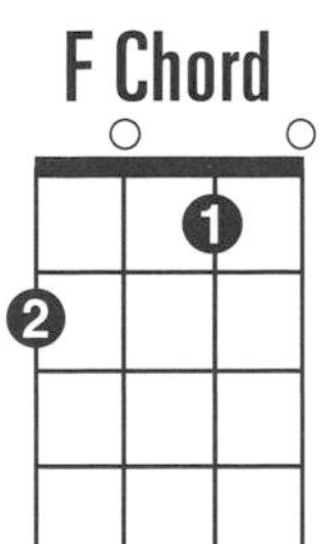

G7 Chord

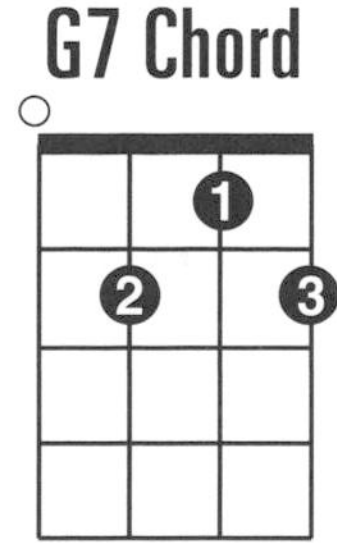

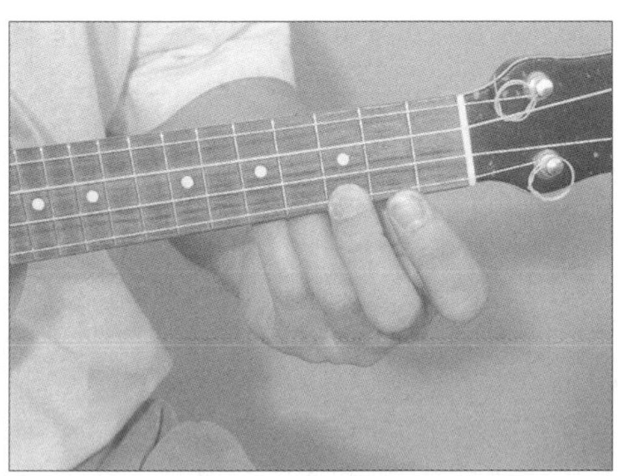

A **chord** is a combination of three or more notes played together. The chord frames above are like maps of your ukulele's fretboard. As you've seen with single notes, the dots show which strings to depress at which frets. The numbers on the dots tell you which fingers to use. To play a C chord, for example, use the tip of the second finger of your left hand and depress the A string just behind the third fret. Strum all four strings with your right hand, and voilà! Now try the F and G7 chords.

Practice these chords by brushing down with your thumb across all four strings. Strum once for each slash in the measure. Note: concentrate on using your fingertips to depress the strings where shown, so that your fingers don't touch any of the wrong strings.

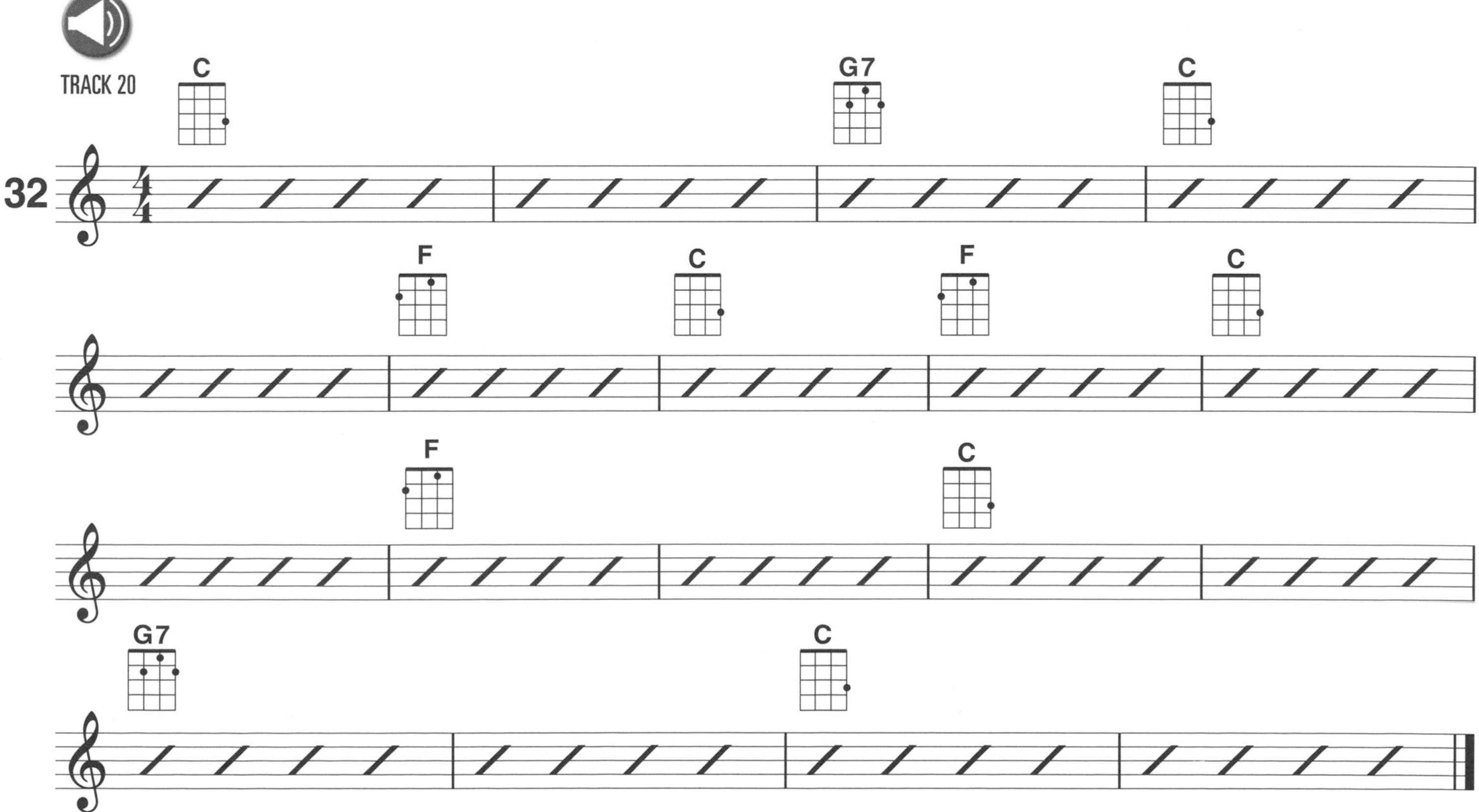

STRUMMING CHORDS

Once you've learned some basic chords, it's time to begin working on some simple strumming techniques. The most basic way to strum chords is with your thumb, as shown.

THUMB BRUSH STRUM

With your hand relaxed, let your thumb gently brush across the strings in a downward pattern.

Each time you brush down across all four strings, lift your hand back up without touching the strings and bring your hand back down to brush again. Do this until you can get a smooth rhythmic beat.

33

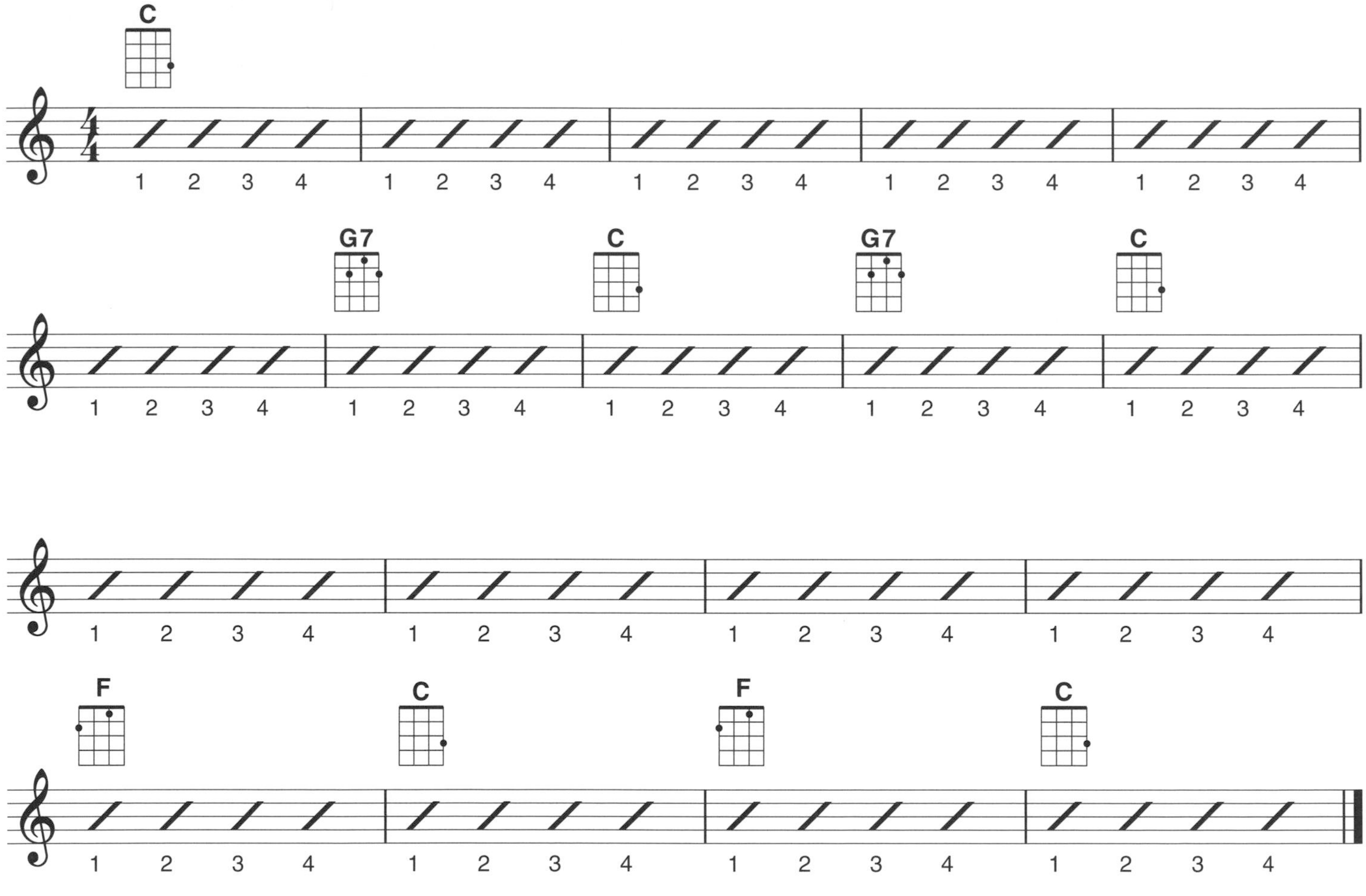

C

1 2 3 4 | 1 2 3 4 | 1 2 3 4 | 1 2 3 4 | 1 2 3 4

G7 C G7 C

1 2 3 4 | 1 2 3 4 | 1 2 3 4 | 1 2 3 4 | 1 2 3 4

1 2 3 4 | 1 2 3 4 | 1 2 3 4 | 1 2 3 4

F C F C

1 2 3 4 | 1 2 3 4 | 1 2 3 4 | 1 2 3 4

Using this familiar two-chord melody, practice the thumb brush strum while singing the words to "Hush Little Baby."

34

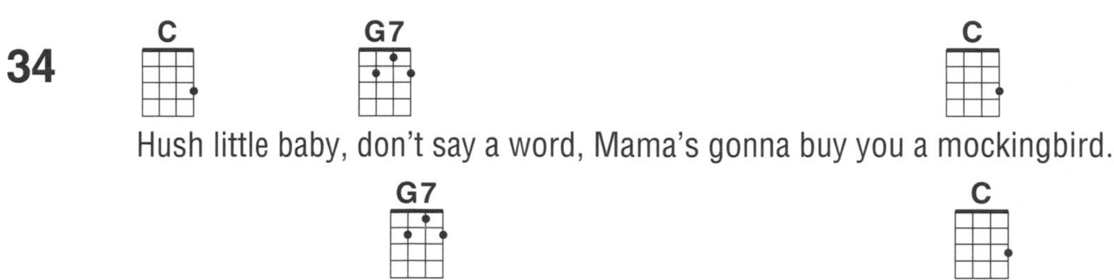

FIRST-FINGER STRUM

The thumb brush may be the most basic way to strum, but the first-finger strum is the most common way to strum your ukulele. Make a loose fist with your right hand and let your first (pointer) finger curl out as shown. Place your hand over the lower fretboard and using the tip of your finger, strum down.

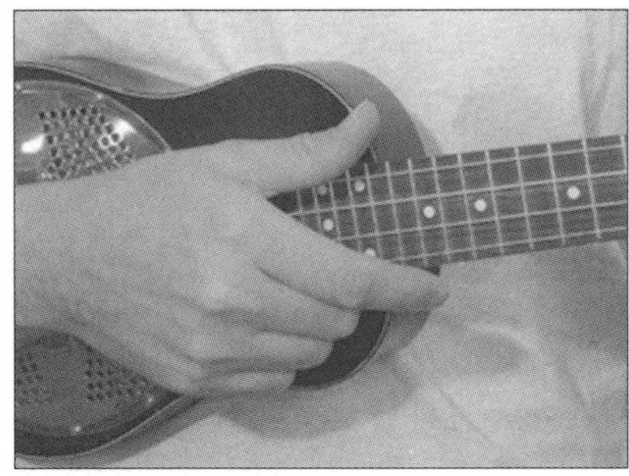

As you did with the thumb, brush down across all four strings, lift your hand back up without touching the strings, then brush down again.

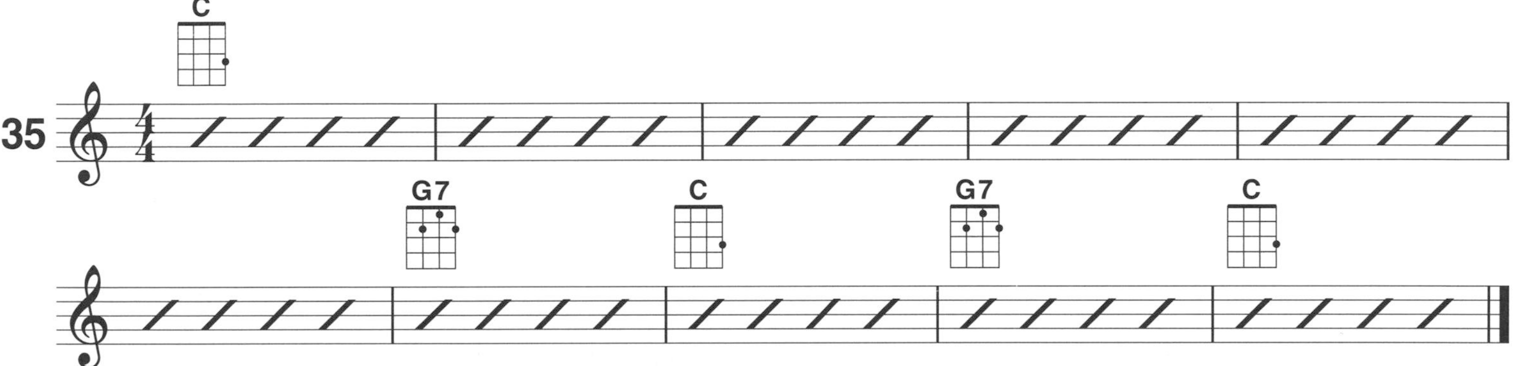

12-BAR BLUES

The basic blues progression below is called a **12-bar blues**, because it has twelve measures. From rock to country to pop, the 12-bar blues is the foundation upon which much of American music rests. It is the heartbeat of Chuck Berry, Bill Haley, Jerry Lee Lewis, and hundreds of others.

Practice this chord progression strumming slowly with this rhythmic strum pattern: down, down–up, down–up, down–up.

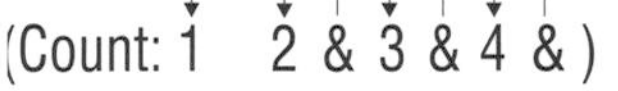

GENERIC BLUES

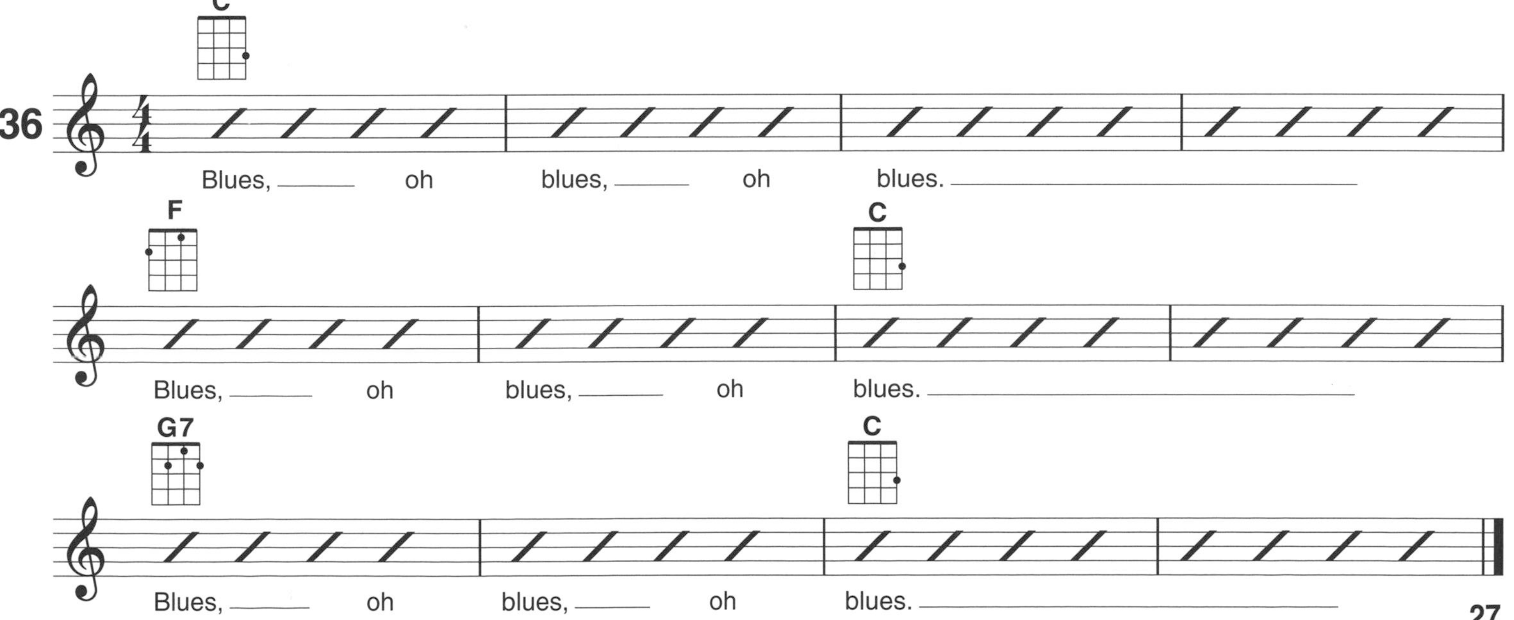

FINGER AND THUMB STRUM

Now that you are comfortable strumming with your thumb and your first finger, let's combine them to create an interesting rhythm. The time signature is 4/4, four beats per measure. The count is "1–2–3–and–4."

1. Brush down with your finger on beat 1.

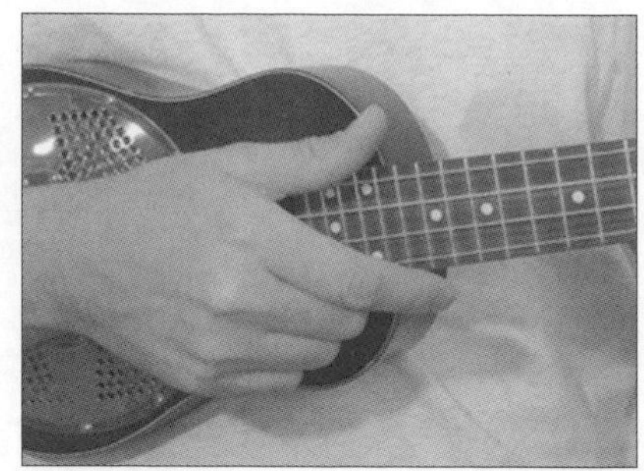

2. Brush down with your finger again on beat 2.

3. Brush down again with your finger following quickly with your thumb, on beat 3.

4. Following quickly, brush up with your finger on the "and" of beat 3 (the eighth note after beat 3).

5. Brush down with your finger again on beat 4.

Listen to Track #21 to get a feel for this new strum pattern. There are many variations that you can play. Below is a graphic example of the main strum pattern and a slight variation of it, both of which you'll hear on Track #21. The arrows represent downstrokes and upstrokes; F = finger, T = thumb.

Practice this very slowly until you can keep a steady rhythmic beat of "1–2–a–3–and–4." It helps to count out loud.

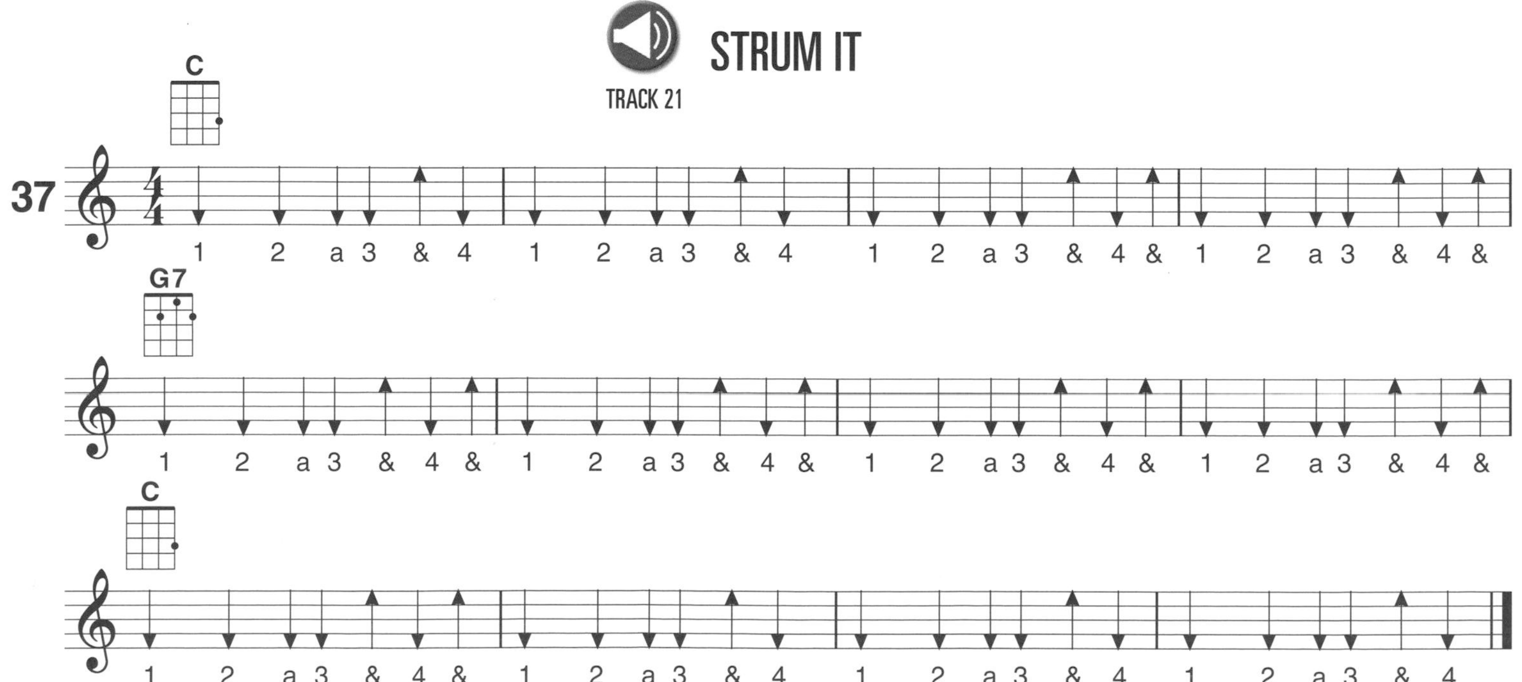

THE G CHORD FAMILY

G, C, D7, and Em Chords

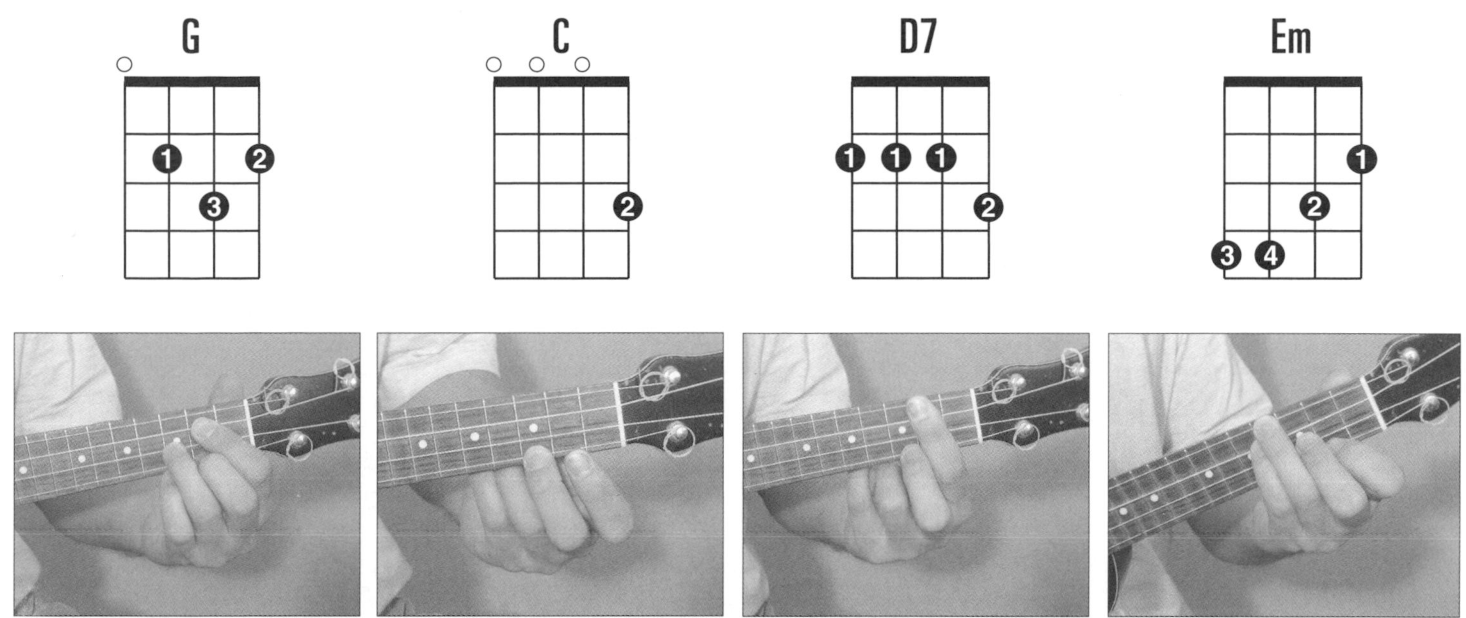

Repeat this progression until you can change chords smoothly. Try playing it with the finger strum pattern heard on the audio.

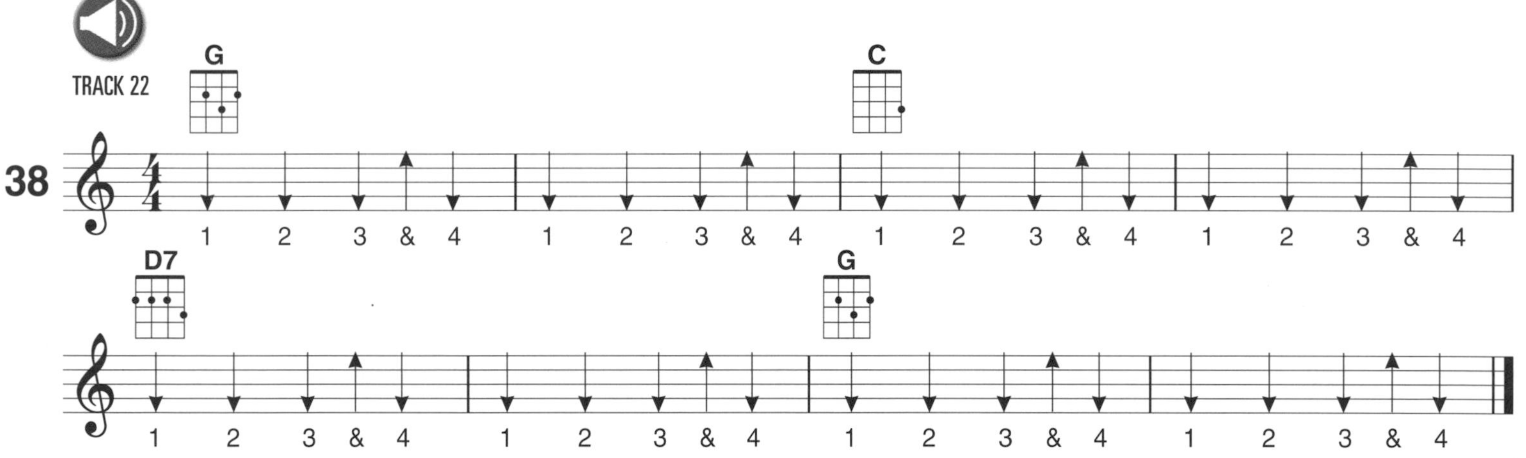

Now try the "Ooh-Wah Uke" progression in the key of G. Use the finger and thumb strum and variation that you just learned.

OOH-WAH UKE

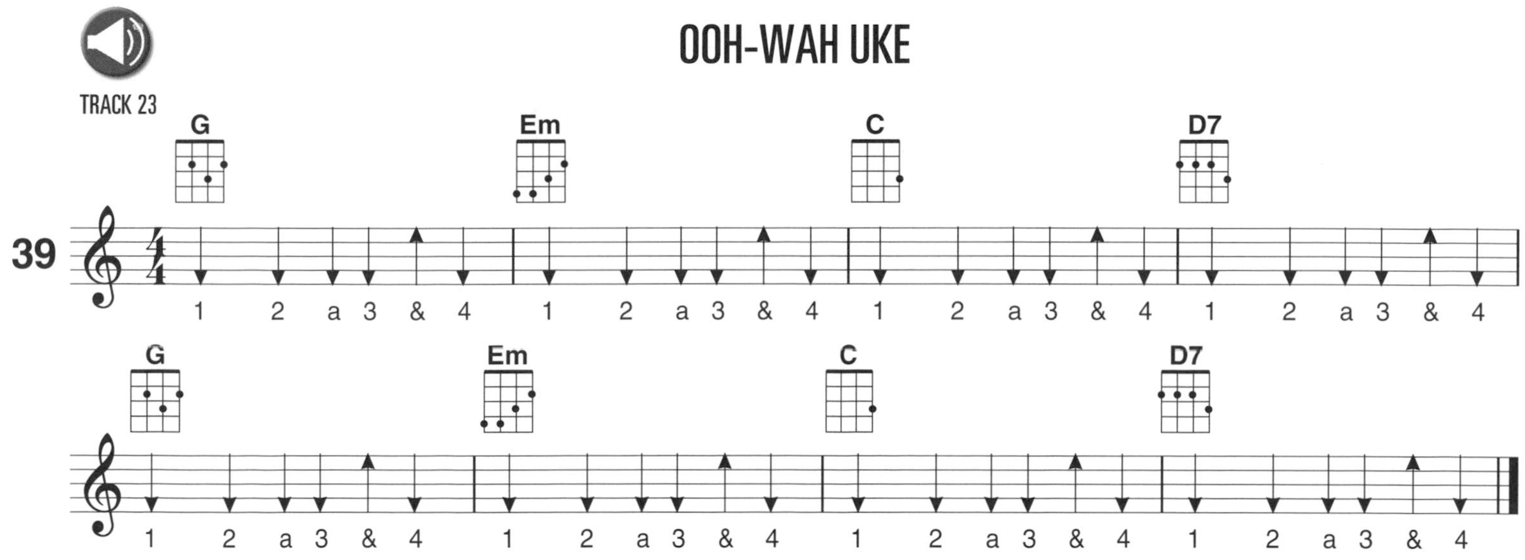

First, become comfortable with picking out this melody. Then go back and learn the rhythm part by strumming the chords.

BOIL 'EM CABBAGE DOWN

TRACK 24
slow/fast

Bluegrass

40

3/4 TIME

While most of the songs we have studied so far have had four beats per measure, **3/4 time** has only three beats per measure. One of the most common 3/4 patterns is called **waltz time**. A waltz is an old-fashioned dance that originated in Eastern Europe around the beginning of the eighteenth century. Today, this rhythm is an important part of American music.

THREE BEATS PER MEASURE
QUARTER NOTE (♩) = ONE BEAT

We count: ONE–two–three,
ONE–two–three,
ONE–two–three.

Or we count: OOM–pah–pah,
OOM–pah–pah,
OOM–pah–pah.

There are literally thousands of songs in 3/4 or waltz time, including "Goodnight Irene," "Tennessee Waltz," "Melody of Love," "After the Ball," "Scarborough Fair," "Streets of Laredo," and "Norwegian Wood."

Here's a 3/4 picking exercise using the G and B notes. Count as you pick.

WALTZ

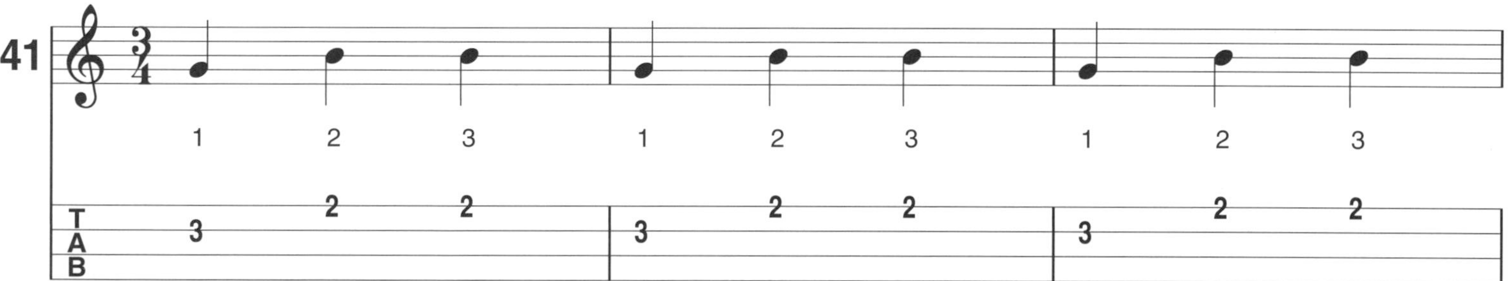

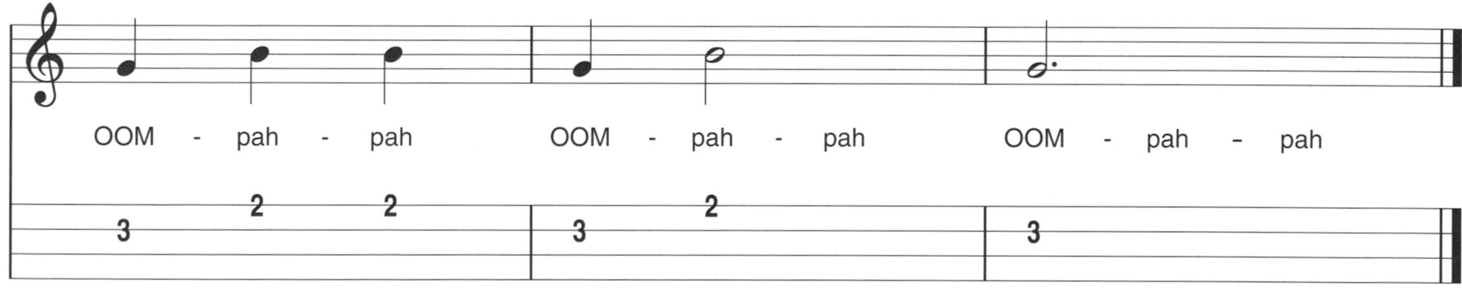

Hawaii's late Queen Liliuakalami once said that the word ukulele meant "the gift that came home." *Uku* means "gift," and *lele* translates as "to come."

—*Old Time Herald*

Try this exercise in 3/4 time using the thumb brush strum.

42
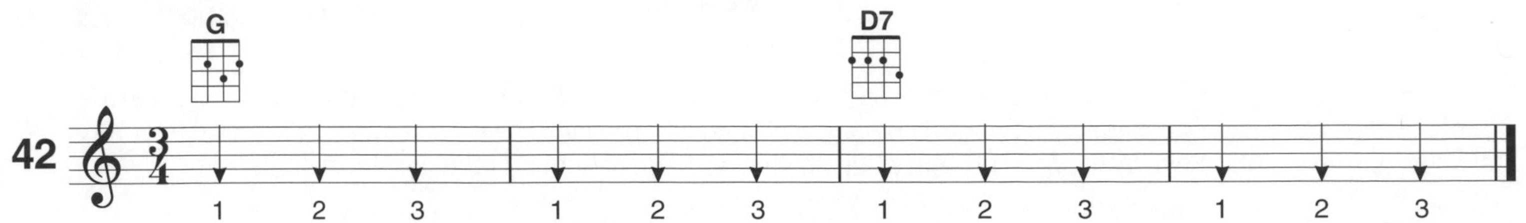

PLAYING THE 3/4 STRUM

Here's one of the many ways to strum in 3/4 time:

1. Position your pointer finger over the fretboard as if you're about to strum;
2. finger a G chord;
3. strum down on beat 1, putting emphasis on that beat;
4. strum down again on beat 2;
5. follow that quickly with an up-strum on the "and" of beat 2;
6. finish with one final strum on beat 3.

The whole thing looks like this:

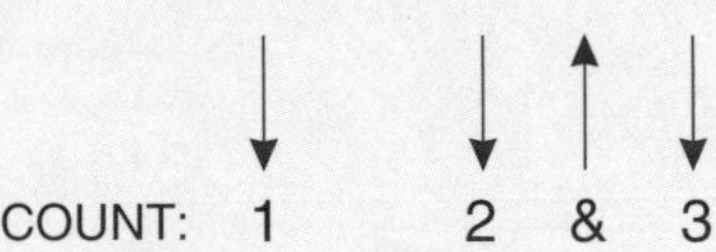

Now let's give it a try.

WALTZ STRUM

43
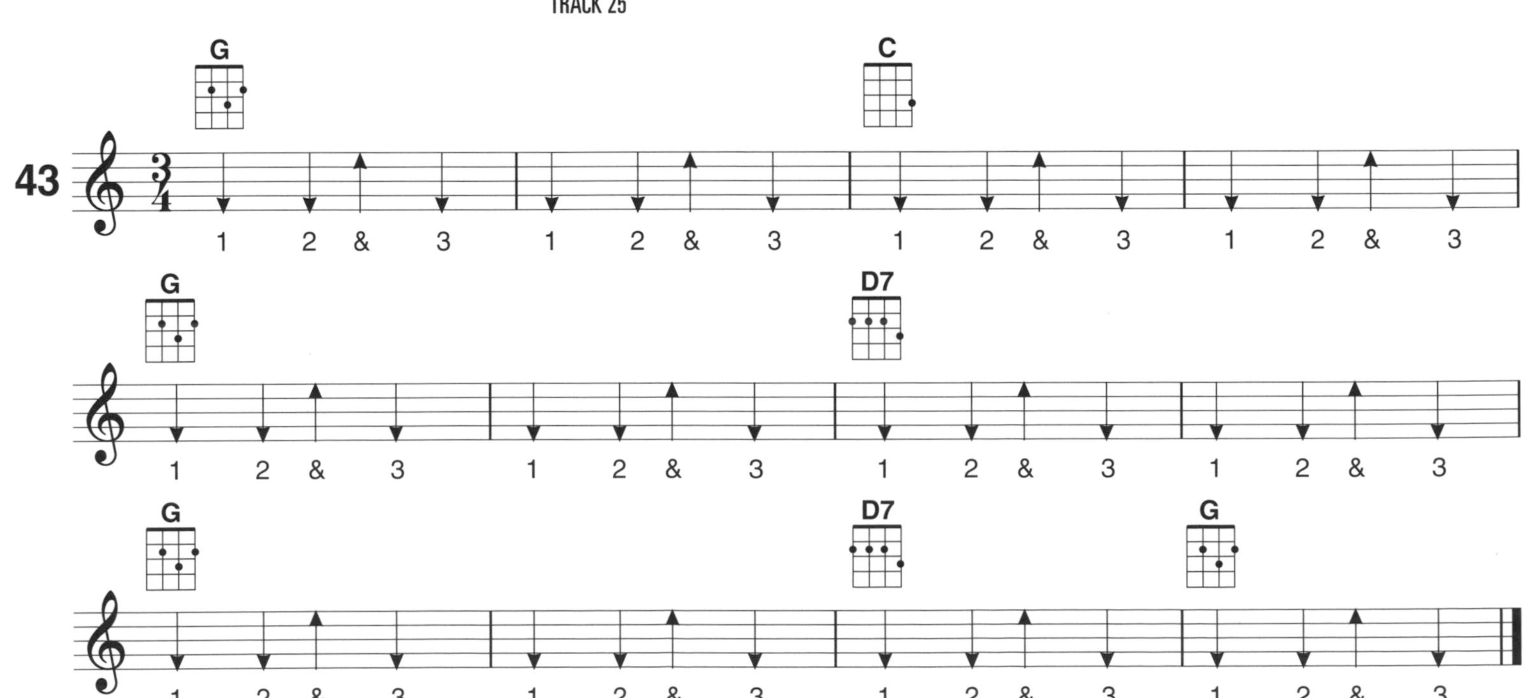

Play this well-known melody, then play the chord part using the 3/4 strum.

AMAZING GRACE

TRACK 26

By John Newton

Arrangment by
Lil' Rev and John Nicolson

44

John Newton was the captain of a slave ship. While sailing on the high seas, he experienced a religious conversion and returned to Africa to set his captives free. He went on to pen many classic hymns, but this one took on a life of its own.

THE F CHORD FAMILY

F, B♭, and C7 Chords

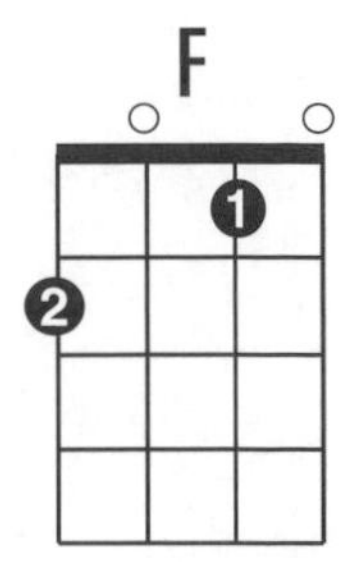

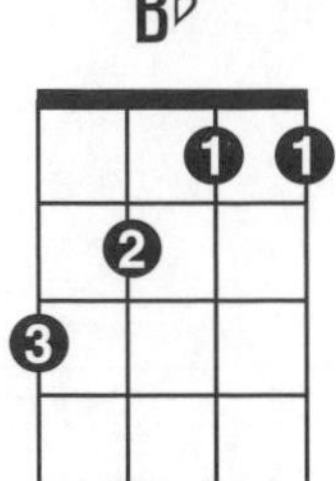

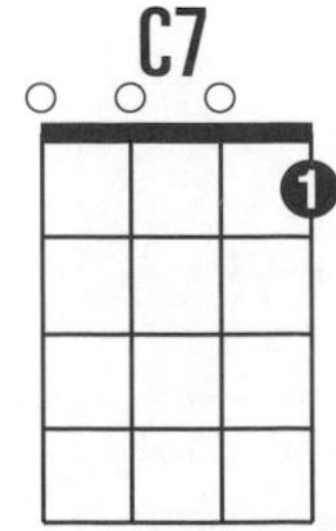

Try playing the F chord all by itself.

Now let's add the C7 chord.

HUSH LITTLE BABY

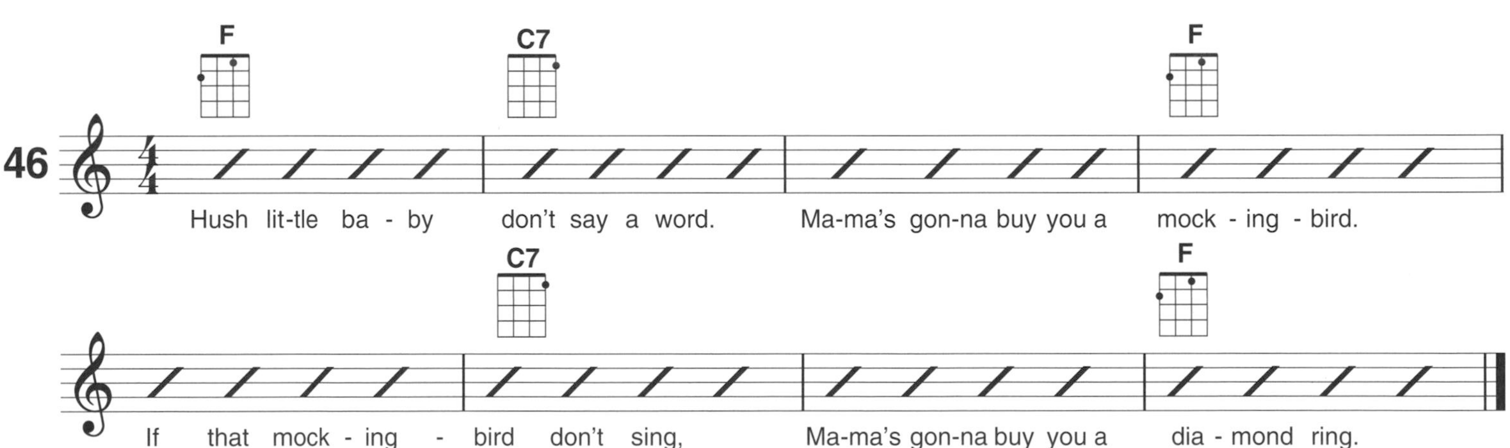

Finally, let's add the B♭ chord.

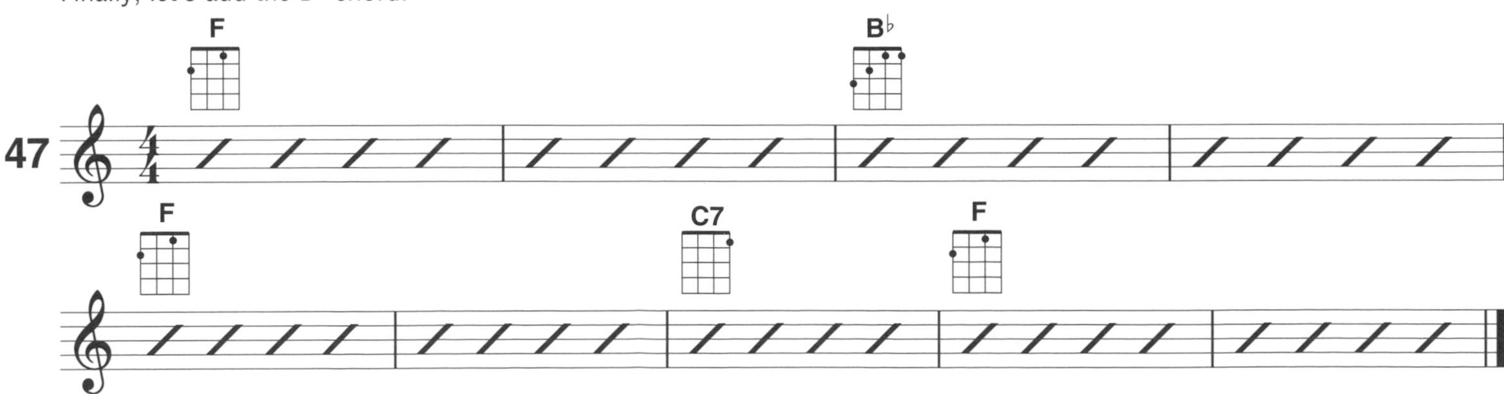

Try strumming the following exercise à la "Rolling in My Sweet Baby's Arms." The finger strum pattern is easy to hear and follow. Your goal is to change chords smoothly without breaking the flow. When you can do this, you'll be ready to learn other songs in the key of F.

ROLLING

TRACK 27

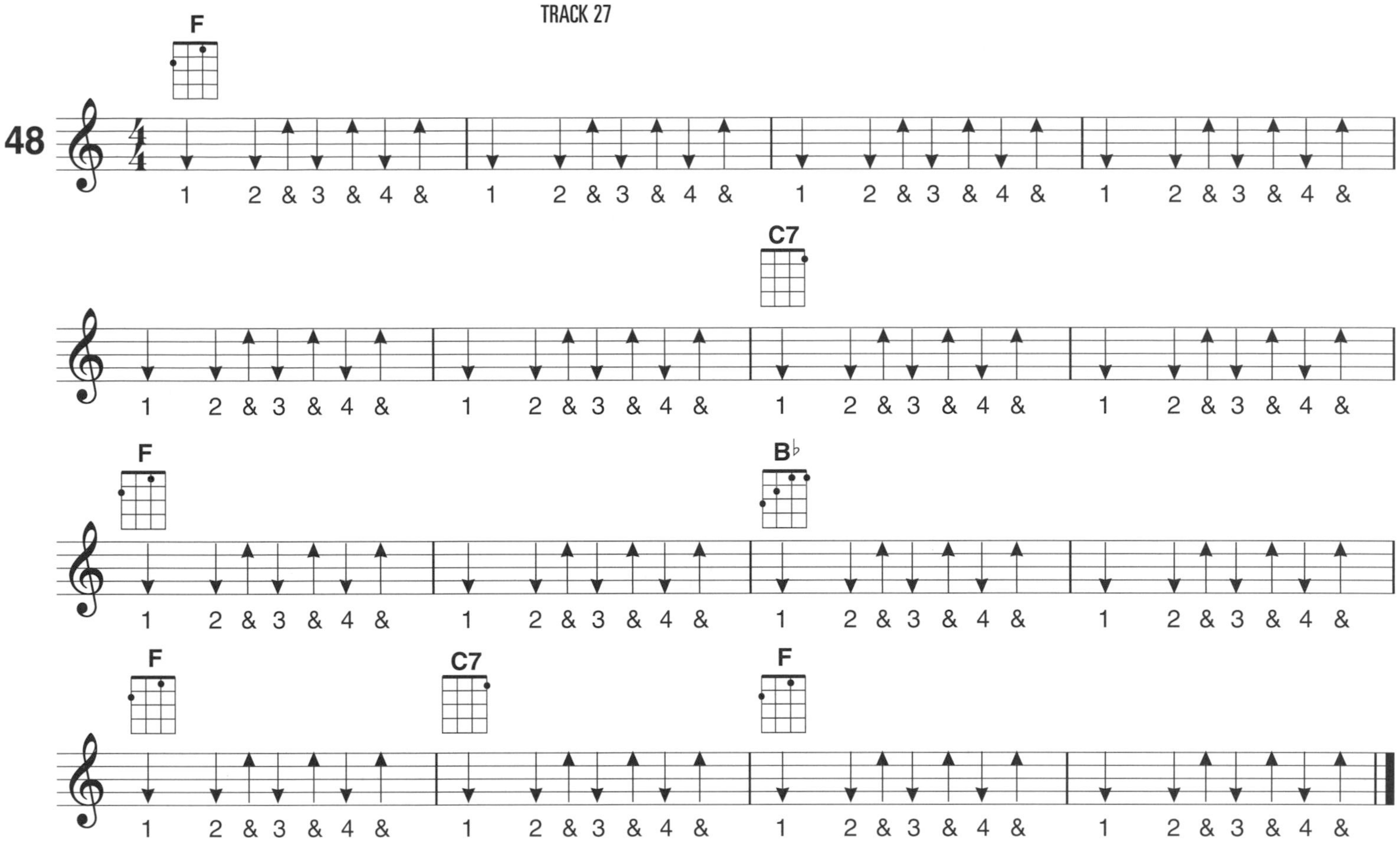

48

F

1 2 & 3 & 4 & 1 2 & 3 & 4 & 1 2 & 3 & 4 & 1 2 & 3 & 4 &

C7

1 2 & 3 & 4 & 1 2 & 3 & 4 & 1 2 & 3 & 4 & 1 2 & 3 & 4 &

F B♭

1 2 & 3 & 4 & 1 2 & 3 & 4 & 1 2 & 3 & 4 & 1 2 & 3 & 4 &

F C7 F

1 2 & 3 & 4 & 1 2 & 3 & 4 & 1 2 & 3 & 4 & 1 2 & 3 & 4 &

JUKING THE UKE

TRACK 28

While the most common type of blues structure is the 12-bar (because it has twelve measures), blues tunes come in all shapes and sizes, from eight, twelve, sixteen, to even thirty-two bars. Here's an eight-bar example. The finger strum pattern is easy to hear and follow.

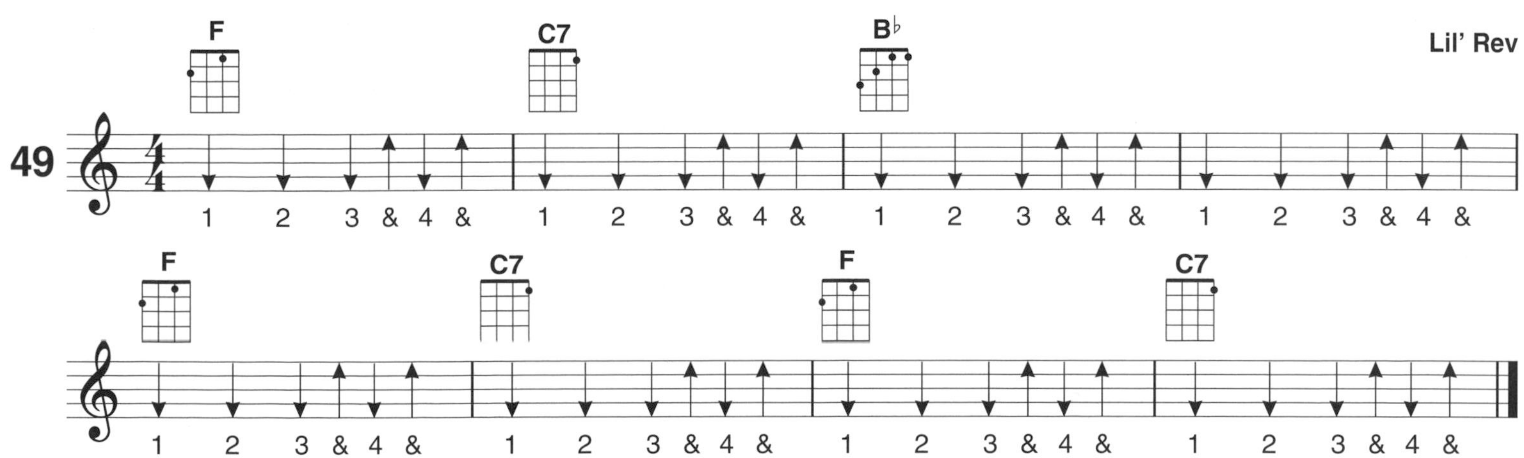

SHARPS AND FLATS

The symbol ♯ stands for **sharp** and raises the pitch by a half step (or one fret). When you see the sharp symbol before a note on the staff line, you raise that note by playing up one fret. Conversely, when you see the **flat** symbol (♭), you play that note one fret down.

Now try playing the chords to this tune along with the audio.

KEY SIGNATURES

One convenient way to avoid assigning a flat (♭) to every B in a piece of music is to simply put a flat sign at the beginning of each line. Then every time you see a B note, you play a B♭. This is called a **key signature** and it works for all kinds of sharps and flats. The exercises below use the key signature.

B-FLAT (B♭)

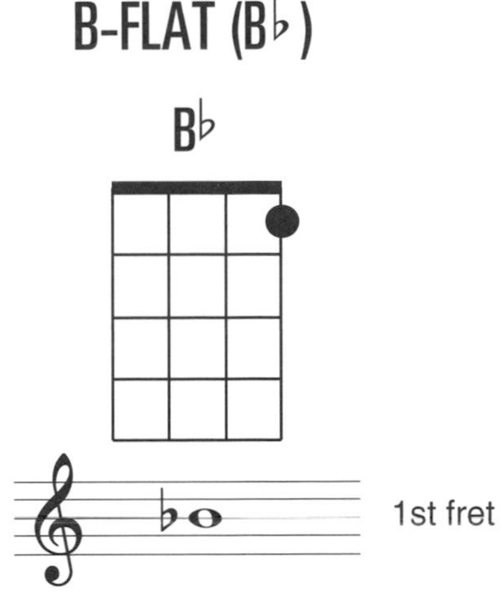

51

52

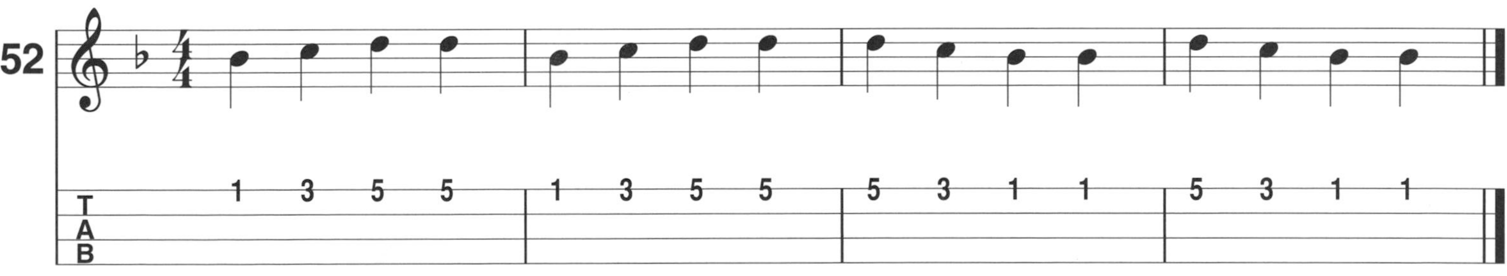

PRACTICE TIP

Regular practice is essential. Practicing a half hour each day is better than practicing two hours every four days. Find a regular time of the day that works for you.

THE F MAJOR SCALE

Now that you know the B♭ note, you know all the notes in the F major scale. The key signature (with B flatted) tells us that we're in the key of F. Notice the new note high F. Play this with your pinky finger on the 8th fret of the first string.

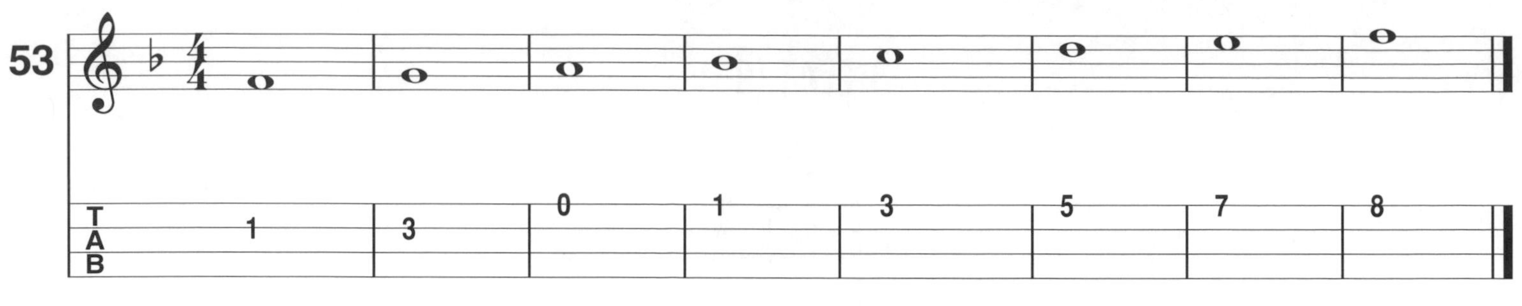

CLEMENTINE

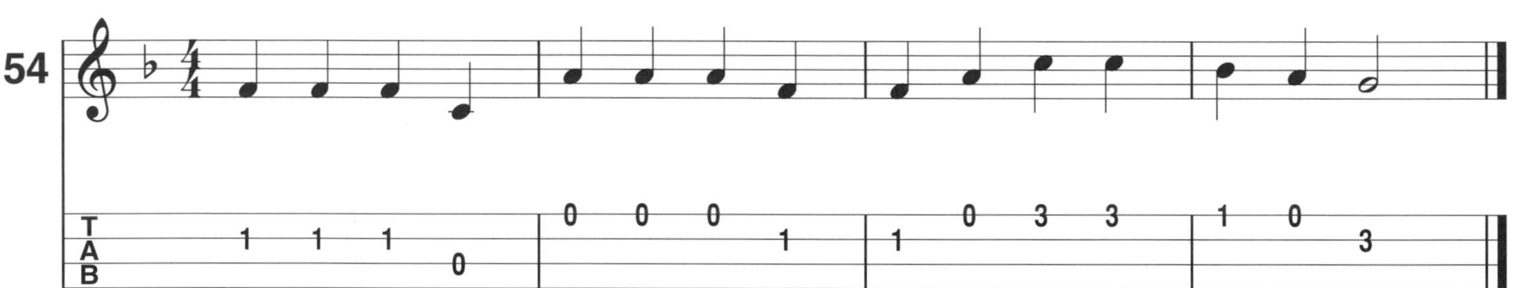

Moving up the F major scale:

TRACK 31

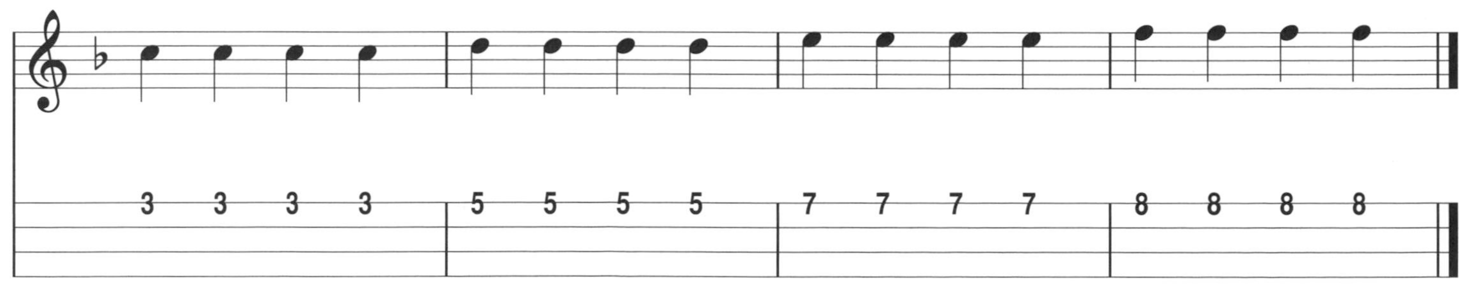

Now let's try playing a basic melody in the key of F using our thumb to pick each note. Go slowly first and gradually pick up speed.

PAW PAW PATCH

TRACK 32

Traditional Folk

Here's a great melody for you to practice in the key of F. After you can pick the melody well, go back and try to sing and strum while tapping out the rhythm with your foot.

SKIP TO MY LOU

TRACK 33

American Game Song

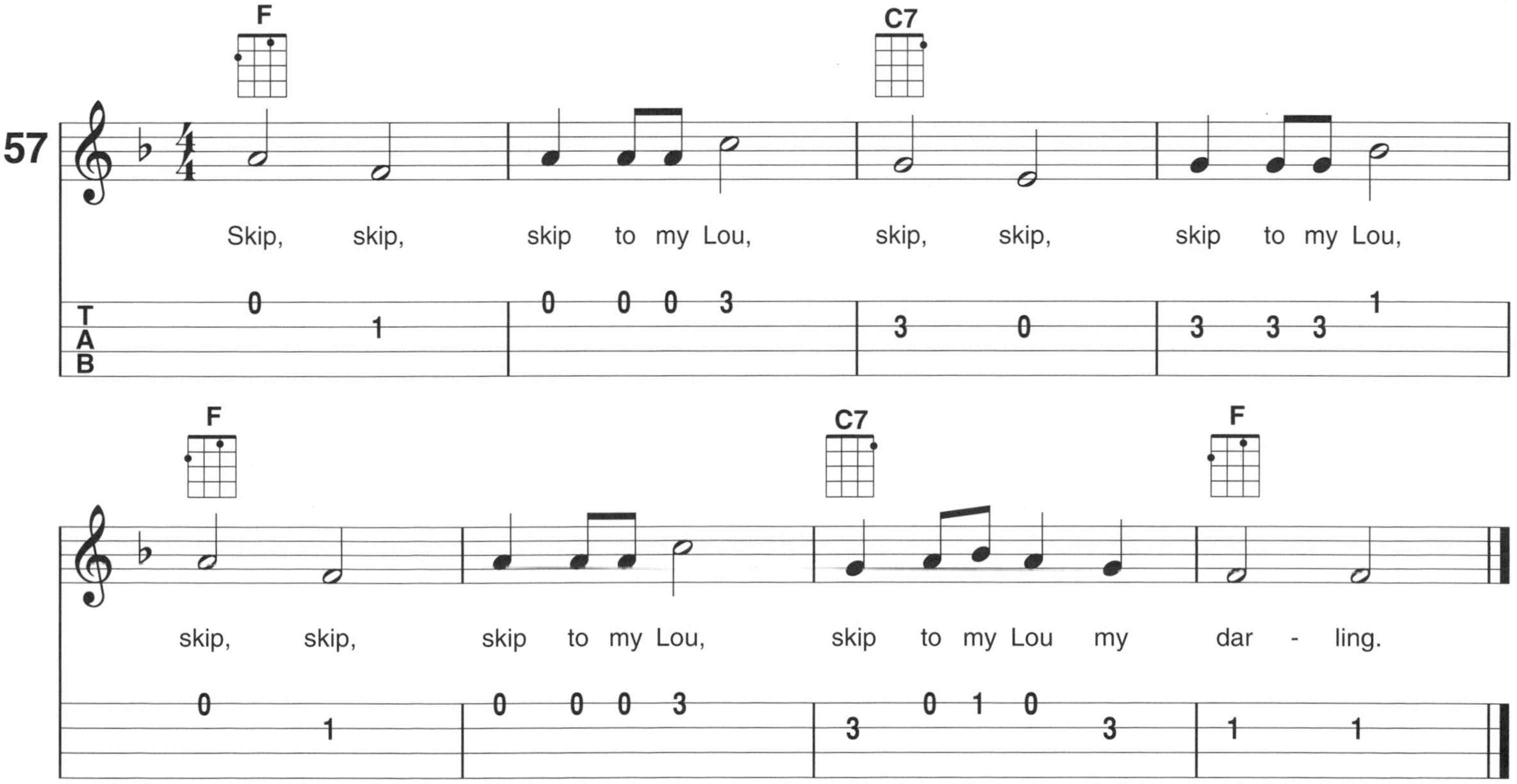

57

F C7

Skip, skip, skip to my Lou, skip, skip, skip to my Lou,

T
A
B

0 1 | 0 0 0 3 | 3 0 | 3 3 3 1

F C7 F

skip, skip, skip to my Lou, skip to my Lou my dar - ling.

0 1 | 0 0 0 3 | 3 0 1 0 3 | 1 1

Notice the new key signature in these next two songs. Remember to play every F note one half step higher to F♯.

IN THE MOON'S PALE SHIMMER
(Au Claire de la Lune)

TRACK 34

French Folk Song

Watch for F♯s in the thirteenth and fifteenth measures.

SHE'LL BE COMING 'ROUND THE MOUNTAIN

TRACK 35

Folk Song

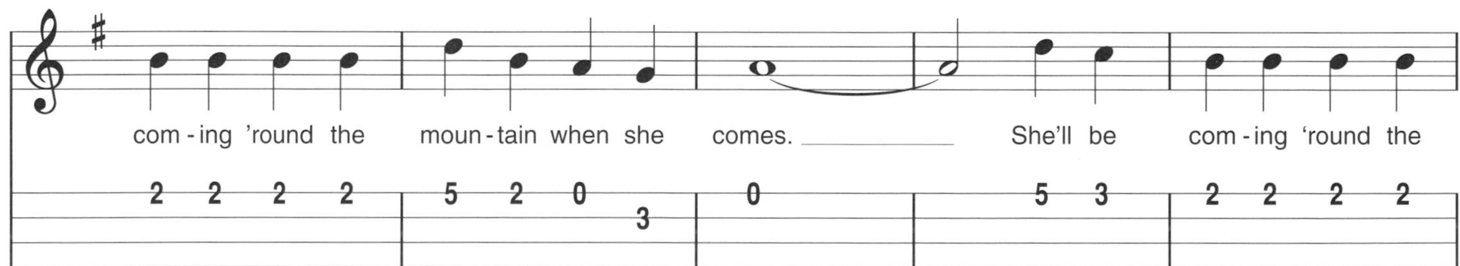

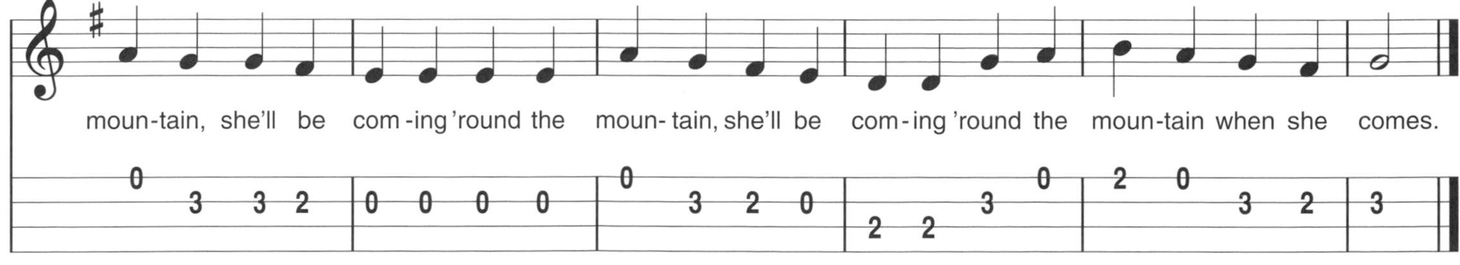

THE SINGLE ROLL STROKE

The roll stroke is a lively rhythmic strumming technique that emphasizes the downbeat of the strum by unraveling your right-hand fingers one-by-one. When properly executed, it should sound like one continuous flowing beat.

Think of flicking a tiny ball of paper off a desk with one finger. Then, imagine flicking four tiny balls of paper (one after the other) with one continuous motion of your four fingers. This is in effect what you are doing with a roll stroke.

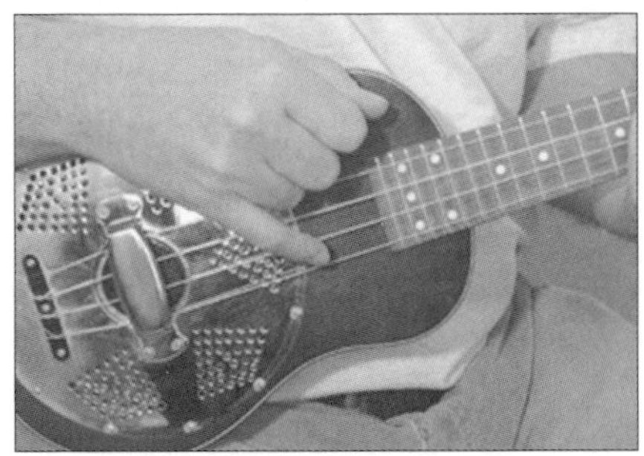

1. Bring your right-hand pinky down across all four strings.

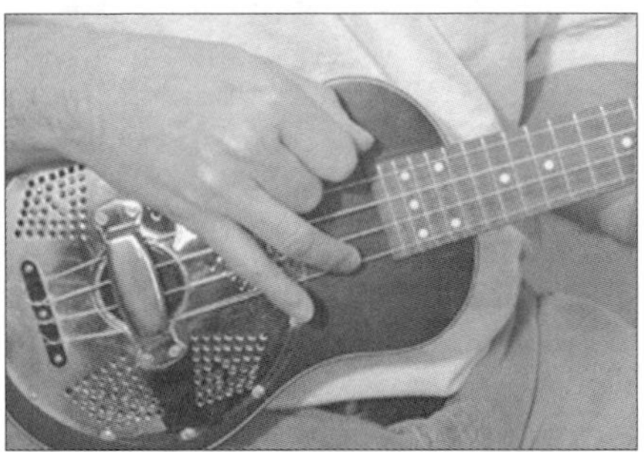

2. Let your third (ring) finger follow right after your pinky.

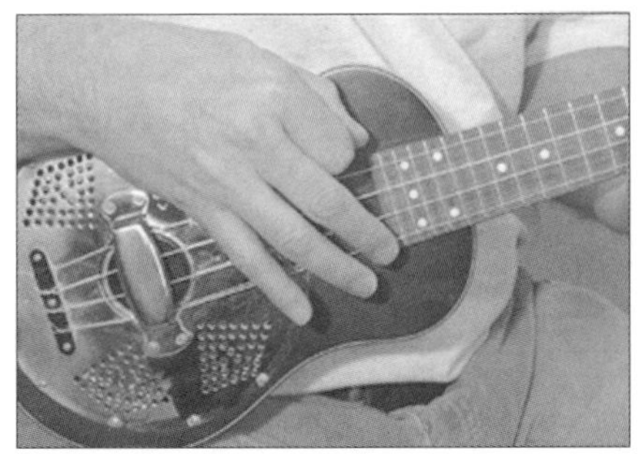

3. Now your second (middle) finger follows down across all four strings.

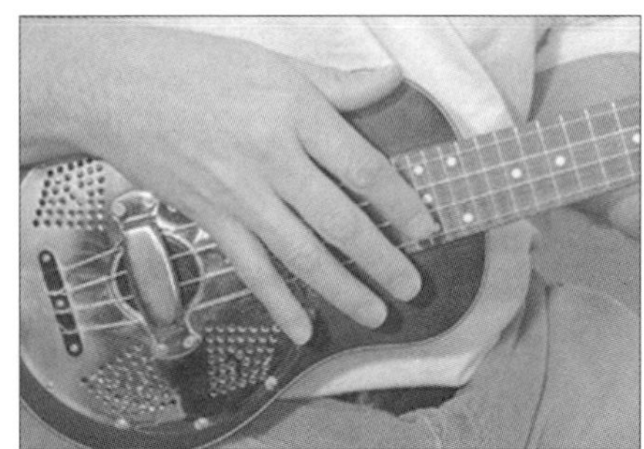

4. Finally, bring your pointer finger down across all of the strings.

Think of your fingers unraveling in a steady progression, one after the next. When this is mastered, you can try adding your thumb, which will follow right after the pointer finger in its downward motion.

At the end of "Shave and a Haircut," try the roll stroke on the D7 chord, then quickly over the G chord. This may take a little practice, but it's well worth the effort. When notes and tablature are shown in stacks as seen below, this indicates a chord, or a group of notes played simultaneously.

SHAVE AND A HAIRCUT

TRACK 36

This lick is traditionally used to end songs. When you have it up to speed, you can use it to end songs in the key of G (including "Boil 'Em Cabbage Down").

Beverly Uke-a-Billy Challenge: See if you can figure out how to play this lick in other keys.

PLAYING TREMOLO

Tremolo is a very beautiful and pleasing sound when played on the ukulele. Here's how to do it:

1. Spread the fingers of your right hand as shown.

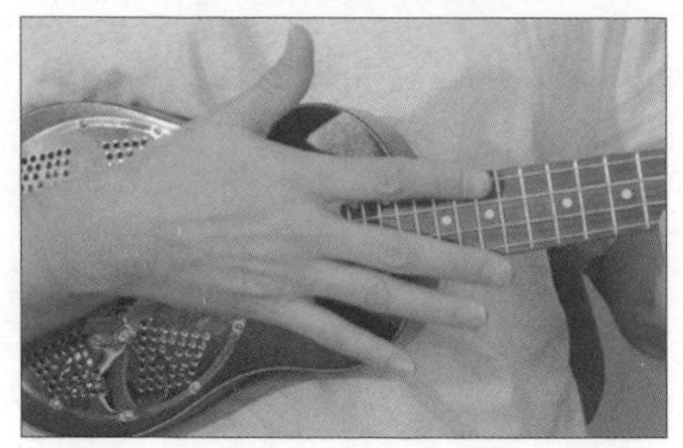
2. Position your pointer over the tenth fret.

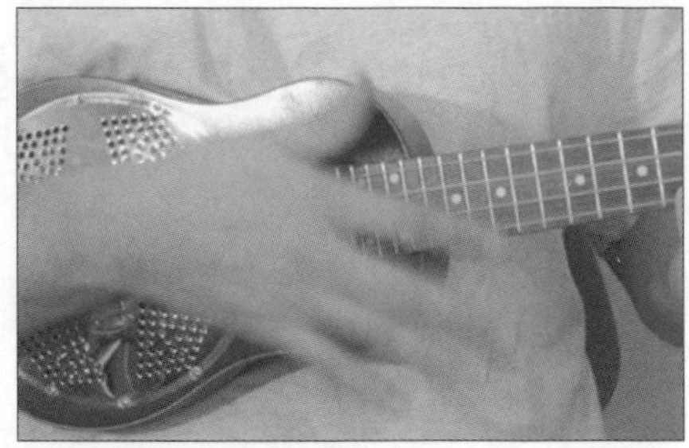
3. Using the pad of your fingertip, gently yet rapidly rub all four strings in a continuous and even up-and-down motion.

The musical symbol we will use for tremolo is (≡).

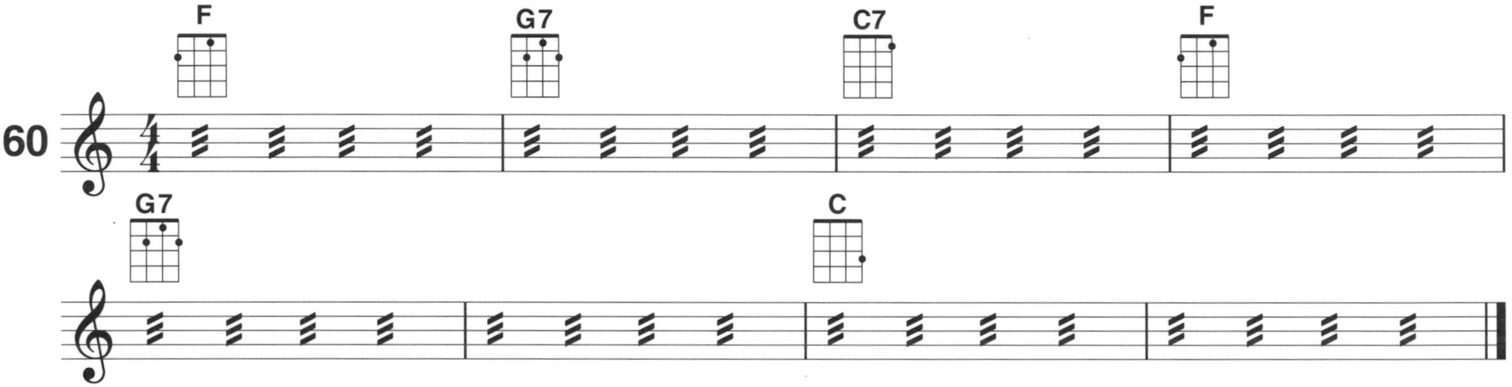

Go back to page 20 and review the melody for "Aura Lee." Once you have it in your head, play this chord progression using tremolo. Notice the new E7 chord. This is just like the D7 chord fingering that you know, but up two frets. There is also another new chord here that is easy to play: Am. Look at the next page for the Am chord fingering. Count "1–2–3–4" for each measure. Then try playing this along with audio track #14.

AURA LEE

TRACK 37

The Am Chord

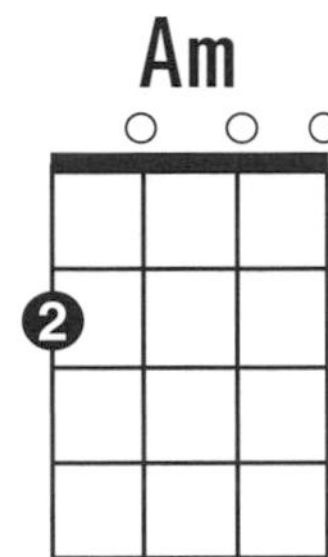

Familiarize yourself with this new chord, and get re-acquainted with the C, F, and G7 chord shapes. Then try playing "Doo-Wop Uke" using tremolo. Work toward keeping the tremolo going smoothly by switching from chord to chord without losing the beat. Remember to use the pad of your pointer finger.

DOO-WOP UKE

TRACK 38

62

C Am F G7

C Am F G7

C Am F G7

C Am F G7

RESTS

Music is made up of both sound and silence. Silence is represented by musical symbols called **rests**. They are just as important as the notes you play. Each type of note has a corresponding rest of the same name and duration:

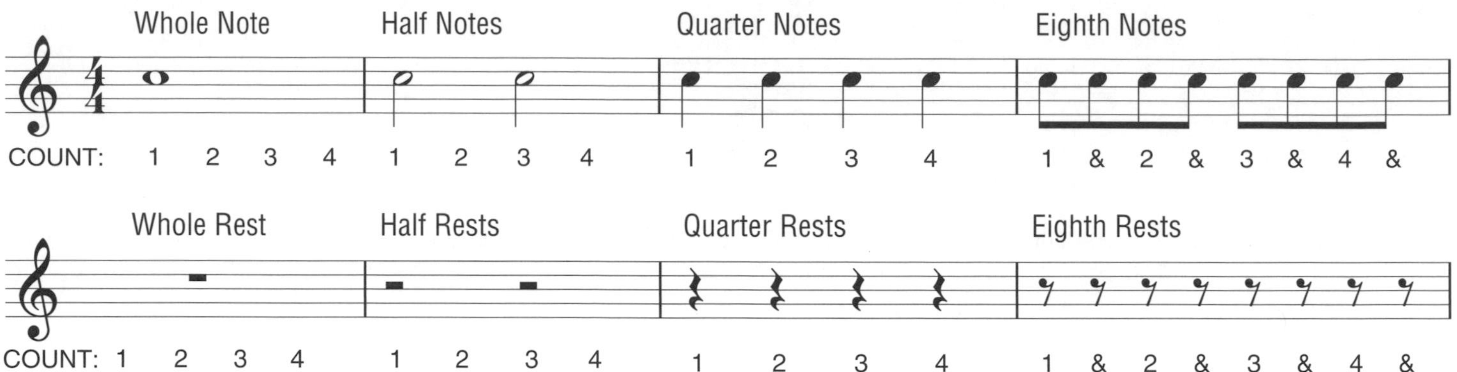

Remember to count while you do these exercises.

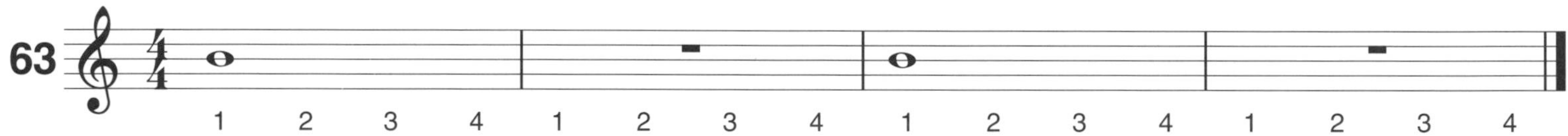

Sometimes it helps to tap your foot during rests to keep time.

"Goodnight Ladies" contains both quarter rests and eighth rests. Notice the key signature!

GOODNIGHT LADIES

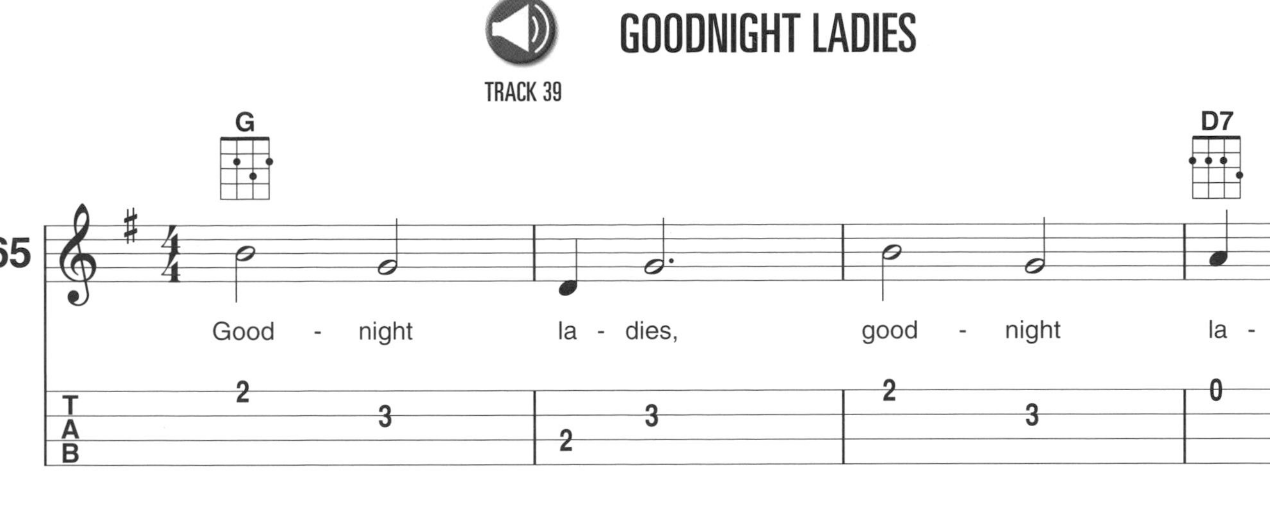

MERRILY WE ROLL ALONG

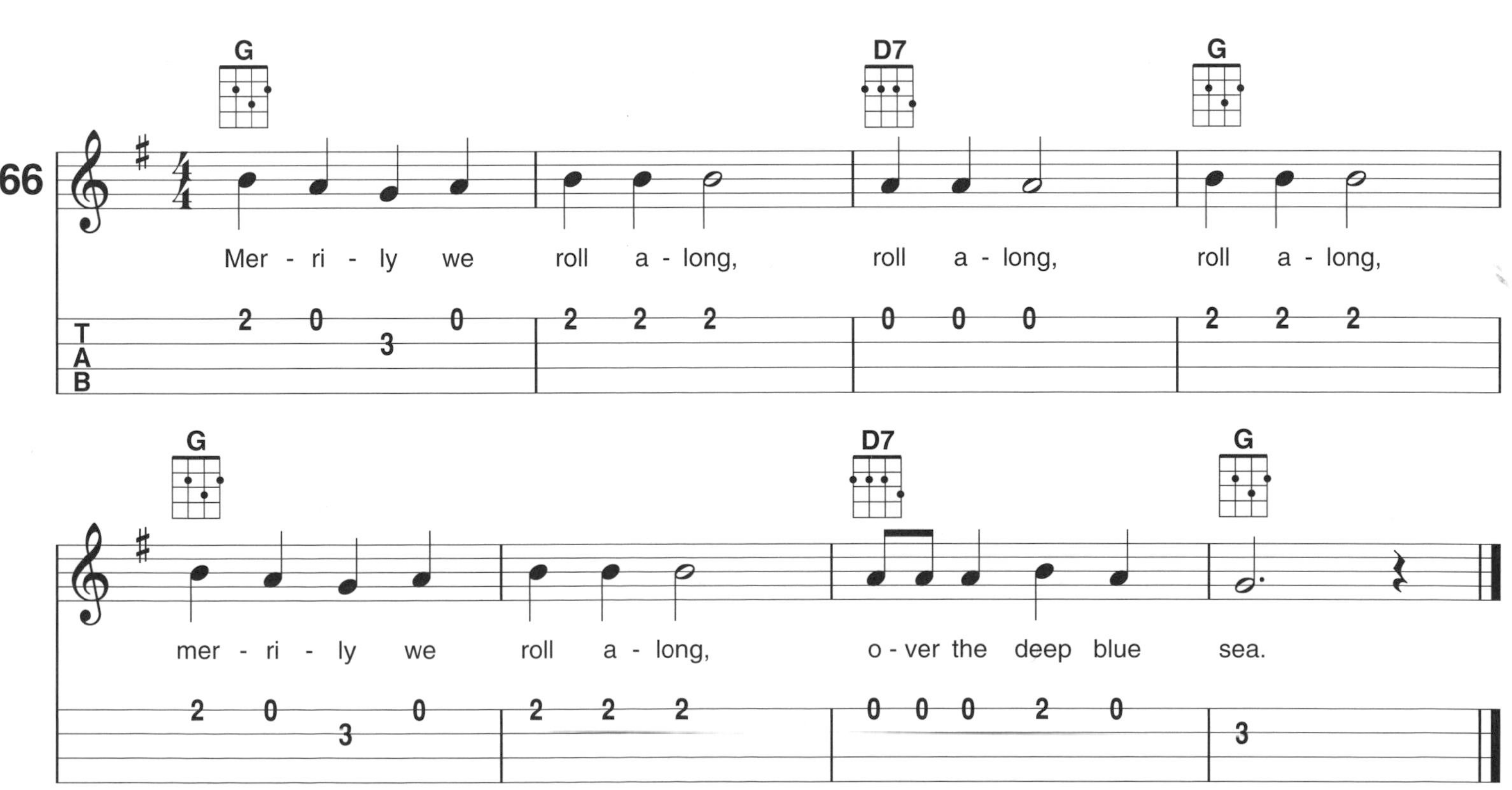

THE E MINOR CHORD FAMILY

Em, Am, and B7 Chords

You already used the Am in "Doo Wop Uke"; now meet its relatives in the E minor family.

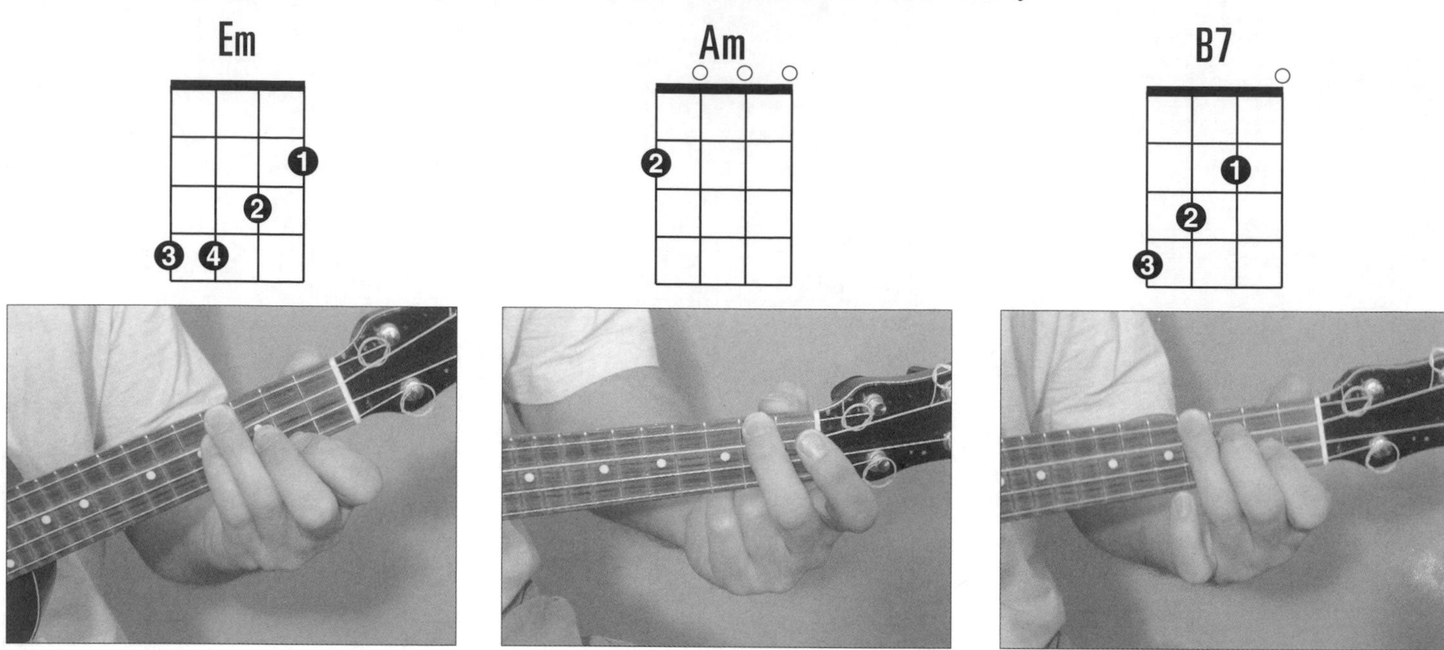

Minor chords offer a nice contrast to the bright sounds of the major and seventh chords we have seen. Some folks describe the sound of minor chords as "spooky" or "sad."

Let's start by strumming the Em chord.

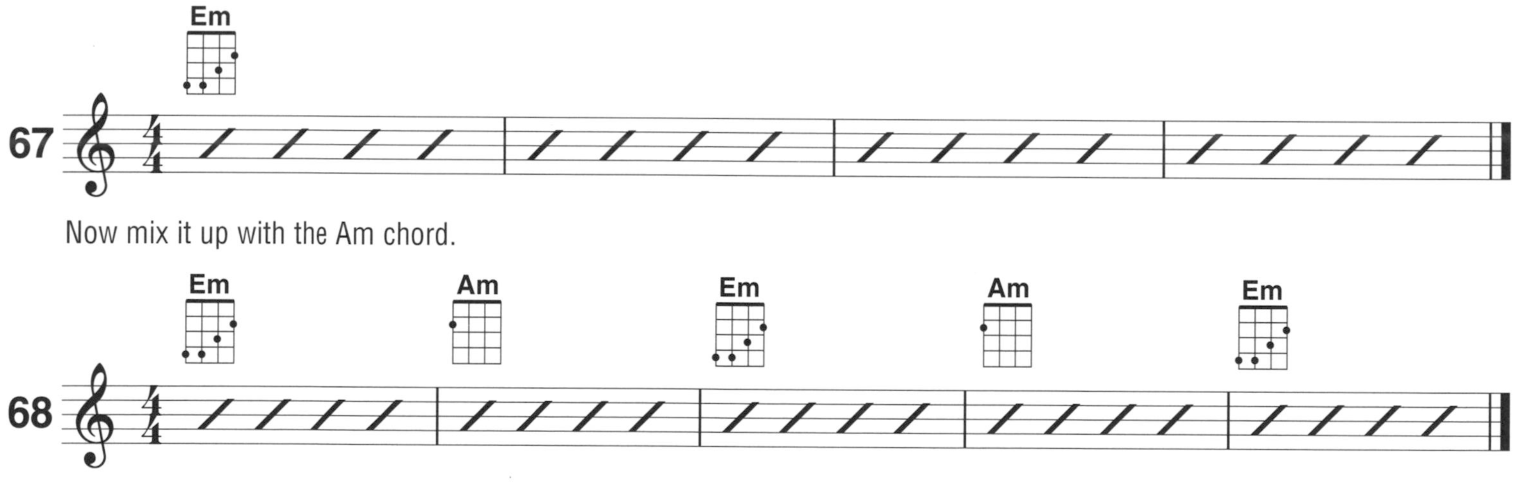

Now mix it up with the Am chord.

Try this 8-bar minor blues progression.

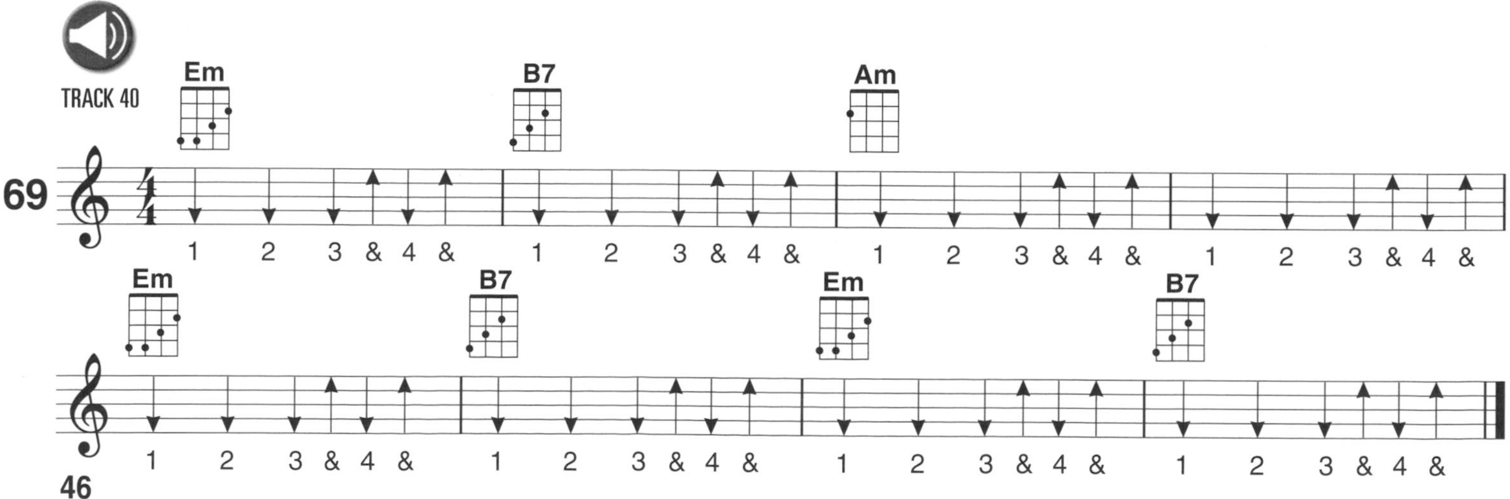

Here's a typical 12-bar minor blues progression in Em. Remember to count "1–2–3–4." Listen to the different strum variations that are played on Track #40. Try mixing it up as you play this tune and use several different strum patterns that you've learned.

THE HAUNTED UKE BLUES

TRACK 41

Blues Progression

70

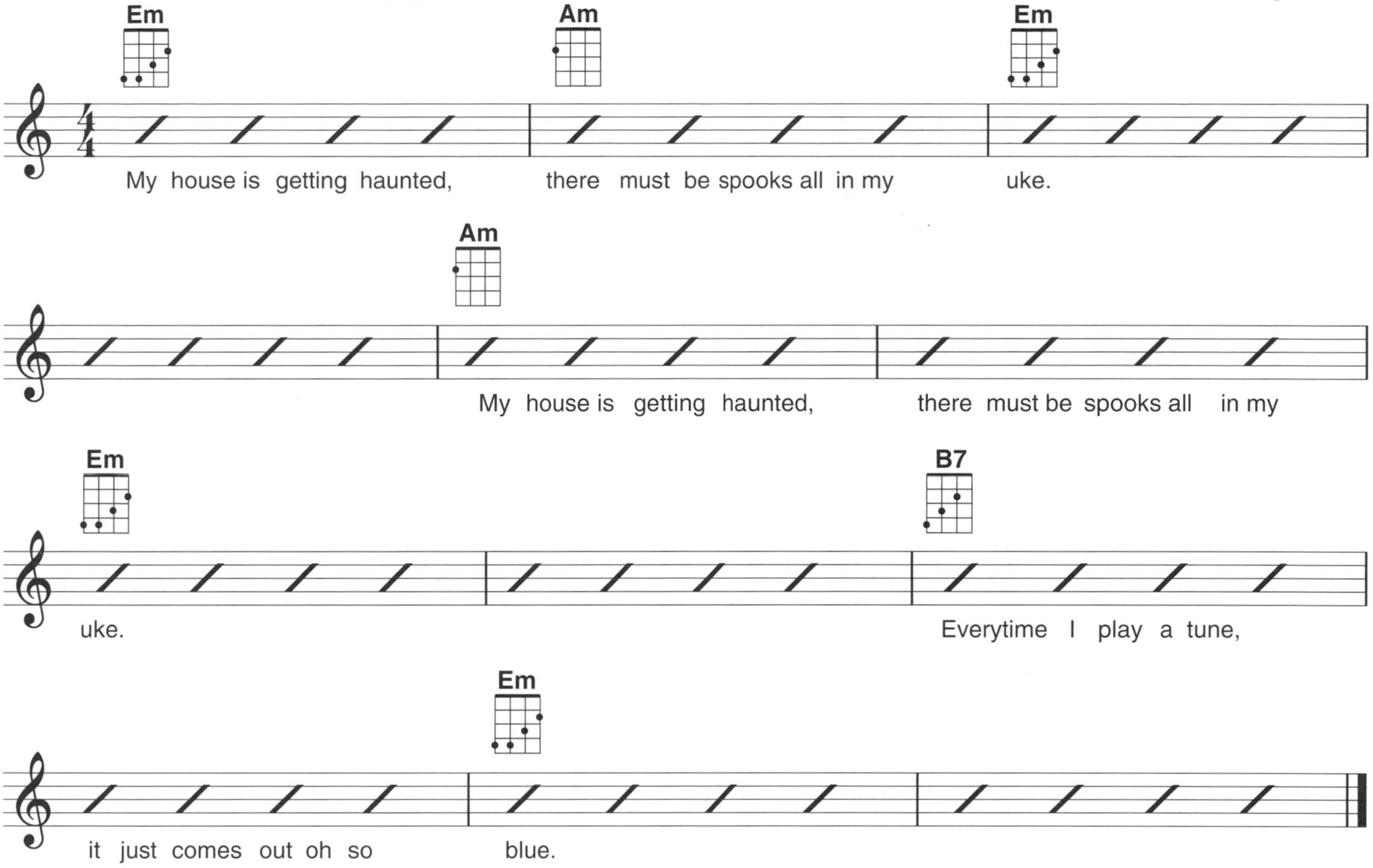
Em
Am
Em
My house is getting haunted,
there must be spooks all in my
uke.
Am
My house is getting haunted,
there must be spooks all in my
Em
B7
uke.
Everytime I play a tune,
Em
it just comes out oh so
blue.

Try picking out this minor melody using your thumb.

HEY, HO, NOBODY HOME

TRACK 42

English Folk Melody

71

Em
Hey, ho, no - bod - y home, meat nor drink nor
T
A
B
0 2 0 0 0 2 0 0 2 2
mon - ey have I none yet will I be mer - ry.
3 3 3 3 2 2 0 2 0 0 0

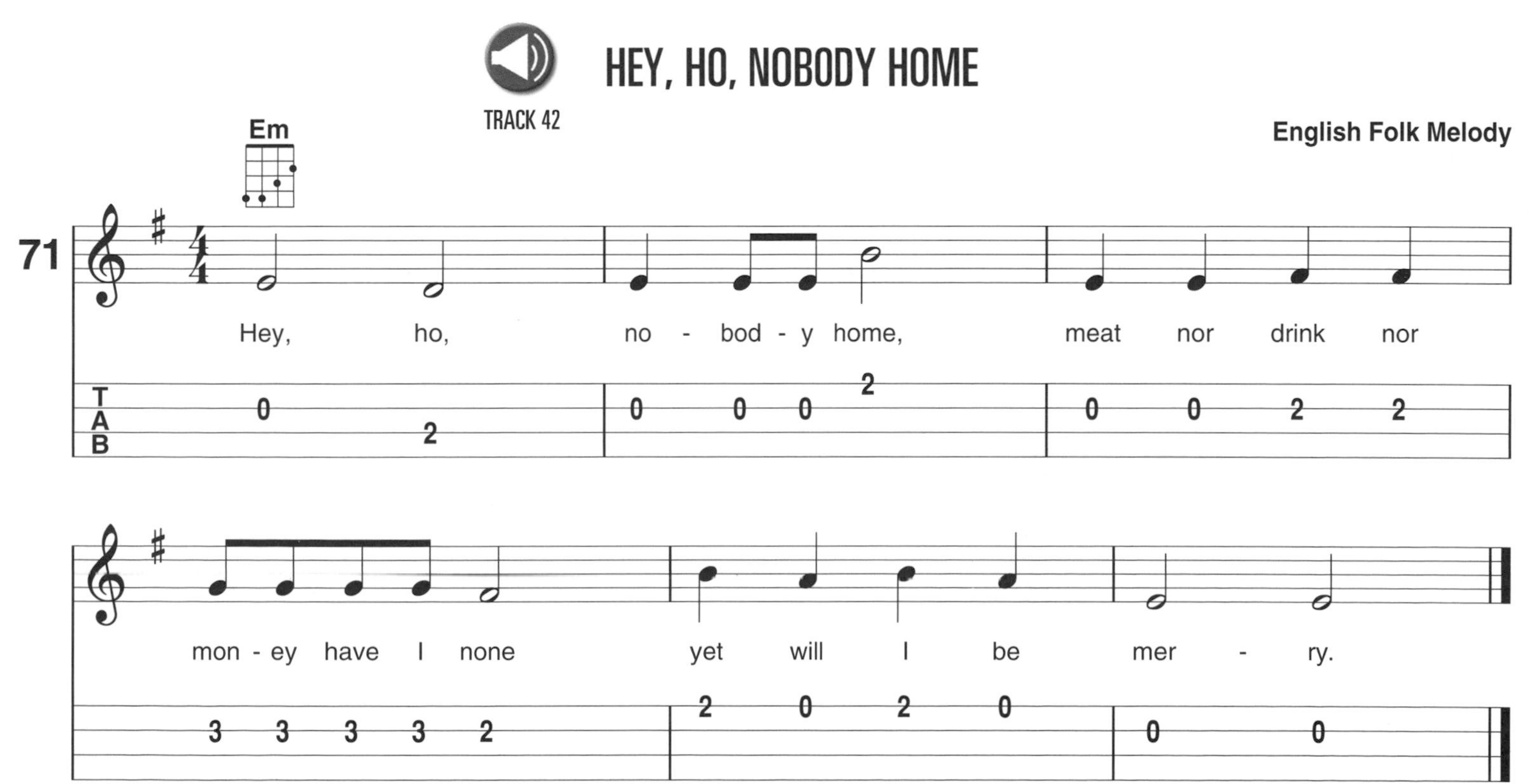

MORE CHORDS

Get familiar with the chord positions shown, then practice changing between the chords.

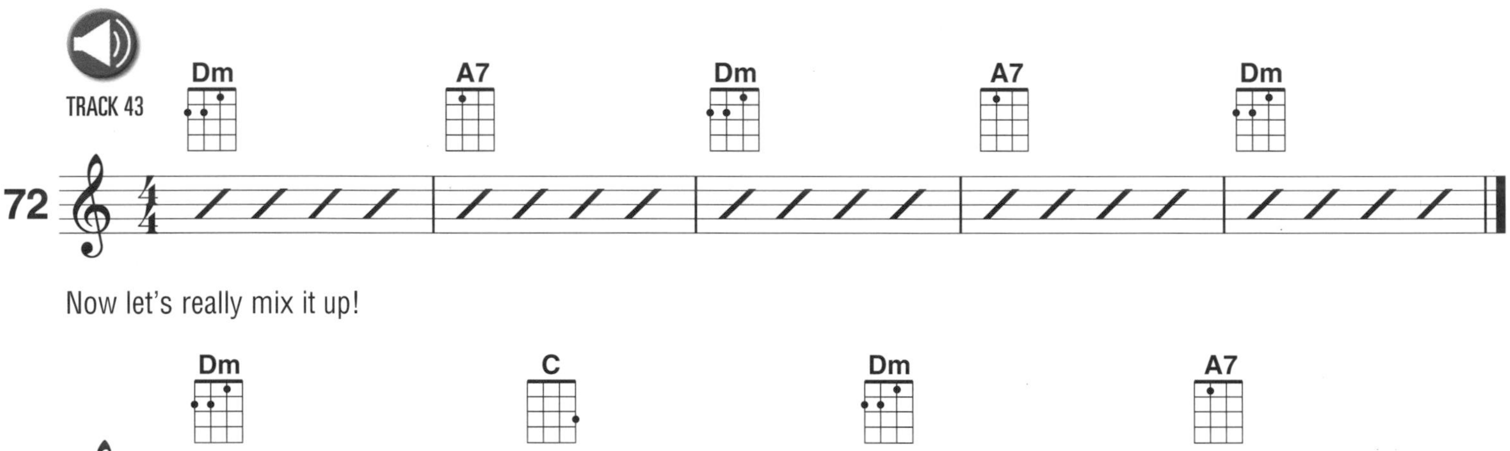

Now let's really mix it up!

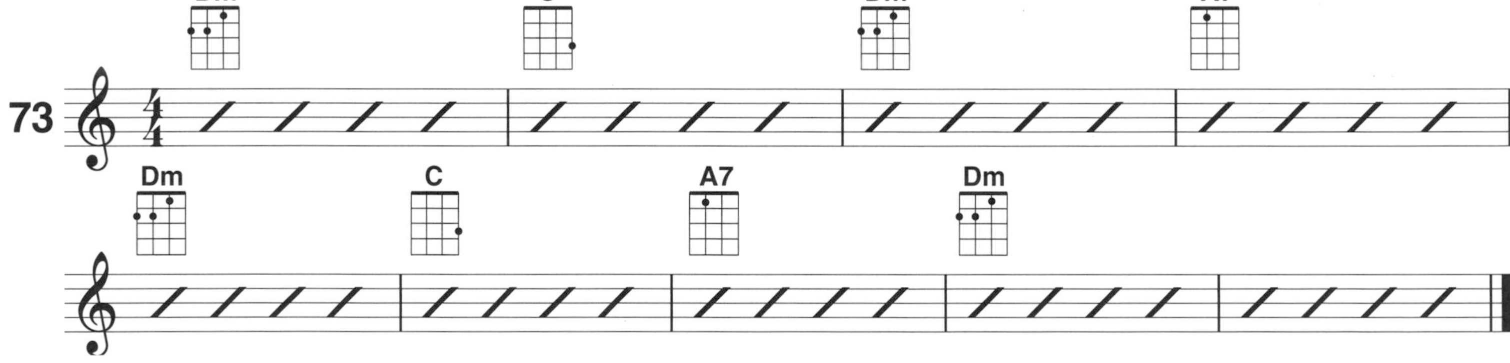

Here's a challenge: try changing chords every one or two beats instead of every four. Practice slowly at first and gradually work up to speed.

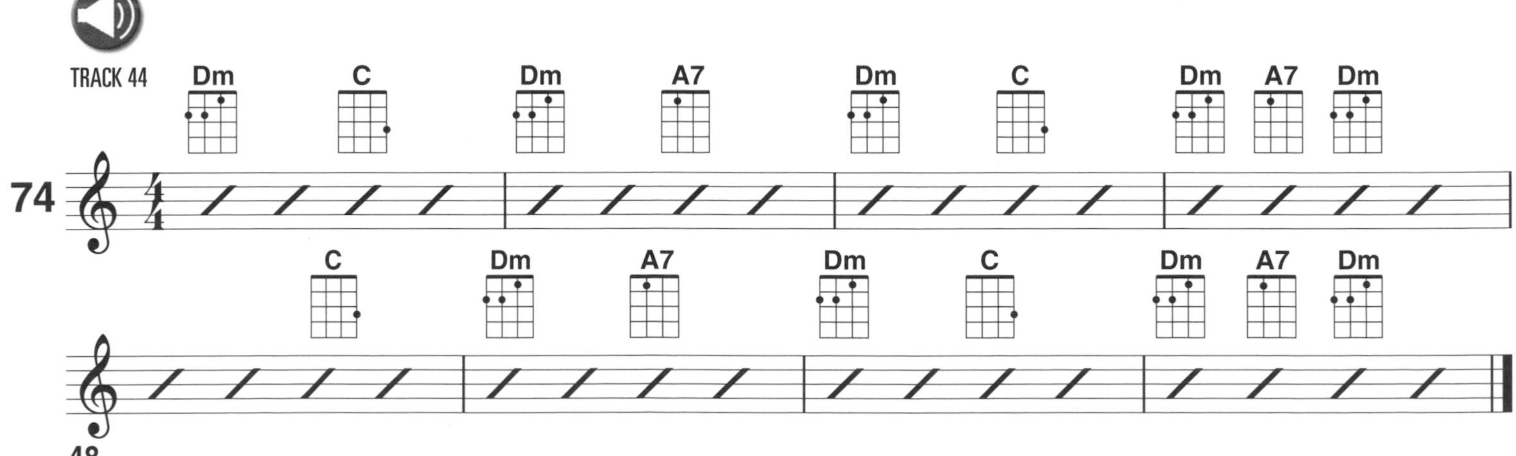

Now that you're familiar with the Dm chord, let's play a minor melody. Go slowly and pay attention to each note's time value. Gradually work up to playing a little faster. There's a new chord in "Scarborough Fair" that you haven't seen yet, the A chord. You can find this chord and many others in the Chord Chart at the back of the book.

CHORD CHART

Here are all the chords we used in the ukulele method, and some other common chords you may encounter in your ukulele adventures.

MAJOR **MINOR** **7TH**

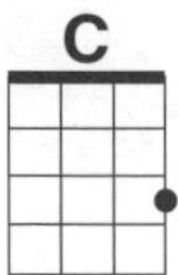

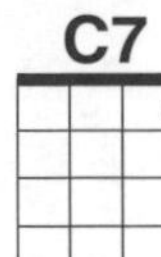

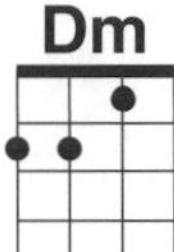

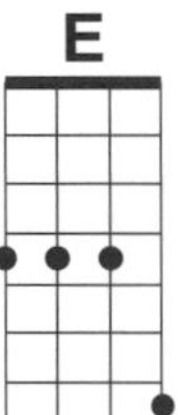

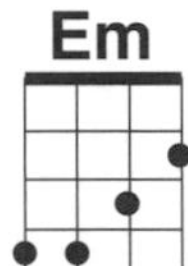

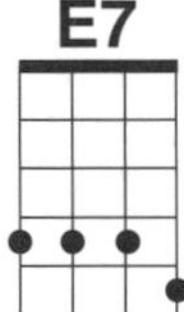

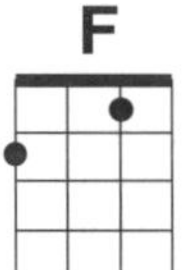

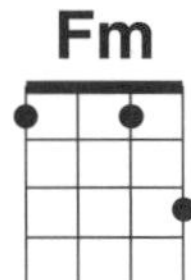

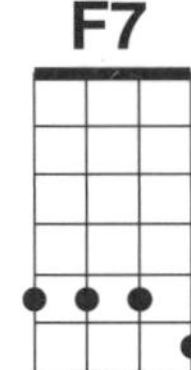

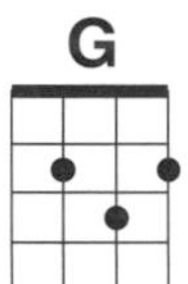

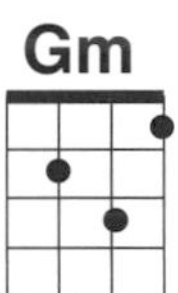

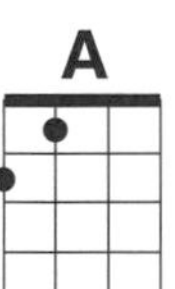

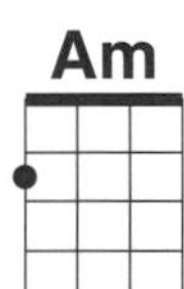

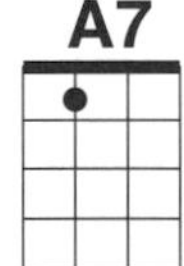

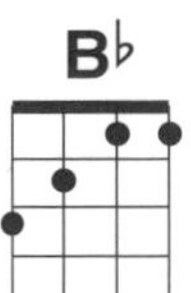

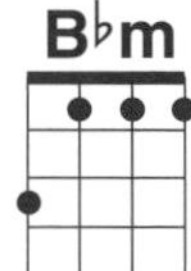

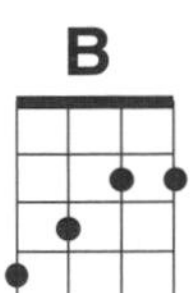

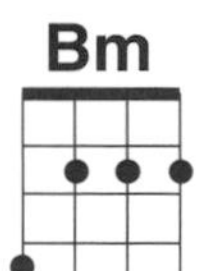

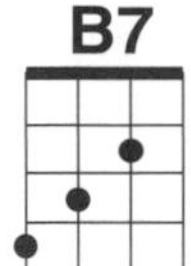

INTRODUCTION TO THE CHORD FINDER

This ukulele chord finder is an extensive reference guide to over 1,000 chords. Twenty-eight different chord qualities are covered for each key, and each chord quality is presented in three different voicings. Open strings are used when possible, but at least one voicing from each quality will be a moveable form. This allows for many unique voicings but also provides practical chord forms that can be transposed to any key. One thing to remember is that many of these moveable forms are also unique. So, just because you've learned two moveable shapes for C7, for example, that doesn't mean there aren't any more moveable seventh chord shapes in the book. Usually, you'll find other moveable voicings for the same chord by looking at other keys throughout the book.

A fingerboard chart of the entire ukulele neck through fret 12 is provided below for reference.

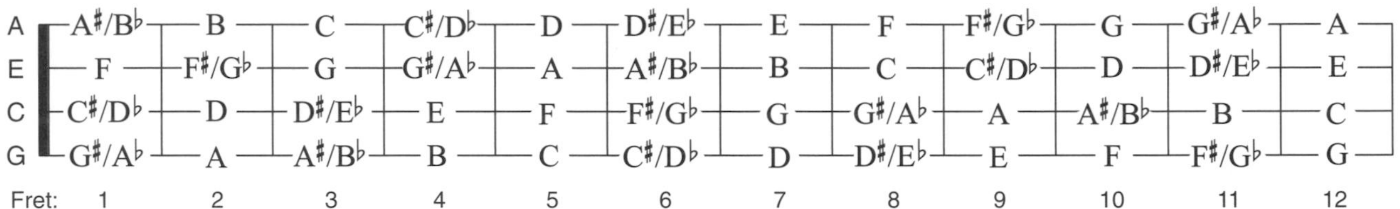

	1	2	3	4	5	6	7	8	9	10	11	12
A	A♯/B♭	B	C	C♯/D♭	D	D♯/E♭	E	F	F♯/G♭	G	G♯/A♭	A
E	F	F♯/G♭	G	G♯/A♭	A	A♯/B♭	B	C	C♯/D♭	D	D♯/E♭	E
C	C♯/D♭	D	D♯/E♭	E	F	F♯/G♭	G	G♯/A♭	A	A♯/B♭	B	C
G	G♯/A♭	A	A♯/B♭	B	C	C♯/D♭	D	D♯/E♭	E	F	F♯/G♭	G

Fret: 1 2 3 4 5 6 7 8 9 10 11 12

The chords throughout this book are presented in chord grid fashion. In case you're not familiar with this type of notation, below is a detailed explanation of how they're read.

The four vertical lines represent the strings on the ukulele.
The lowest string (G) is on the left, moving through to the highest string (E) on the right.

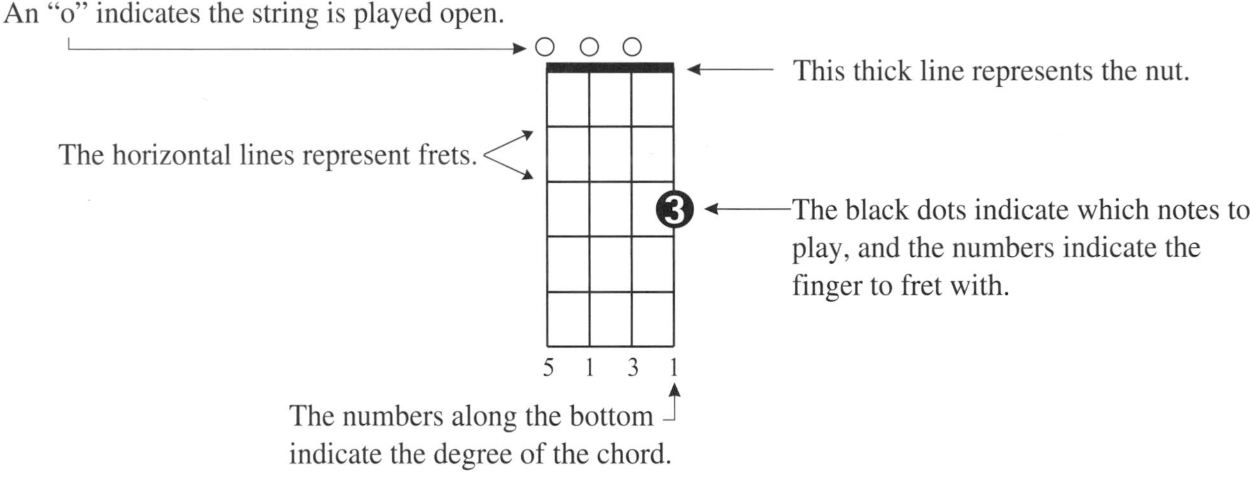

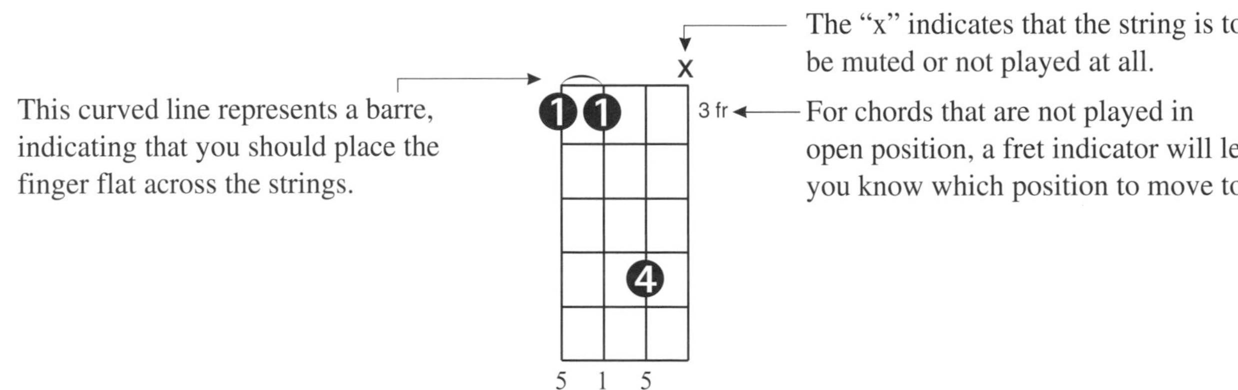

CHORD CONSTRUCTION

This section is intended to provide a basic knowledge of chords, how to build them, and how to use them. Some of you may already know this; if so, skip ahead! If not, read on and learn how to impress your friends who don't know.

TRIADS

A chord is simply a collection of notes deliberately arranged in a harmonious (or sometimes non-harmonious) fashion. The most common type of chord is called a *triad.* The name triad is telling of the number of notes in the chord—three. Triads can be one of four different qualities: major, minor, augmented, or diminished. Below, we find what's known as a C Major triad:

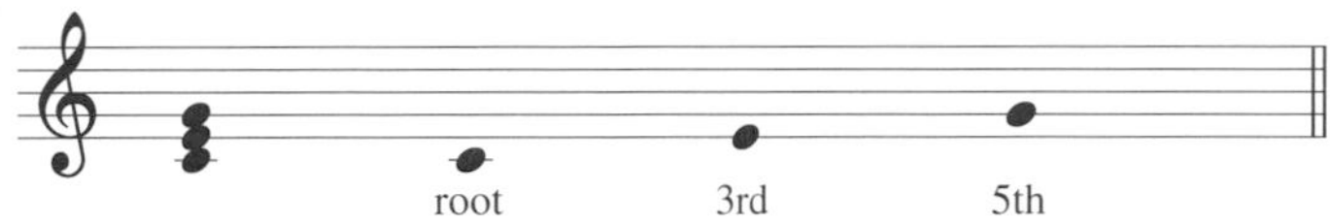

The words "root," "third," and "fifth" below the notes on the staff indicate how each note functions within the chord. A root note is the foundation of the chord and the note after which the chord will be named.

INTERVALS

The other two notes in our C triad (the 3rd and the 5th) are responsible for the *quality* of the chord. The notes C and E are an interval (or distance) of a major 3rd apart. Intervals are comprised of two components: a *number* and a *quality.*

In the case of the number, we can determine that C to E is a *3rd* by simply counting through the musical alphabet. Starting from C: C is one, D is two, and E is three. (The word "root" is many times used interchangeably with the number "1." For all practical purposes, they mean the same thing.) From C to G is a 5th, and we can confirm this by again counting up from C: C(1)–D(2)–E(3)–F(4)–G(5).

Determining the quality of an interval is not quite as easy as the number, but it's not too difficult. It will require a bit of memorization, but it's very logical. Below we'll find all twelve of the notes in the chromatic scale and their intervals measured from a C root note:

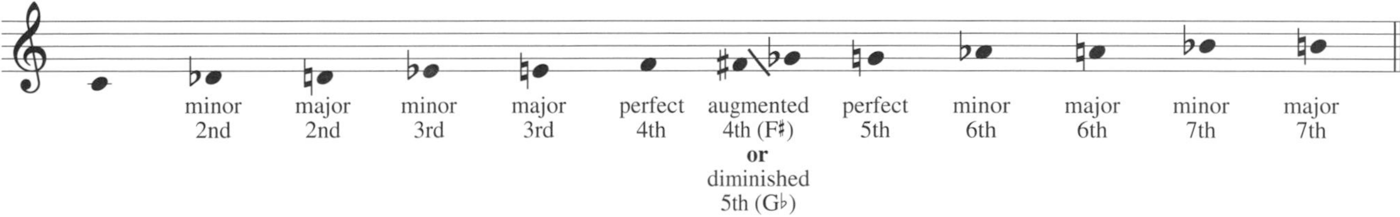

This example tells us a great deal about intervals. We can see a few formulas here at work. The first thing we should notice is that a minor interval is always one half step smaller than a major interval. C to E is a major 3rd, whereas C to E♭ is a minor 3rd. C to A is a major 6th, whereas C to A♭ is a minor 6th, etc. The next thing we should notice is how 4ths and 5ths work. We can see that an augmented interval is always one half step greater than a perfect one, and a diminished interval is always one half step smaller.

Any triad of one of the four above-mentioned qualities will contain a root, 3rd, and 5th. Other types of triads you may encounter include 6 chords, sus4 chords, and sus2 chords. Theses chords are the product of (in the case of sus4 and sus2 chords) replacing the 3rd with another note or (in the case of 6 chords) replacing the 5th (or sometimes adding to it) with another note.

Below are several different qualities of triads which will allow us to examine these intervals at work and note how they affect the names of these chords:

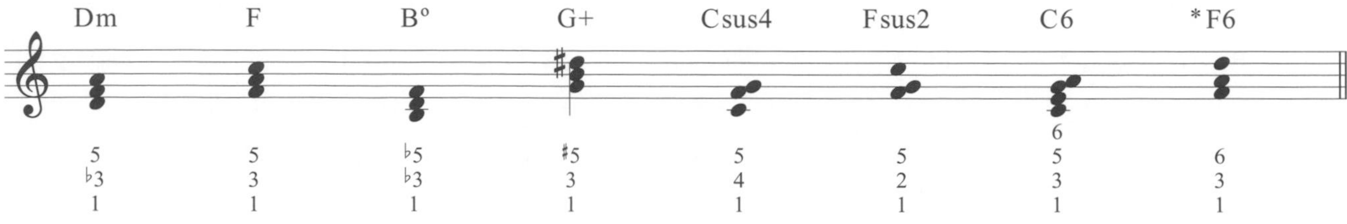

The symbol ° stands for diminished, while the symbol + stands for augmented.
* Note that the 5th tone may or may not be present in a 6 chord.

7TH CHORDS

Beyond the triad, we'll encounter many more chords, most commonly 7th chords. These chords will not only contain the root, 3rd, and 5th, but also the 7th. Below are a few common 7th chords. (Note that the 7th interval may be major or minor independent of the 3rd, thus affecting the name of the chord.)

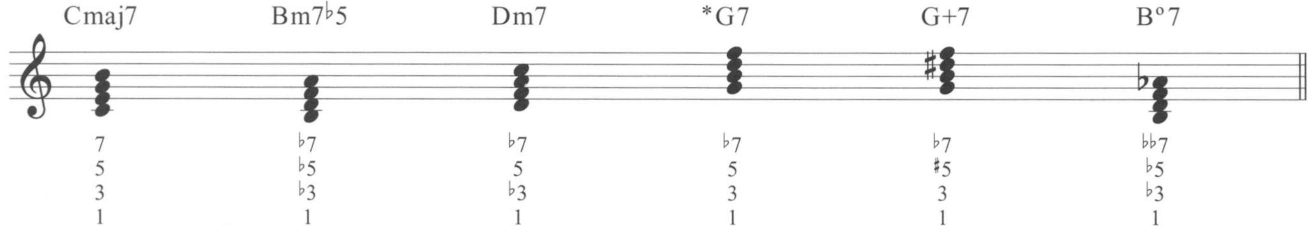

* Note that the G7 chord contains a major 3rd and a minor 7th. This type of chord is referred to as a *dominant 7th.*

EXTENSIONS

Finally, beyond 7th chords, we have extensions. The concept of extensions is a bit complicated and will only be touched upon here, as it requires more extensive study than is possible within the scope of this book. Basically, extended chords continue the process of stacking notes onto a triad that we began with the 7th chord. Instead of only adding the 7th to the chord, however, in a 9th chord we'll add the 7th and the 9th. In an 11th chord, we'll add the 7th, 9th, and 11th to our triad, etc. Now, here's the catch: not all of the notes need to be present in an extended chord. The general rule is, if the 7th is present, then notes other than the root, 3rd, and 5th are extensions and therefore numbered an octave higher (9, 11, 13). Since we're only capable of playing four notes at a time on the ukulele, we must decide which notes are important and which notes we can omit. Generally speaking, you'll want to include the root, 3rd, 7th, and the extension. The C13 chord below demonstrates this concept:

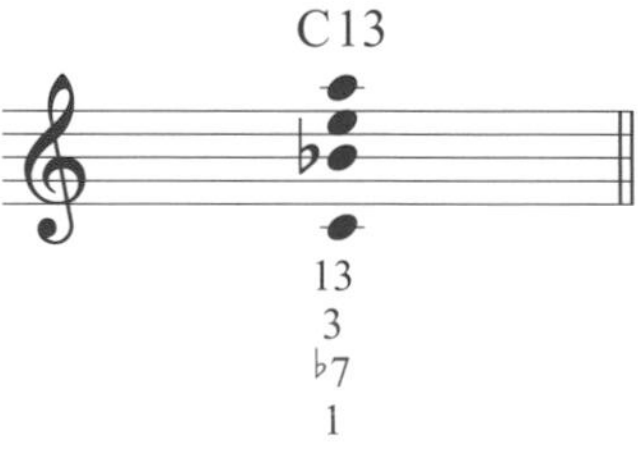

Note that there is no 5th (G) present in this chord, but the presence of the 7th (B♭) tells us that this chord is called C13, rather than some kind of C6 chord.

Extended chords may contain either the major 3rd or the perfect 11th, but usually not both. These two notes can clash with one another, since the 11th is equivalent to the 4th, only a half step away from the 3rd. In the C13 chord above, the 11th was omitted. In a chord where the 11th is specified, the major 3rd is usually omitted. There may be some cases where your ear tells you it is OK to use a chord with both notes. This book includes examples of both options, with emphasis on the common practice. Minor chords do not have this problem and may include the 11th and minor 3rd together.

INVERSIONS

Since the ukulele only has four strings, chords will often be voiced in *inversion*. A chord is inverted when a note other than the root is in the bass. In a triad, which contains three different notes, there are three basic possibilities for the vertical organization of the notes: root position, first inversion, and second inversion. Chords in root position contain the root of the chord in the bass; in other words, they are not inversions. A first inversion chord, however, contains the 3rd in the bass, while a second inversion chord contains the 5th in the bass. This is demonstrated below:

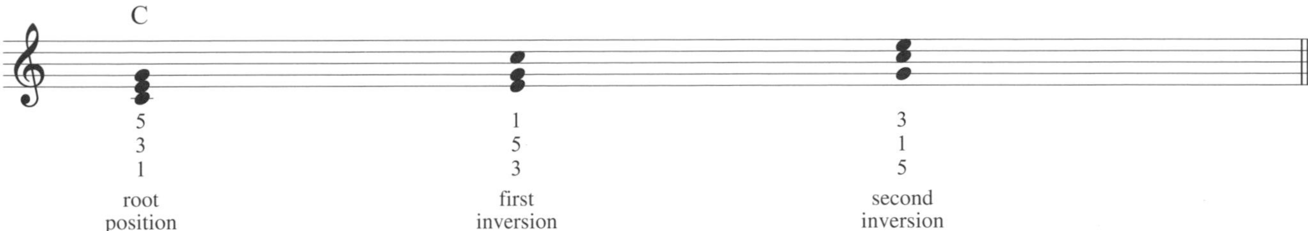

In a seventh chord or an extended chord, which contains four different notes, we have another inversion possibility. In addition to the first and second inversions, we can also have a third inversion, which places the 7th of the chord in the bass.

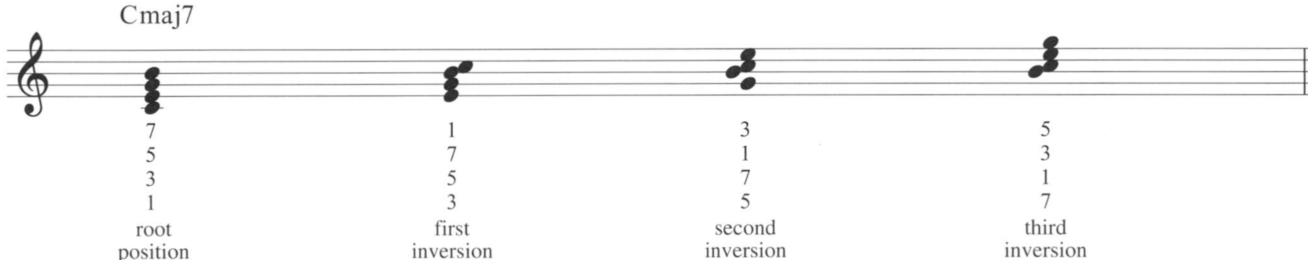

Occasionally, extended chords will feature an extension (9th, 11th, or 13th) in the bass. While these chords are inversions as well, they aren't typically numbered as with the triads and seventh chords. For instance, the chord below would most likely be called "D9 with E in the bass," or "D9 with the 9th in the bass," or simply "D9 over E."

Again, this section is intended to be a basic tutorial on the concept of chord construction and chord theory. If you're interested in furthering your knowledge on this subject, I suggest you take a look at some of the many books dedicated to chord construction and theory.

CHORD QUALITIES

Below is a list of the twenty-eight different chord qualities presented in this book, their abbreviations, and their formulas:

CHORD TYPE	ABBREVIATION	FORMULA
Major	C	1–3–5
Minor	Cm	1–♭3–5
Augmented	C+	1–3–♯5
Diminished	C°	1–♭3–♭5
Fifth (Power Chord)	C5	1–5
Added Ninth	Cadd9	1–3–5–9
Minor Added Ninth	Cm(add9)	1–♭3–5–9
Suspended Fourth	Csus4	1–4–5
Suspended Second	Csus2	1–2–5
Sixth	C6	1–3–5–6
Minor Sixth	Cm6	1–♭3–5–6
Major Seventh	Cmaj7	1–3–5–7
Major Ninth	Cmaj9	1–3–5–7–9
Minor Seventh	Cm7	1–♭3–5–♭7
Minor, Major Seventh	Cm(maj7)	1–♭3–5–7
Minor Seventh, Flat Fifth	Cm7♭5	1–♭3–♭5–♭7
Minor Ninth	Cm9	1–♭3–5–♭7–9
Minor Eleventh	Cm11	1–♭3–5–♭7–9–11
Seventh	C7	1–3–5–♭7
Seventh, Suspended Fourth	C7sus4	1–4–5–♭7
Augmented Seventh	C+7	1–3–♯5–♭7
Seventh, Flat Fifth	C7♭5	1–3–♭5–♭7
Ninth	C9	1–3–5–♭7–9
Seventh, Sharp Ninth	C7♯9	1–3–5–♭7–♯9
Seventh, Flat Ninth	C7♭9	1–3–5–♭7–♭9
Eleventh	C11	1–3–5–♭7–9–11*
Thirteenth	C13	1–3–5–♭7–9–11–13 **
Diminished Seventh	C°7	1–♭3–♭5–♭♭7

* The 3rd is sometimes omitted from an eleventh chord.
** The 11th is sometimes omitted from a thirteenth chord.

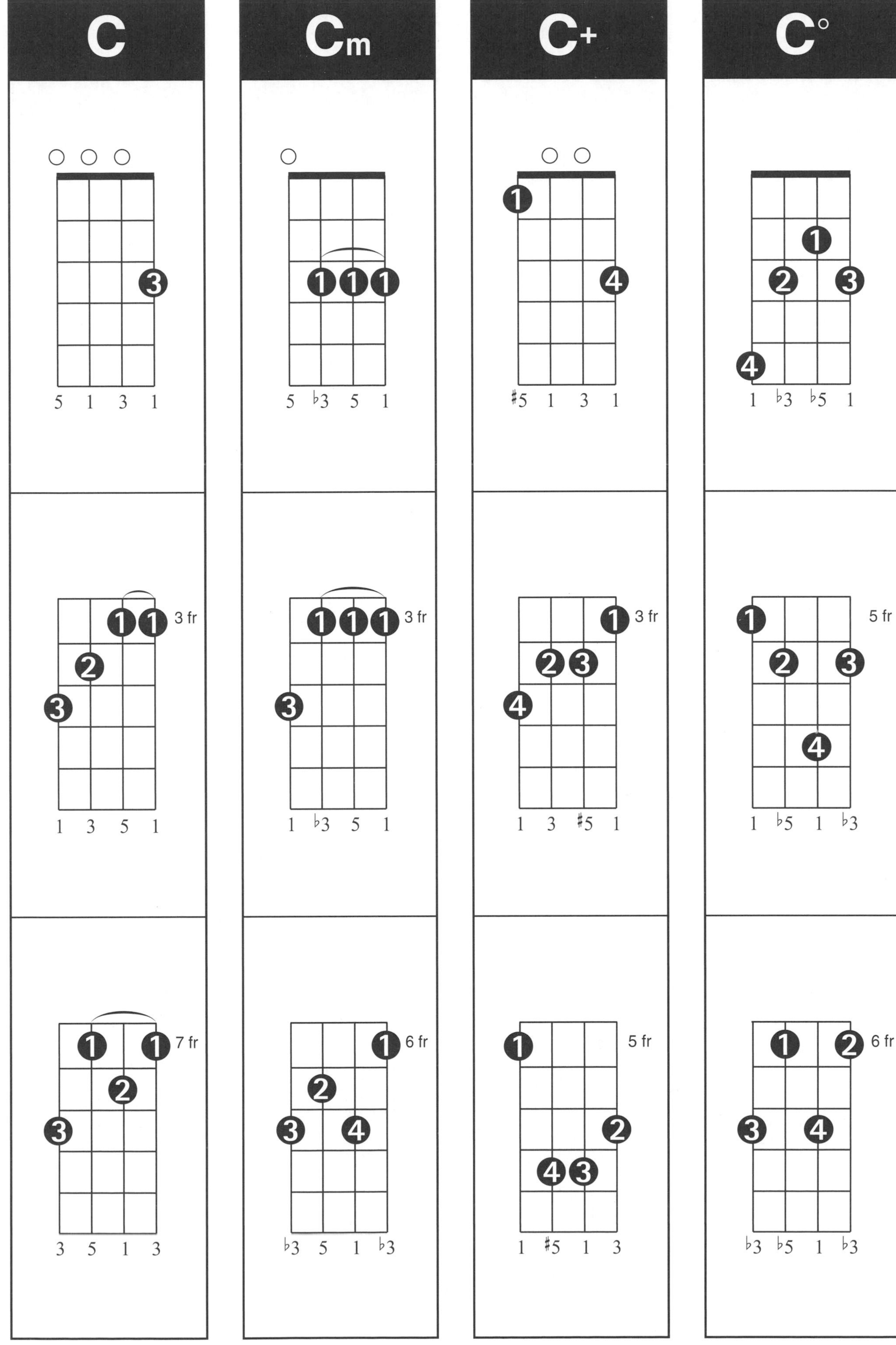
C
Cm
C+
C°
5 1 3 1
5 ♭3 5 1
♯5 1 3 1
1 ♭3 ♭5 1
3 fr
1 3 5 1
3 fr
1 ♭3 5 1
3 fr
1 3 ♯5 1
5 fr
1 ♭5 1 ♭3
7 fr
3 5 1 3
6 fr
♭3 5 1 ♭3
5 fr
1 ♯5 1 3
6 fr
♭3 ♭5 1 ♭3

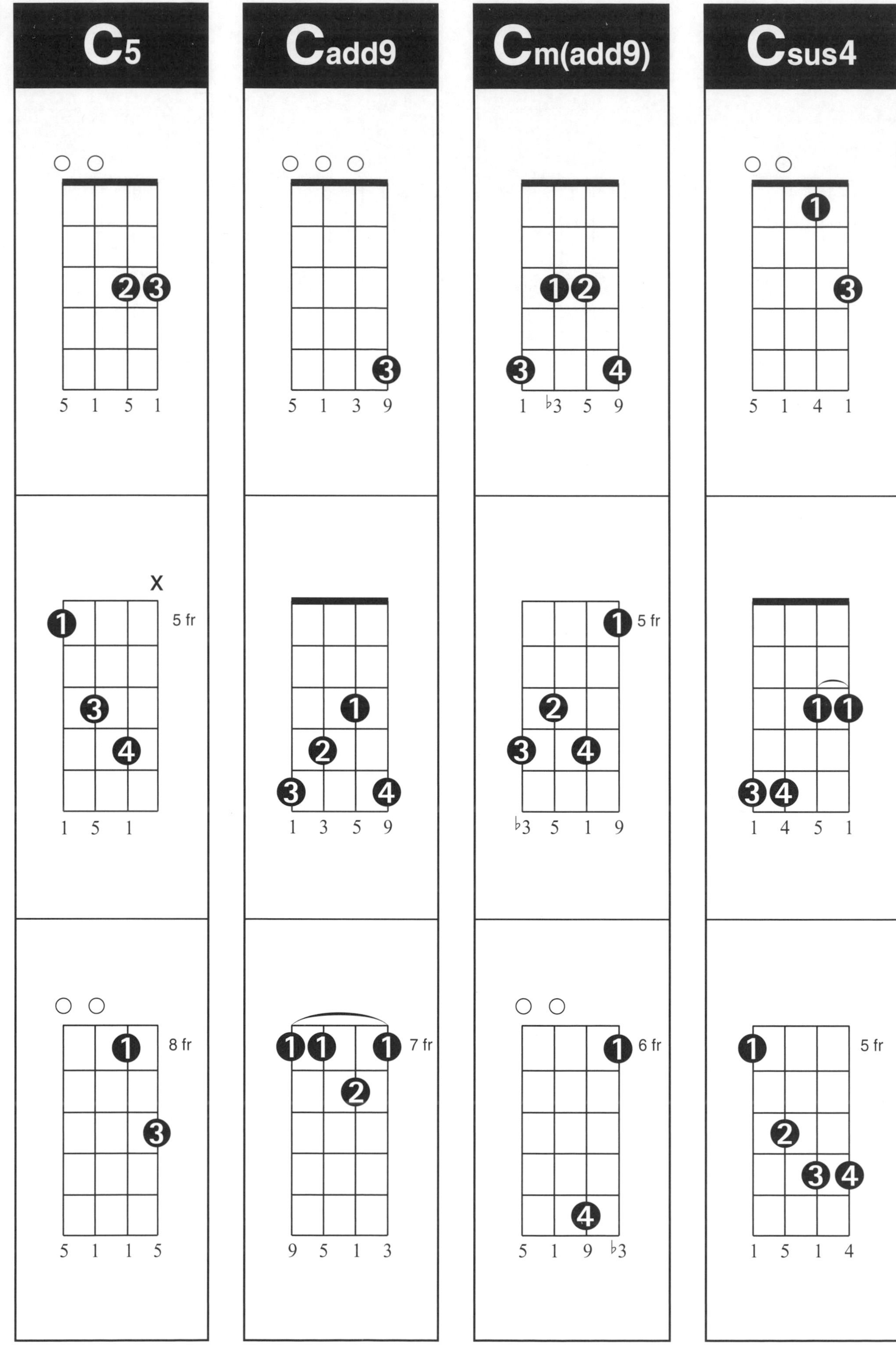
C5
Cadd9
Cm(add9)
Csus4
5 1 5 1
5 1 3 9
1 ♭3 5 9
5 1 4 1
X
5 fr
1 5 1
1 3 5 9
5 fr
♭3 5 1 9
1 4 5 1
8 fr
5 1 1 5
7 fr
9 5 1 3
6 fr
5 1 9 ♭3
5 fr
1 5 1 4

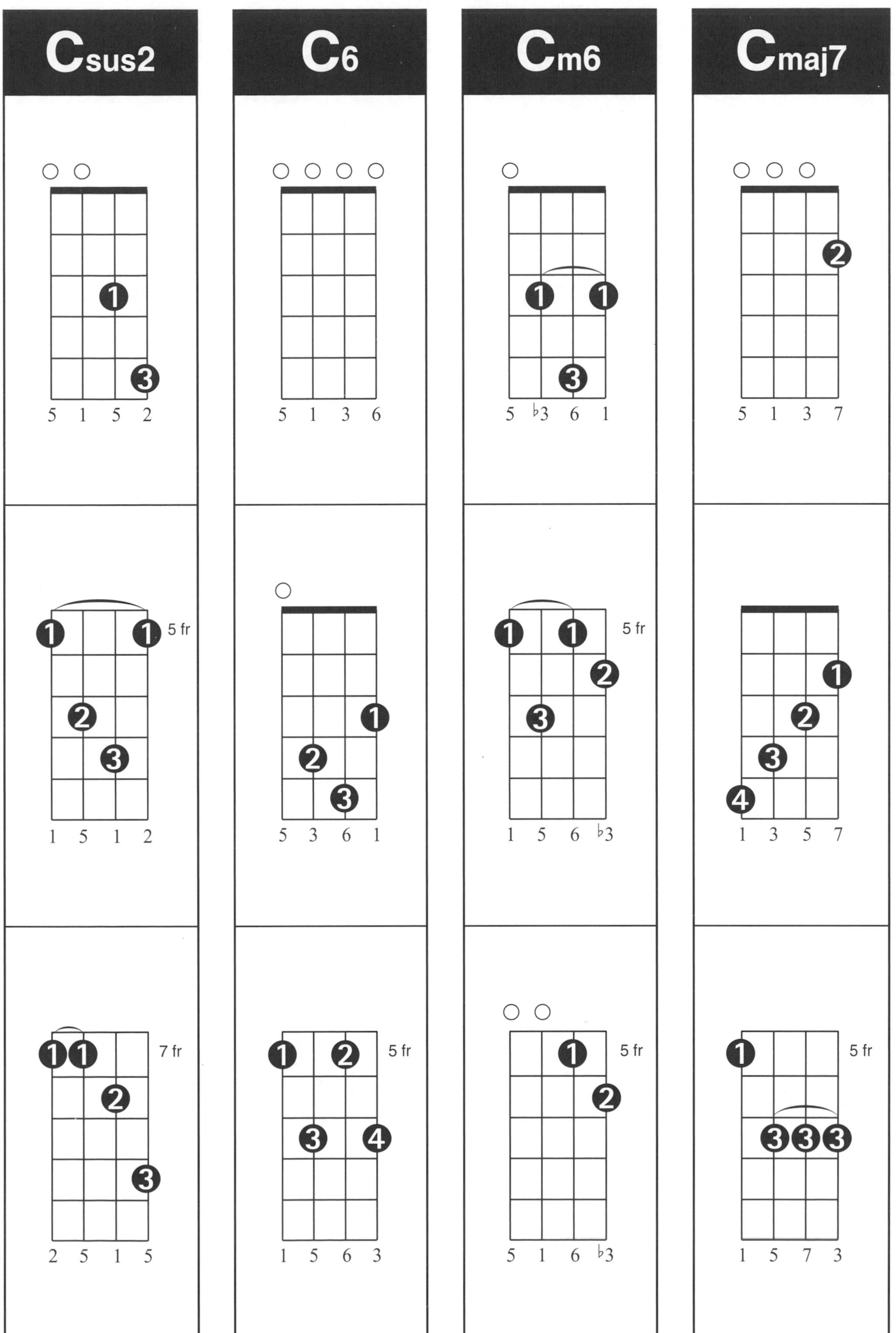
Csus2
C6
Cm6
Cmaj7
5 1 5 2
5 1 3 6
5 ♭3 6 1
5 1 3 7
5 fr
1 5 1 2
5 3 6 1
5 fr
1 5 6 ♭3
1 3 5 7
7 fr
2 5 1 5
5 fr
1 5 6 3
5 fr
5 1 6 ♭3
5 fr
1 5 7 3

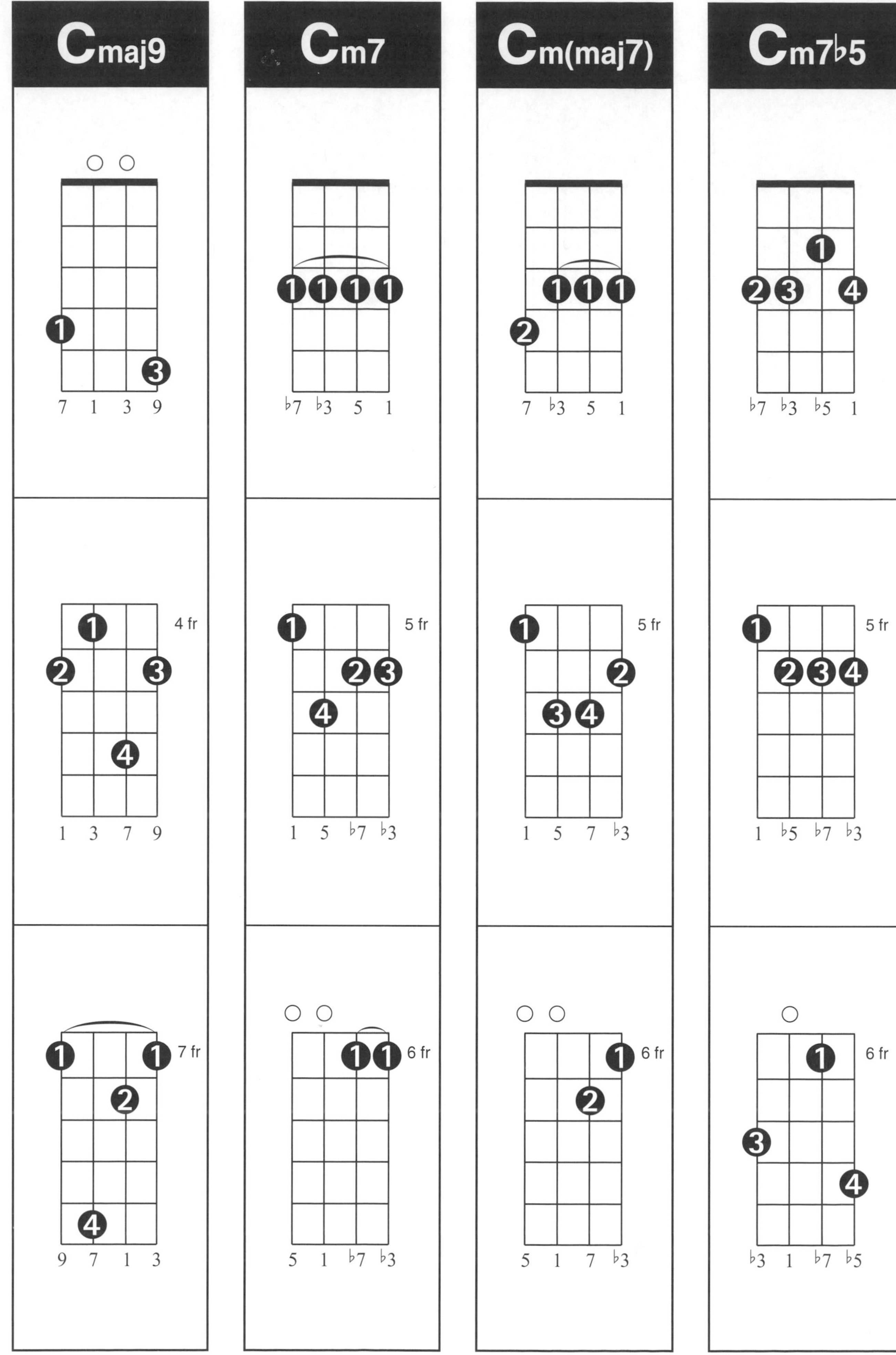

Cmaj9
Cm7
Cm(maj7)
Cm7♭5
7 1 3 9
♭7 ♭3 5 1
7 ♭3 5 1
♭7 ♭3 ♭5 1
4 fr
5 fr
5 fr
5 fr
1 3 7 9
1 5 ♭7 ♭3
1 5 7 ♭3
1 ♭5 ♭7 ♭3
7 fr
6 fr
6 fr
6 fr
9 7 1 3
5 1 ♭7 ♭3
5 1 7 ♭3
♭3 1 ♭7 ♭5

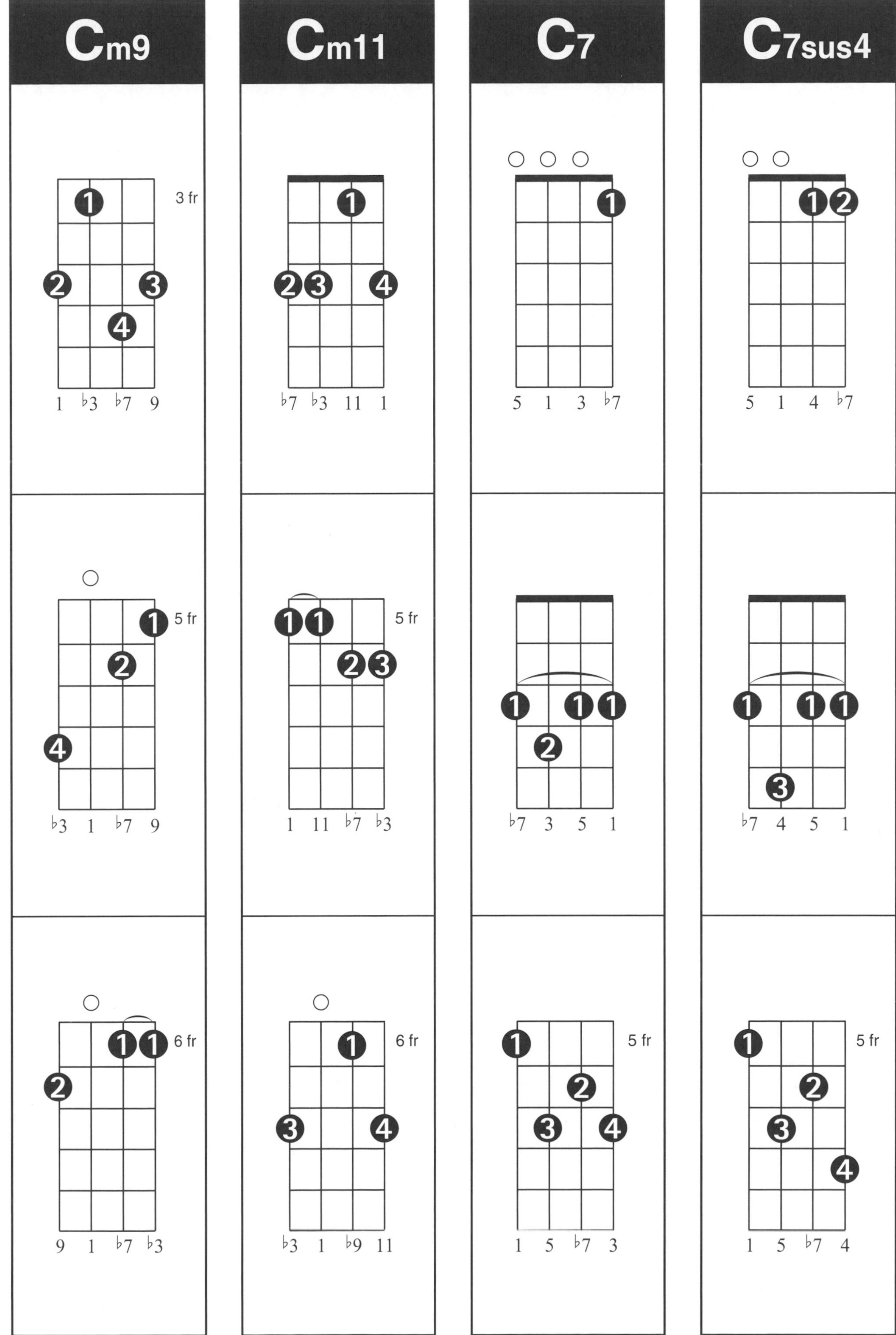
Cm9
3 fr
1 ♭3 ♭7 9
5 fr
♭3 1 ♭7 9
6 fr
9 1 ♭7 ♭3
Cm11
♭7 ♭3 11 1
5 fr
1 11 ♭7 ♭3
6 fr
♭3 1 ♭9 11
C7
5 1 3 ♭7
♭7 3 5 1
5 fr
1 5 ♭7 3
C7sus4
5 1 4 ♭7
♭7 4 5 1
5 fr
1 5 ♭7 4

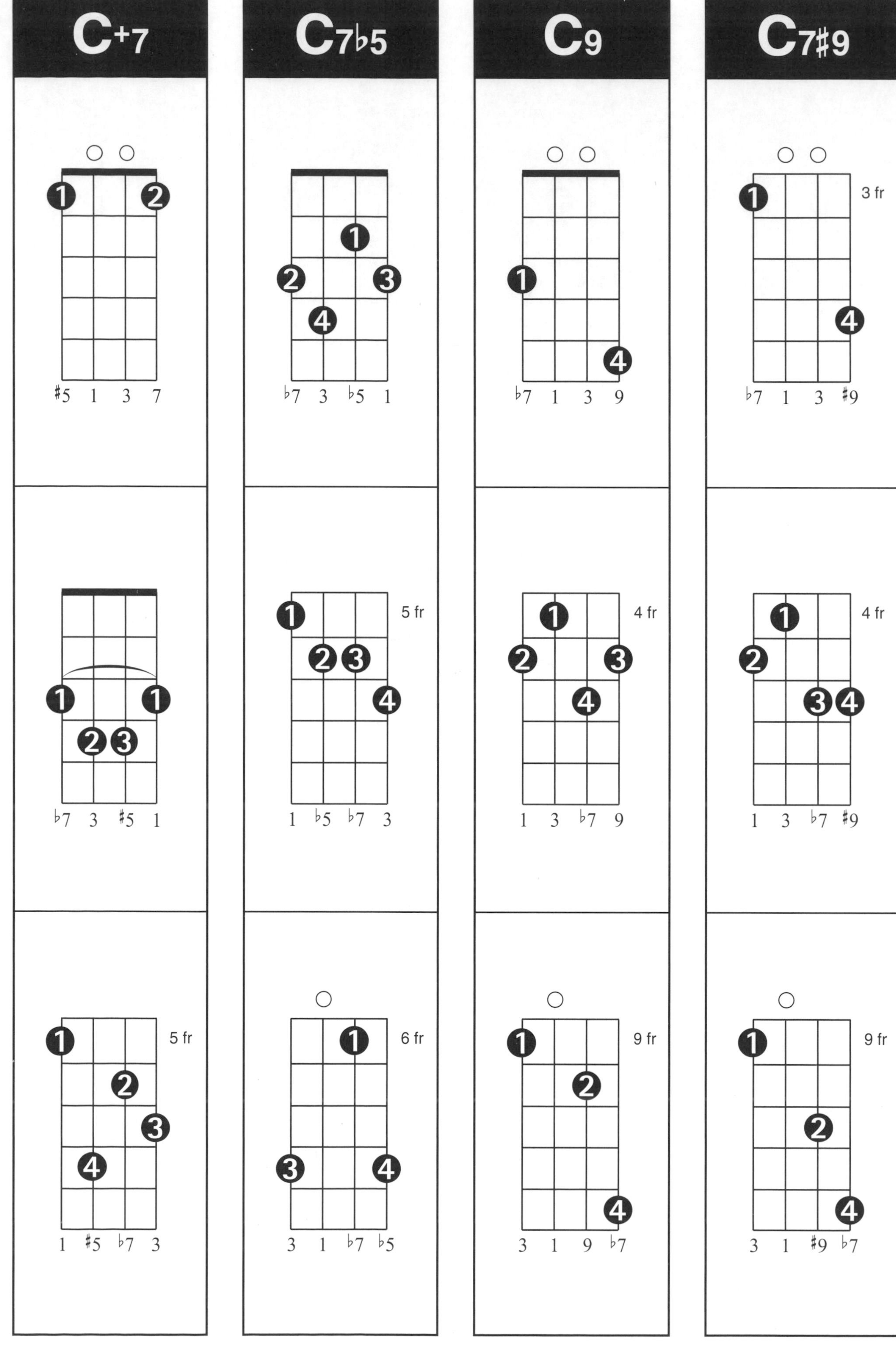
C+7
C7♭5
C9
C7♯9
♯5 1 3 7
♭7 3 ♭5 1
♭7 1 3 9
3 fr
♭7 1 3 ♯9
♭7 3 ♯5 1
5 fr
1 ♭5 ♭7 3
4 fr
1 3 ♭7 9
4 fr
1 3 ♭7 ♯9
5 fr
1 ♯5 ♭7 3
6 fr
3 1 ♭7 ♭5
9 fr
3 1 9 ♭7
9 fr
3 1 ♯9 ♭7

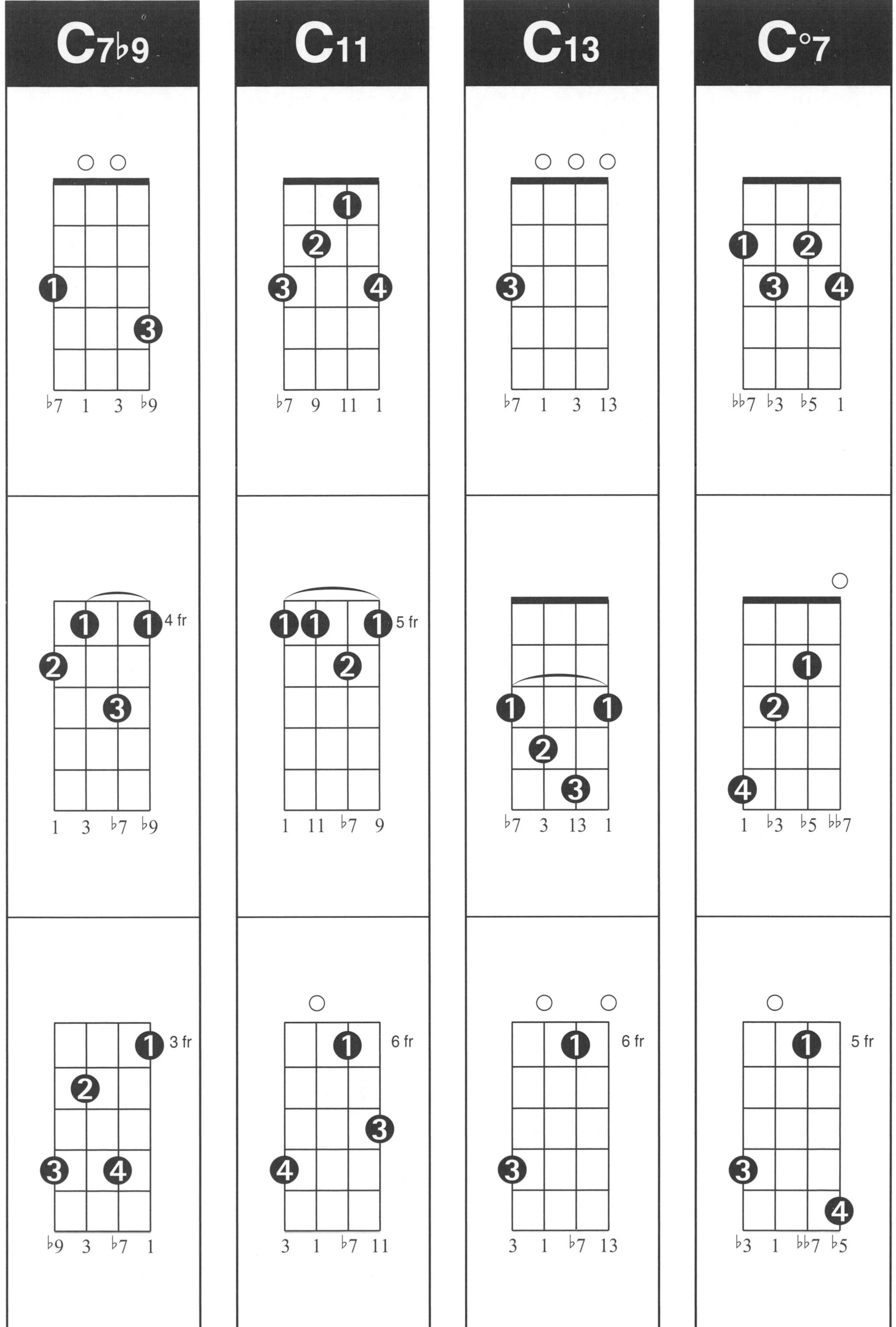
C7♭9
C11
C13
C°7
♭7 1 3 ♭9
♭7 9 11 1
♭7 1 3 13
♭♭7 ♭3 ♭5 1
4 fr
5 fr
1 3 ♭7 ♭9
1 11 ♭7 9
♭7 3 13 1
1 ♭3 ♭5 ♭♭7
3 fr
6 fr
6 fr
5 fr
♭9 3 ♭7 1
3 1 ♭7 11
3 1 ♭7 13
♭3 1 ♭♭7 ♭5

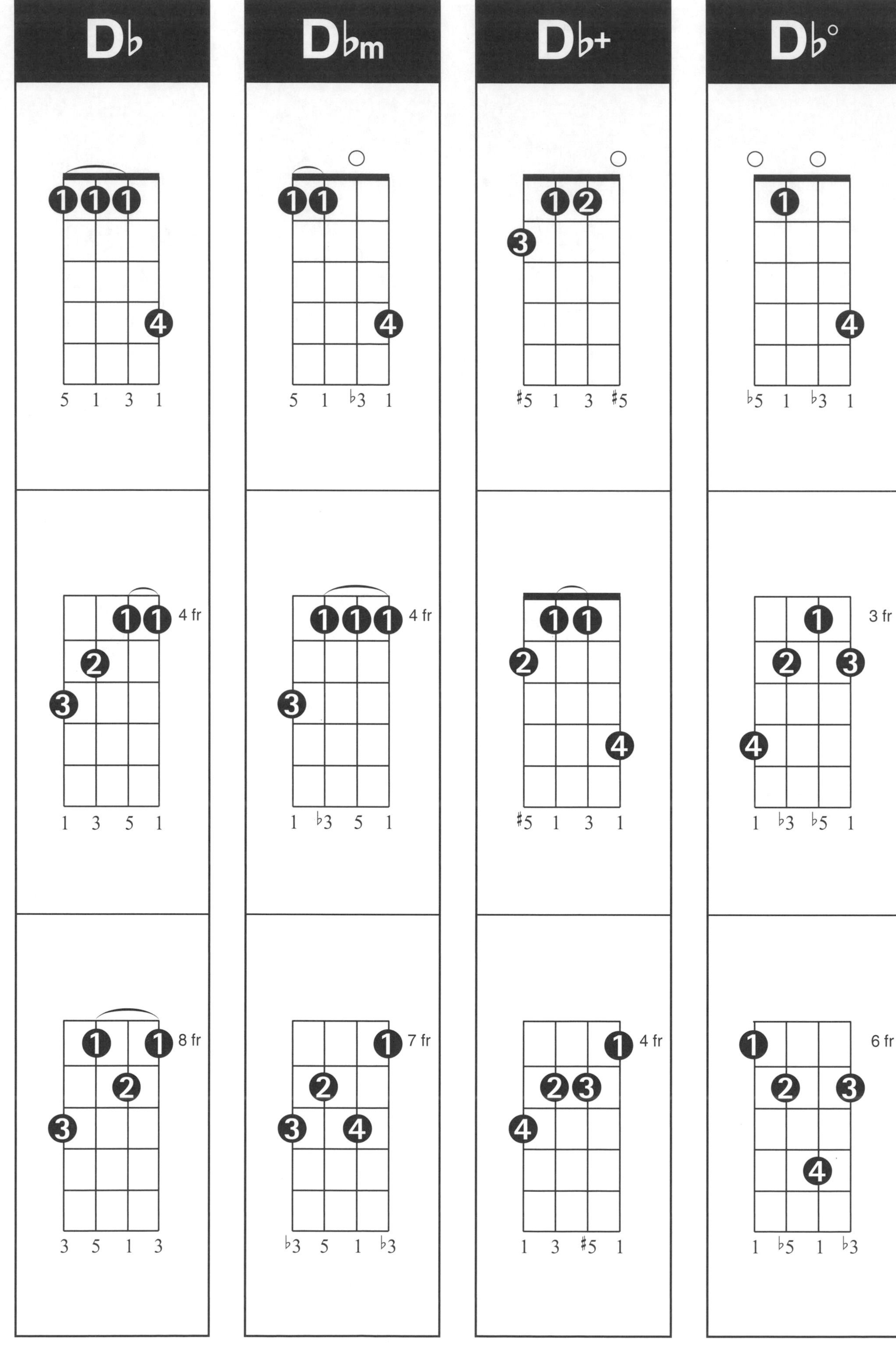

D♭
D♭m
D♭+
D♭°
5 1 3 1
5 1 ♭3 1
♯5 1 3 ♯5
♭5 1 ♭3 1
4 fr
1 3 5 1
4 fr
1 ♭3 5 1
♯5 1 3 1
3 fr
1 ♭3 ♭5 1
8 fr
3 5 1 3
7 fr
♭3 5 1 ♭3
4 fr
1 3 ♯5 1
6 fr
1 ♭5 1 ♭3

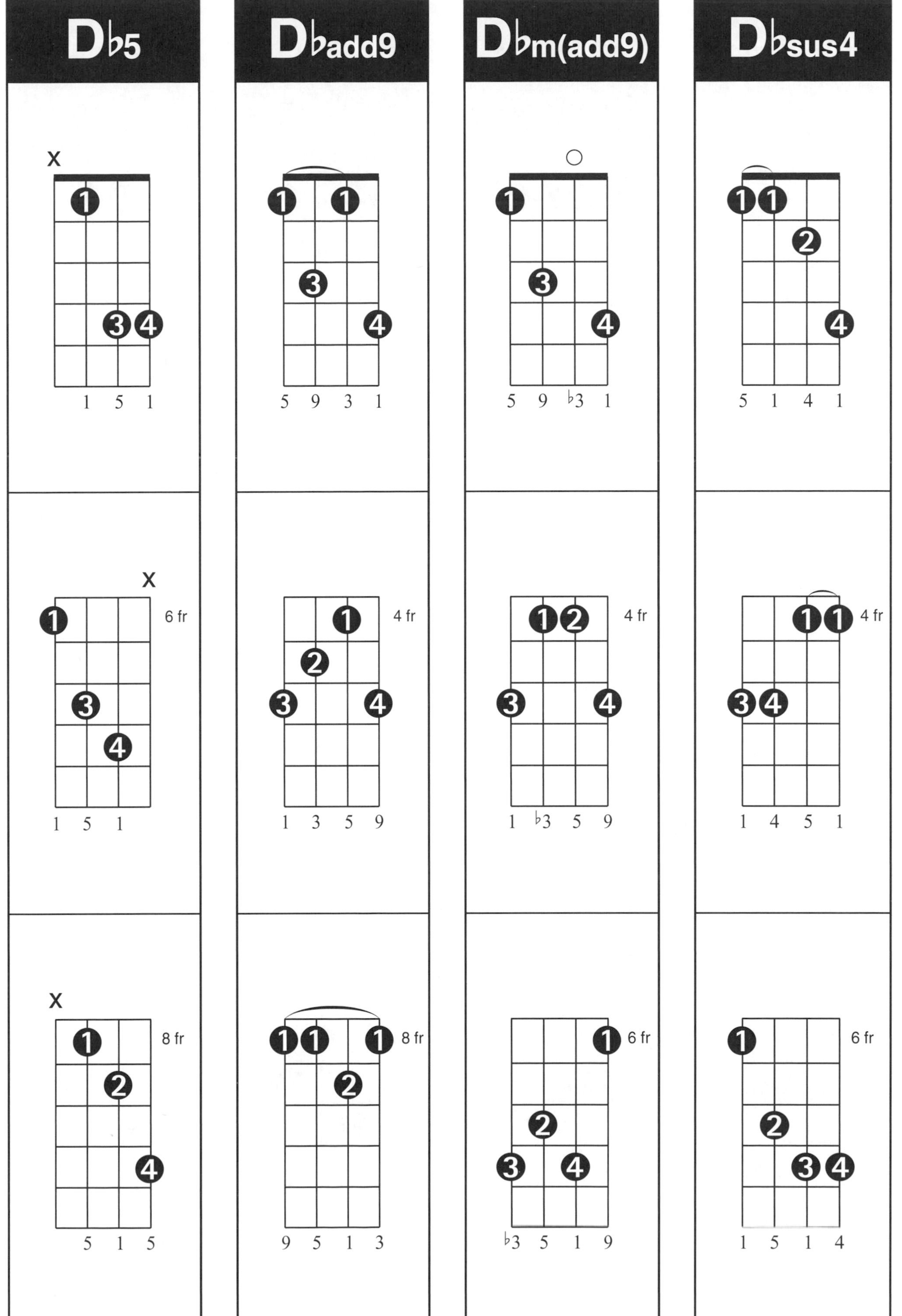

D♭5
D♭add9
D♭m(add9)
D♭sus4
1 5 1
5 9 3 1
5 9 ♭3 1
5 1 4 1
6 fr
4 fr
4 fr
4 fr
1 5 1
1 3 5 9
1 ♭3 5 9
1 4 5 1
8 fr
8 fr
6 fr
6 fr
5 1 5
9 5 1 3
♭3 5 1 9
1 5 1 4

D♭sus2

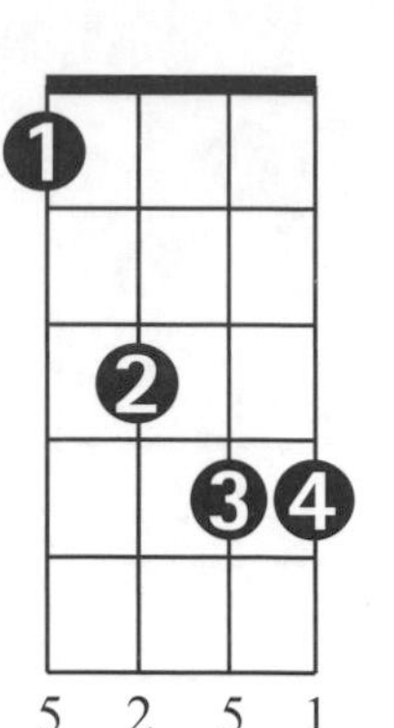

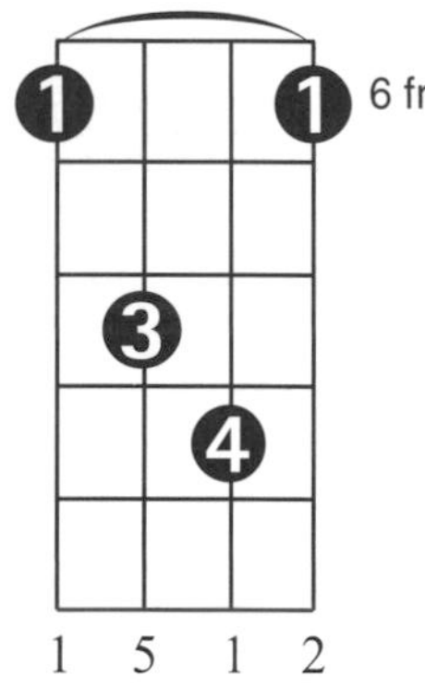

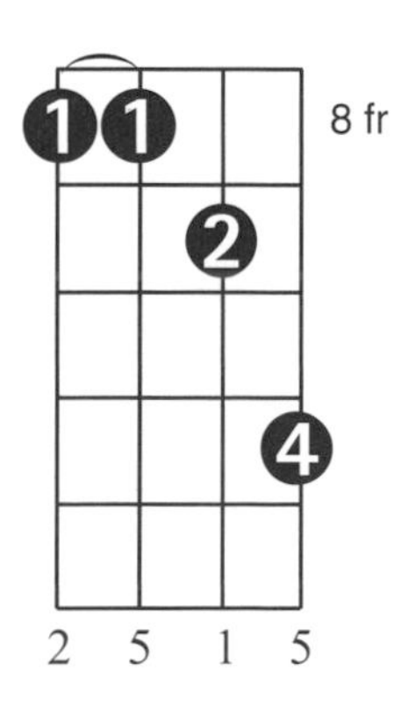

D♭6

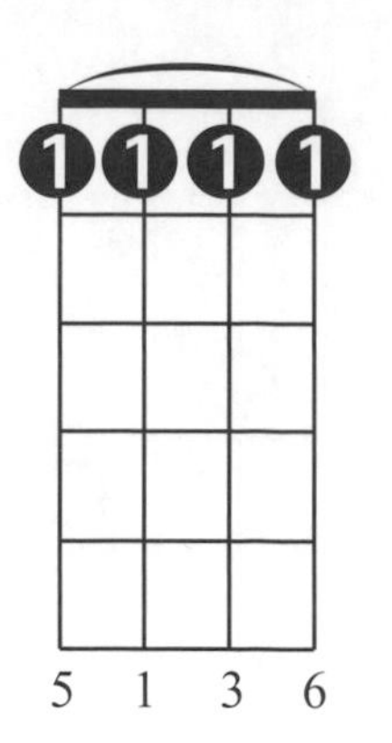

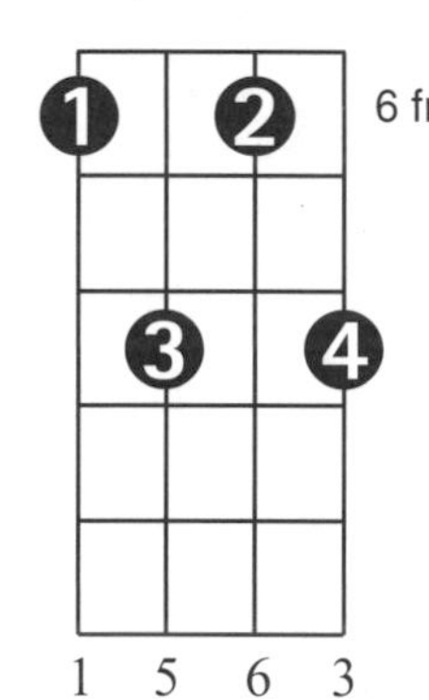

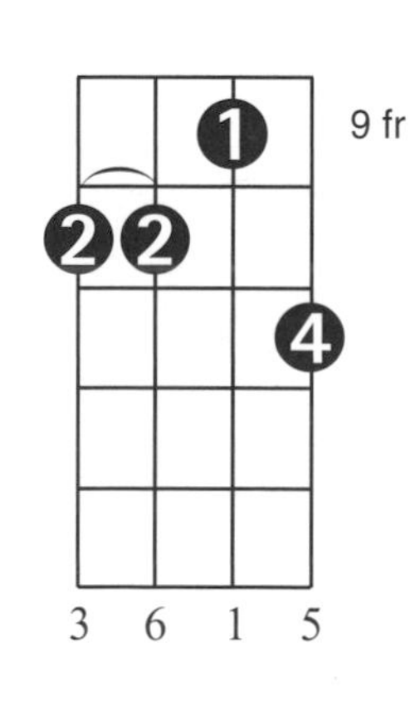

D♭m6

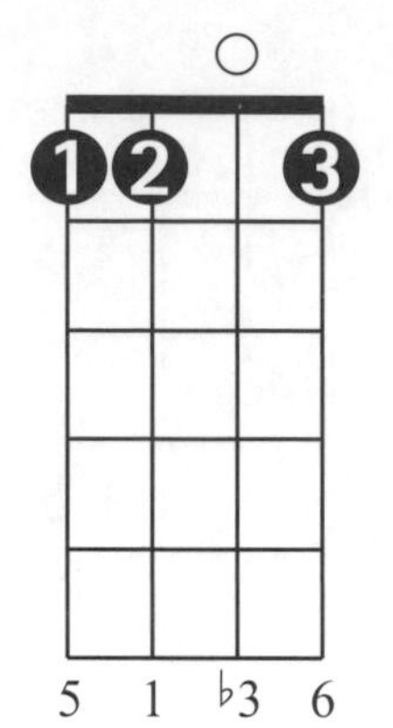

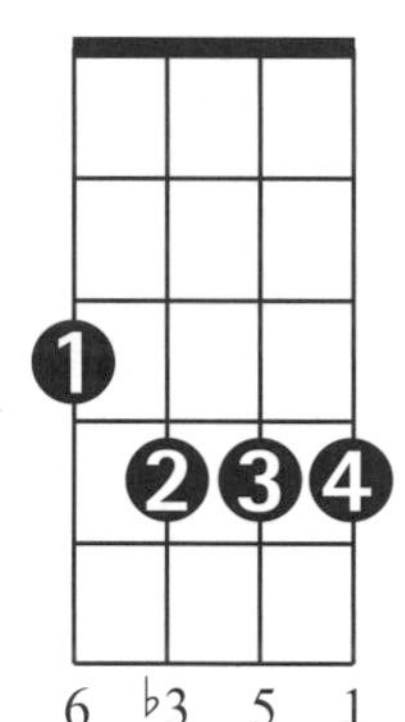

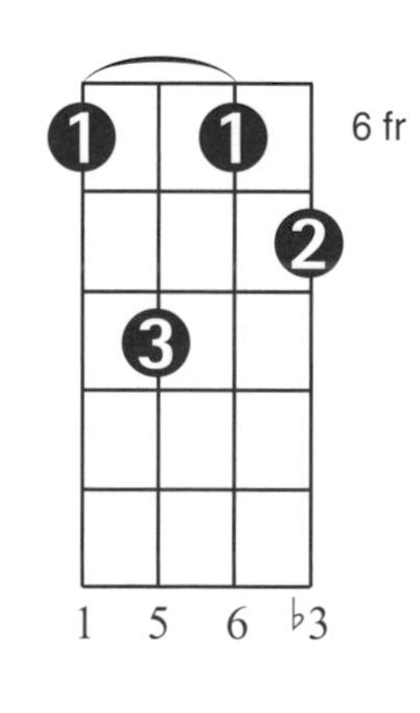

D♭maj7

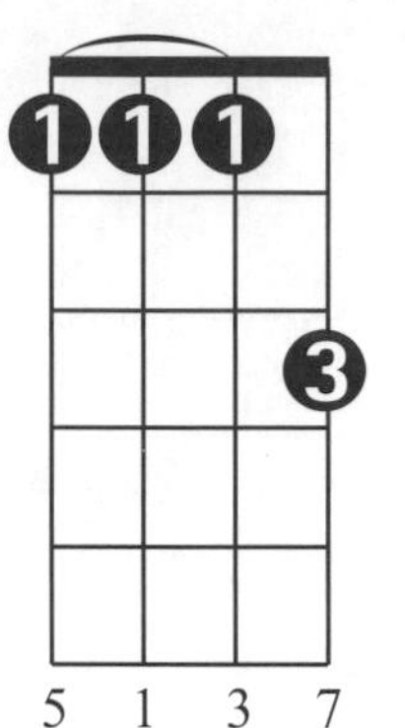

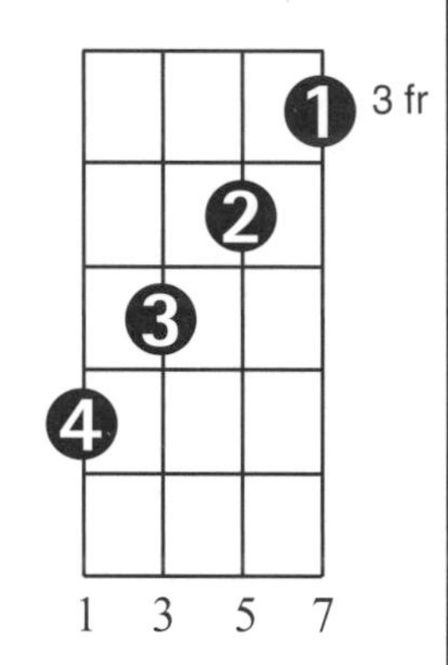

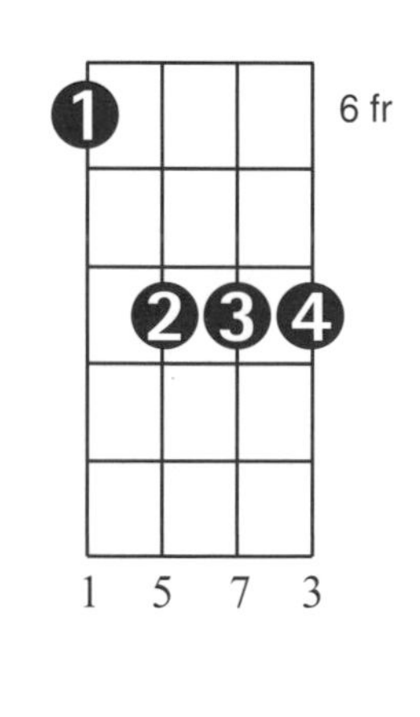

D♭maj9	D♭m7	D♭m(maj7)	D♭m7♭5
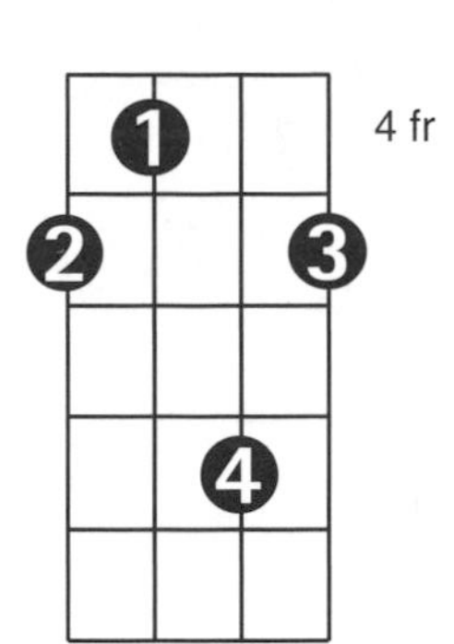	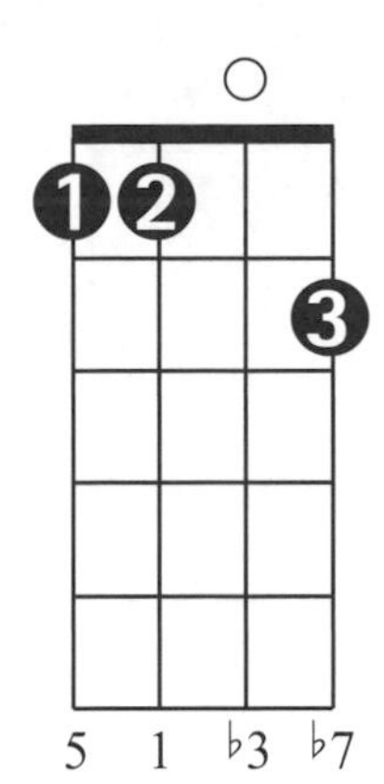	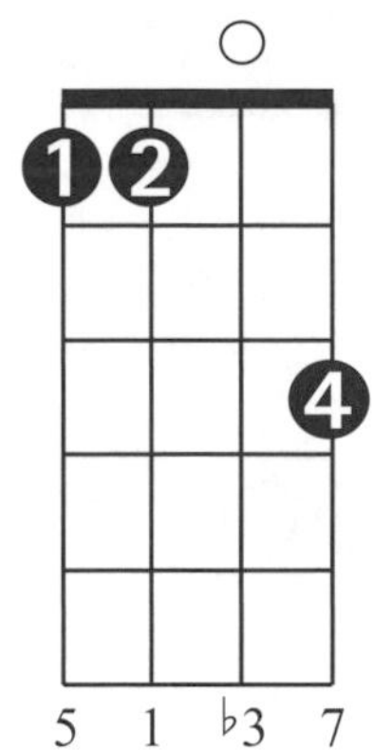	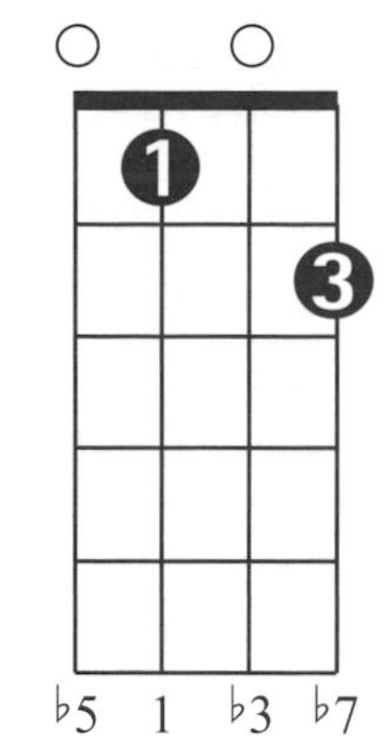
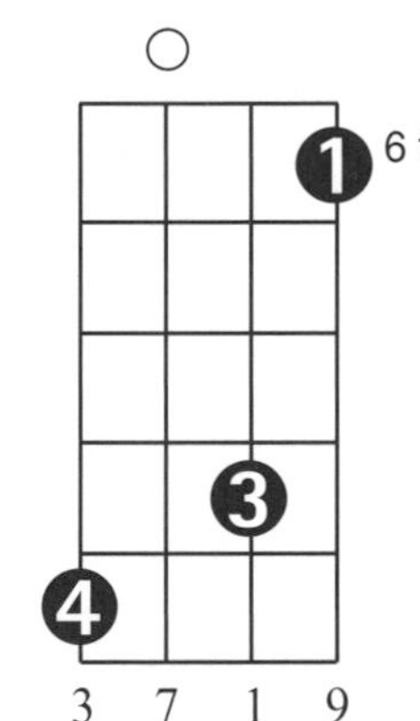	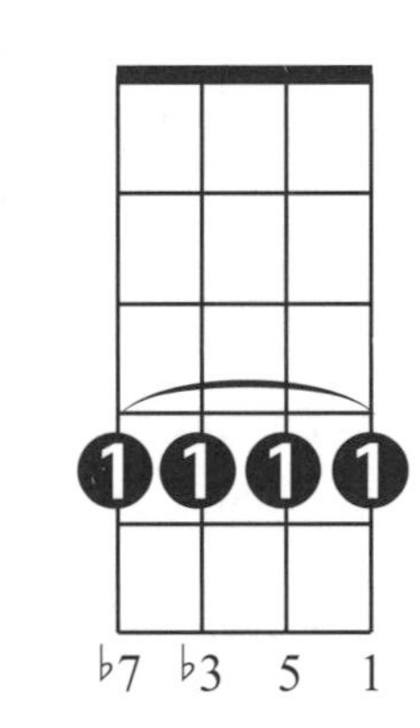	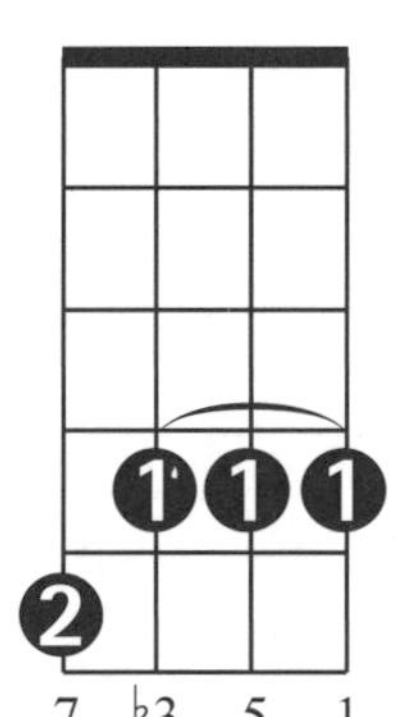	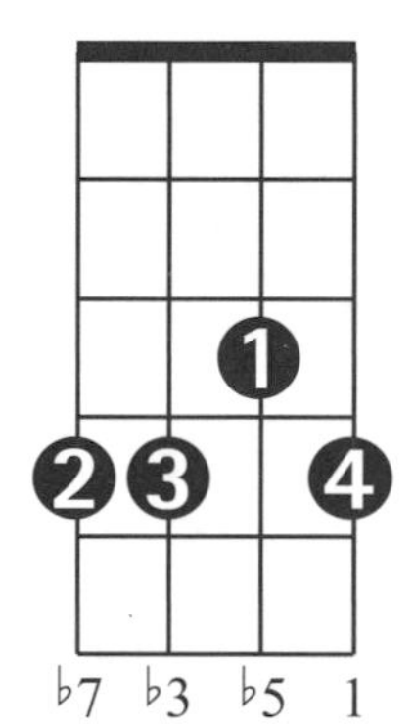
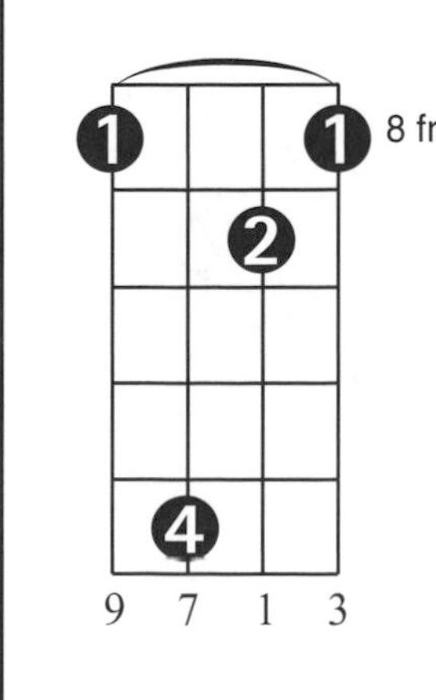	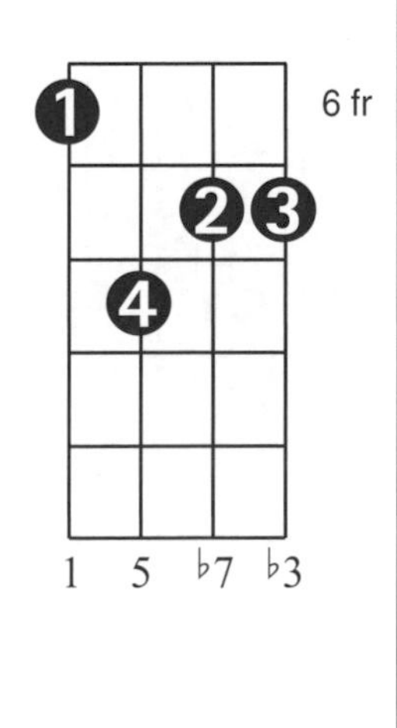	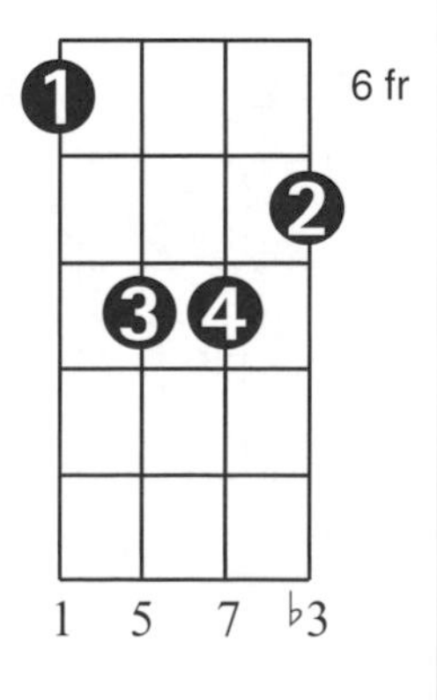	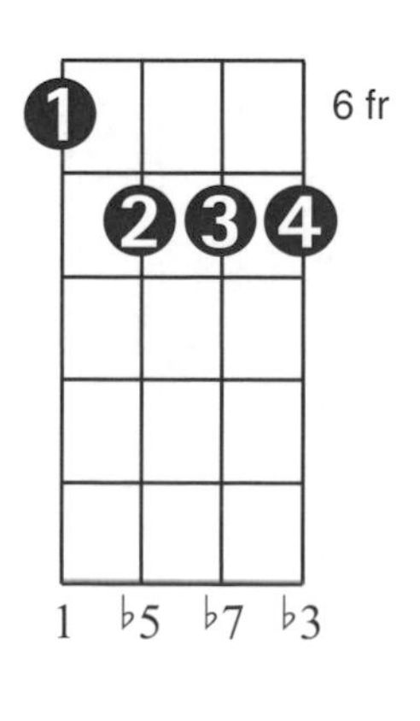

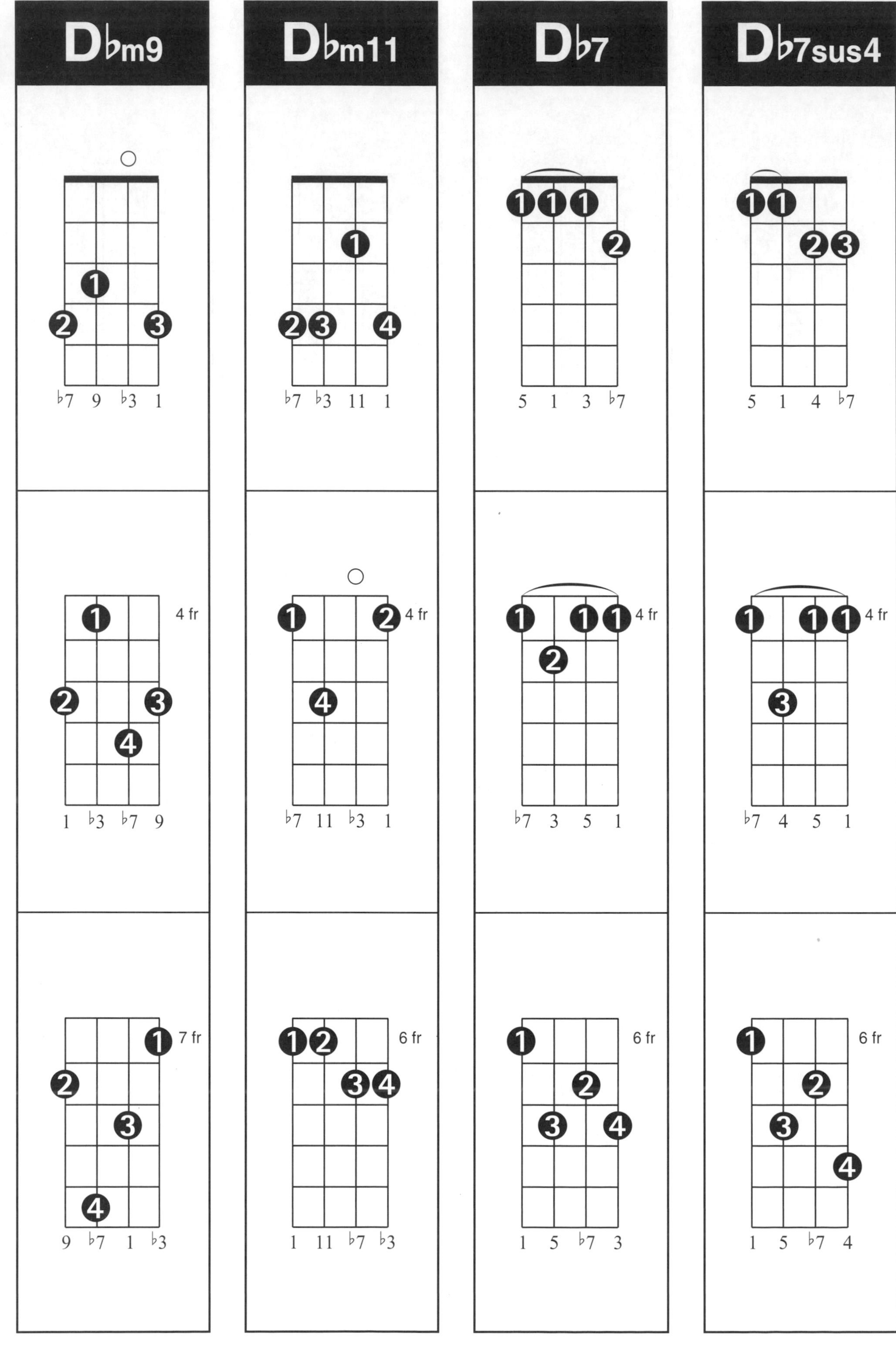

D♭m9
D♭m11
D♭7
D♭7sus4
♭7 9 ♭3 1
♭7 ♭3 11 1
5 1 3 ♭7
5 1 4 ♭7
4 fr
4 fr
4 fr
4 fr
1 ♭3 ♭7 9
♭7 11 ♭3 1
♭7 3 5 1
♭7 4 5 1
7 fr
6 fr
6 fr
6 fr
9 ♭7 1 ♭3
1 11 ♭7 ♭3
1 5 ♭7 3
1 5 ♭7 4

D♭+7	D♭7♭5	D♭9	D♭7♯9
♯5 1 3 ♭7	♭5 1 3 ♭7	♭7 9 3 1	♭7 3 ♯9 1
♭7 3 ♯5 1	♭7 3 ♭5 1	5 fr 1 3 ♭7 9	5 fr 1 3 ♭7 ♯9
5 fr 1 3 ♭7 ♯5	6 fr 1 ♭5 ♭7 3	8 fr 9 ♭7 1 3	4 fr ♭7 3 5 ♯9

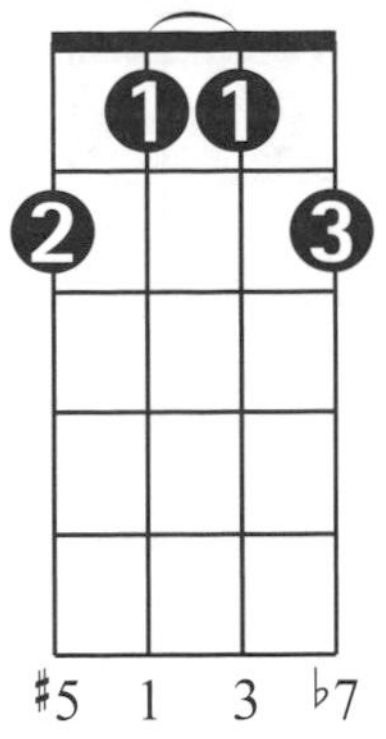

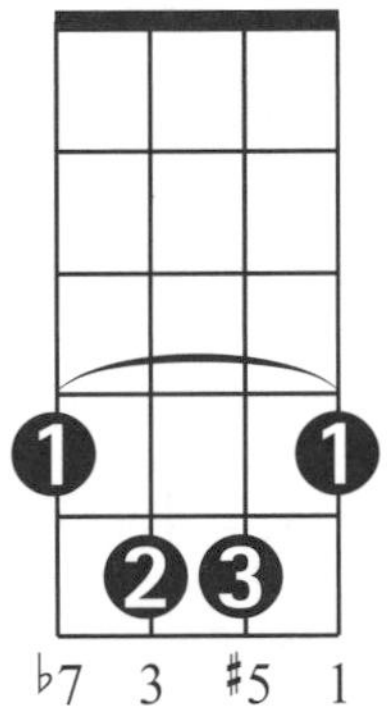

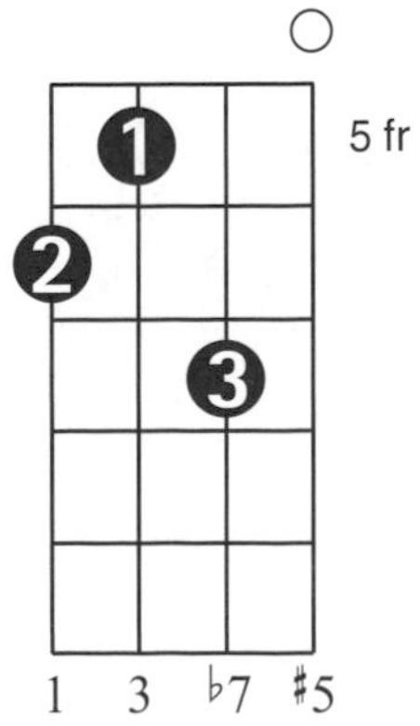

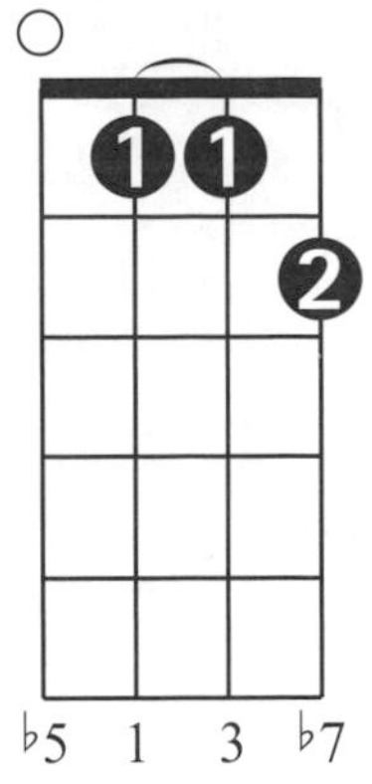

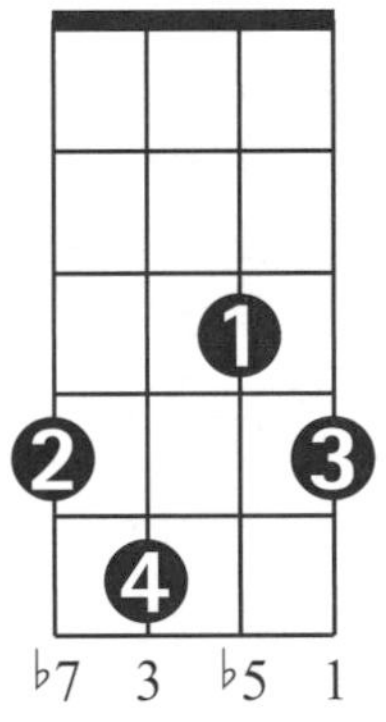

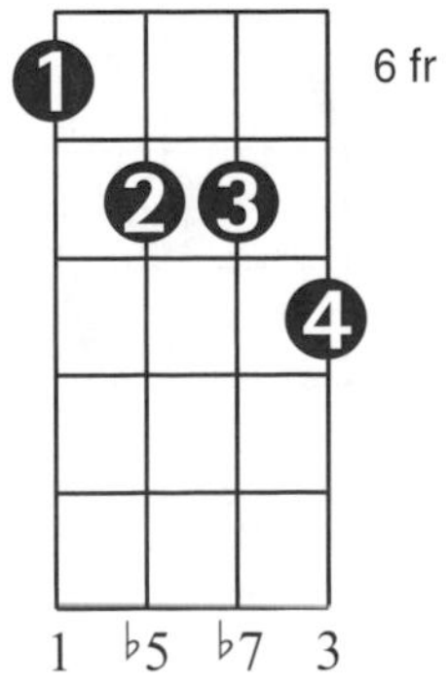

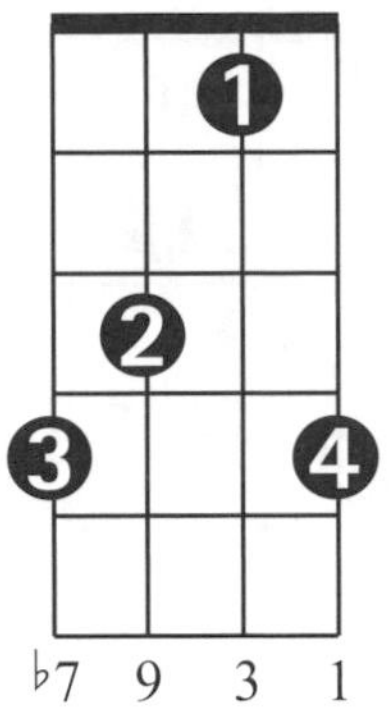

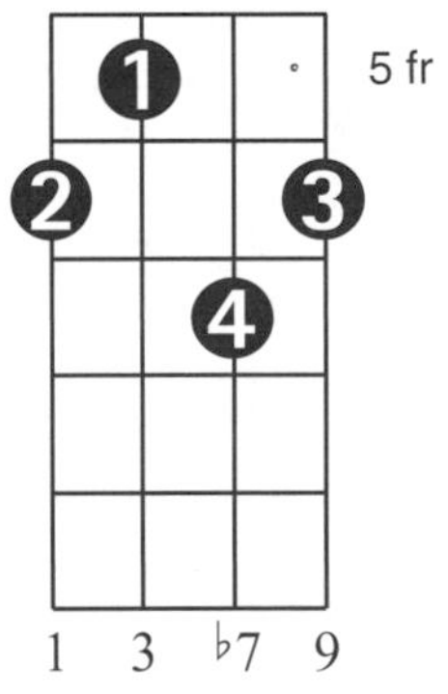

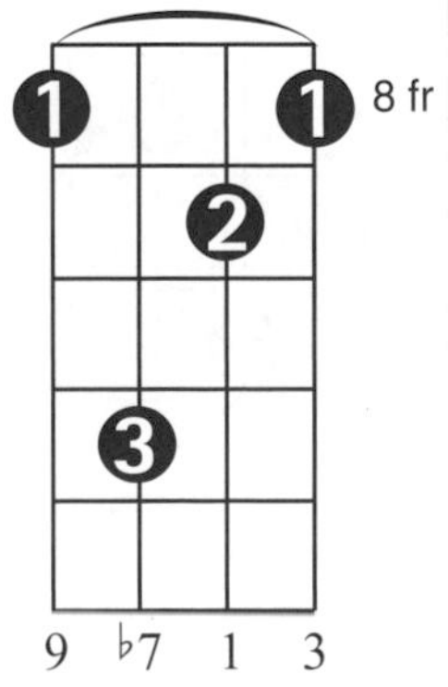

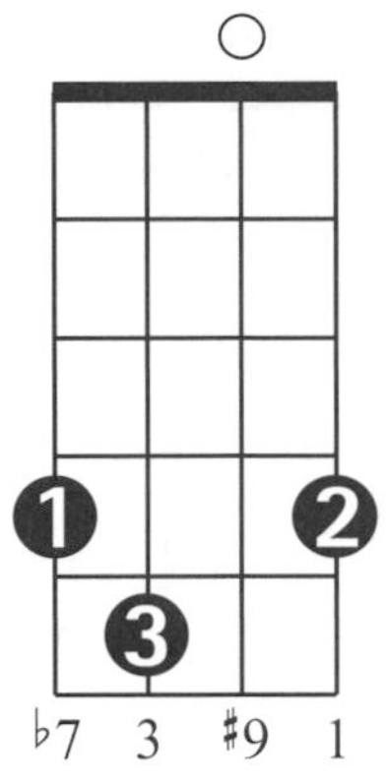

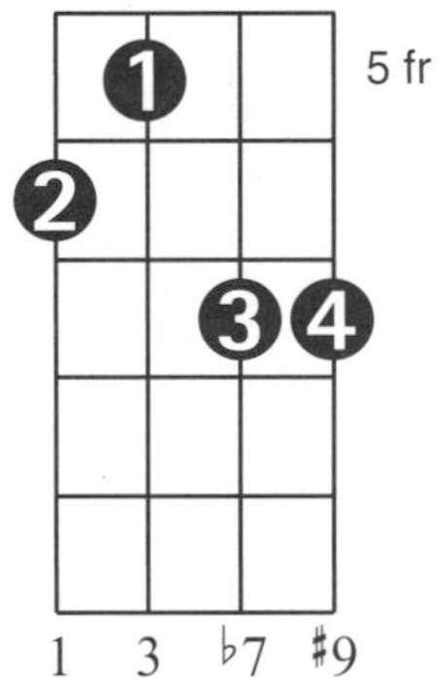

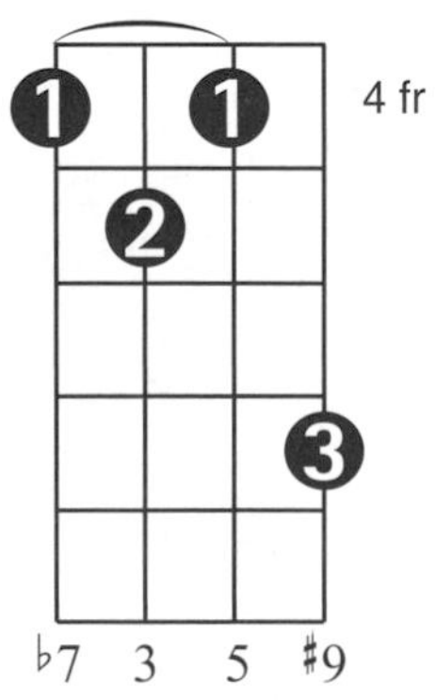

D♭7♭9	D♭11	D♭13	D♭°7
♭7 1 3 ♭9	♭7 9 11 1	♭7 1 3 13	♭5 1 ♭3 ♭♭7
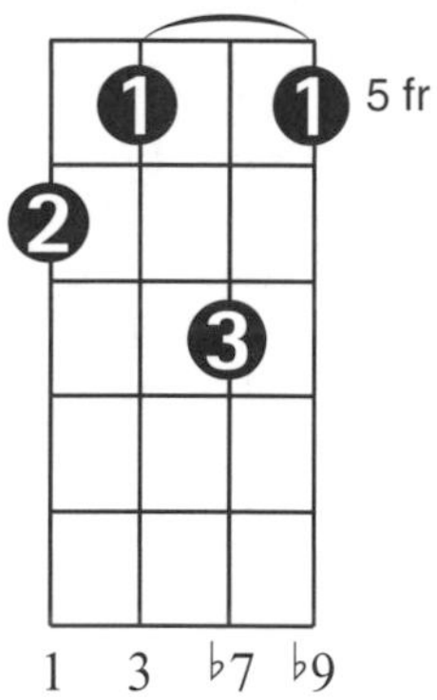 5 fr 1 3 ♭7 ♭9	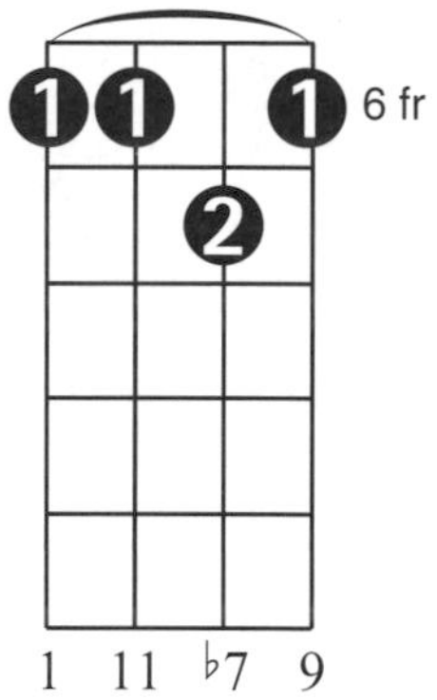 6 fr 1 11 ♭7 9	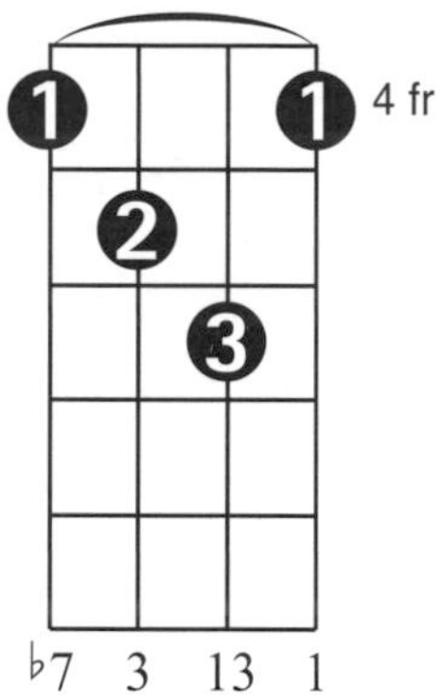 4 fr ♭7 3 13 1	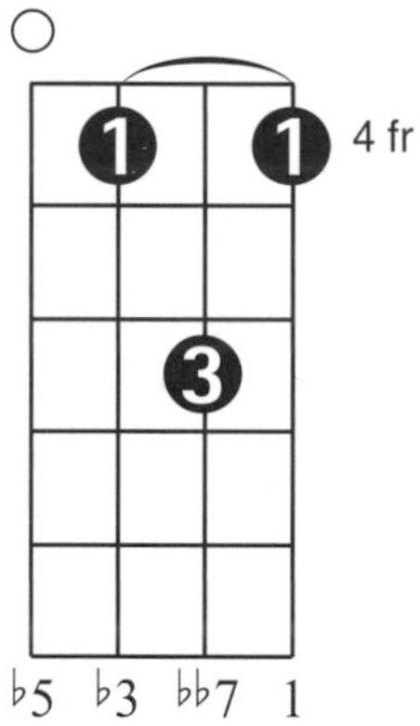 4 fr ♭5 ♭3 ♭♭7 1
7 fr ♭9 ♭7 1 3	9 fr 3 ♭7 1 11	6 fr 1 13 ♭7 3	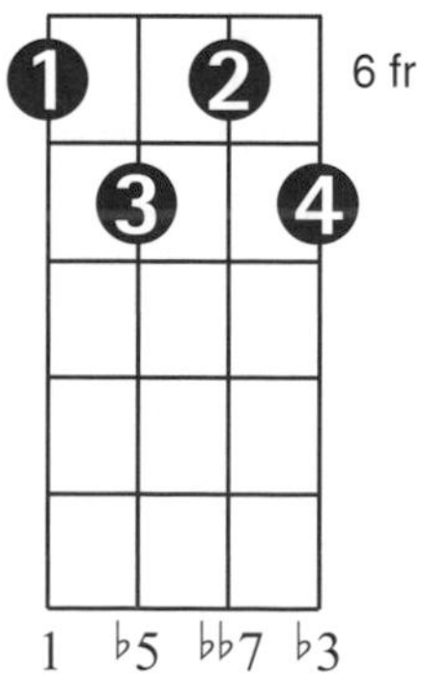 6 fr 1 ♭5 ♭♭7 ♭3

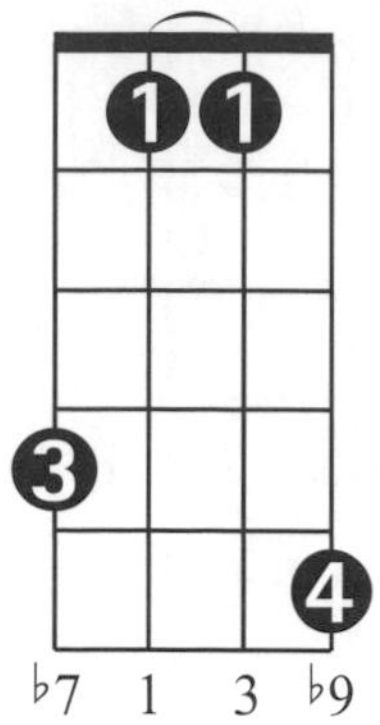

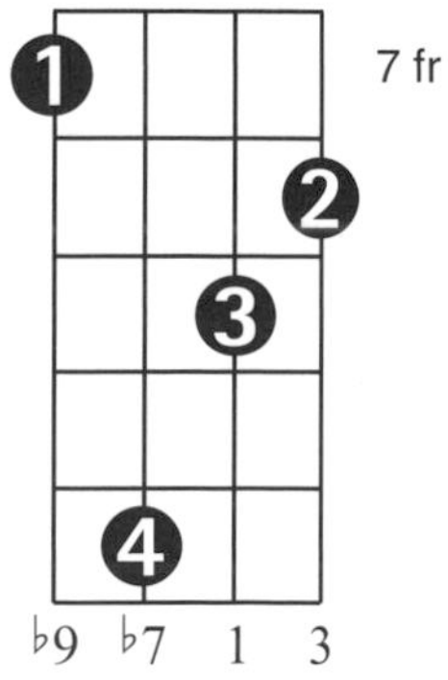

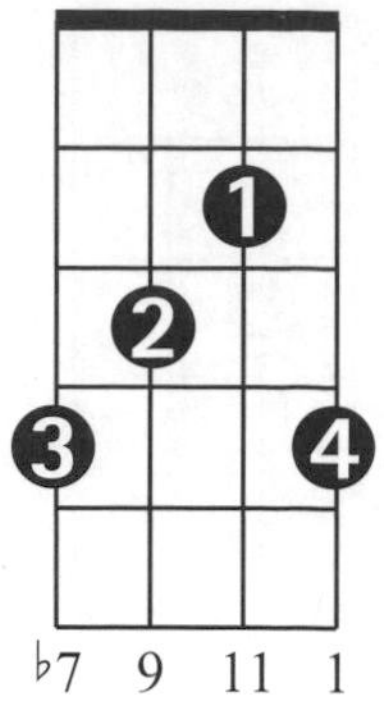

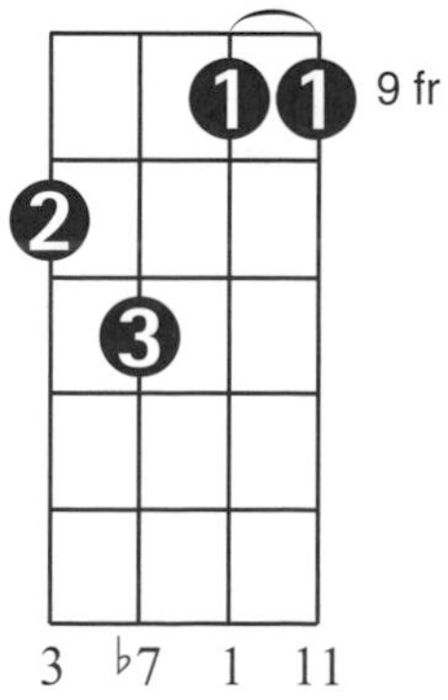

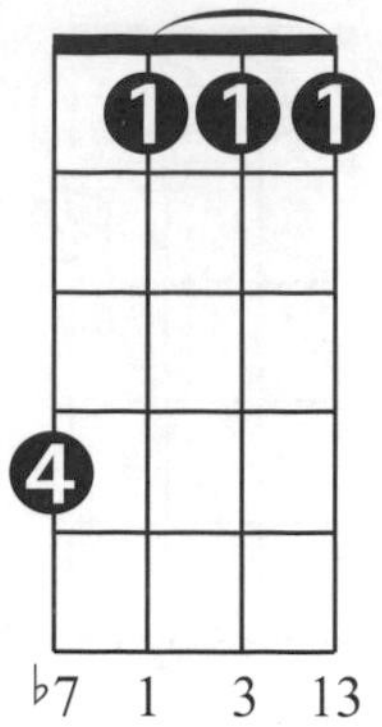

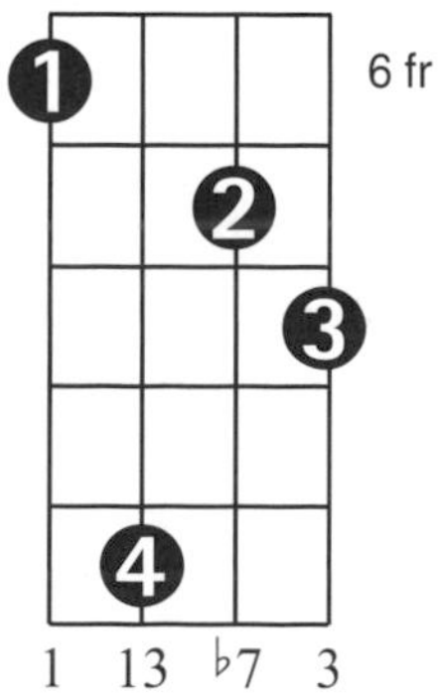

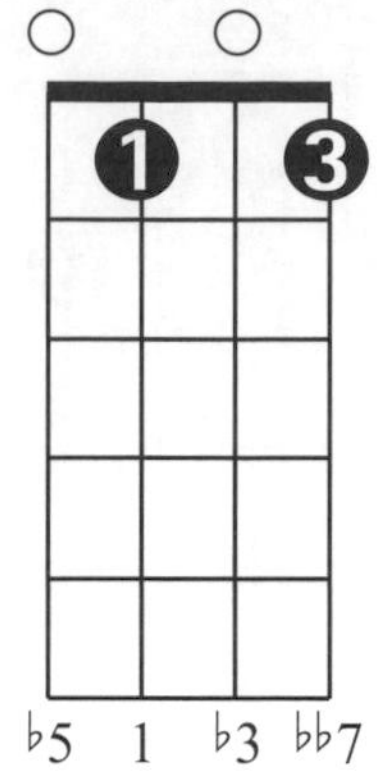

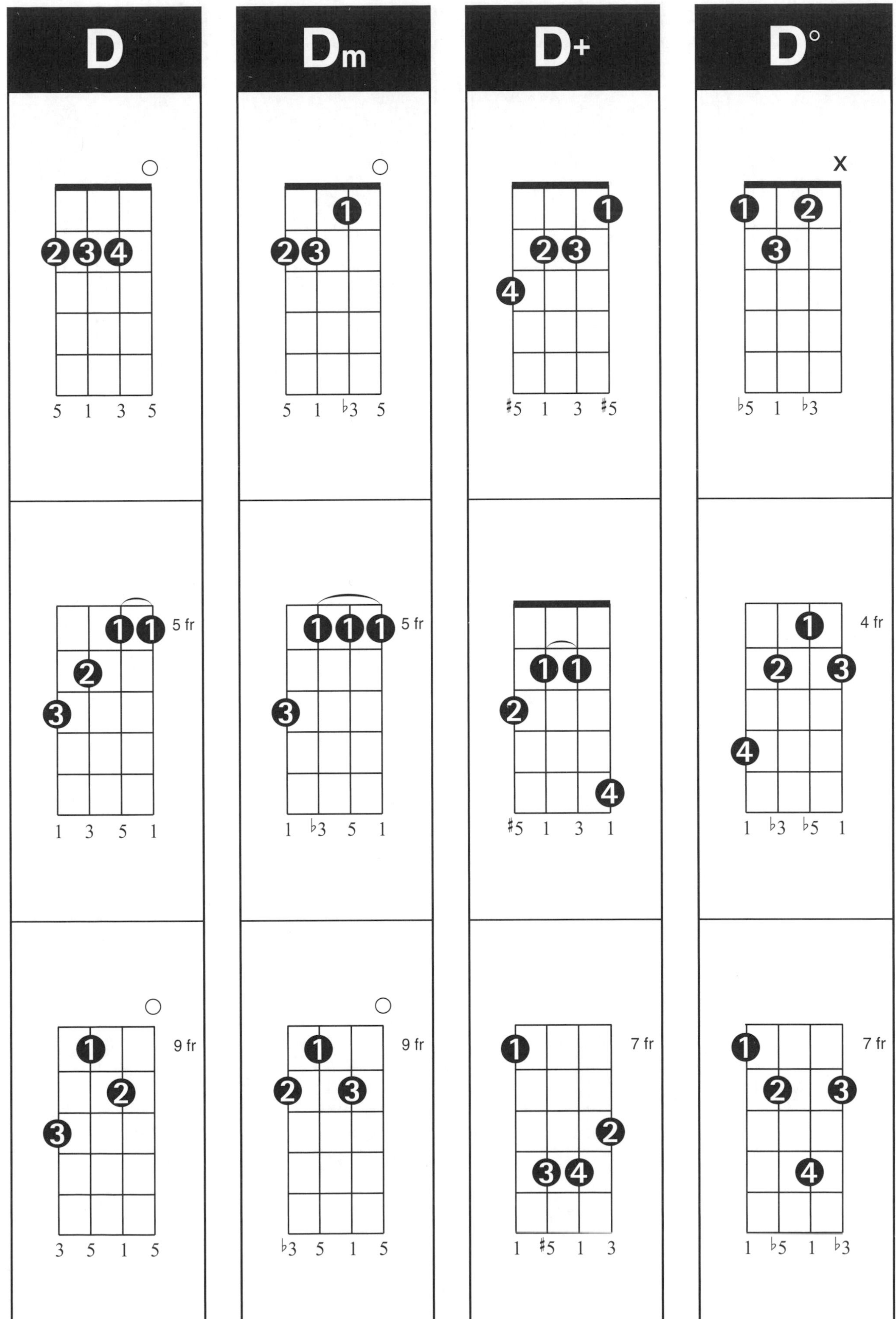
D
Dm
D+
D°
5 1 3 5
5 1 ♭3 5
♯5 1 3 ♯5
♭5 1 ♭3
5 fr
1 3 5 1
5 fr
1 ♭3 5 1
♯5 1 3 1
4 fr
1 ♭3 ♭5 1
9 fr
3 5 1 5
9 fr
♭3 5 1 5
7 fr
1 ♯5 1 3
7 fr
1 ♭5 1 ♭3

D

D5	Dadd9	Dm(add9)	Dsus4
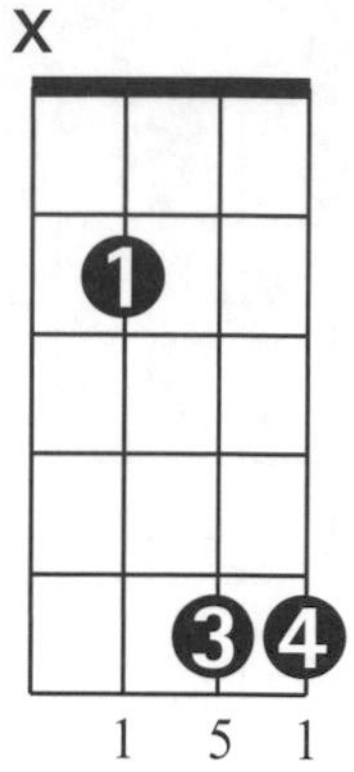 x; 1 5 1	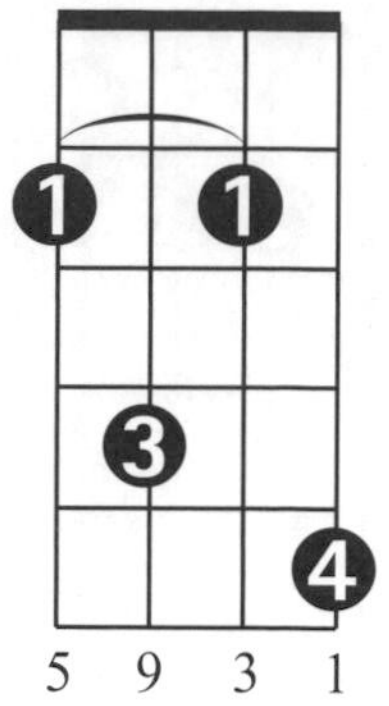 5 9 3 1	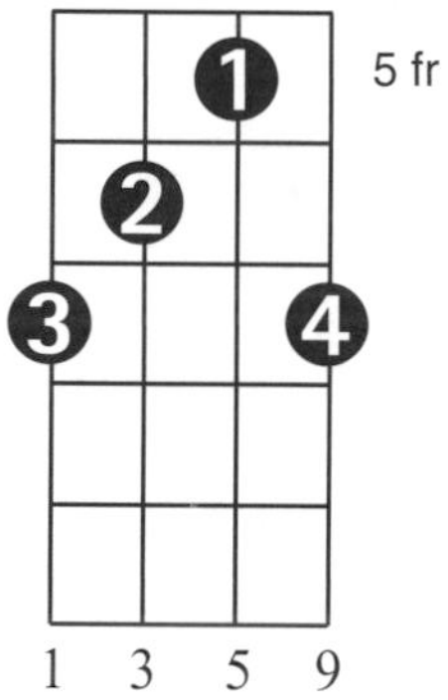 5 fr; 1 ♭3 5 9	4 1 4 5
7 fr; 1 5 1 5	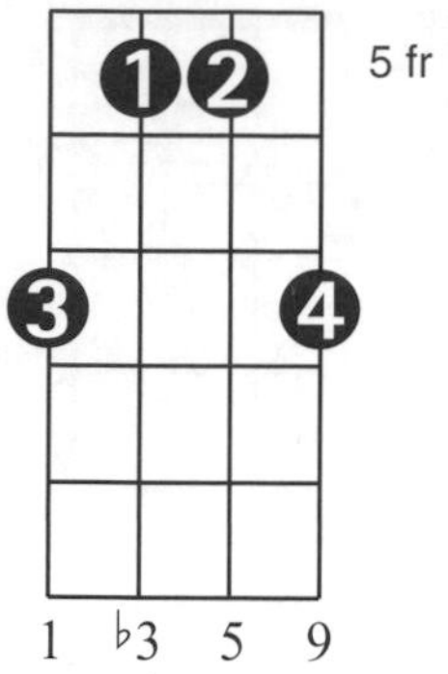 5 fr; 1 3 5 9	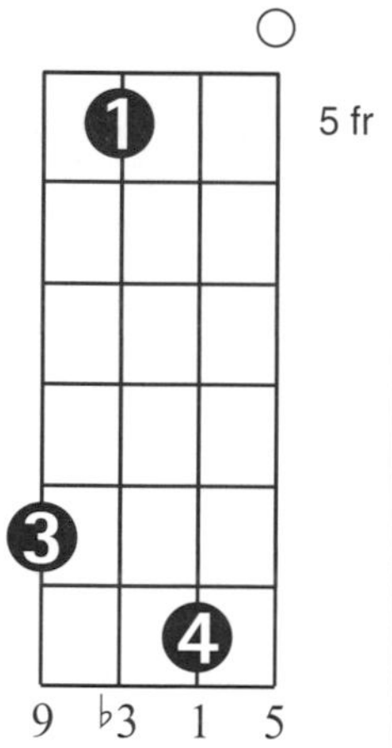 5 fr; 9 ♭3 1 5	5 1 4 1
x; 9 fr; 5 1 5	6 fr; 9 3 1 5	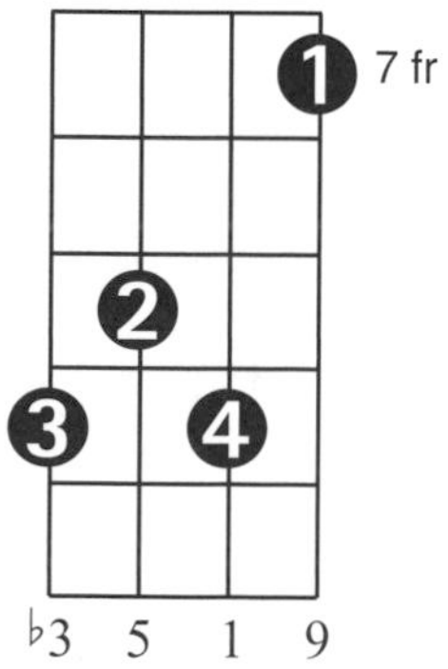 7 fr; ♭3 5 1 9	5 fr; 1 4 5 1

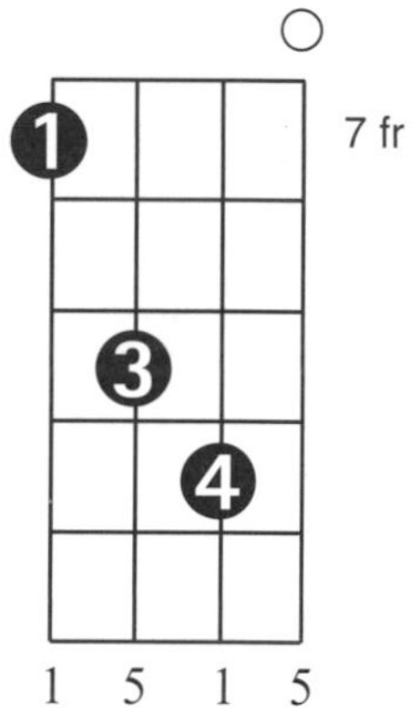

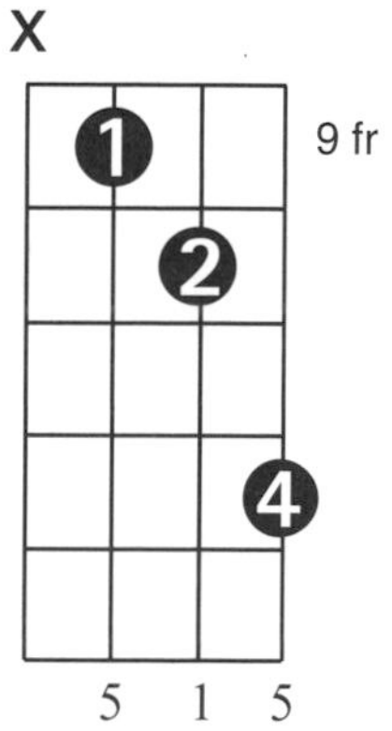

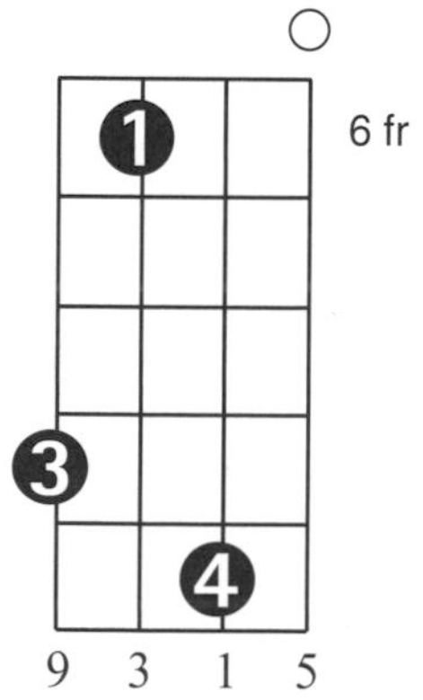

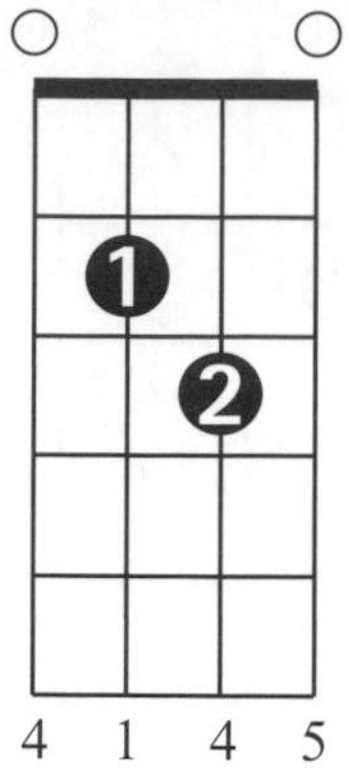

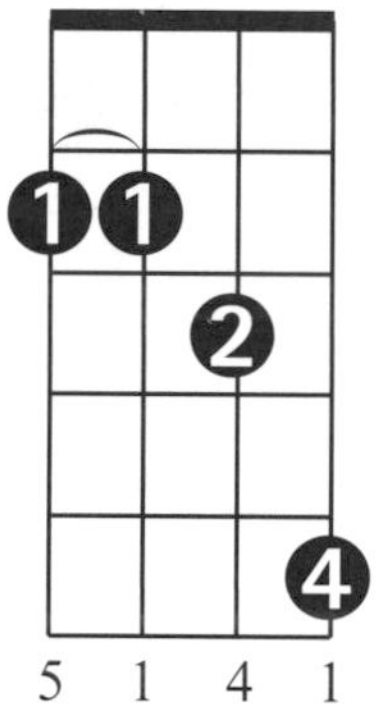

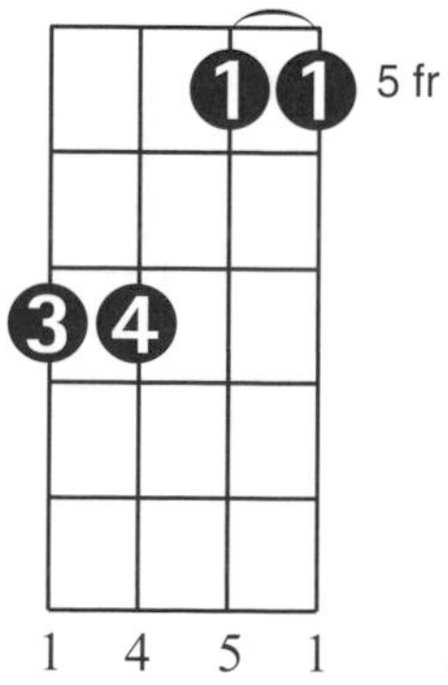

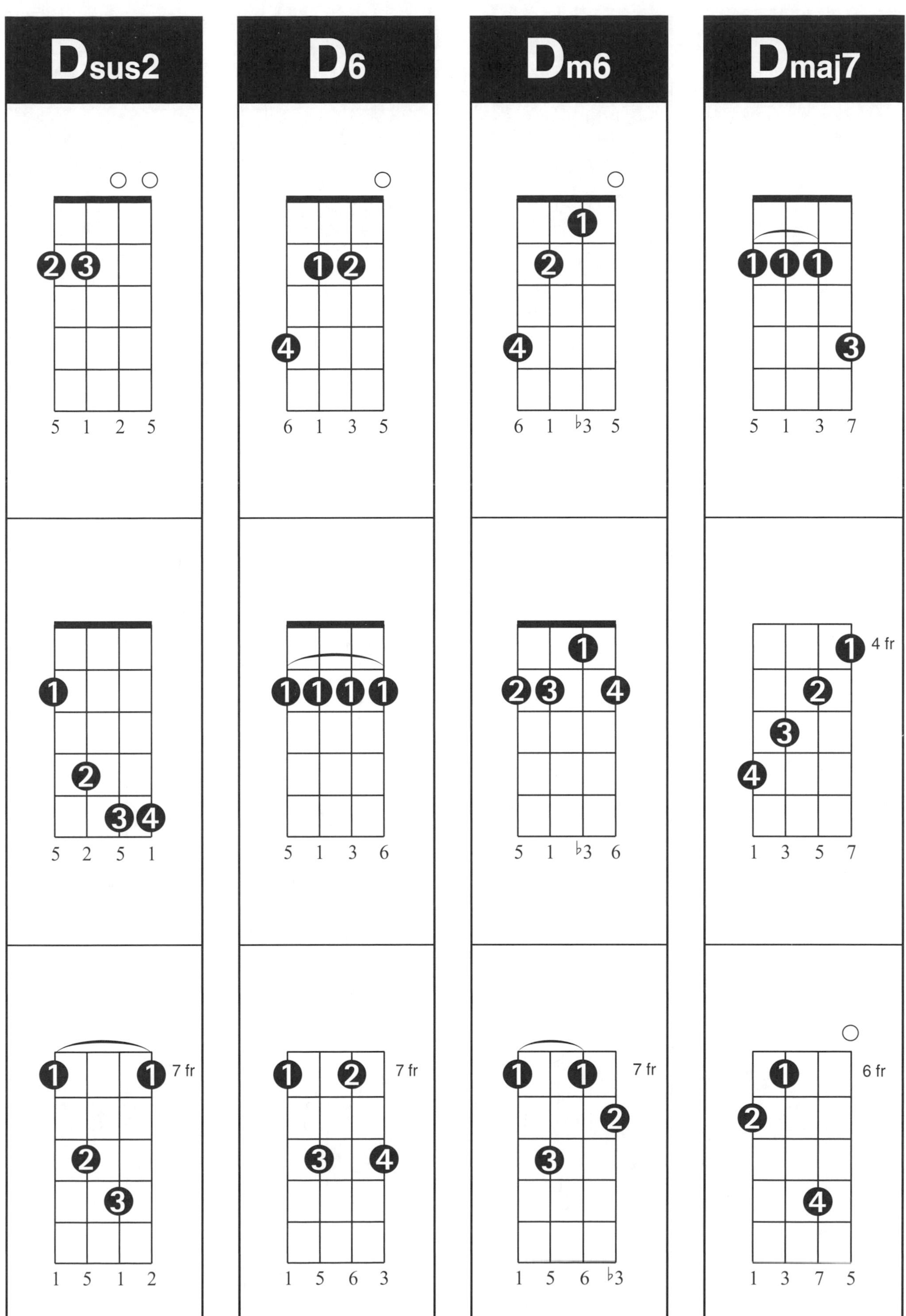
Dsus2
D6
Dm6
Dmaj7
5 1 2 5
6 1 3 5
6 1 ♭3 5
5 1 3 7
5 2 5 1
5 1 3 6
5 1 ♭3 6
4 fr
1 3 5 7
7 fr
1 5 1 2
7 fr
1 5 6 3
7 fr
1 5 6 ♭3
6 fr
1 3 7 5

D

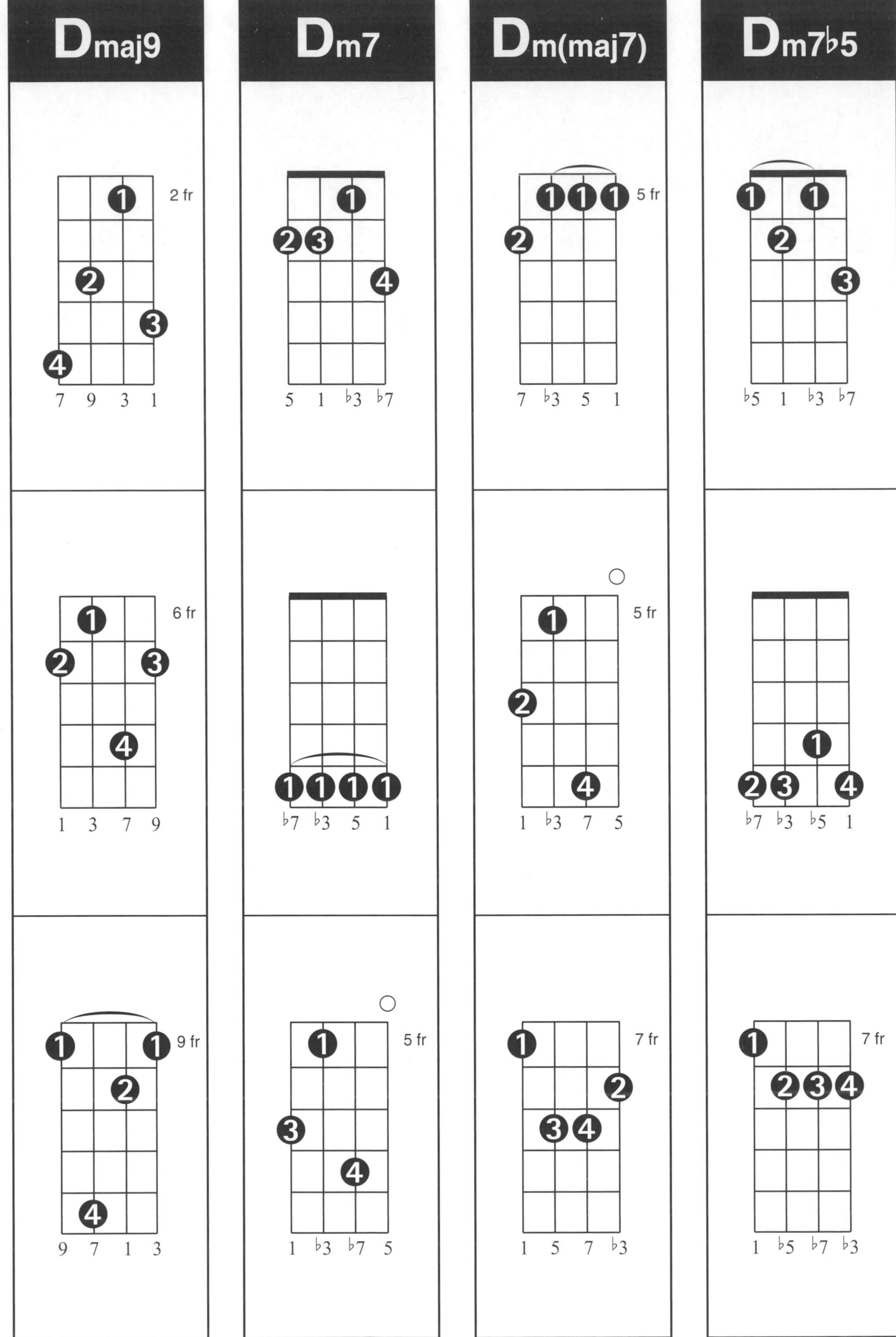
Dmaj9
2 fr
7 9 3 1
6 fr
1 3 7 9
9 fr
9 7 1 3
Dm7
5 1 ♭3 ♭7
♭7 ♭3 5 1
5 fr
1 ♭3 ♭7 5
Dm(maj7)
5 fr
7 ♭3 5 1
5 fr
1 ♭3 7 5
7 fr
1 5 7 ♭3
Dm7♭5
♭5 1 ♭3 ♭7
♭7 ♭3 ♭5 1
7 fr
1 ♭5 ♭7 ♭3

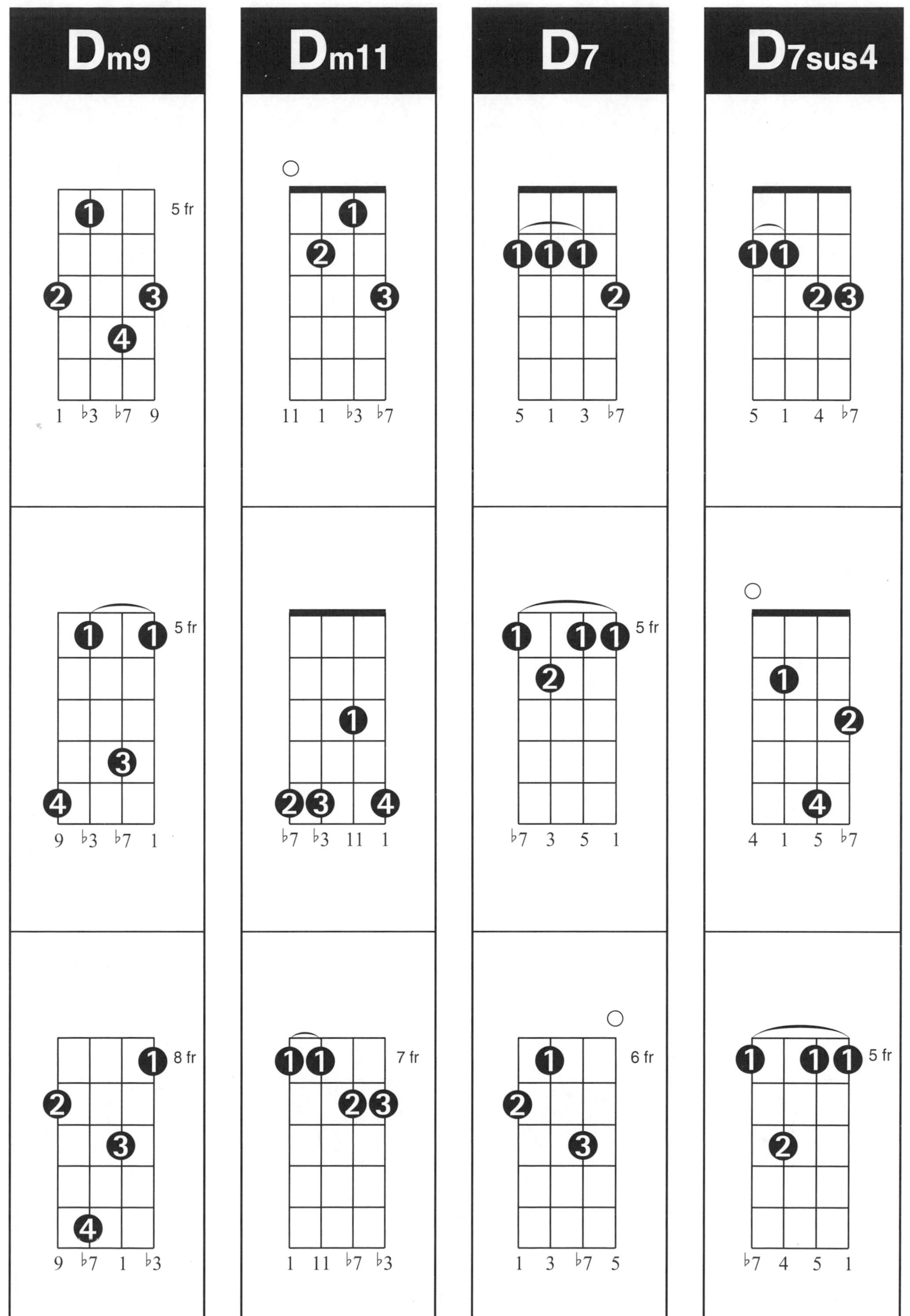

Dm9
Dm11
D7
D7sus4
5 fr
1 ♭3 ♭7 9
11 1 ♭3 ♭7
5 1 3 ♭7
5 1 4 ♭7
5 fr
9 ♭3 ♭7 1
♭7 ♭3 11 1
5 fr
♭7 3 5 1
4 1 5 ♭7
8 fr
9 ♭7 1 ♭3
7 fr
1 11 ♭7 ♭3
6 fr
1 3 ♭7 5
5 fr
♭7 4 5 1

D

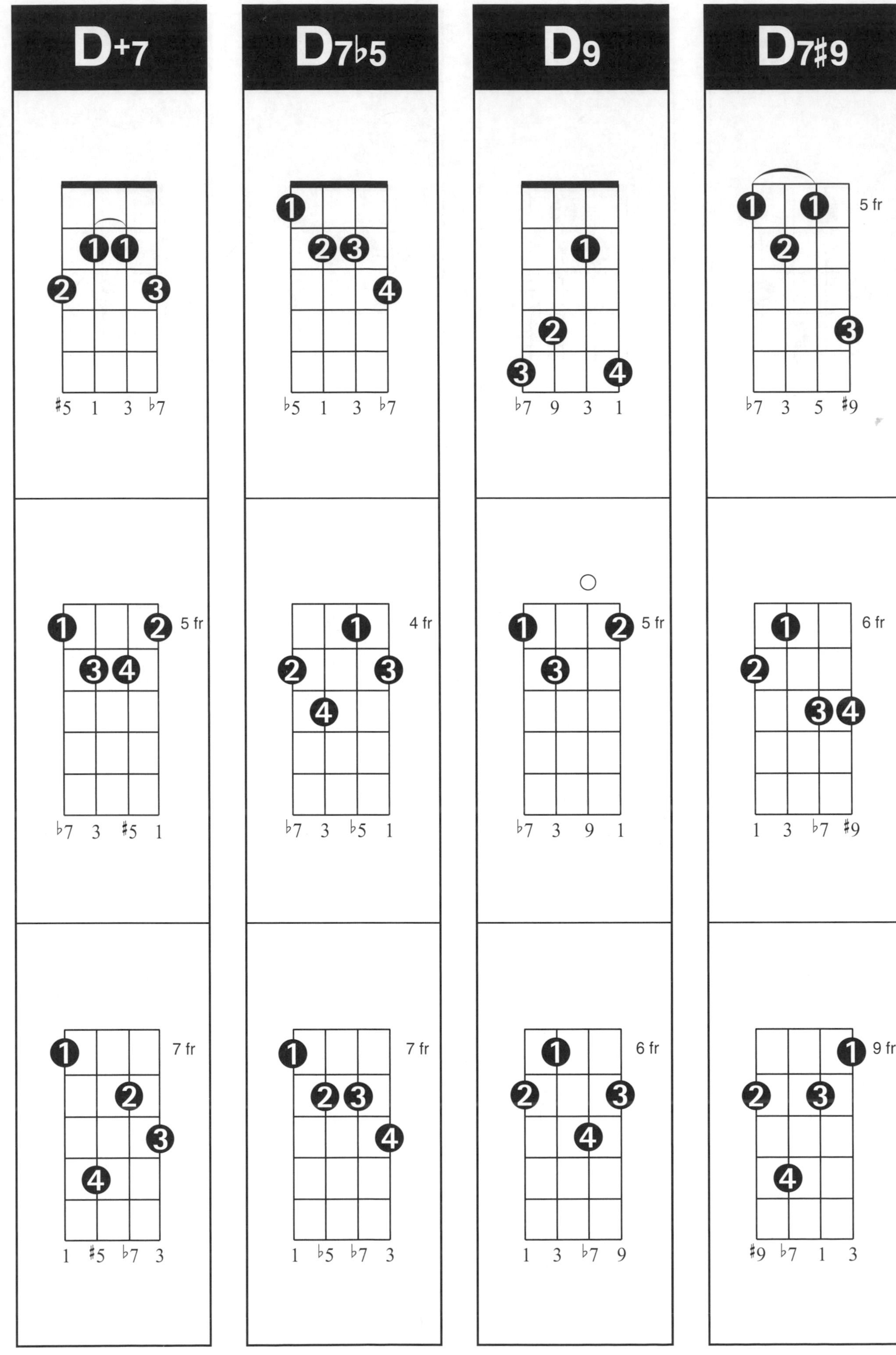
D+7
D7♭5
D9
D7♯9
D
♯5 1 3 ♭7
♭5 1 3 ♭7
♭7 9 3 1
♭7 3 5 ♯9
5 fr
♭7 3 ♯5 1
4 fr
♭7 3 ♭5 1
5 fr
♭7 3 9 1
6 fr
1 3 ♭7 ♯9
7 fr
1 ♯5 ♭7 3
7 fr
1 ♭5 ♭7 3
6 fr
1 3 ♭7 9
9 fr
♯9 ♭7 1 3

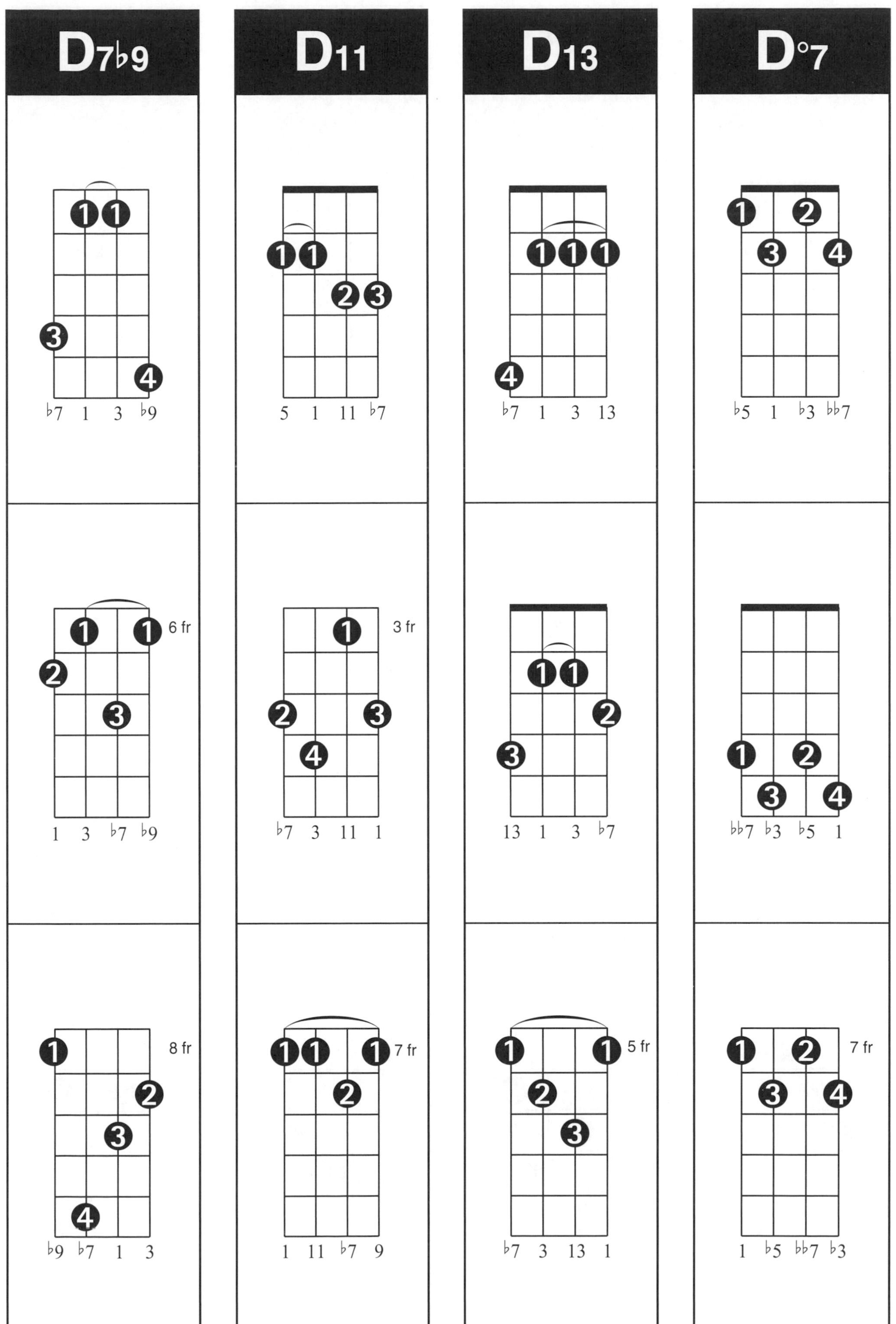
D7♭9
D11
D13
D°7
6 fr
3 fr
8 fr
7 fr
5 fr
7 fr
♭7 1 3 ♭9
5 1 11 ♭7
♭7 1 3 13
♭5 1 ♭3 ♭♭7
1 3 ♭7 ♭9
♭7 3 11 1
13 1 3 ♭7
♭♭7 ♭3 ♭5 1
♭9 ♭7 1 3
1 11 ♭7 9
♭7 3 13 1
1 ♭5 ♭♭7 ♭3

D

E♭/D♯

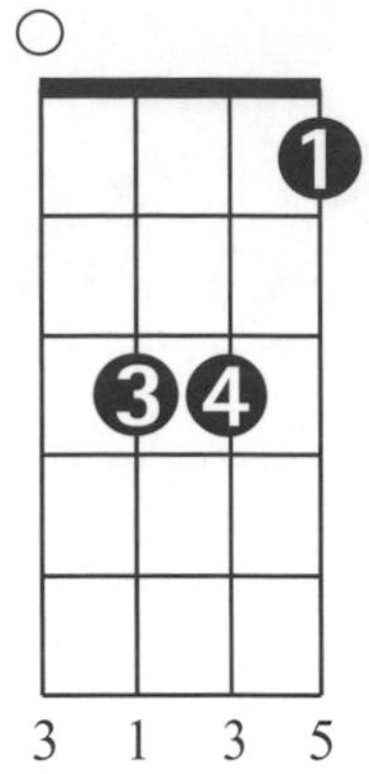

E♭	E♭m	E♭+	E♭°
3 1 3 5	5 1 ♭3 5	3 1 3 ♯5	♭5 1 ♭3 ♭5
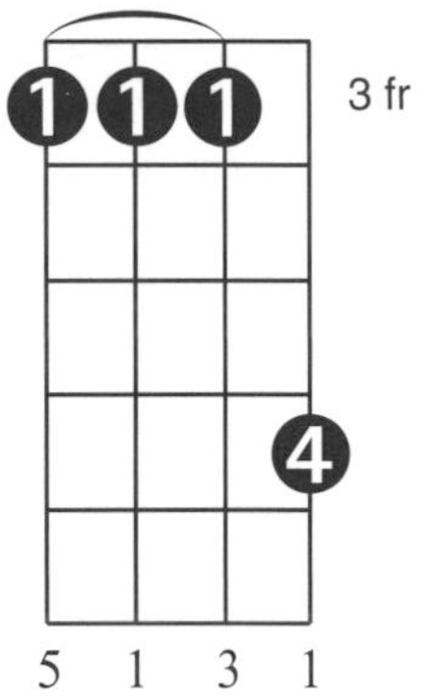 3 fr 5 1 3 1	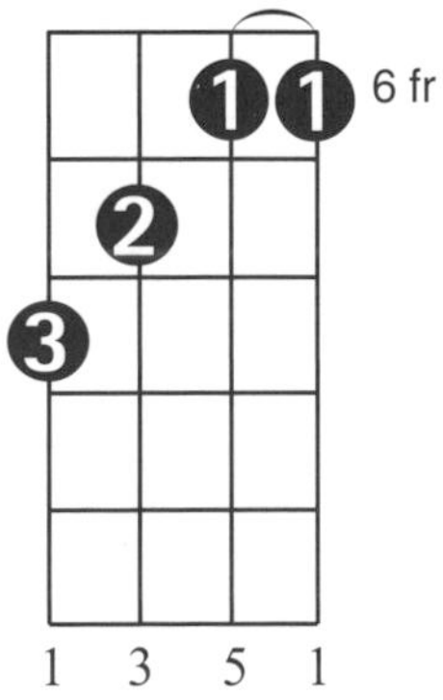 6 fr 1 ♭3 5 1	3 fr ♯5 1 3 1	5 fr 1 ♭3 ♭5 1
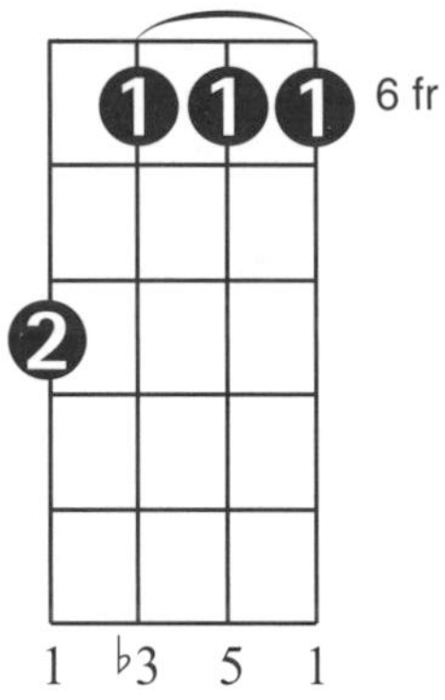 6 fr 1 3 5 1	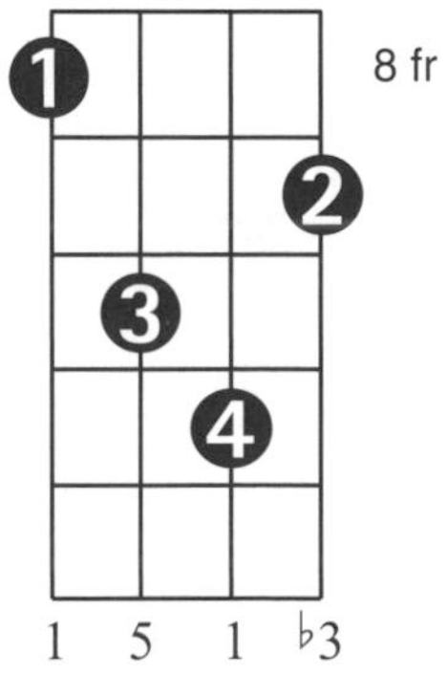 8 fr 1 5 1 ♭3	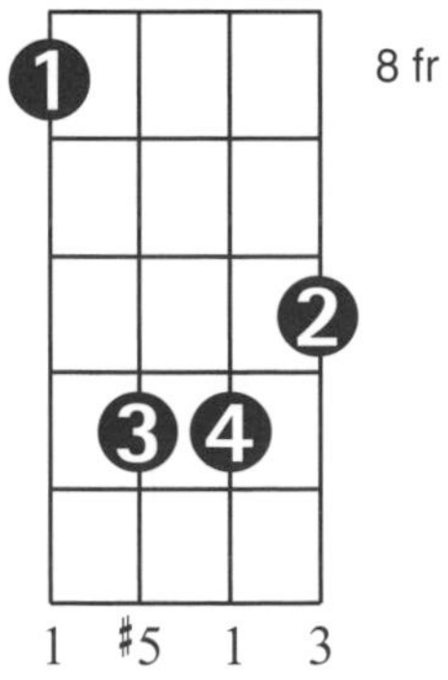 8 fr 1 ♯5 1 3	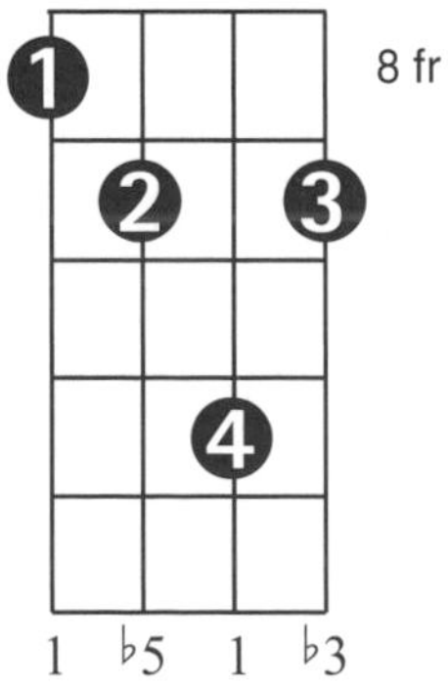 8 fr 1 ♭5 1 ♭3

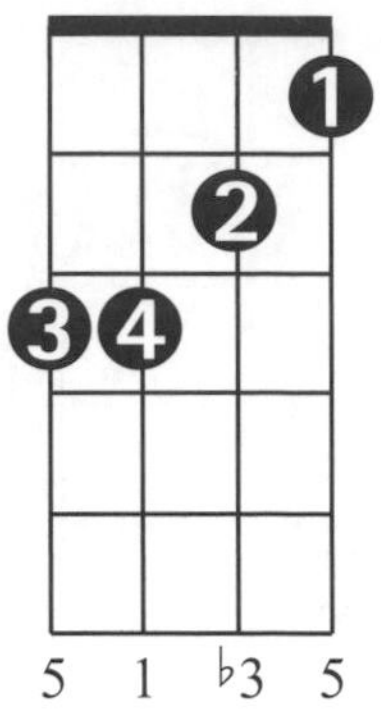

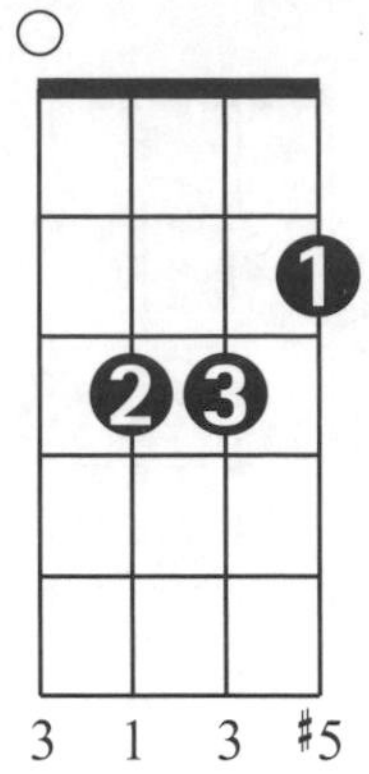

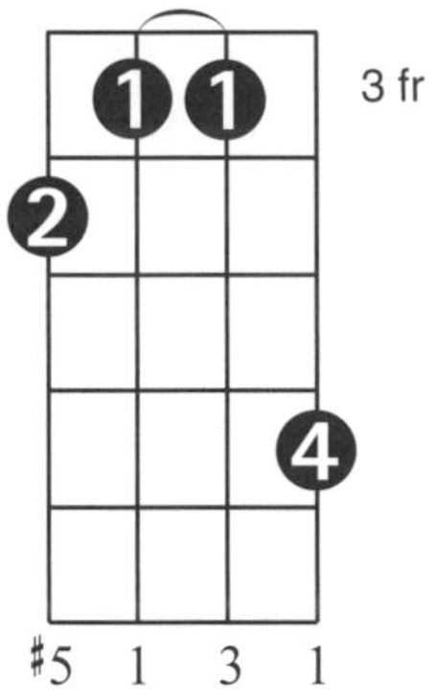

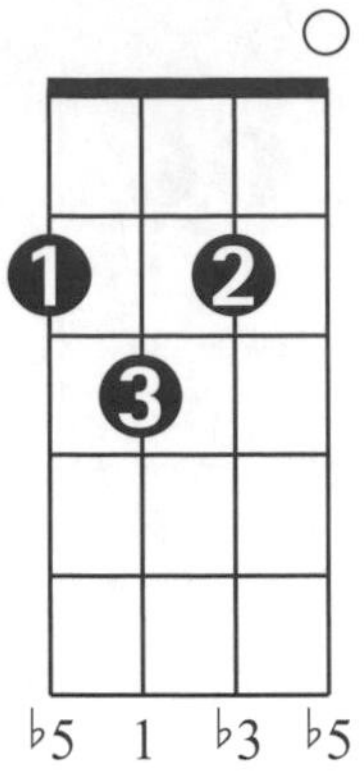

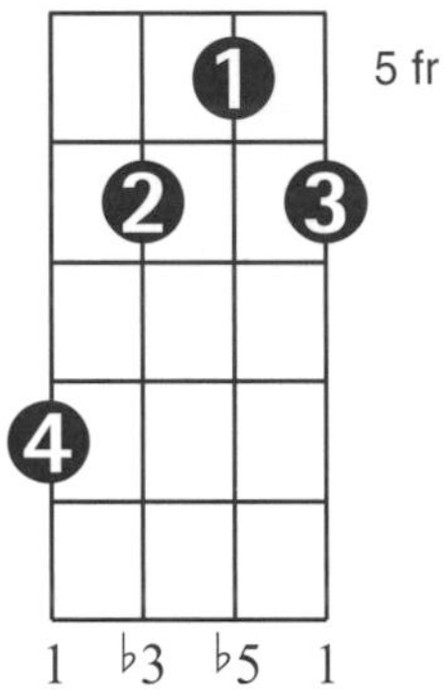

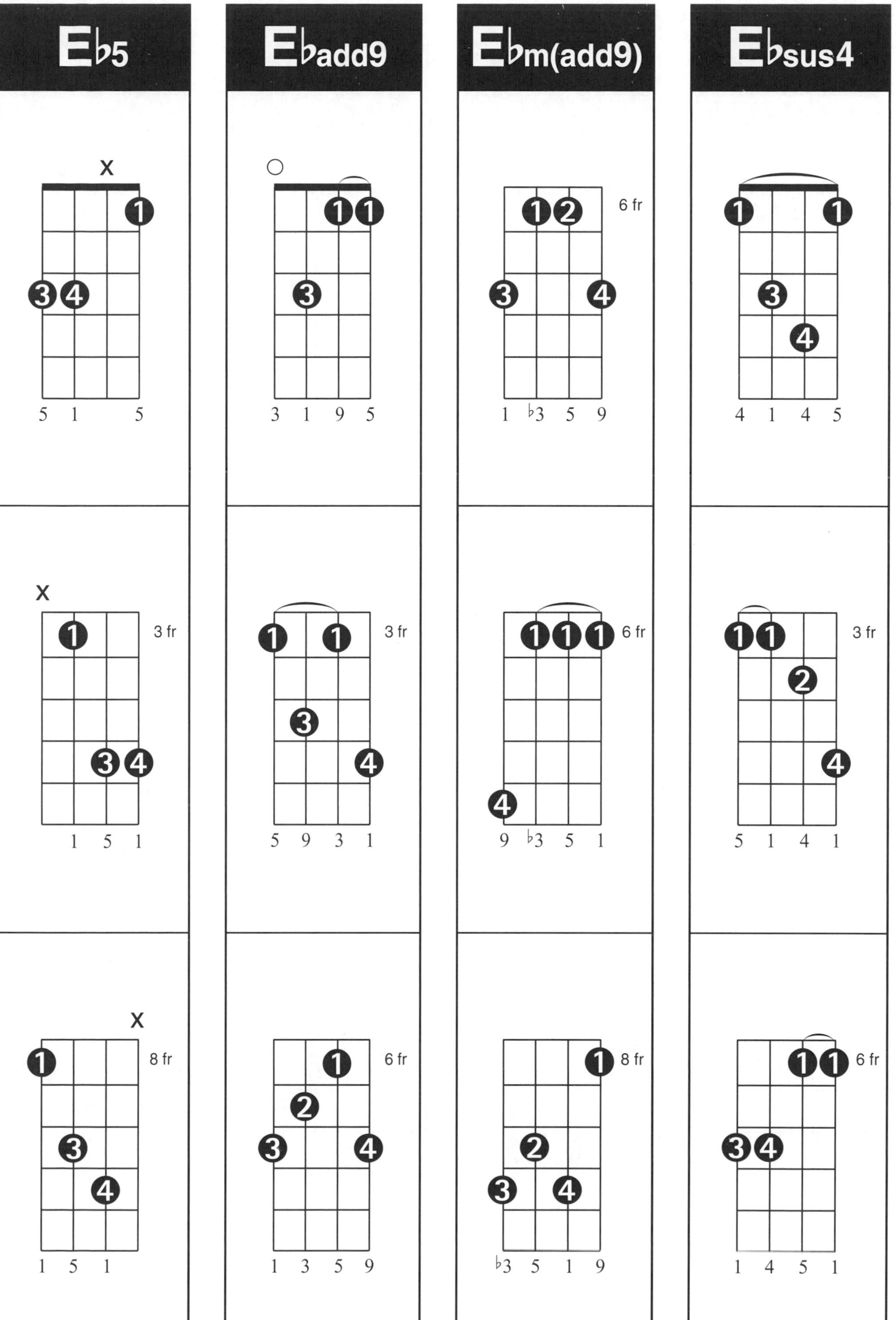

E♭5
E♭add9
E♭m(add9)
E♭sus4
E♭/D♯
x
5 1 5
○
3 1 9 5
6 fr
1 ♭3 5 9
4 1 4 5
x
3 fr
1 5 1
3 fr
5 9 3 1
6 fr
9 ♭3 5 1
3 fr
5 1 4 1
x
8 fr
1 5 1
6 fr
1 3 5 9
8 fr
♭3 5 1 9
6 fr
1 4 5 1

E♭/D♯

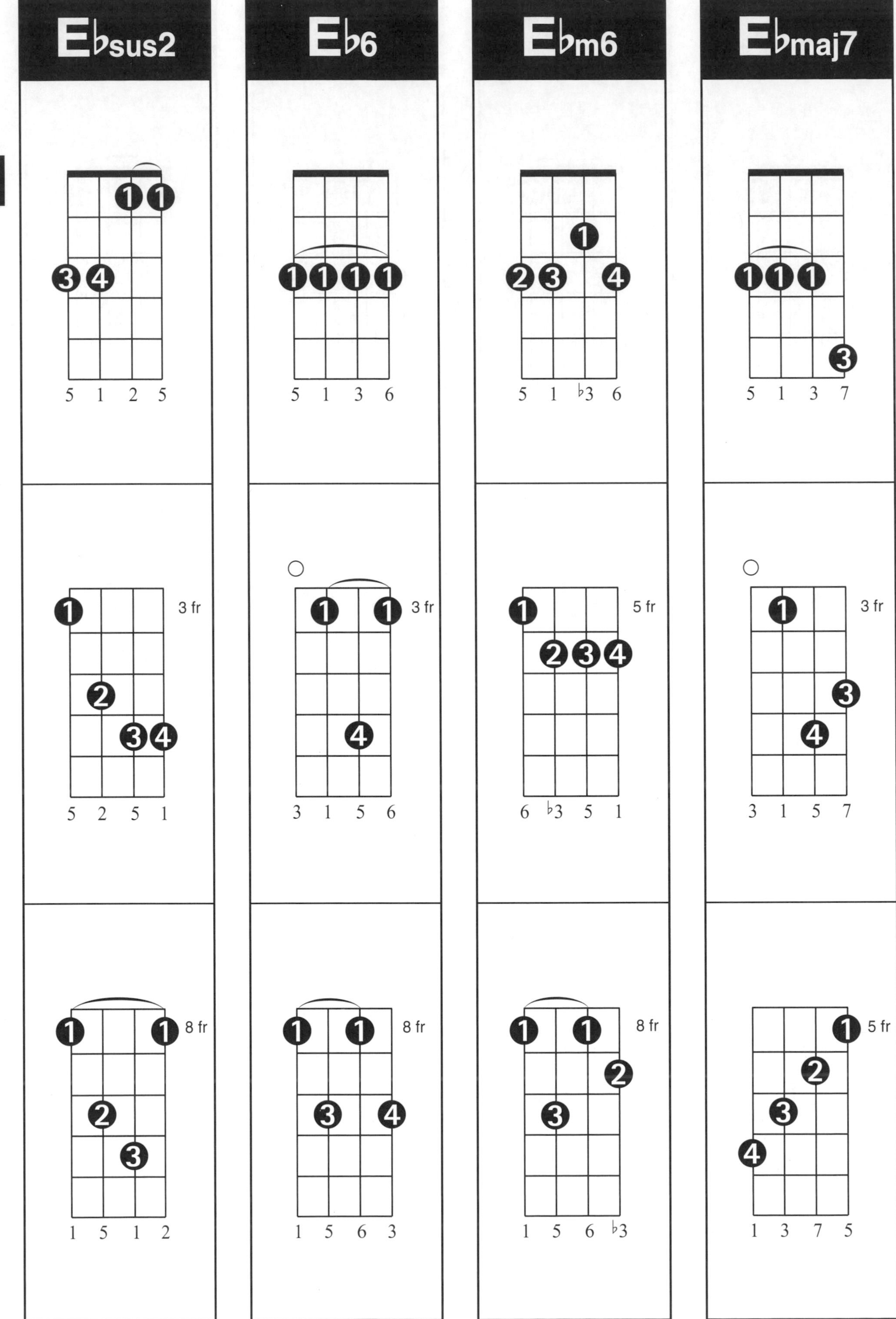

E♭sus2
5 1 2 5
3 fr
5 2 5 1
8 fr
1 5 1 2
E♭6
5 1 3 6
3 fr
3 1 5 6
8 fr
1 5 6 3
E♭m6
5 1 ♭3 6
5 fr
6 ♭3 5 1
8 fr
1 5 6 ♭3
E♭maj7
5 1 3 7
3 fr
3 1 5 7
5 fr
1 3 7 5

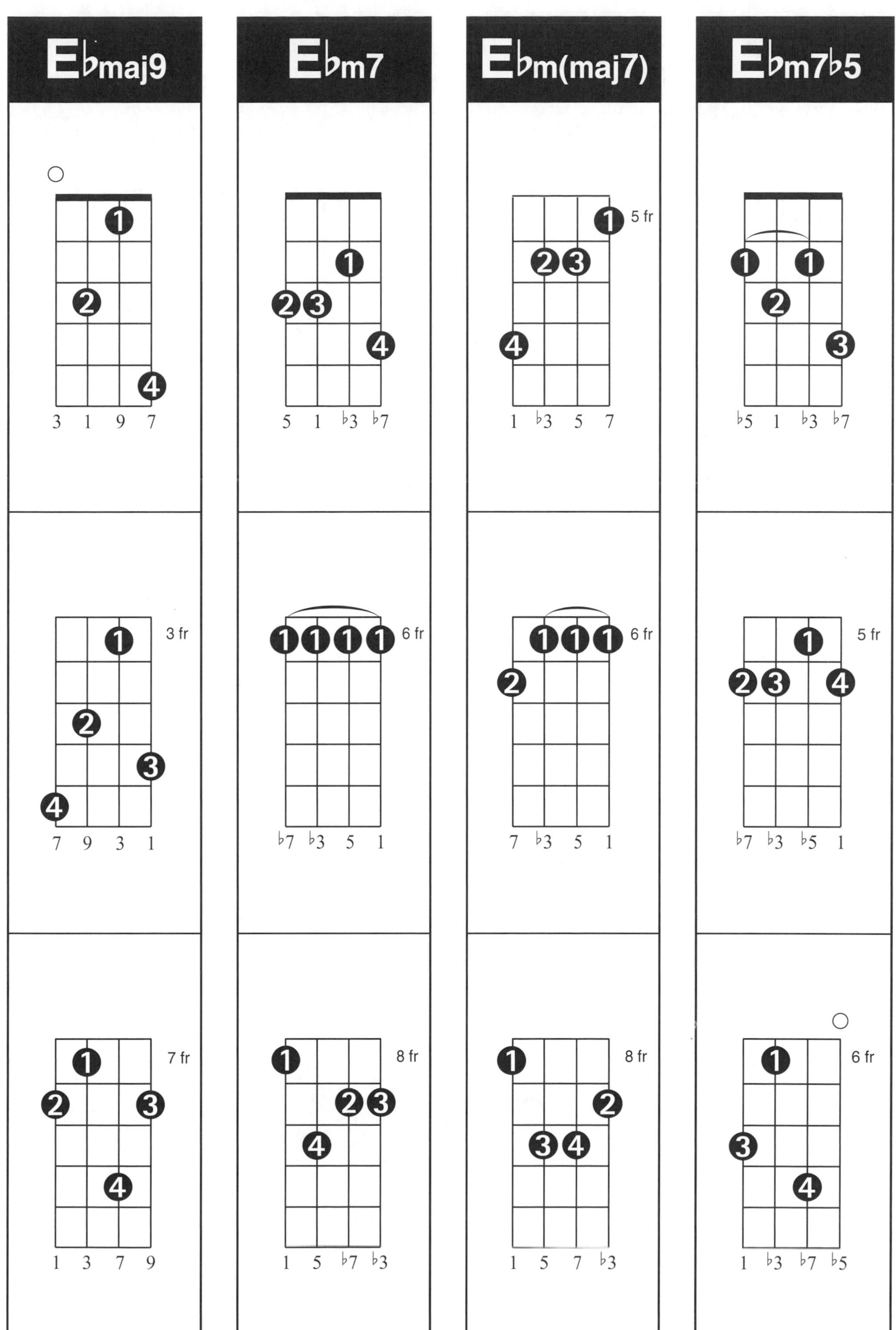
E♭maj9
E♭m7
E♭m(maj7)
E♭m7♭5
3 1 9 7
5 1 ♭3 ♭7
5 fr
1 ♭3 5 7
♭5 1 ♭3 ♭7
3 fr
7 9 3 1
6 fr
♭7 ♭3 5 1
6 fr
7 ♭3 5 1
5 fr
♭7 ♭3 ♭5 1
7 fr
1 3 7 9
8 fr
1 5 ♭7 ♭3
8 fr
1 5 7 ♭3
6 fr
1 ♭3 ♭7 ♭5

E♭/D♯

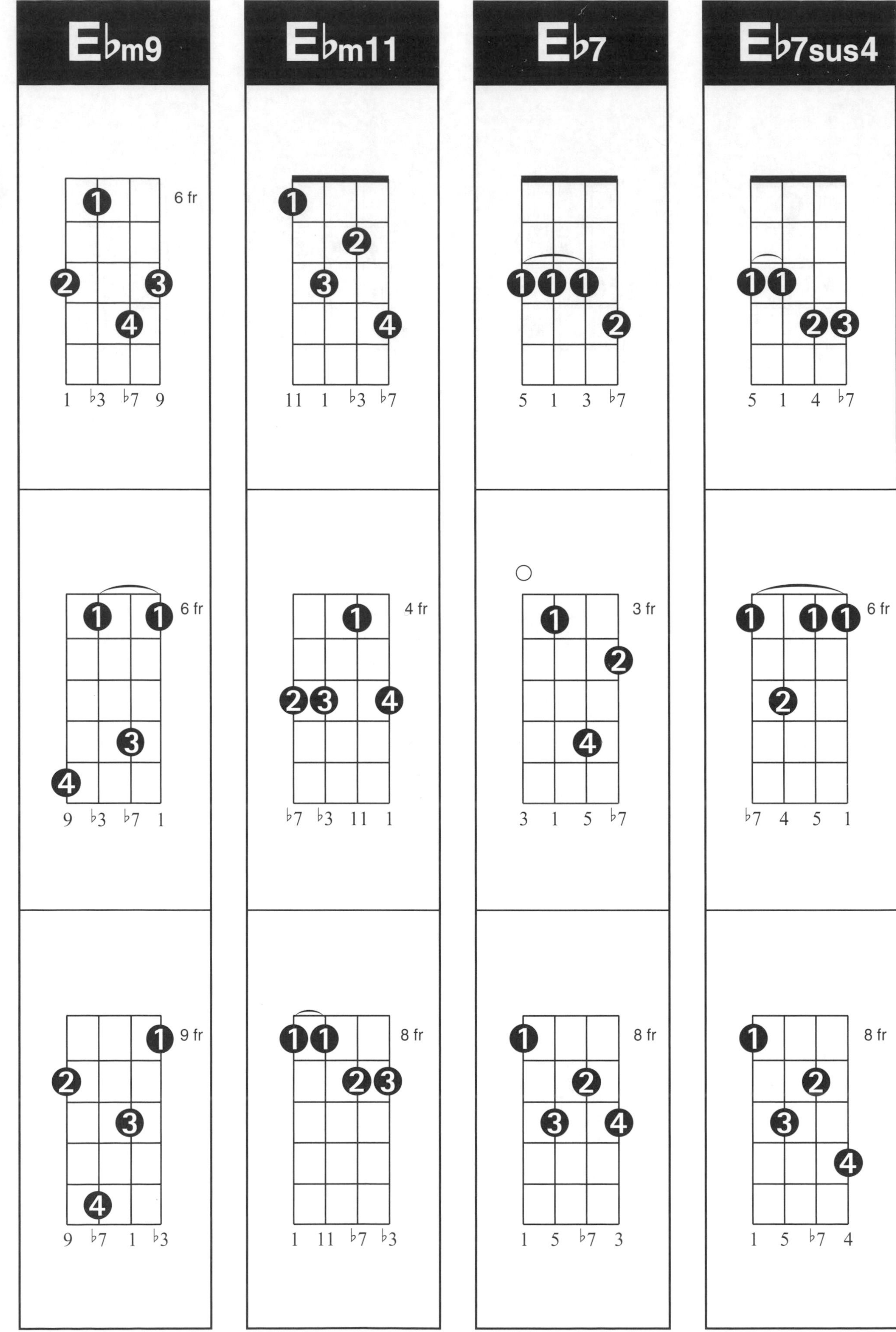
E♭m9
E♭m11
E♭7
E♭7sus4
6 fr
1 ♭3 ♭7 9
11 1 ♭3 ♭7
5 1 3 ♭7
5 1 4 ♭7
6 fr
9 ♭3 ♭7 1
4 fr
♭7 ♭3 11 1
3 fr
3 1 5 ♭7
6 fr
♭7 4 5 1
9 fr
9 ♭7 1 ♭3
8 fr
1 11 ♭7 ♭3
8 fr
1 5 ♭7 3
8 fr
1 5 ♭7 4

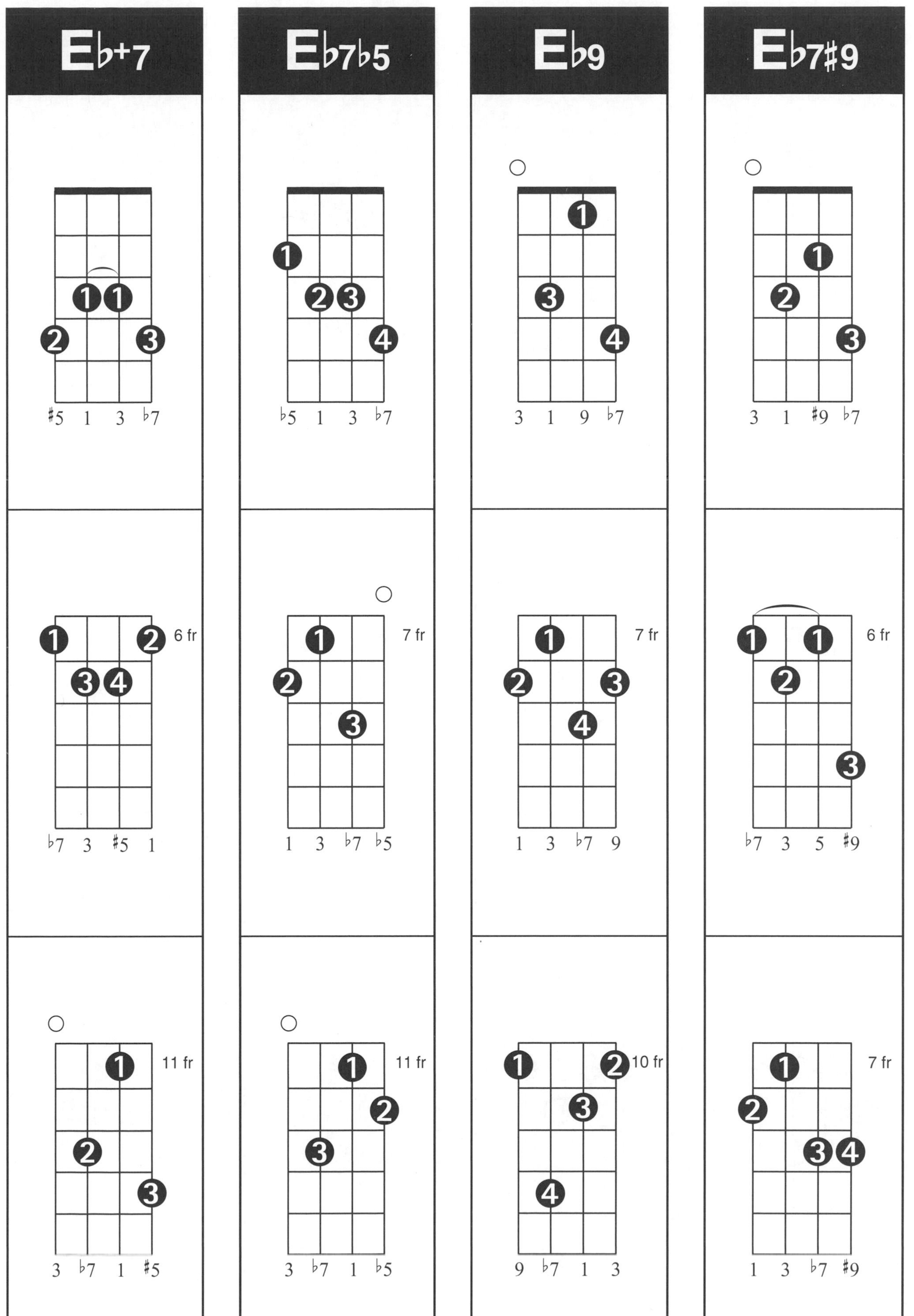

E♭+7
E♭7♭5
E♭9
E♭7♯9
E♭/D♯
♯5 1 3 ♭7
♭5 1 3 ♭7
3 1 9 ♭7
3 1 ♯9 ♭7
6 fr
7 fr
7 fr
6 fr
♭7 3 ♯5 1
1 3 ♭7 ♭5
1 3 ♭7 9
♭7 3 5 ♯9
11 fr
11 fr
10 fr
7 fr
3 ♭7 1 ♯5
3 ♭7 1 ♭5
9 ♭7 1 3
1 3 ♭7 ♯9

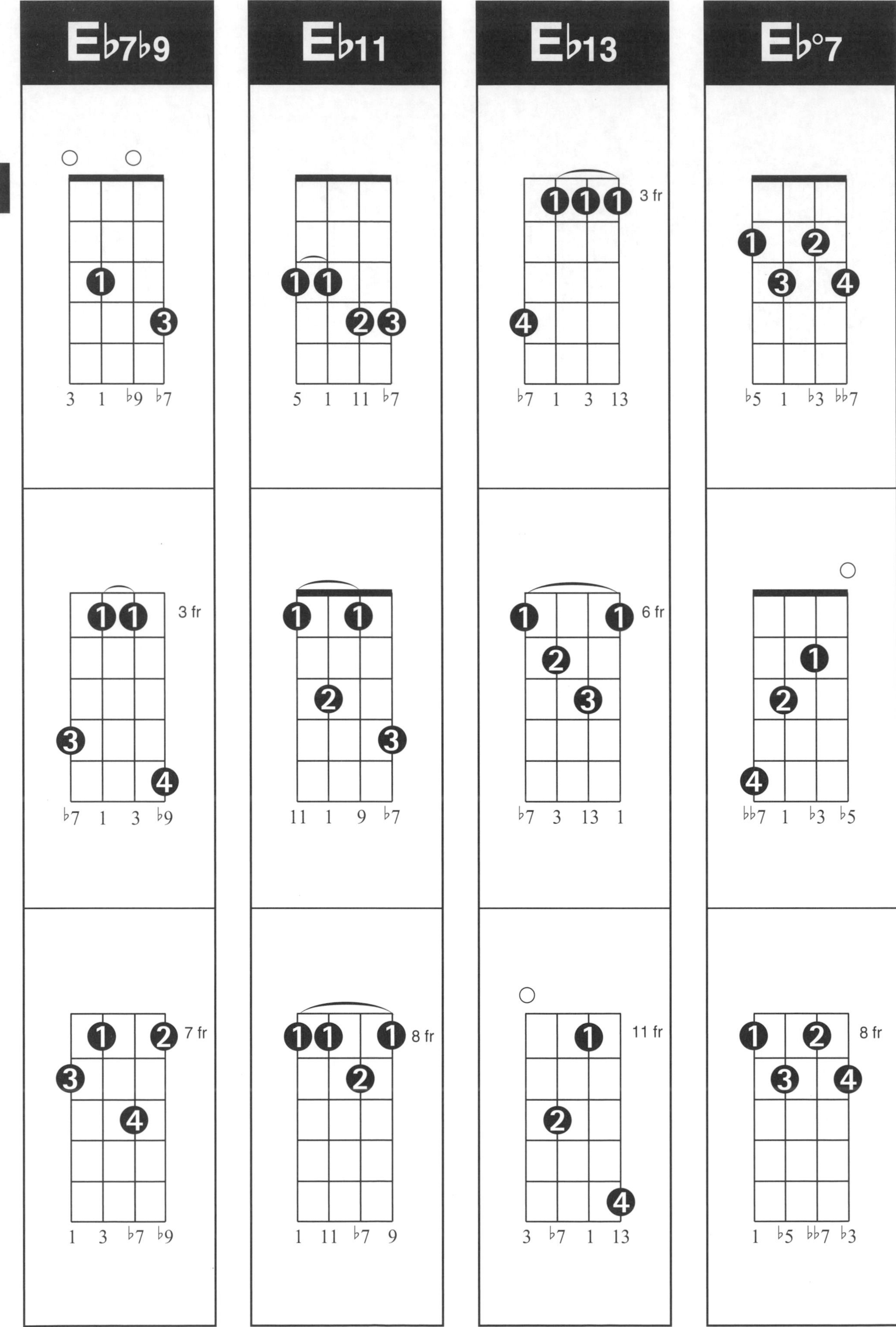
E♭7♭9
3 1 ♭9 ♭7
3 fr
♭7 1 3 ♭9
7 fr
1 3 ♭7 ♭9
E♭11
5 1 11 ♭7
11 1 9 ♭7
8 fr
1 11 ♭7 9
E♭13
3 fr
♭7 1 3 13
6 fr
♭7 3 13 1
11 fr
3 ♭7 1 13
E♭°7
♭5 1 ♭3 ♭♭7
♭♭7 1 ♭3 ♭5
8 fr
1 ♭5 ♭♭7 ♭3

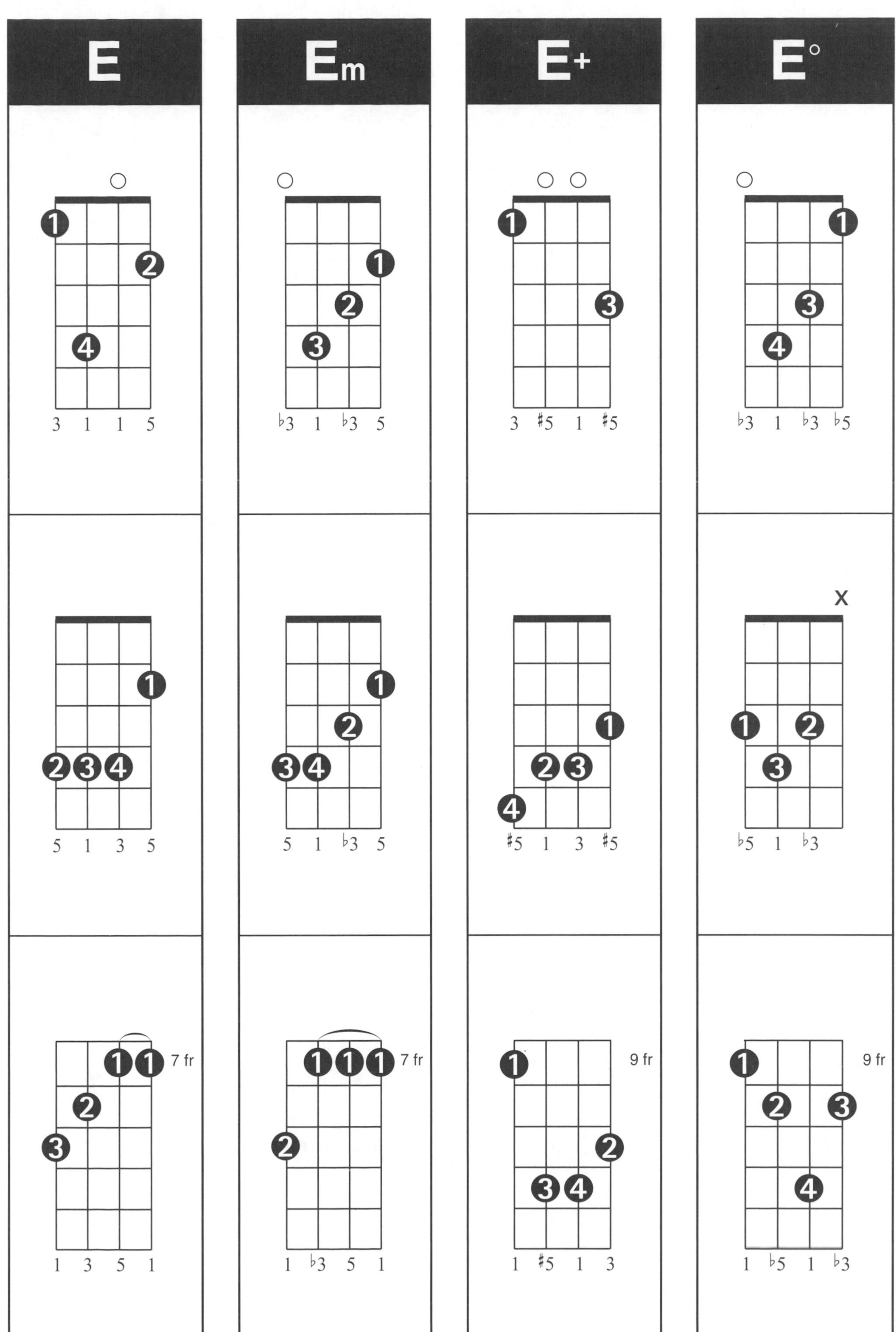
E
Em
E+
E°
3 1 1 5
♭3 1 ♭3 5
3 ♯5 1 ♯5
♭3 1 ♭3 ♭5
5 1 3 5
5 1 ♭3 5
♯5 1 3 ♯5
X
♭5 1 ♭3
7 fr
7 fr
9 fr
9 fr
1 3 5 1
1 ♭3 5 1
1 ♯5 1 3
1 ♭5 1 ♭3

E

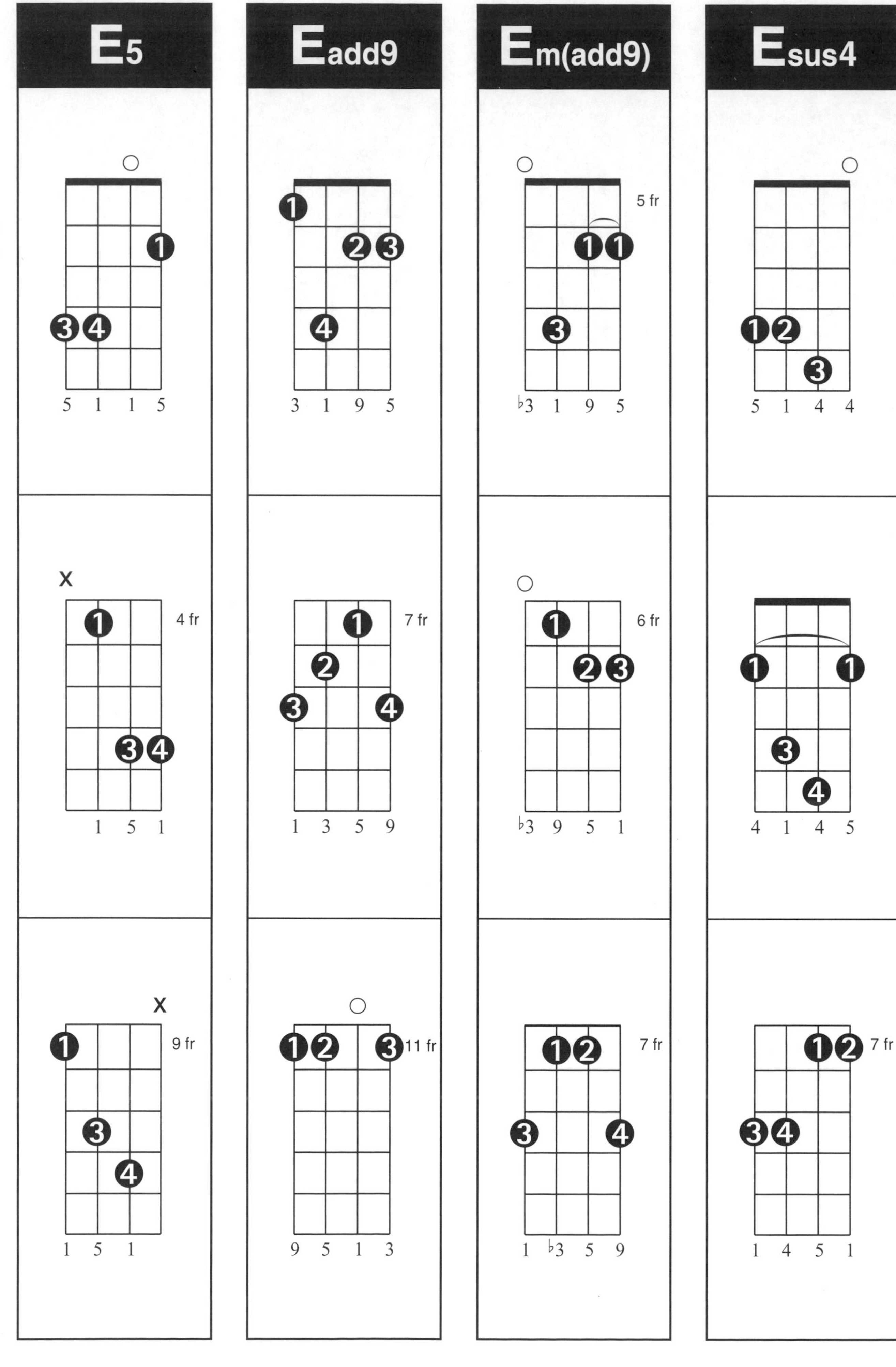
E5
5 1 1 5
X
4 fr
1 5 1
X
9 fr
1 5 1
Eadd9
3 1 9 5
7 fr
1 3 5 9
11 fr
9 5 1 3
Em(add9)
5 fr
♭3 1 9 5
6 fr
♭3 9 5 1
7 fr
1 ♭3 5 9
Esus4
5 1 4 4
4 1 4 5
7 fr
1 4 5 1

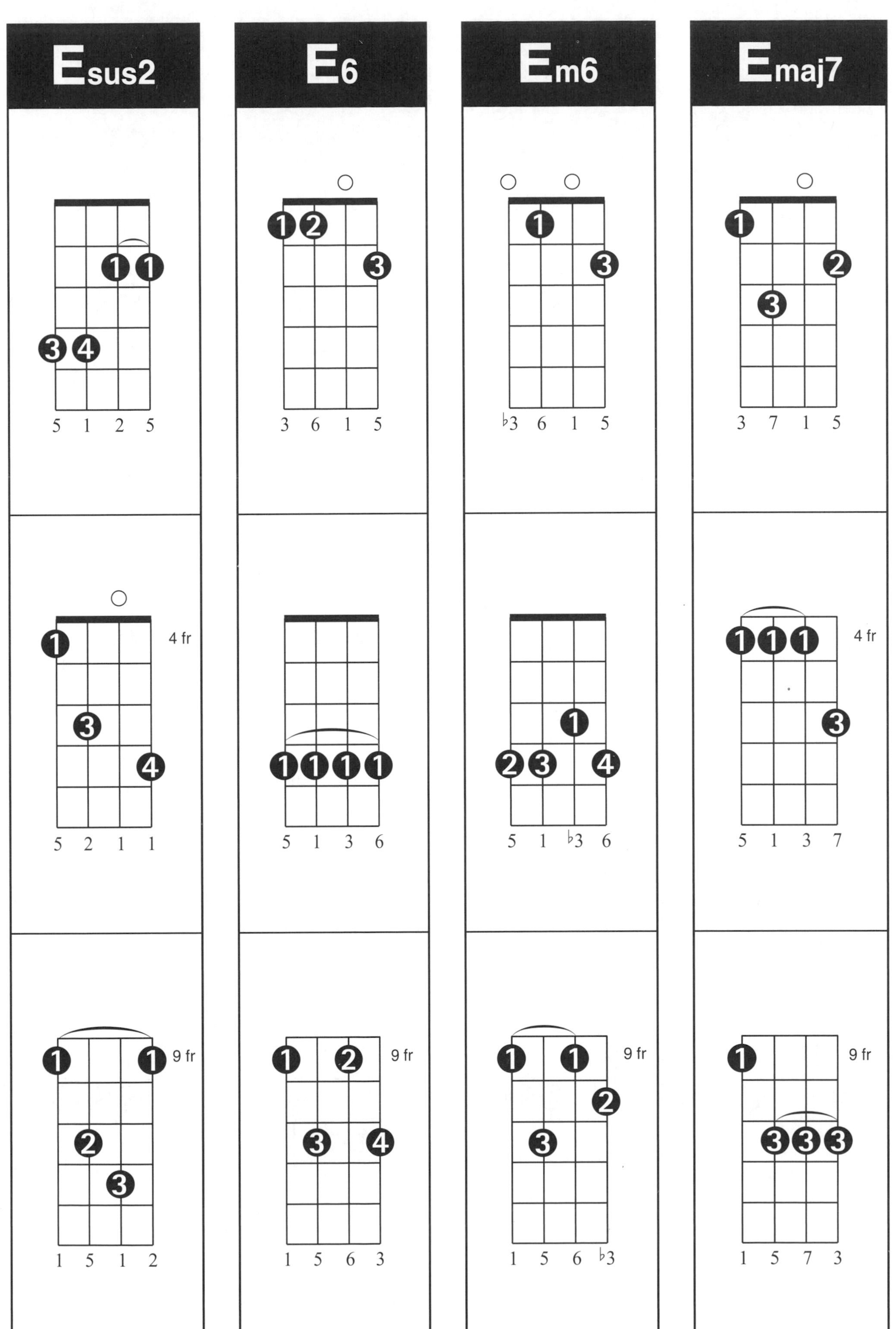
Esus2
E6
Em6
Emaj7
5 1 2 5
3 6 1 5
♭3 6 1 5
3 7 1 5
4 fr
5 2 1 1
5 1 3 6
5 1 ♭3 6
4 fr
5 1 3 7
9 fr
1 5 1 2
9 fr
1 5 6 3
9 fr
1 5 6 ♭3
9 fr
1 5 7 3
E

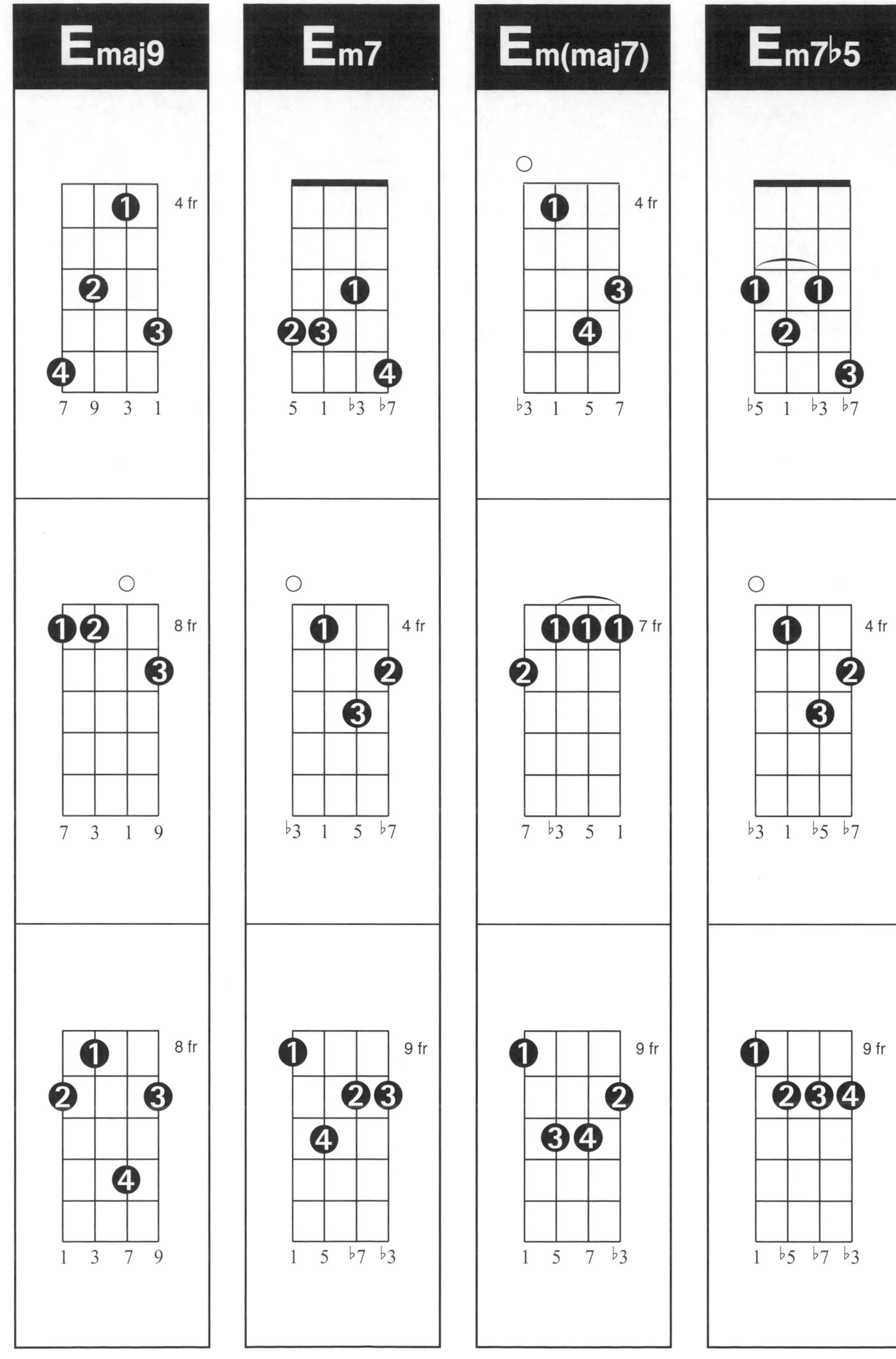
Emaj9
Em7
Em(maj7)
Em7♭5
4 fr
4 fr
7 9 3 1
5 1 ♭3 ♭7
♭3 1 5 7
♭5 1 ♭3 ♭7
8 fr
4 fr
7 fr
4 fr
7 3 1 9
♭3 1 5 ♭7
7 ♭3 5 1
♭3 1 ♭5 ♭7
8 fr
9 fr
9 fr
9 fr
1 3 7 9
1 5 ♭7 ♭3
1 5 7 ♭3
1 ♭5 ♭7 ♭3

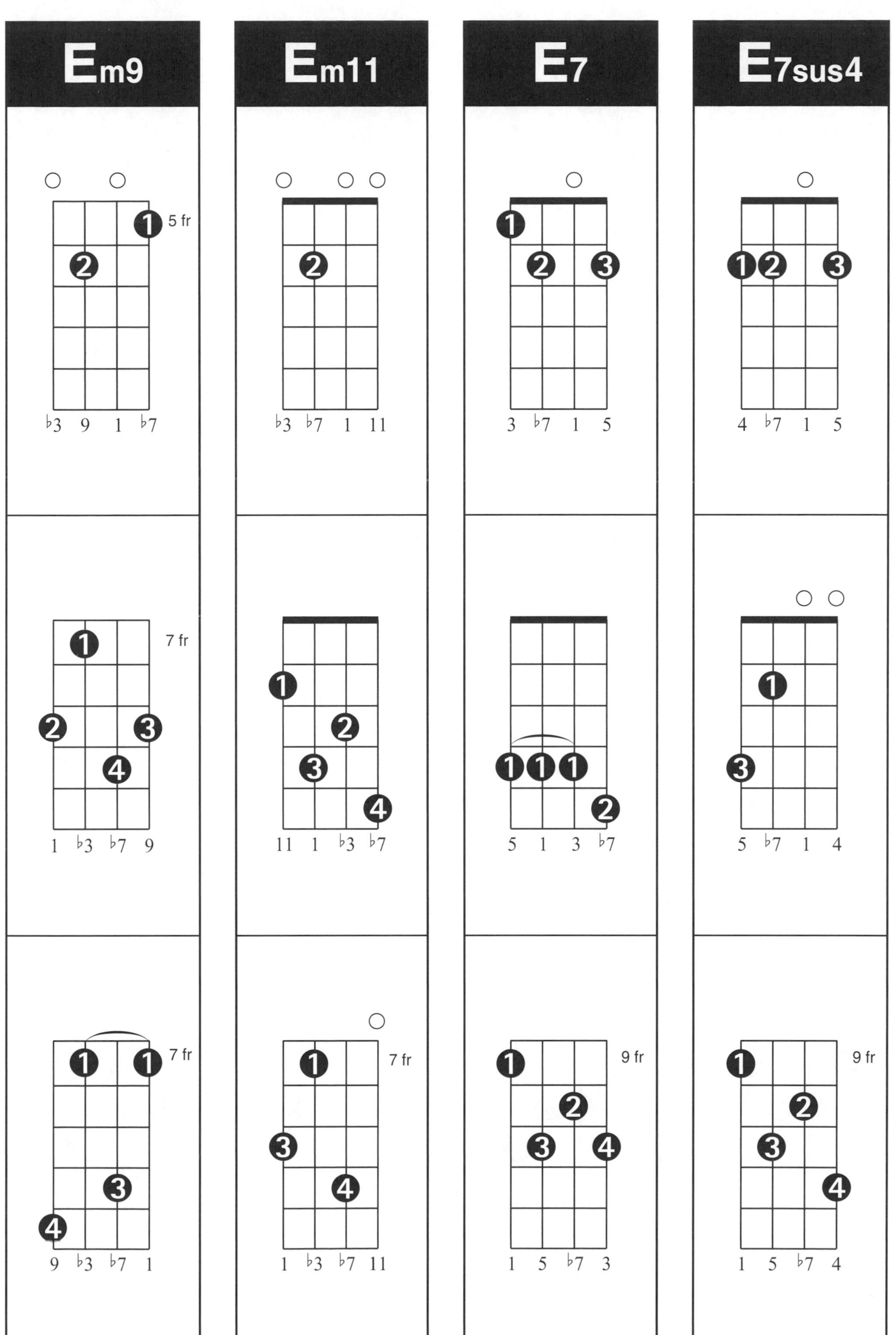
Em9
Em11
E7
E7sus4
5 fr
♭3 9 1 ♭7
♭3 ♭7 1 11
3 ♭7 1 5
4 ♭7 1 5
7 fr
1 ♭3 ♭7 9
11 1 ♭3 ♭7
5 1 3 ♭7
5 ♭7 1 4
7 fr
9 ♭3 ♭7 1
7 fr
1 ♭3 ♭7 11
9 fr
1 5 ♭7 3
9 fr
1 5 ♭7 4

E

E

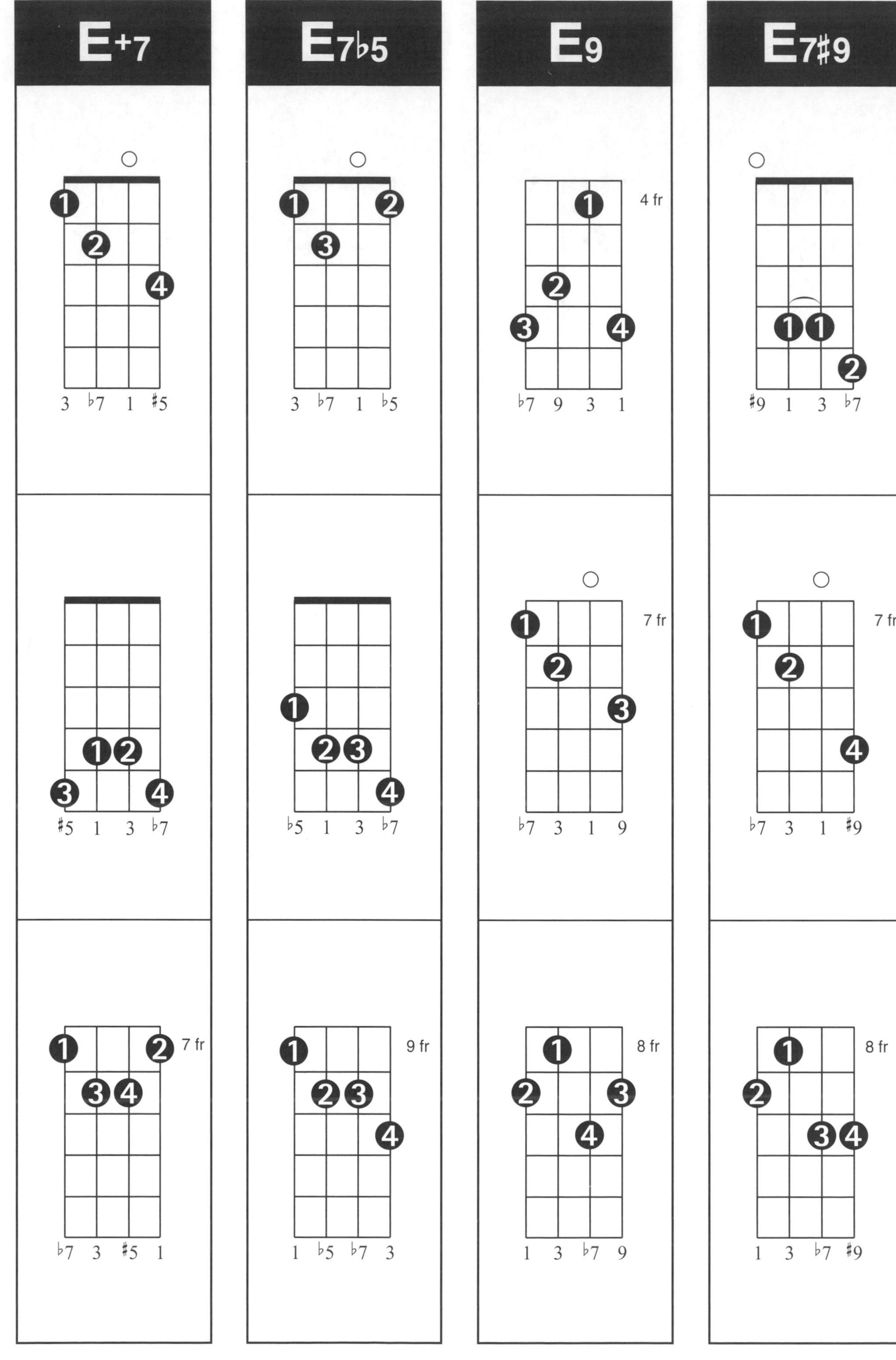
E+7
E7♭5
E9
E7♯9
3 ♭7 1 ♯5
3 ♭7 1 ♭5
4 fr
♭7 9 3 1
♯9 1 3 ♭7
♯5 1 3 ♭7
♭5 1 3 ♭7
7 fr
♭7 3 1 9
7 fr
♭7 3 1 ♯9
7 fr
♭7 3 ♯5 1
9 fr
1 ♭5 ♭7 3
8 fr
1 3 ♭7 9
8 fr
1 3 ♭7 ♯9

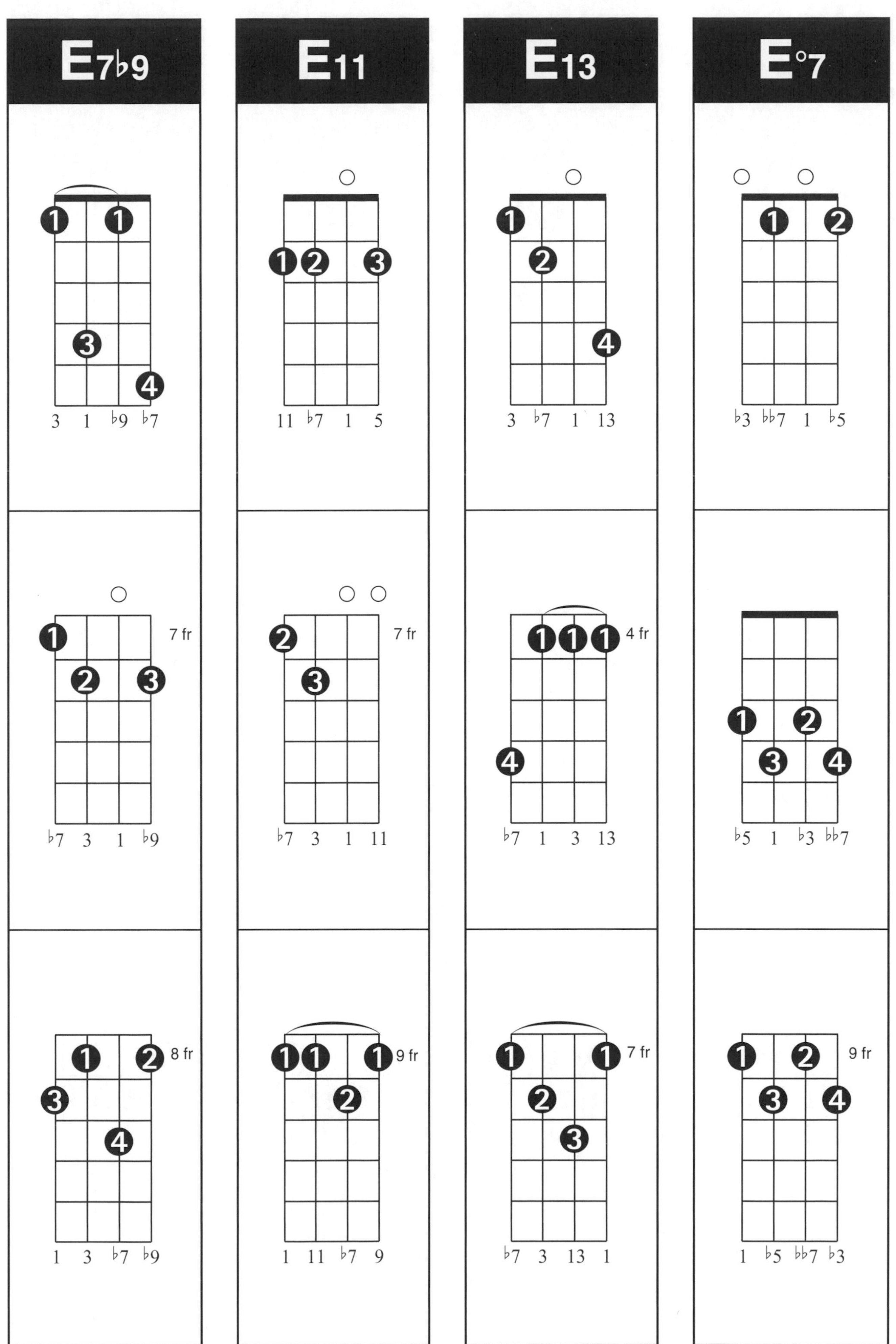

E7♭9
E11
E13
E°7
3 1 ♭9 ♭7
11 ♭7 1 5
3 ♭7 1 13
♭3 ♭♭7 1 ♭5
7 fr
7 fr
4 fr
♭7 3 1 ♭9
♭7 3 1 11
♭7 1 3 13
♭5 1 ♭3 ♭♭7
8 fr
9 fr
7 fr
9 fr
1 3 ♭7 ♭9
1 11 ♭7 9
♭7 3 13 1
1 ♭5 ♭♭7 ♭3

E

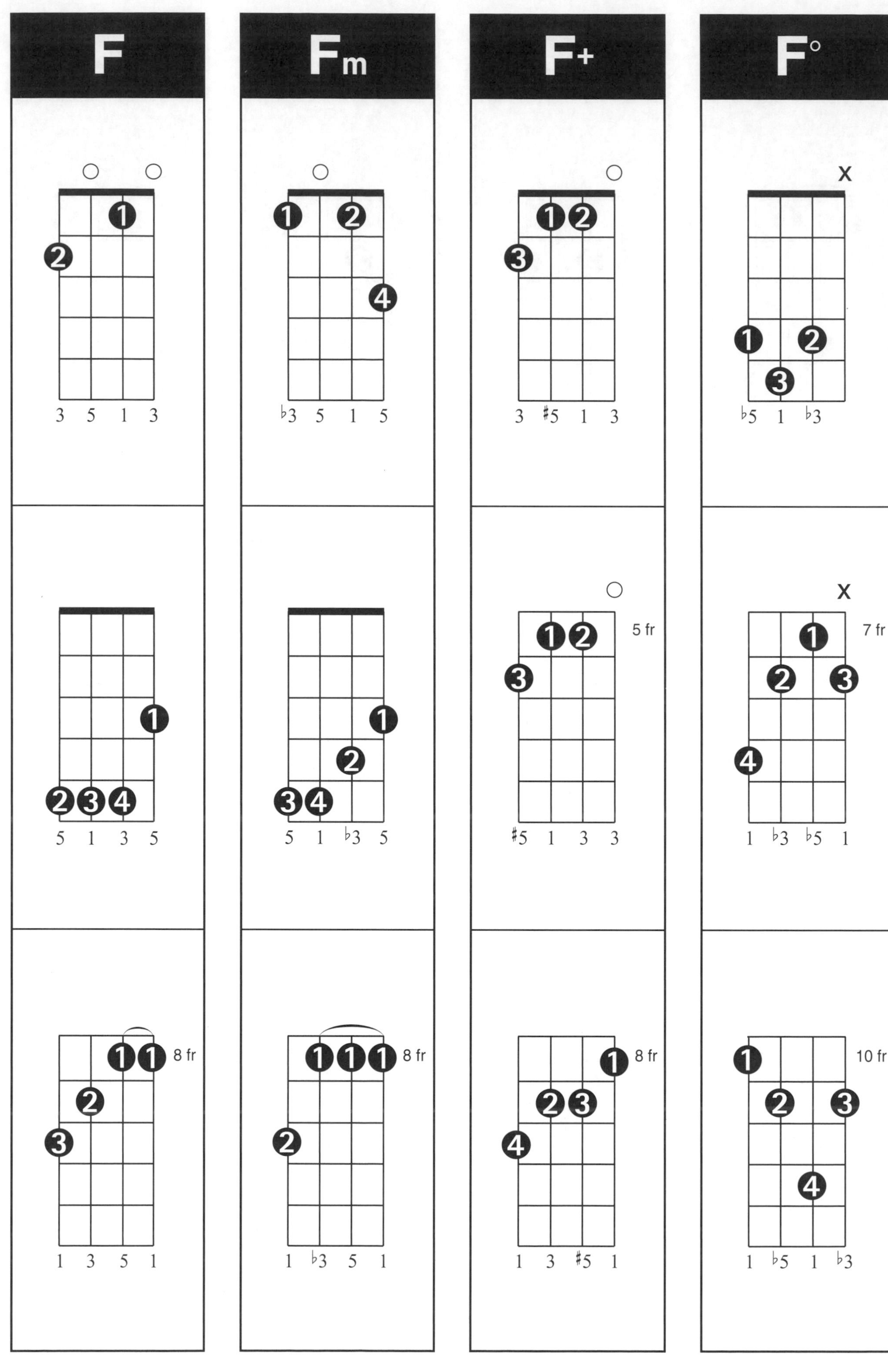
F
Fm
F+
F°
3 5 1 3
♭3 5 1 5
3 ♯5 1 3
♭5 1 ♭3
5 1 3 5
5 1 ♭3 5
5 fr
♯5 1 3 3
7 fr
1 ♭3 ♭5 1
8 fr
1 3 5 1
8 fr
1 ♭3 5 1
8 fr
1 3 ♯5 1
10 fr
1 ♭5 1 ♭3

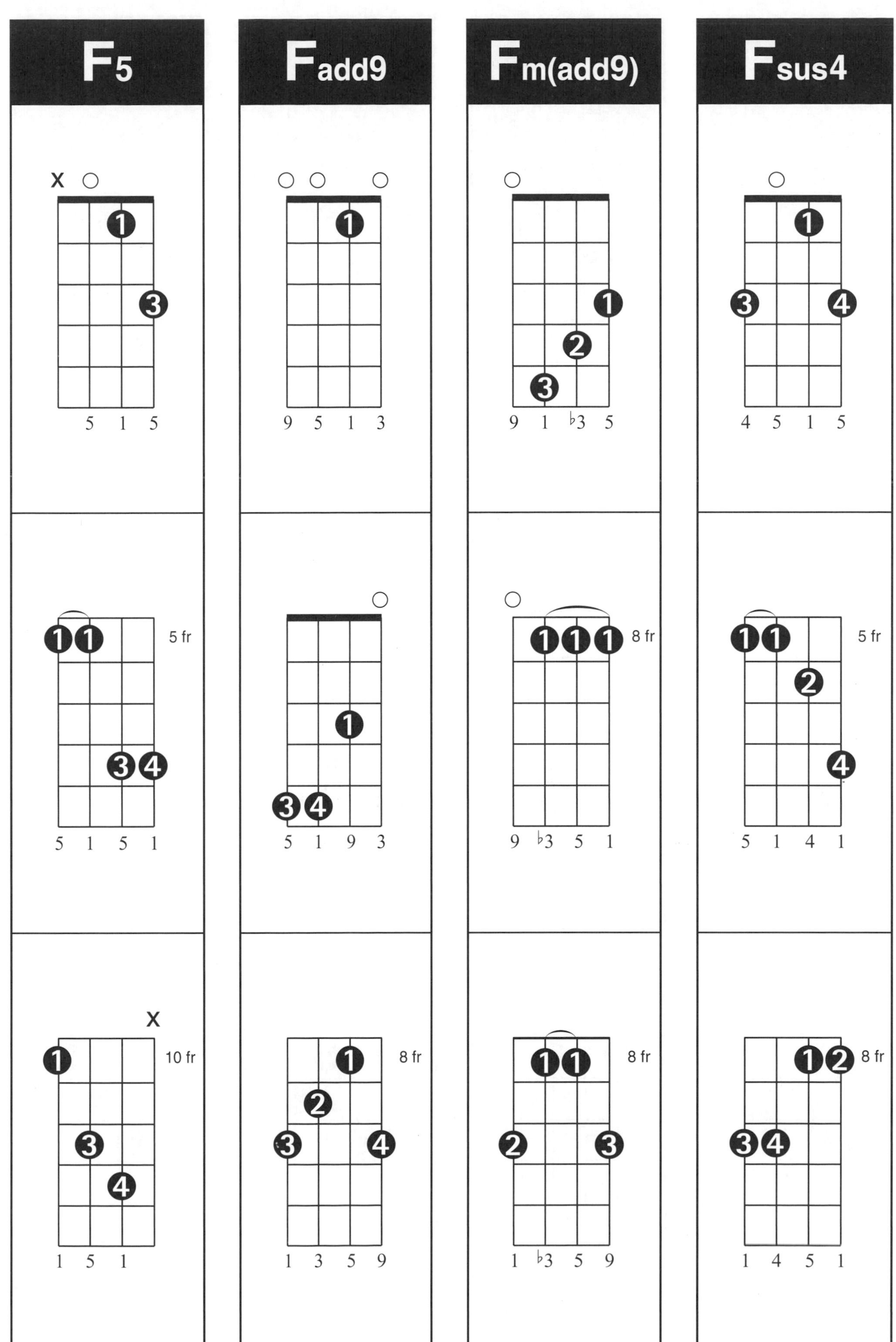

F

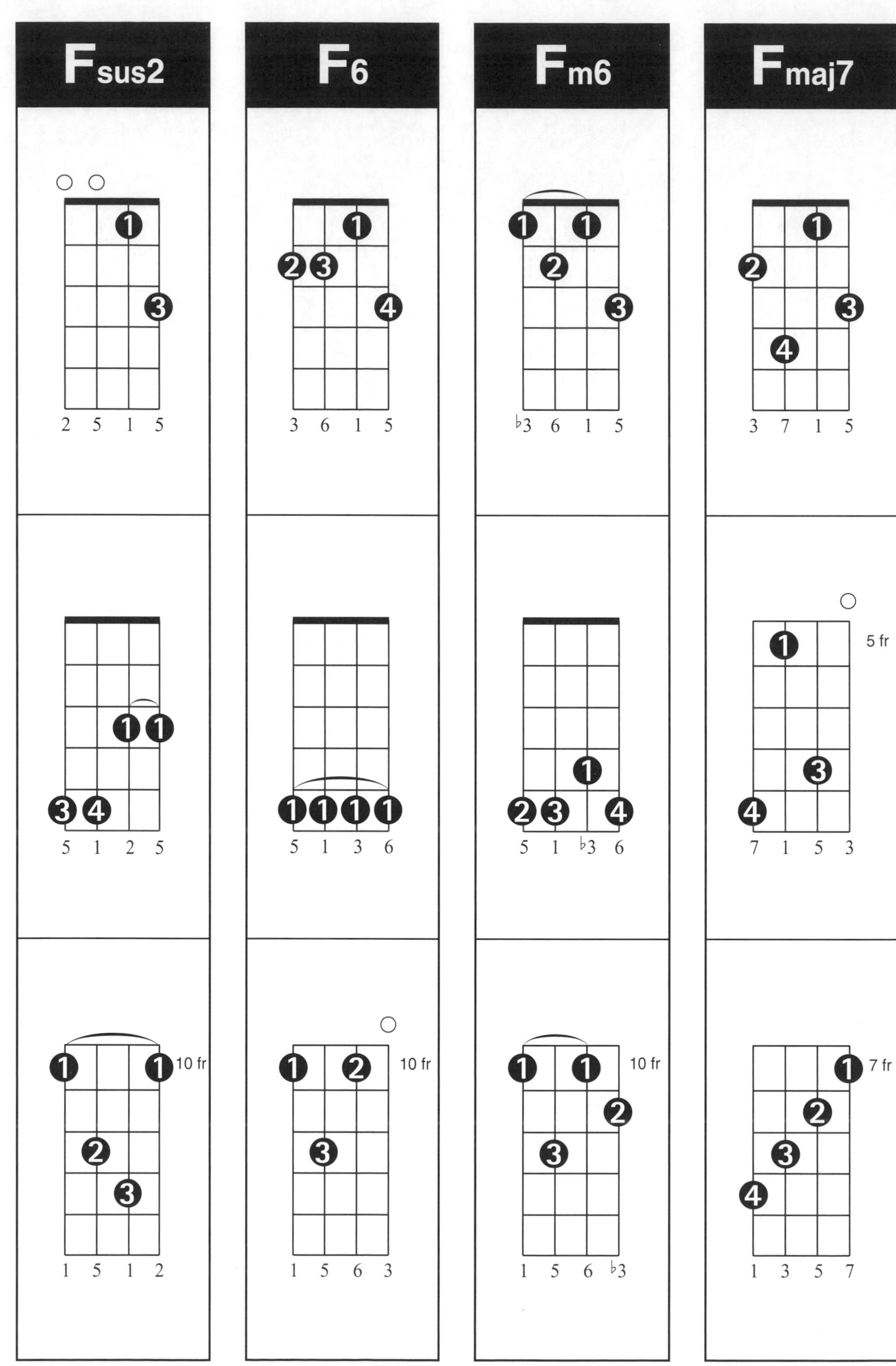

Fsus2
F6
Fm6
Fmaj7
2 5 1 5
3 6 1 5
♭3 6 1 5
3 7 1 5
5 1 2 5
5 1 3 6
5 1 ♭3 6
5 fr
7 1 5 3
10 fr
1 5 1 2
10 fr
1 5 6 3
10 fr
1 5 6 ♭3
7 fr
1 3 5 7
F

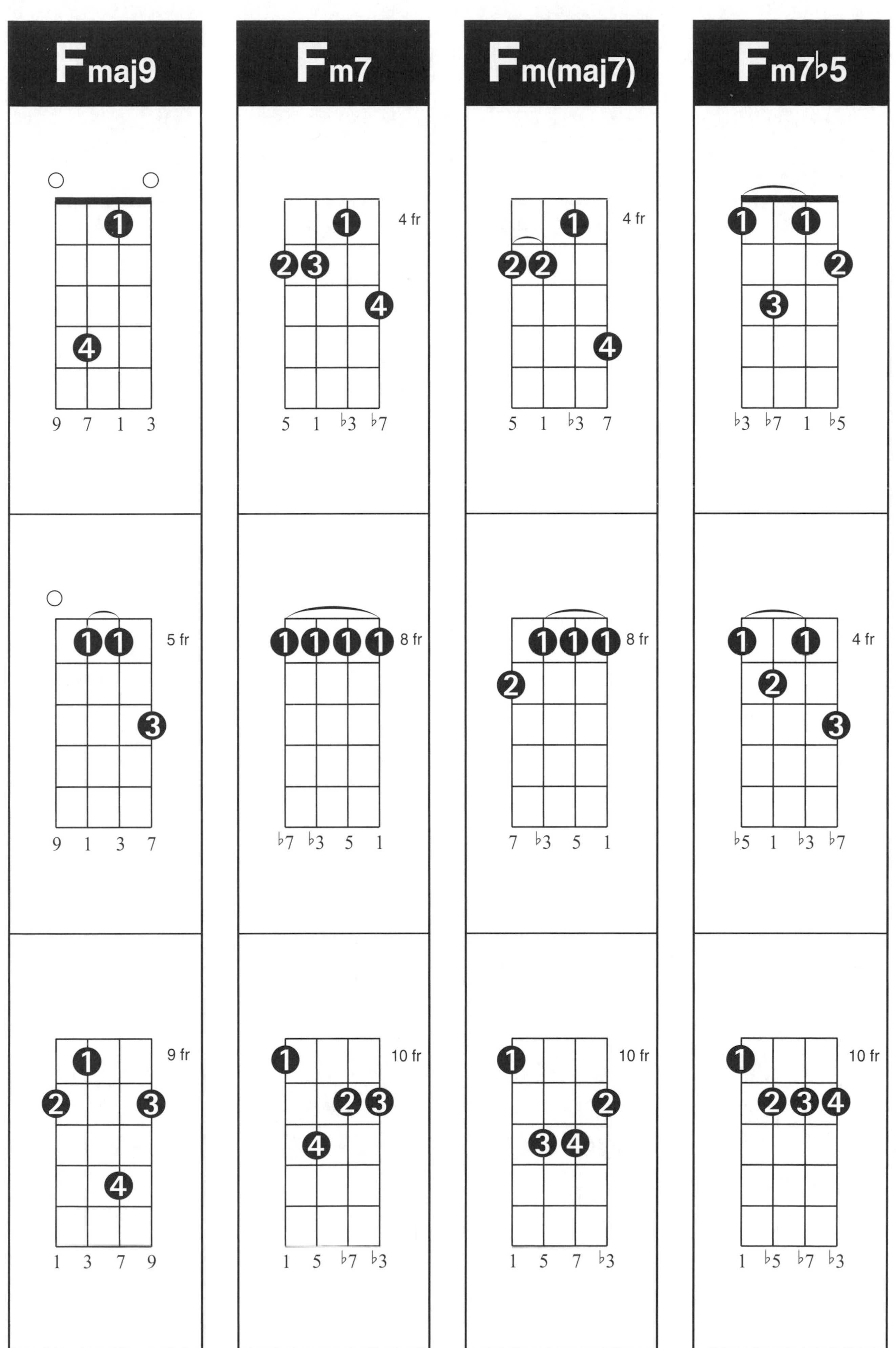
Fmaj9
Fm7
Fm(maj7)
Fm7♭5
4 fr
4 fr
9 7 1 3
5 1 ♭3 ♭7
5 1 ♭3 7
♭3 ♭7 1 ♭5
5 fr
8 fr
8 fr
4 fr
9 1 3 7
♭7 ♭3 5 1
7 ♭3 5 1
♭5 1 ♭3 ♭7
9 fr
10 fr
10 fr
10 fr
1 3 7 9
1 5 ♭7 ♭3
1 5 7 ♭3
1 ♭5 ♭7 ♭3

F

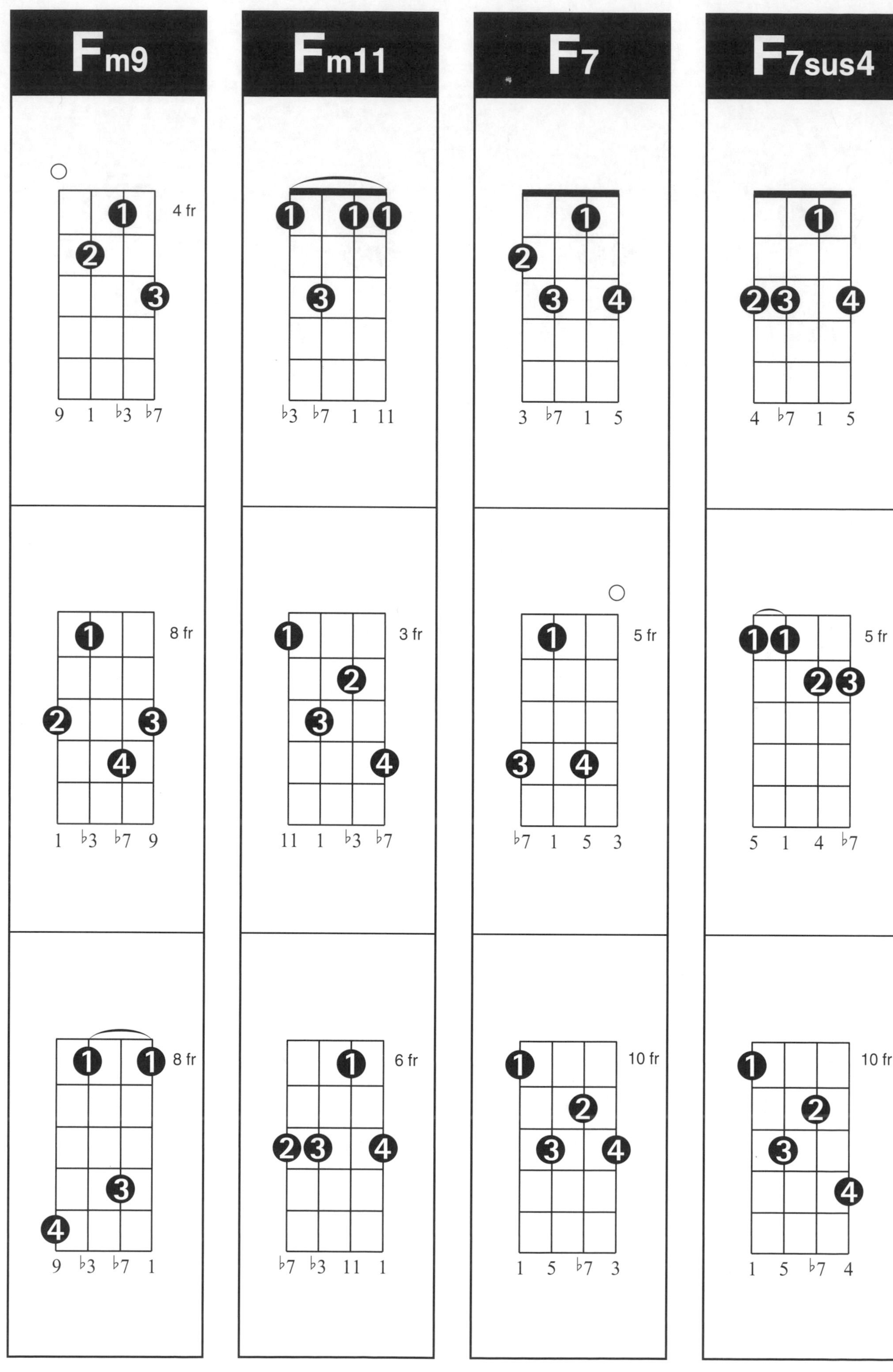
Fm9
Fm11
F7
F7sus4
4 fr
9 1 ♭3 ♭7
♭3 ♭7 1 11
3 ♭7 1 5
4 ♭7 1 5
8 fr
1 ♭3 ♭7 9
3 fr
11 1 ♭3 ♭7
5 fr
♭7 1 5 3
5 fr
5 1 4 ♭7
8 fr
9 ♭3 ♭7 1
6 fr
♭7 ♭3 11 1
10 fr
1 5 ♭7 3
10 fr
1 5 ♭7 4

F

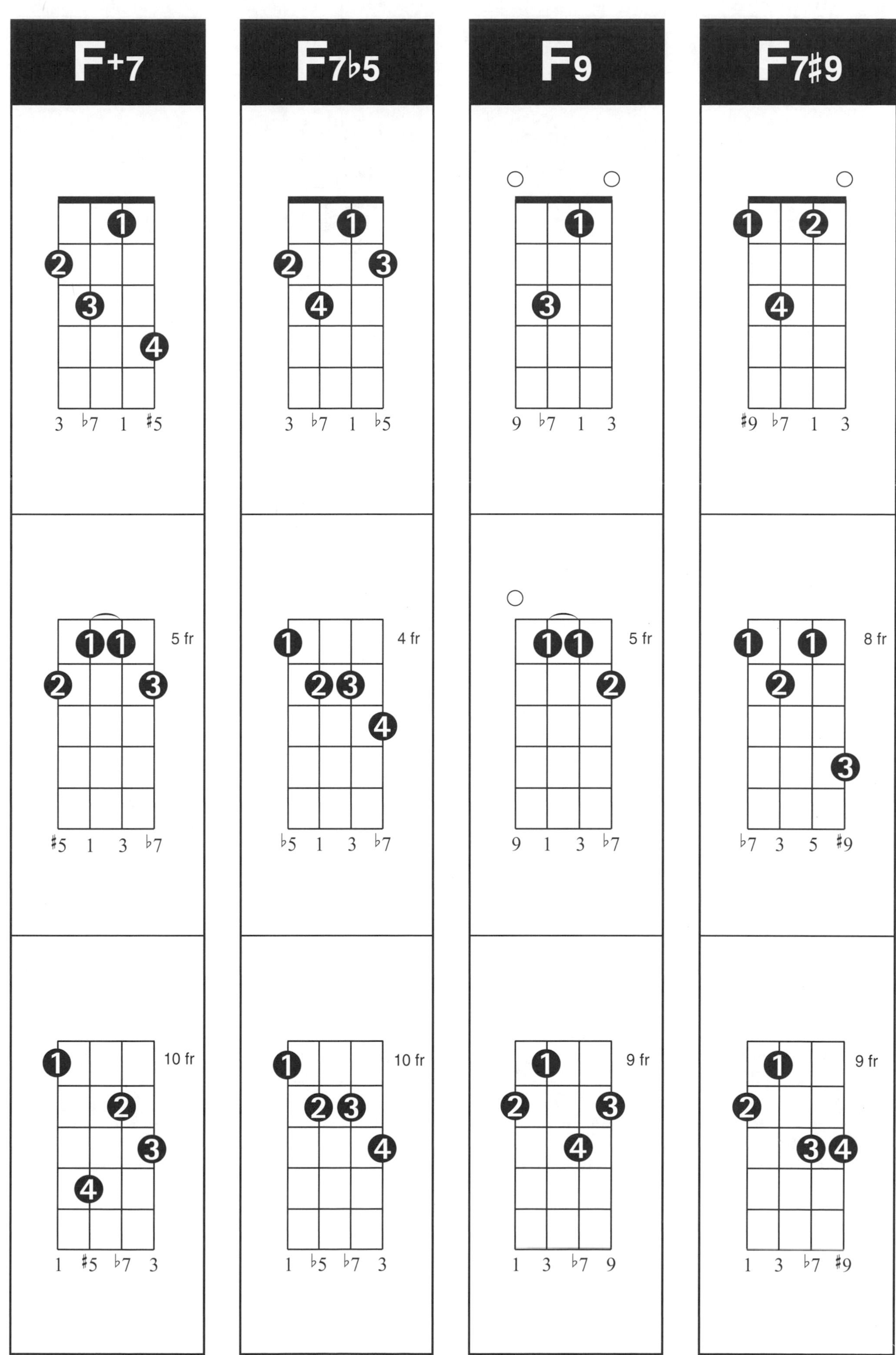
F+7
3 ♭7 1 ♯5
5 fr
♯5 1 3 ♭7
10 fr
1 ♯5 ♭7 3
F7♭5
3 ♭7 1 ♭5
4 fr
♭5 1 3 ♭7
10 fr
1 ♭5 ♭7 3
F9
9 ♭7 1 3
5 fr
9 1 3 ♭7
9 fr
1 3 ♭7 9
F7♯9
♯9 ♭7 1 3
8 fr
♭7 3 5 ♯9
9 fr
1 3 ♭7 ♯9

F

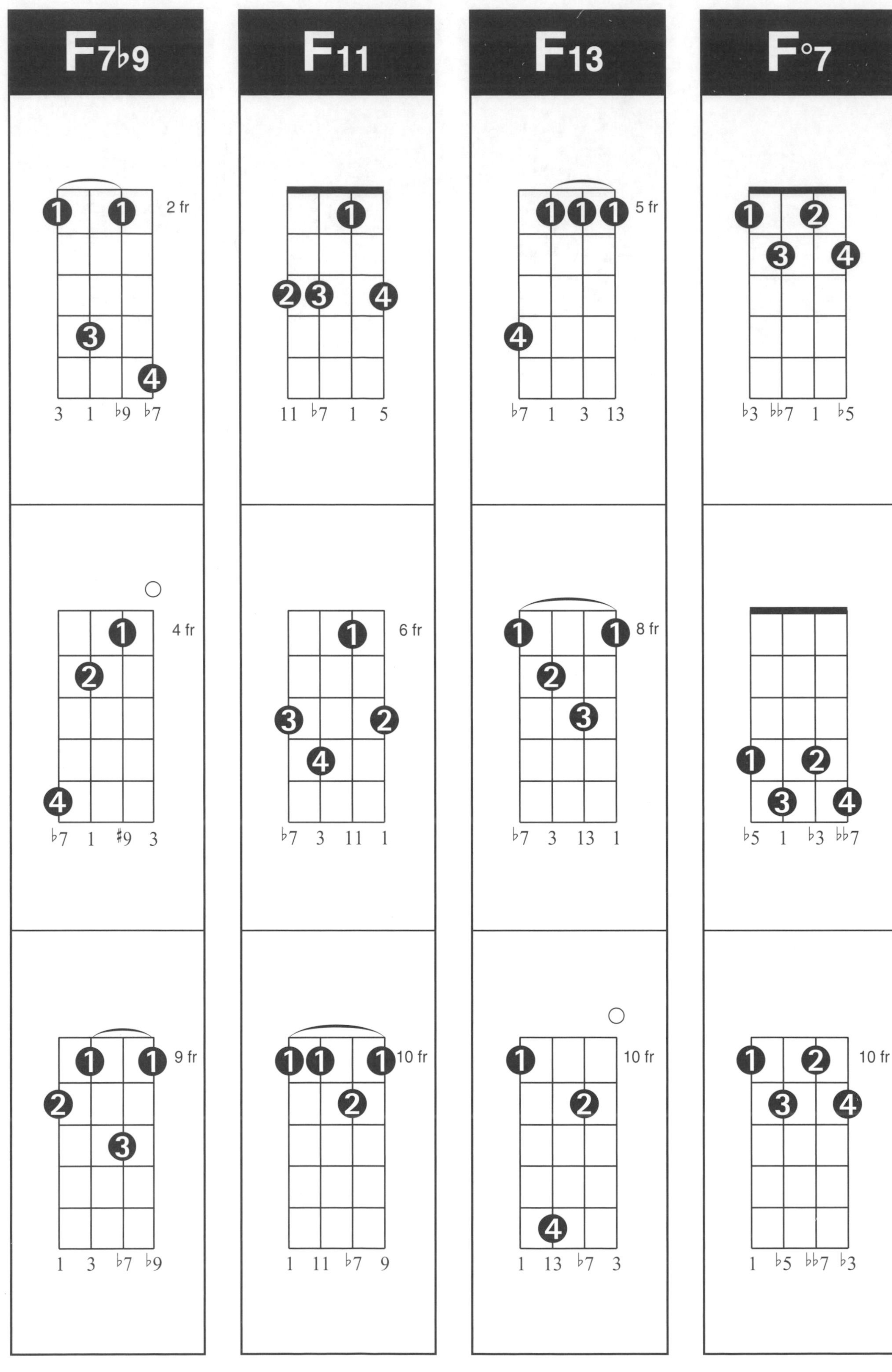
F7♭9
F11
F13
F°7
2 fr
3 1 ♭9 ♭7
11 ♭7 1 5
5 fr
♭7 1 3 13
♭3 ♭♭7 1 ♭5
4 fr
♭7 1 ♯9 3
6 fr
♭7 3 11 1
8 fr
♭7 3 13 1
♭5 1 ♭3 ♭♭7
9 fr
1 3 ♭7 ♭9
10 fr
1 11 ♭7 9
10 fr
1 13 ♭7 3
10 fr
1 ♭5 ♭♭7 ♭3

F

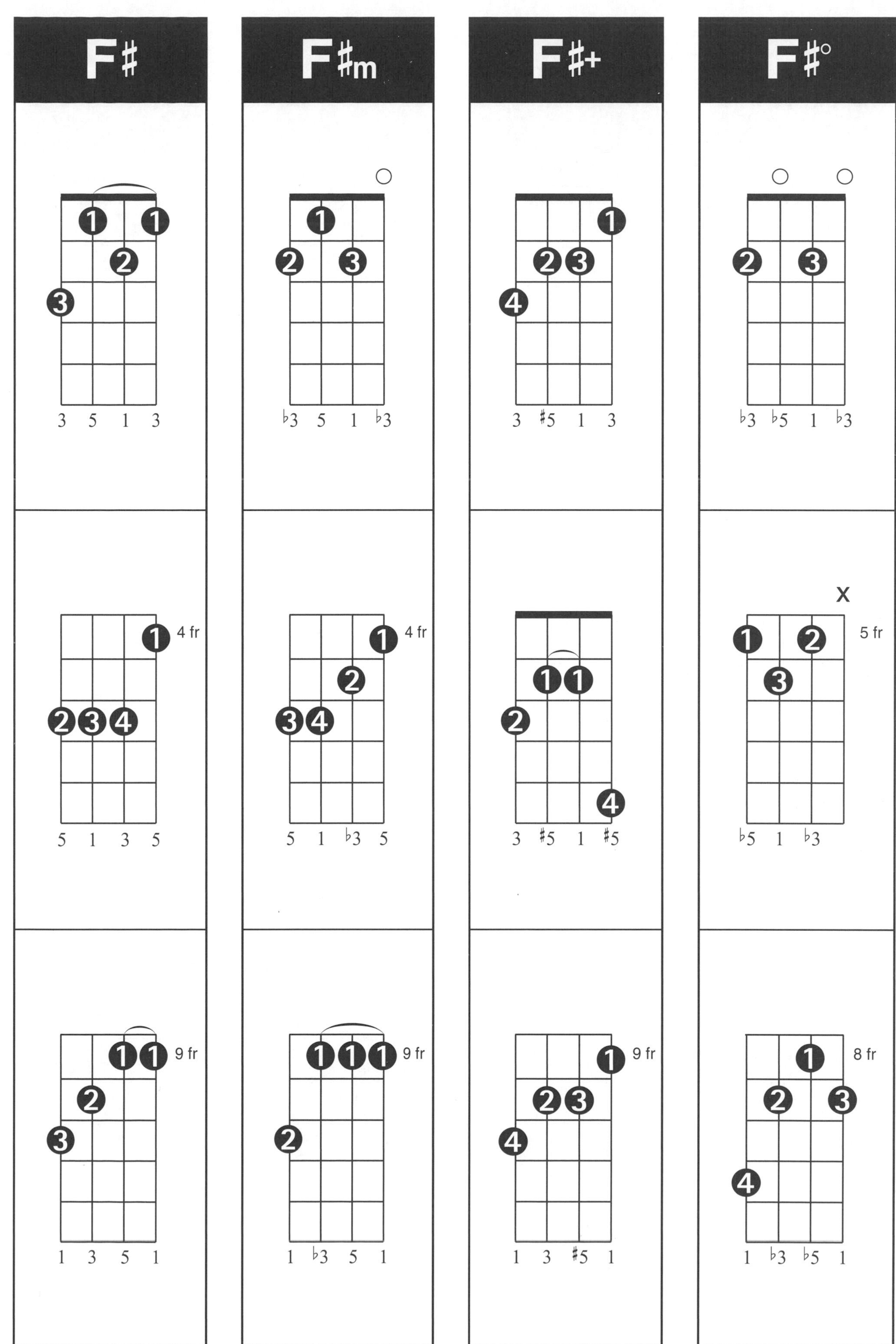
F♯
F♯m
F♯+
F♯°
3 5 1 3
♭3 5 1 ♭3
3 ♯5 1 3
♭3 ♭5 1 ♭3
4 fr
5 1 3 5
4 fr
5 1 ♭3 5
3 ♯5 1 ♯5
X
5 fr
♭5 1 ♭3
9 fr
1 3 5 1
9 fr
1 ♭3 5 1
9 fr
1 3 ♯5 1
8 fr
1 ♭3 ♭5 1

F♯/G♭

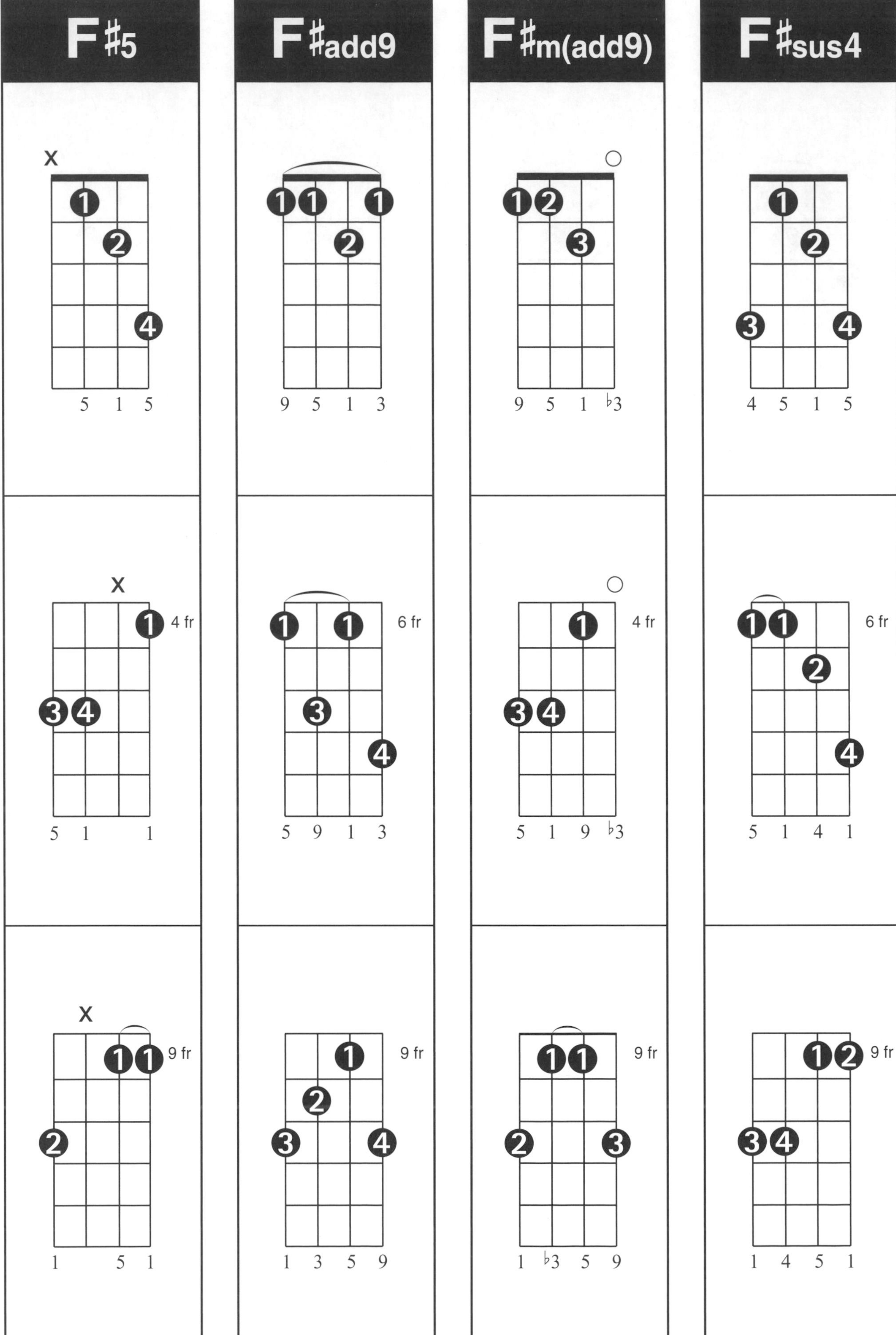

F#5
F#add9
F#m(add9)
F#sus4
F#/G♭
x
5 1 5
9 5 1 3
9 5 1 ♭3
4 5 1 5
x
4 fr
5 1 1
6 fr
5 9 1 3
4 fr
5 1 9 ♭3
6 fr
5 1 4 1
x
9 fr
1 5 1
9 fr
1 3 5 9
9 fr
1 ♭3 5 9
9 fr
1 4 5 1

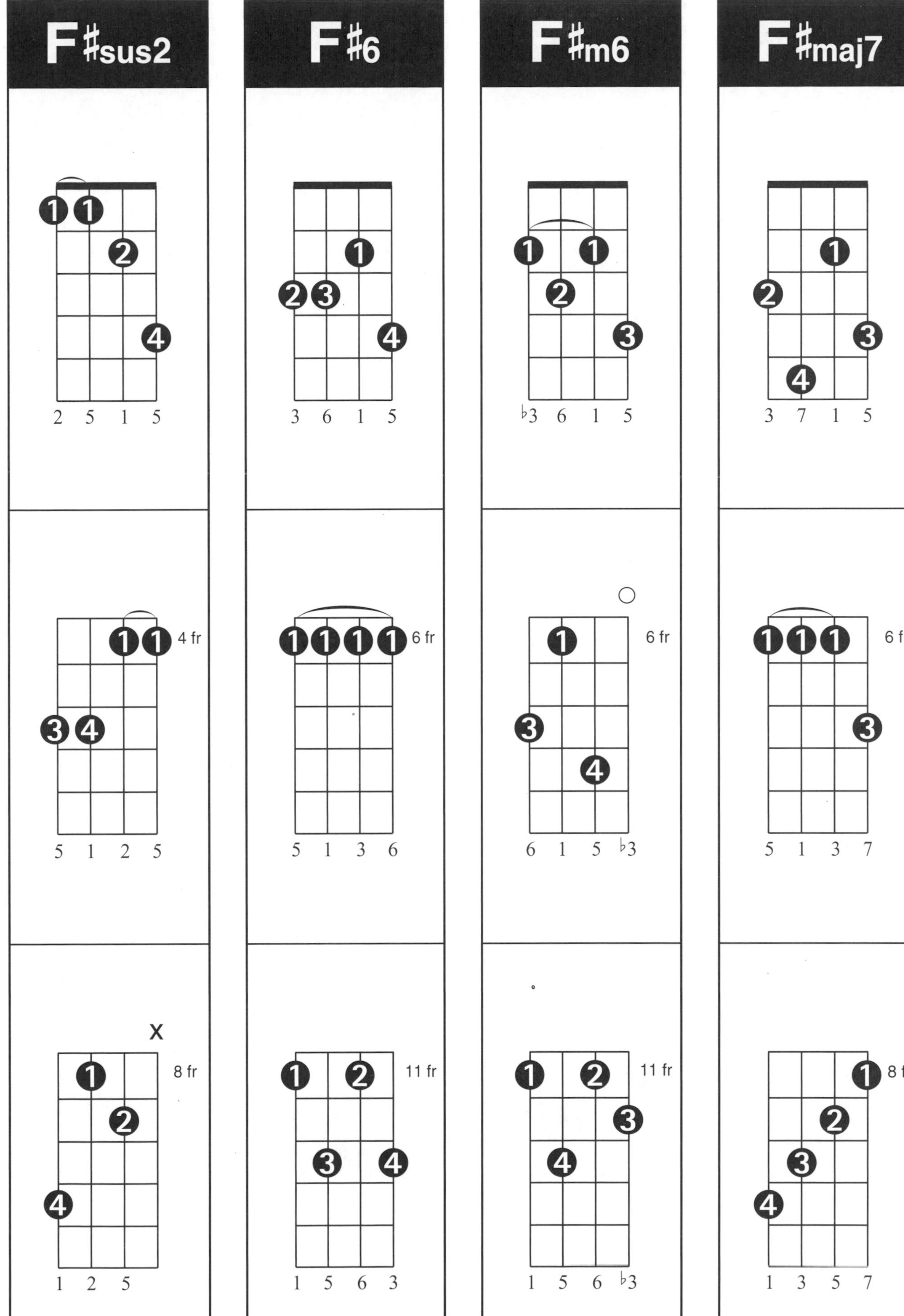
F♯sus2
F♯6
F♯m6
F♯maj7
2 5 1 5
3 6 1 5
♭3 6 1 5
3 7 1 5
4 fr
6 fr
6 fr
6 fr
5 1 2 5
5 1 3 6
6 1 5 ♭3
5 1 3 7
X
8 fr
11 fr
11 fr
8 fr
1 2 5
1 5 6 3
1 5 6 ♭3
1 3 5 7

F♯/G♭

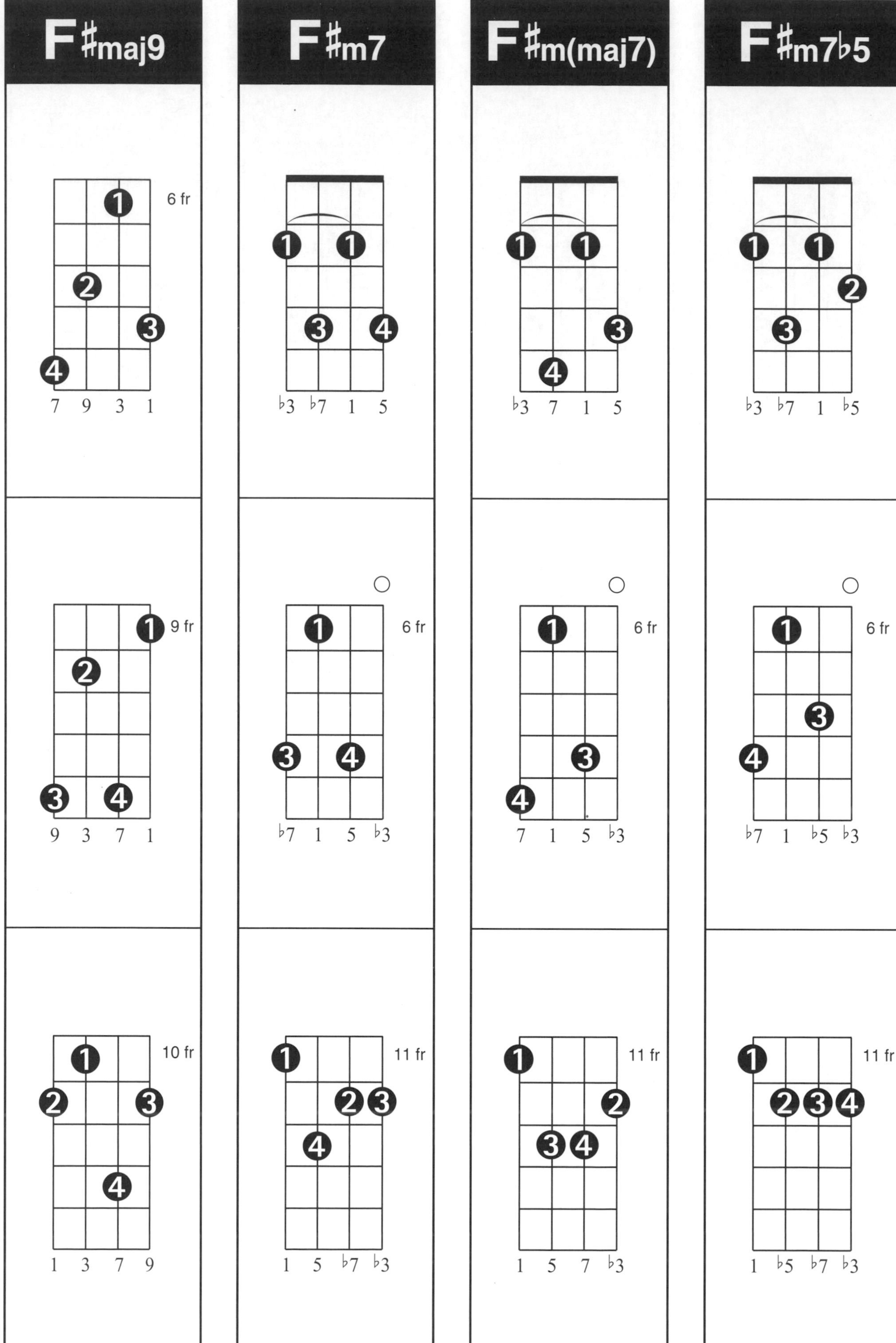
F♯maj9
F♯m7
F♯m(maj7)
F♯m7♭5
6 fr
7 9 3 1
♭3 ♭7 1 5
♭3 7 1 5
♭3 ♭7 1 ♭5
9 fr
9 3 7 1
6 fr
♭7 1 5 ♭3
6 fr
7 1 5 ♭3
6 fr
♭7 1 ♭5 ♭3
10 fr
1 3 7 9
11 fr
1 5 ♭7 ♭3
11 fr
1 5 7 ♭3
11 fr
1 ♭5 ♭7 ♭3

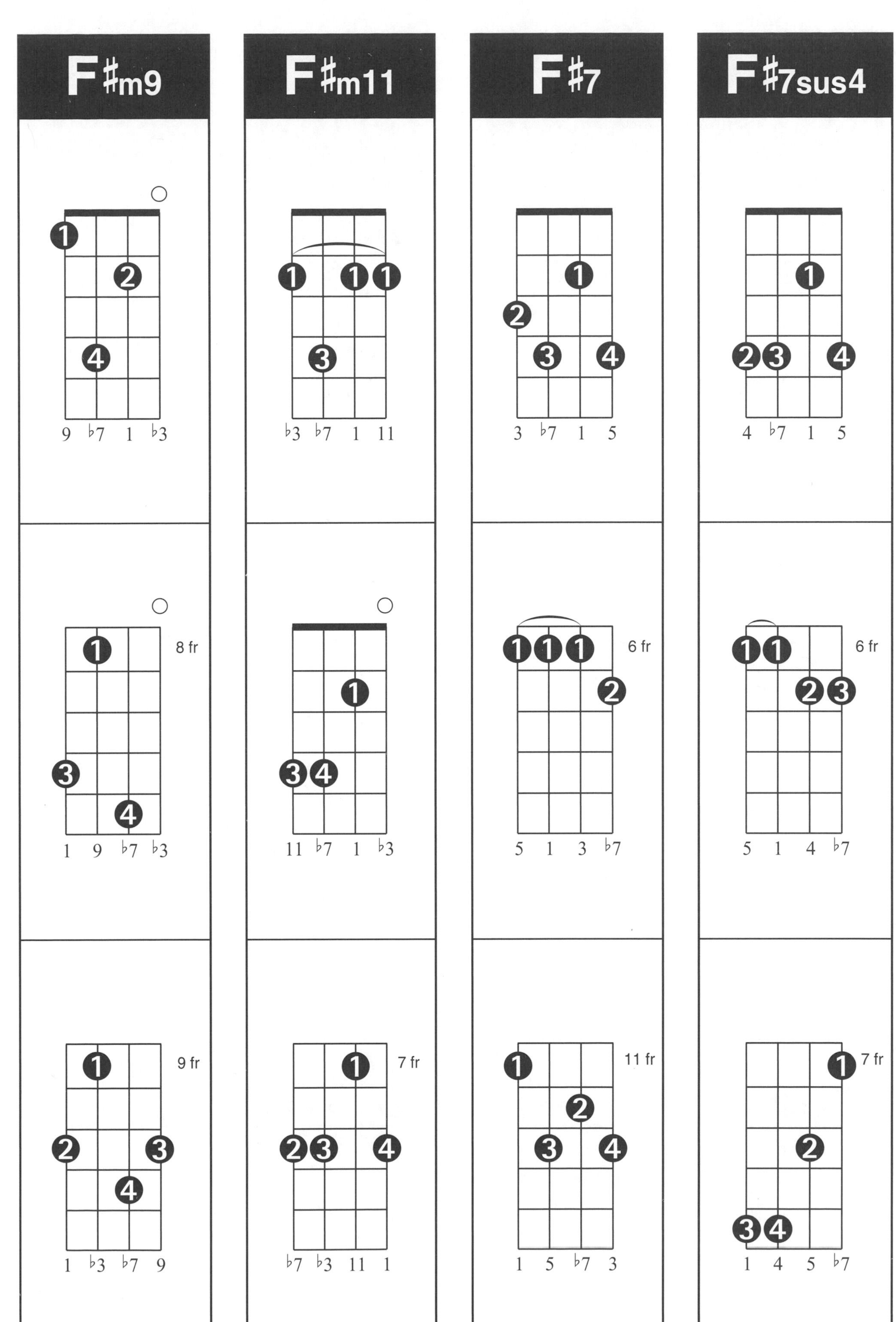
F♯m9
9 ♭7 1 ♭3
8 fr
1 9 ♭7 ♭3
9 fr
1 ♭3 ♭7 9
F♯m11
♭3 ♭7 1 11
11 ♭7 1 ♭3
7 fr
♭7 ♭3 11 1
F♯7
3 ♭7 1 5
6 fr
5 1 3 ♭7
11 fr
1 5 ♭7 3
F♯7sus4
4 ♭7 1 5
6 fr
5 1 4 ♭7
7 fr
1 4 5 ♭7

F♯/G♭

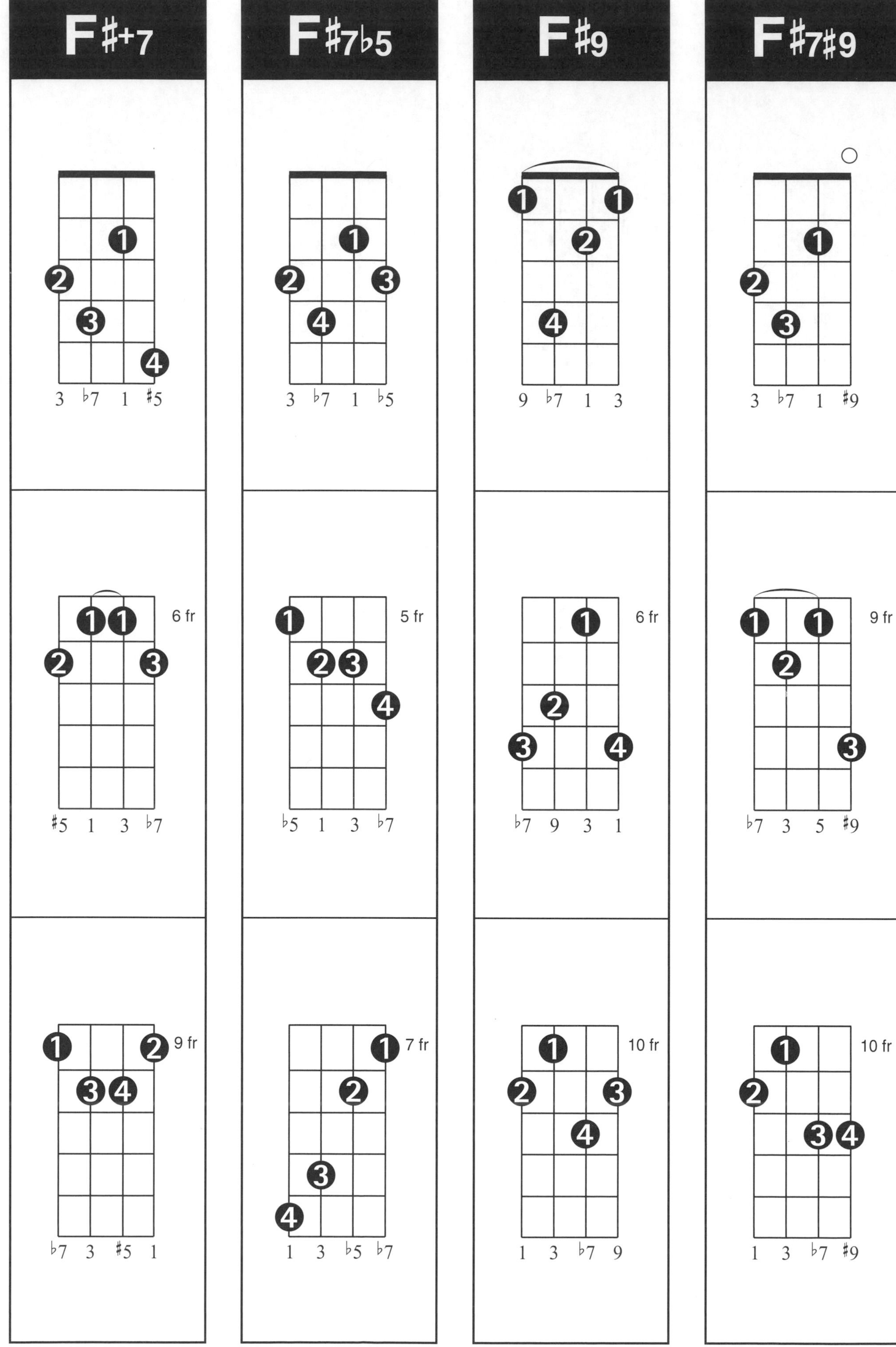
F♯+7
F♯7♭5
F♯9
F♯7♯9
F♯/G♭
3 ♭7 1 ♯5
3 ♭7 1 ♭5
9 ♭7 1 3
3 ♭7 1 ♯9
6 fr
5 fr
6 fr
9 fr
♯5 1 3 ♭7
♭5 1 3 ♭7
♭7 9 3 1
♭7 3 5 ♯9
9 fr
7 fr
10 fr
10 fr
♭7 3 ♯5 1
1 3 ♭5 ♭7
1 3 ♭7 9
1 3 ♭7 ♯9

F♯7♭9

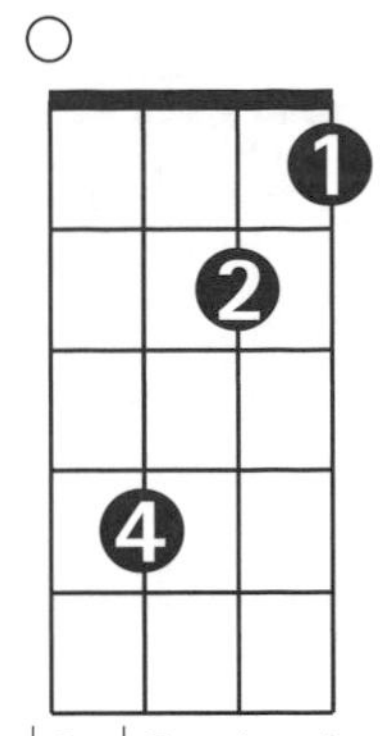

○

♭9 ♭7 1 3

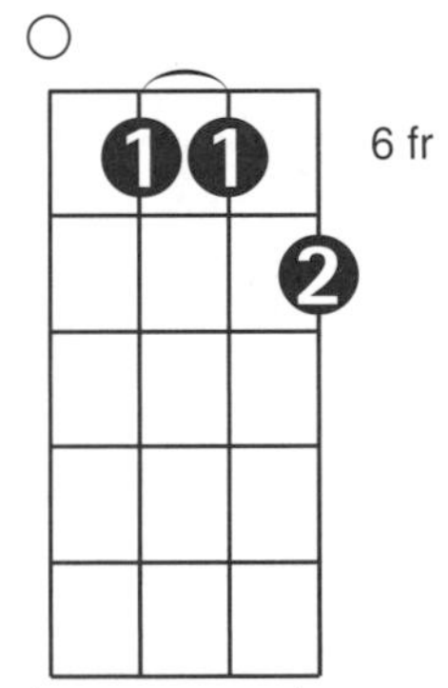

○ 6 fr

♭9 1 3 ♭7

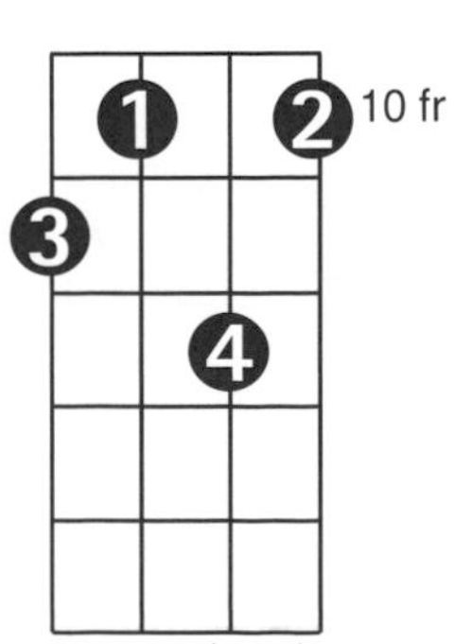

10 fr

1 3 ♭7 ♭9

F♯11

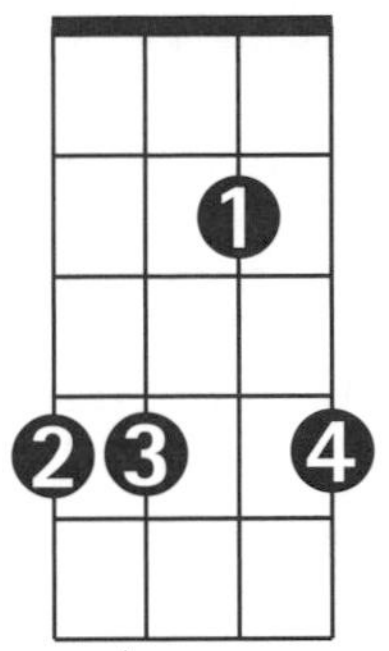

11 ♭7 1 5

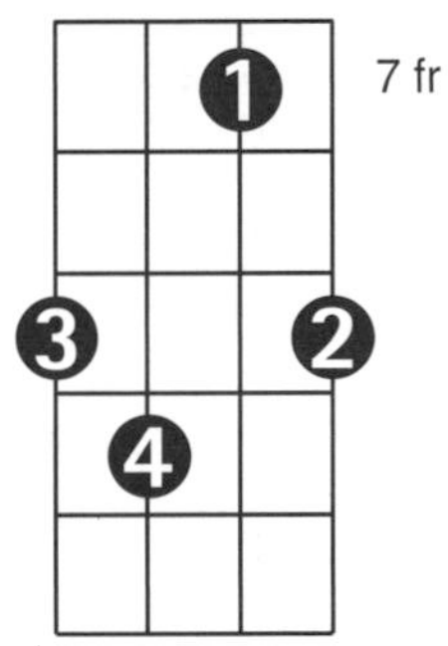

7 fr

♭7 3 11 1

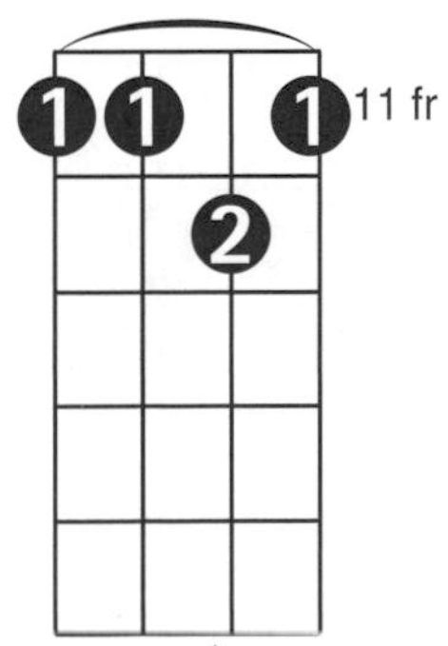

11 fr

1 11 ♭7 9

F♯13

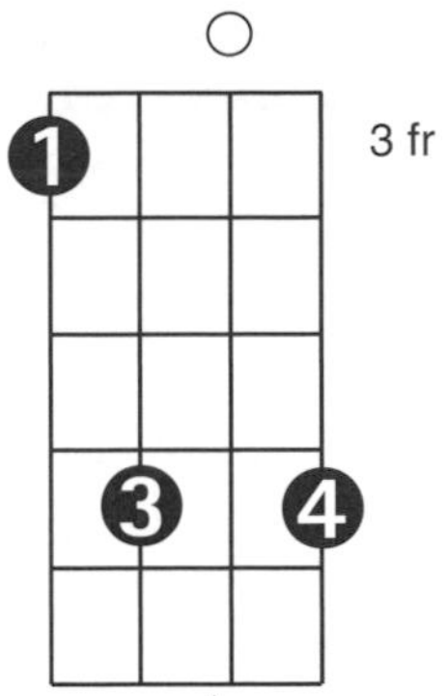

○ 3 fr

3 1 ♭7 13

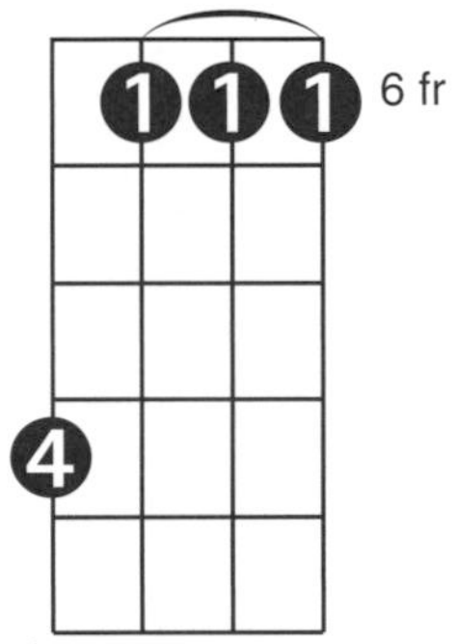

6 fr

♭7 1 3 13

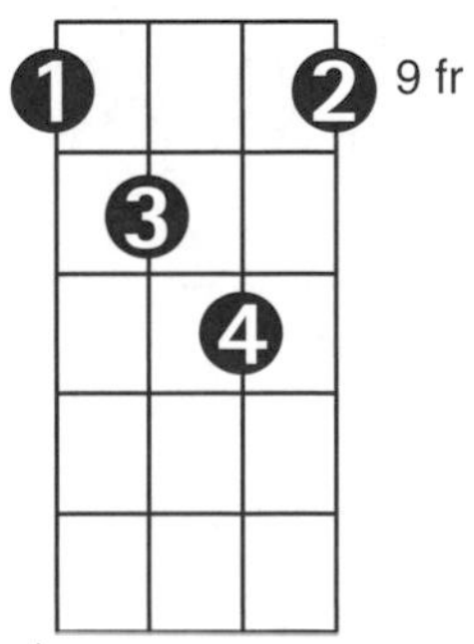

9 fr

♭7 3 13 1

F♯°7

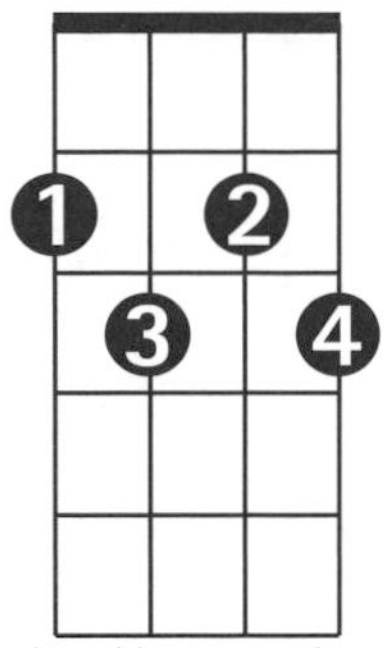

♭3 ♭♭7 1 ♭5

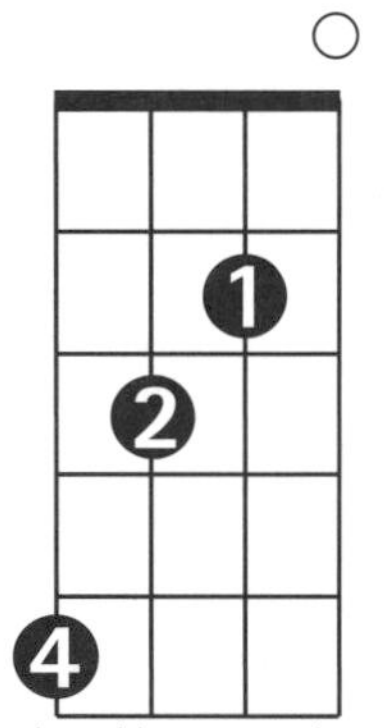

○

♭5 ♭♭7 1 ♭3

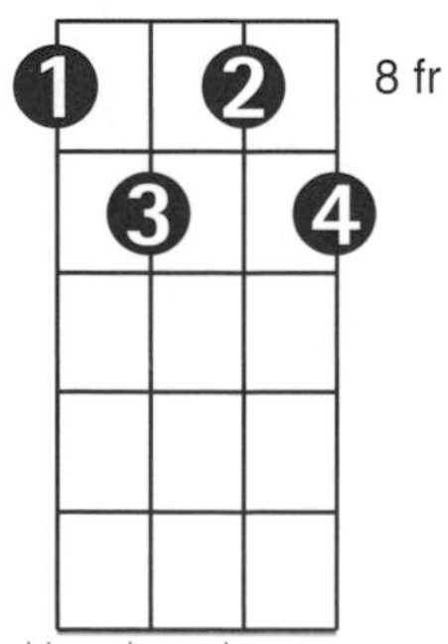

8 fr

♭♭7 ♭3 ♭5 1

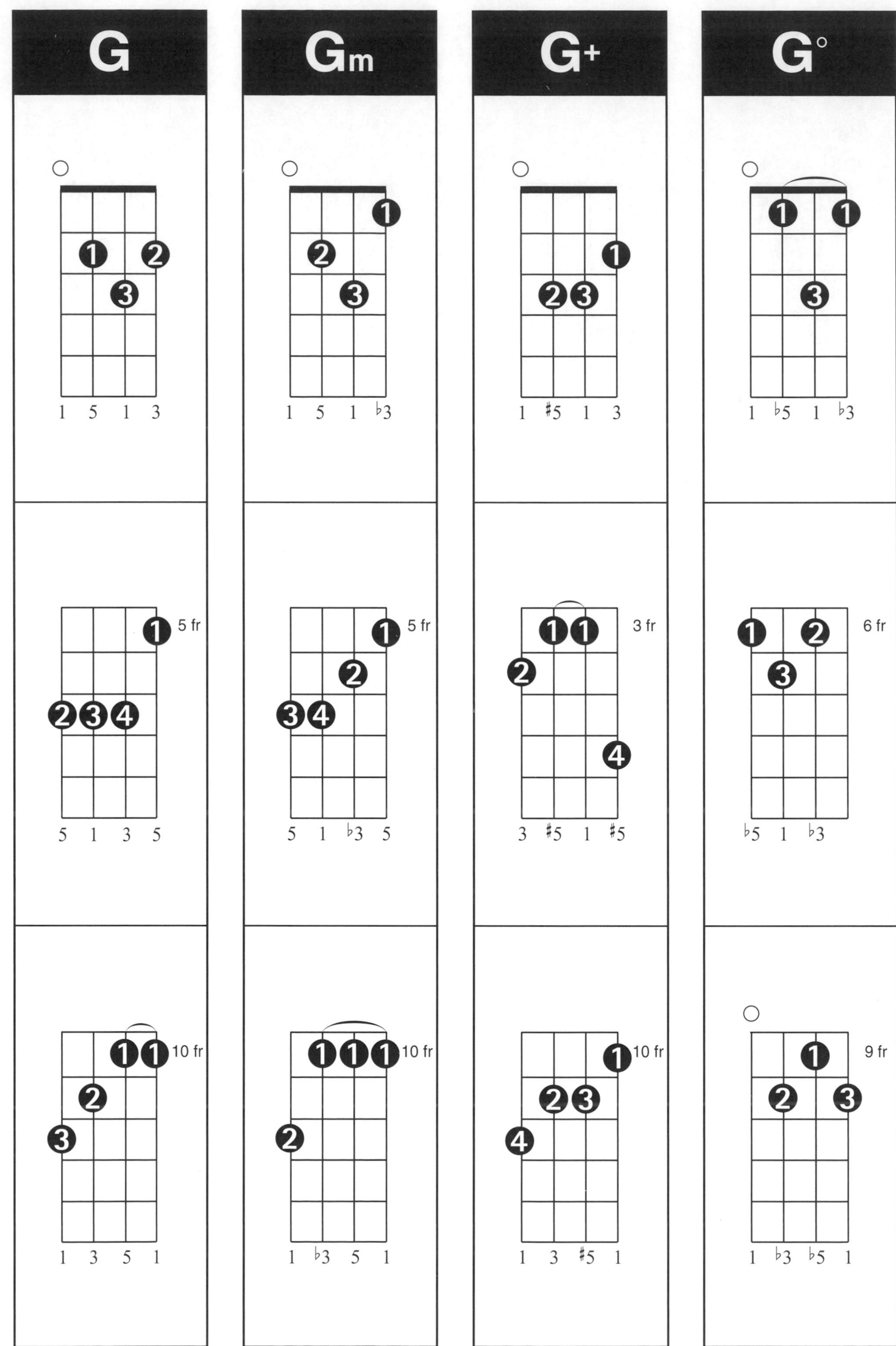
G
Gm
G+
G°
1 5 1 3
1 5 1 ♭3
1 ♯5 1 3
1 ♭5 1 ♭3
5 fr
5 1 3 5
5 fr
5 1 ♭3 5
3 fr
3 ♯5 1 ♯5
6 fr
♭5 1 ♭3
10 fr
1 3 5 1
10 fr
1 ♭3 5 1
10 fr
1 3 ♯5 1
9 fr
1 ♭3 ♭5 1
G

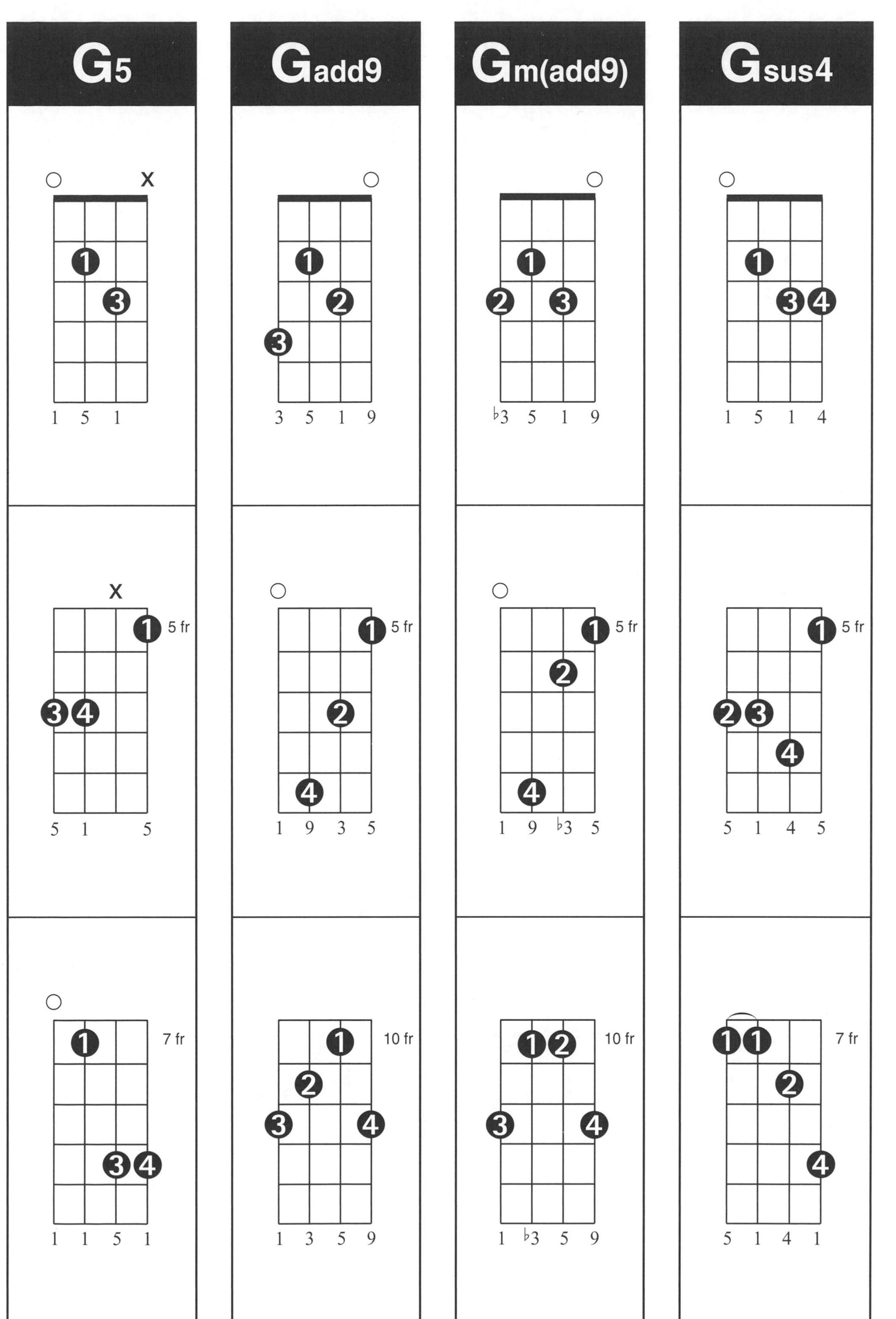
G5
Gadd9
Gm(add9)
Gsus4
1 5 1
3 5 1 9
♭3 5 1 9
1 5 1 4
5 fr
5 1 5
5 fr
1 9 3 5
5 fr
1 9 ♭3 5
5 fr
5 1 4 5
7 fr
1 1 5 1
10 fr
1 3 5 9
10 fr
1 ♭3 5 9
7 fr
5 1 4 1
G

Gsus2

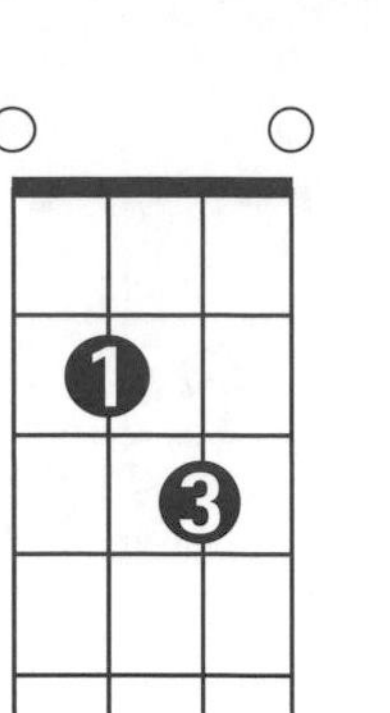

2 5 1 5

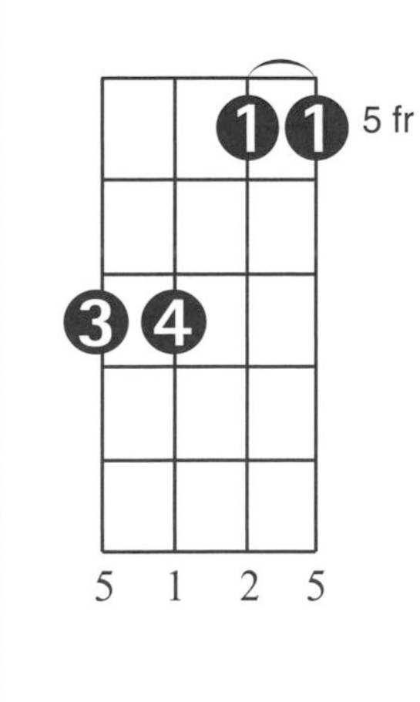

G6

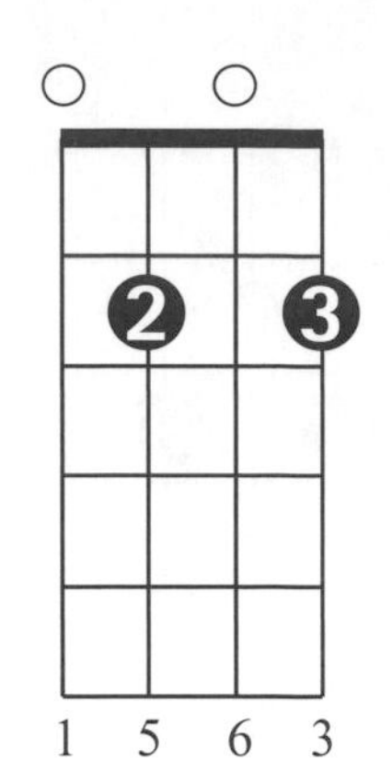

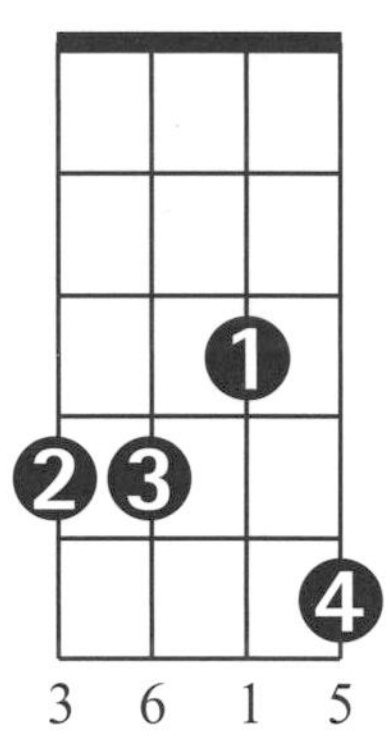

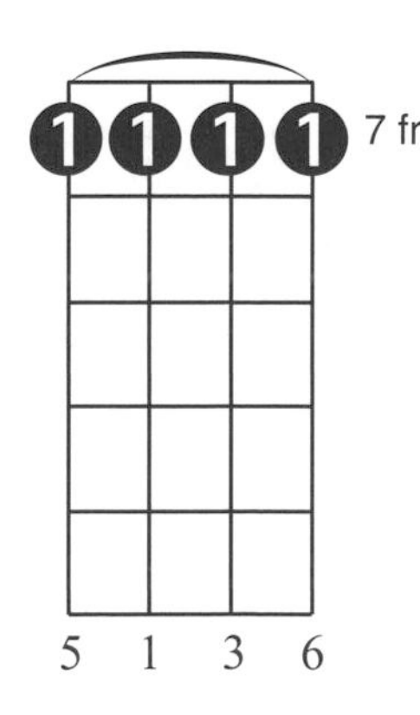

Gm6

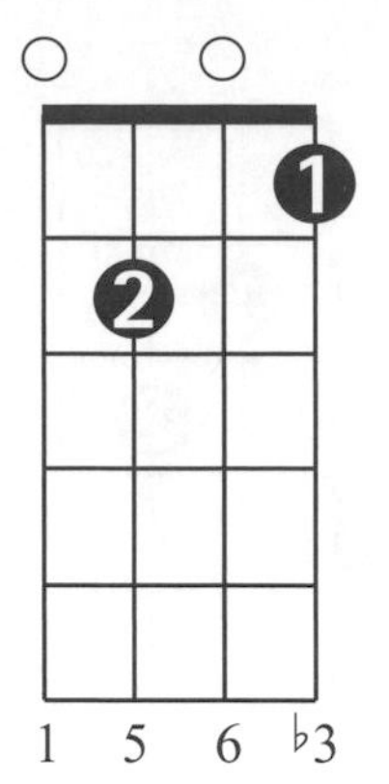

♭3 6 1 5

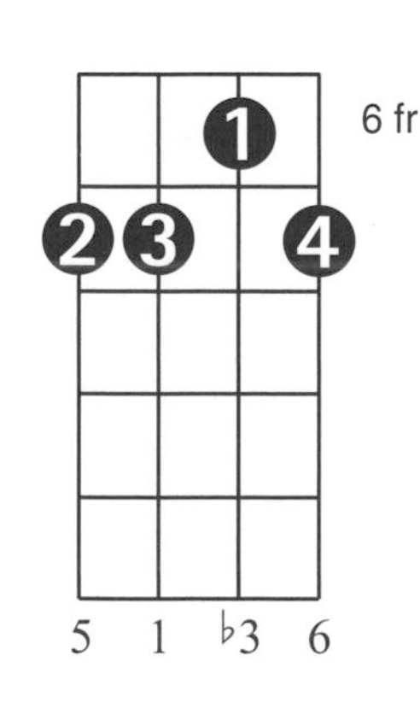

Gmaj7

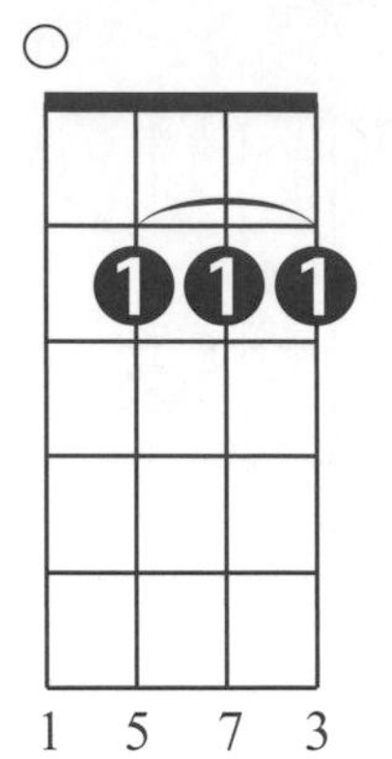

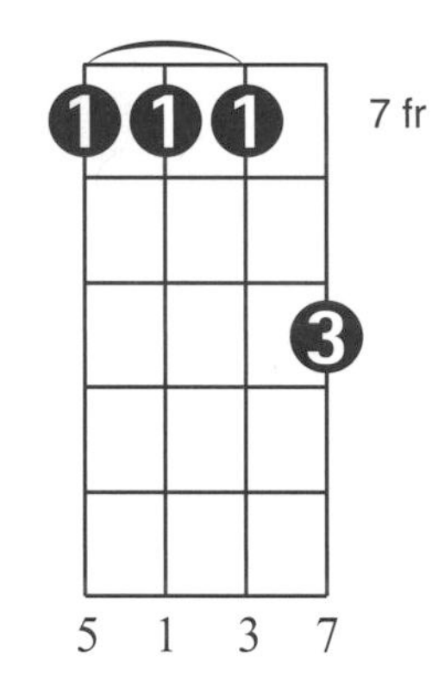

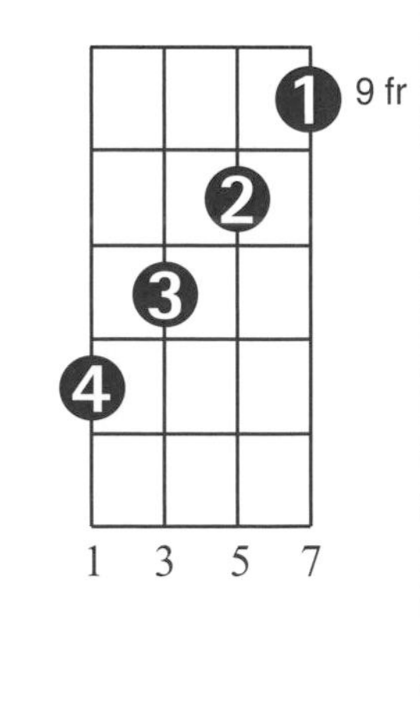

G

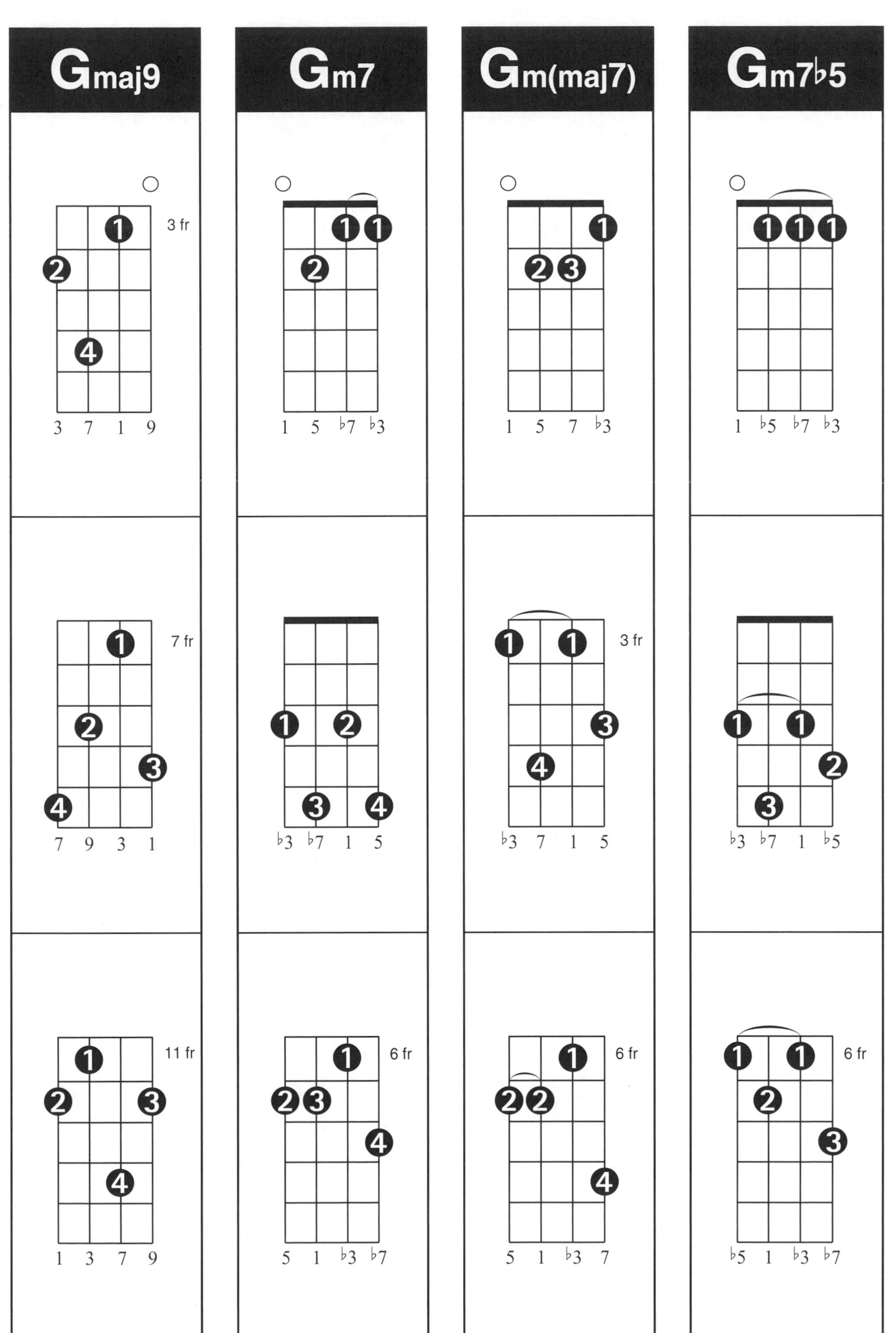
Gmaj9
Gm7
Gm(maj7)
Gm7♭5
3 fr
3 7 1 9
1 5 ♭7 ♭3
1 5 7 ♭3
1 ♭5 ♭7 ♭3
7 fr
7 9 3 1
♭3 ♭7 1 5
3 fr
♭3 7 1 5
♭3 ♭7 1 ♭5
11 fr
1 3 7 9
6 fr
5 1 ♭3 ♭7
6 fr
5 1 ♭3 7
6 fr
♭5 1 ♭3 ♭7
G

Gm9

1 ♭7 9 ♭3

5 fr
1 ♭7 ♭3 9

10 fr
1 ♭3 ♭7 9

Gm11

1 11 ♭7 ♭3

♭3 ♭7 1 11

5 fr
11 1 ♭3 ♭7

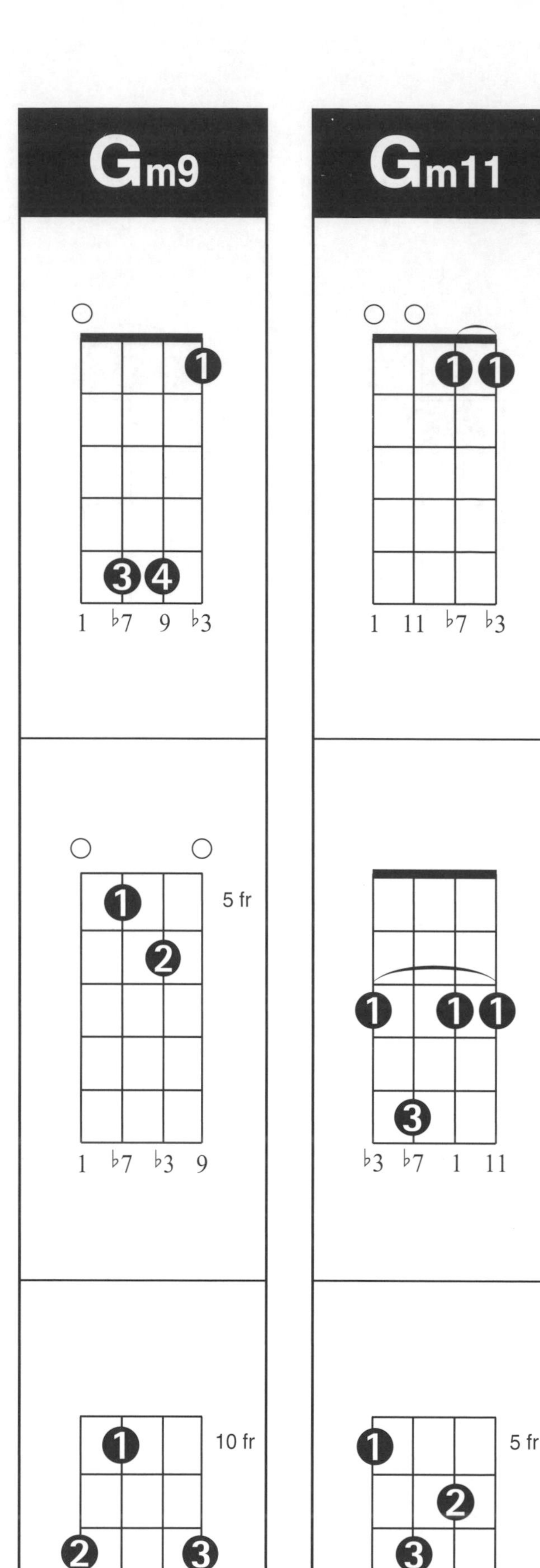

G7

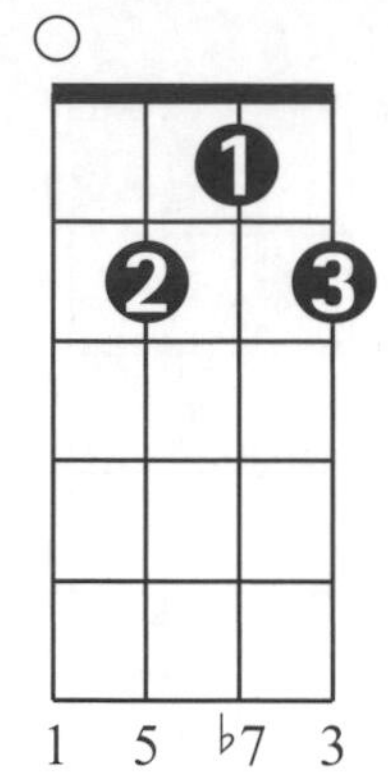

1 5 ♭7 3

5 fr
1 ♭7 3 5

7 fr
5 1 3 ♭7

G7sus4

1 5 ♭7 4

5 fr
1 ♭7 4 5

7 fr
5 1 4 ♭7

G

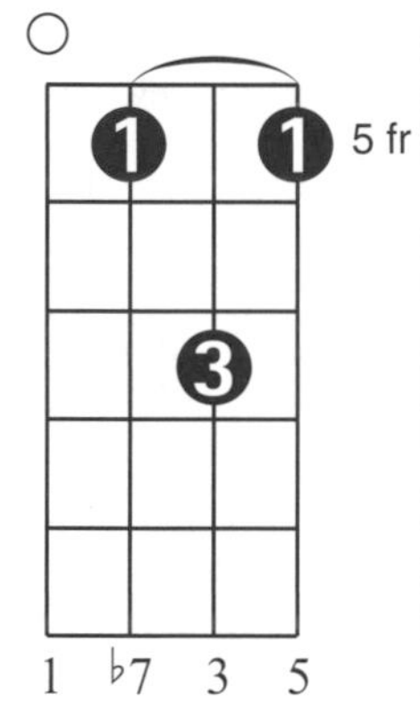

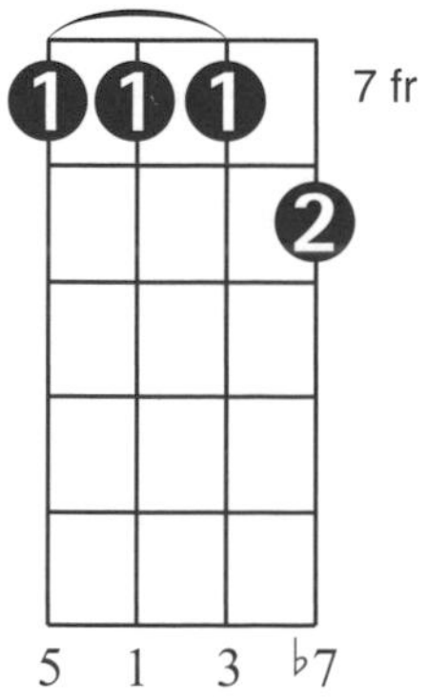

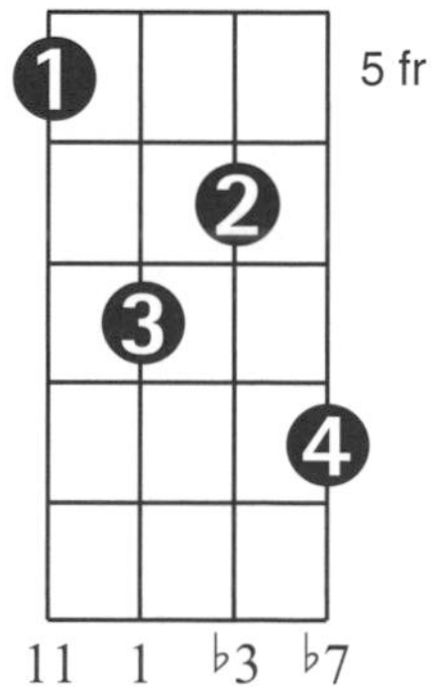

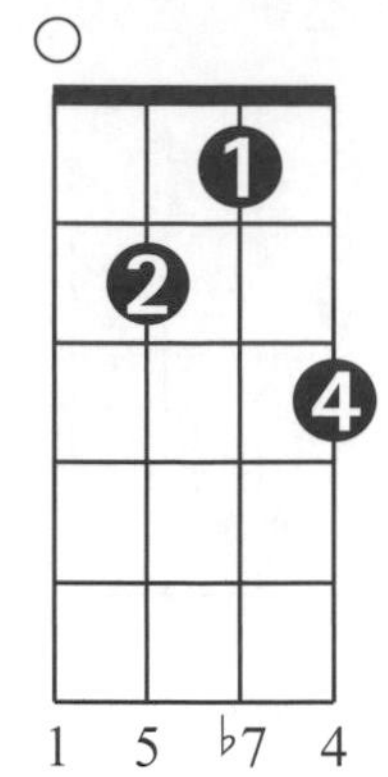

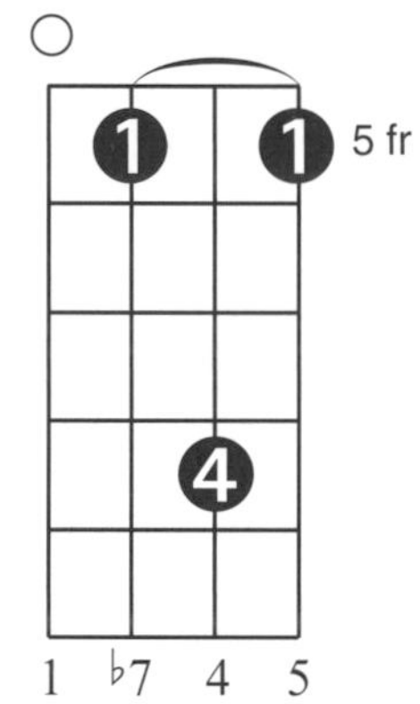

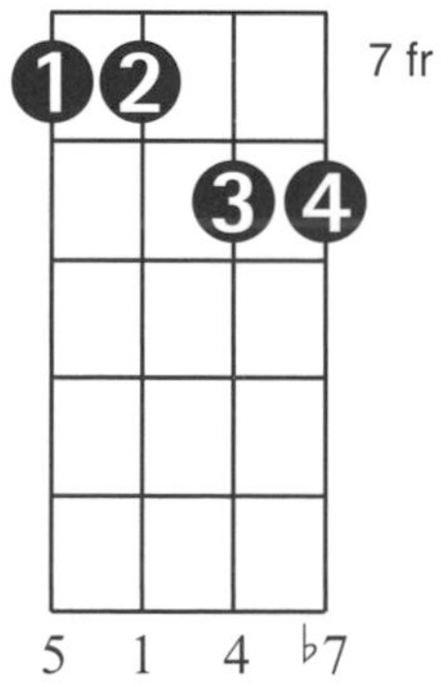

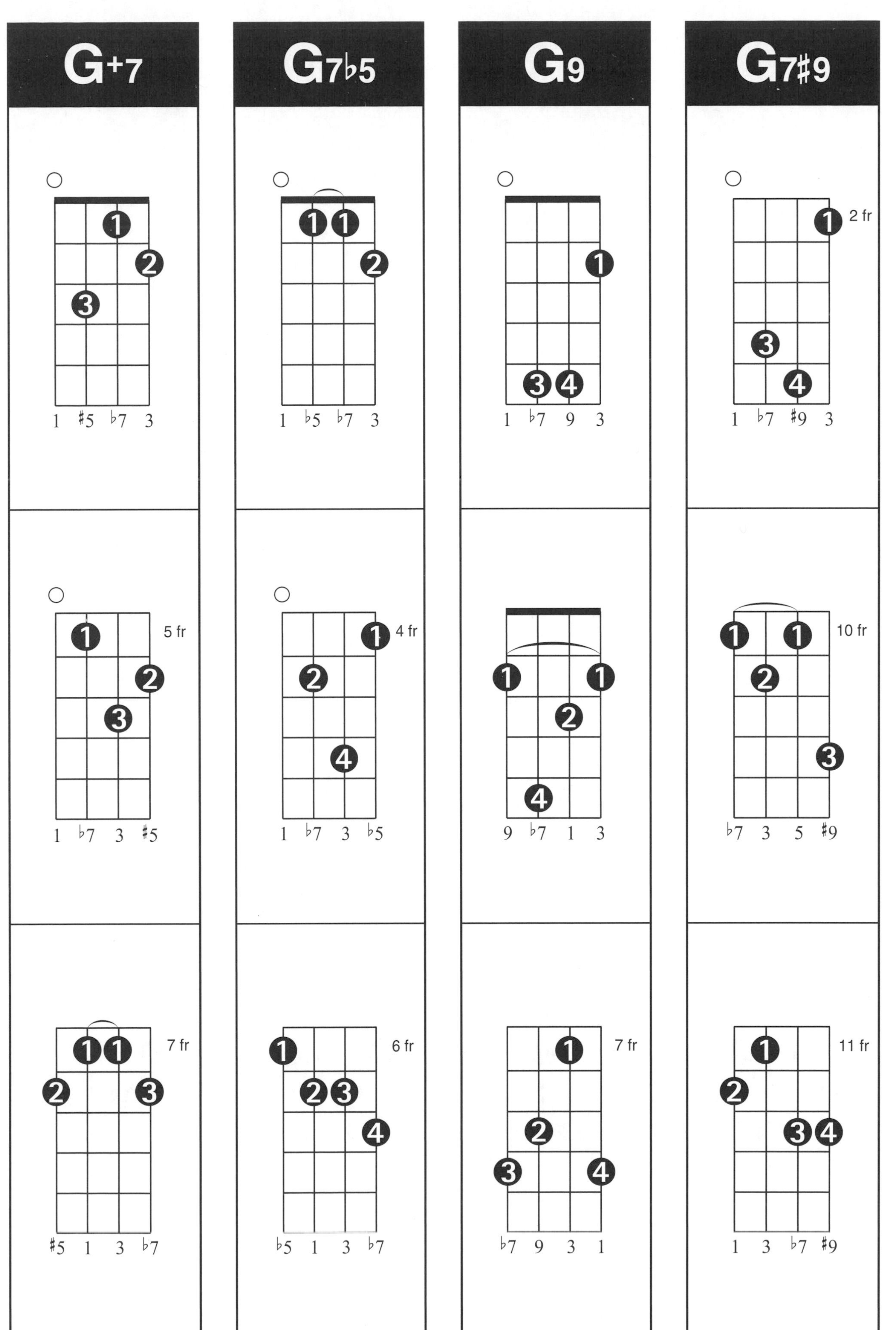
G+7
G7♭5
G9
G7♯9
1 ♯5 ♭7 3
1 ♭5 ♭7 3
1 ♭7 9 3
2 fr
1 ♭7 ♯9 3
G
5 fr
1 ♭7 3 ♯5
4 fr
1 ♭7 3 ♭5
9 ♭7 1 3
10 fr
♭7 3 5 ♯9
7 fr
♯5 1 3 ♭7
6 fr
♭5 1 3 ♭7
7 fr
♭7 9 3 1
11 fr
1 3 ♭7 ♯9

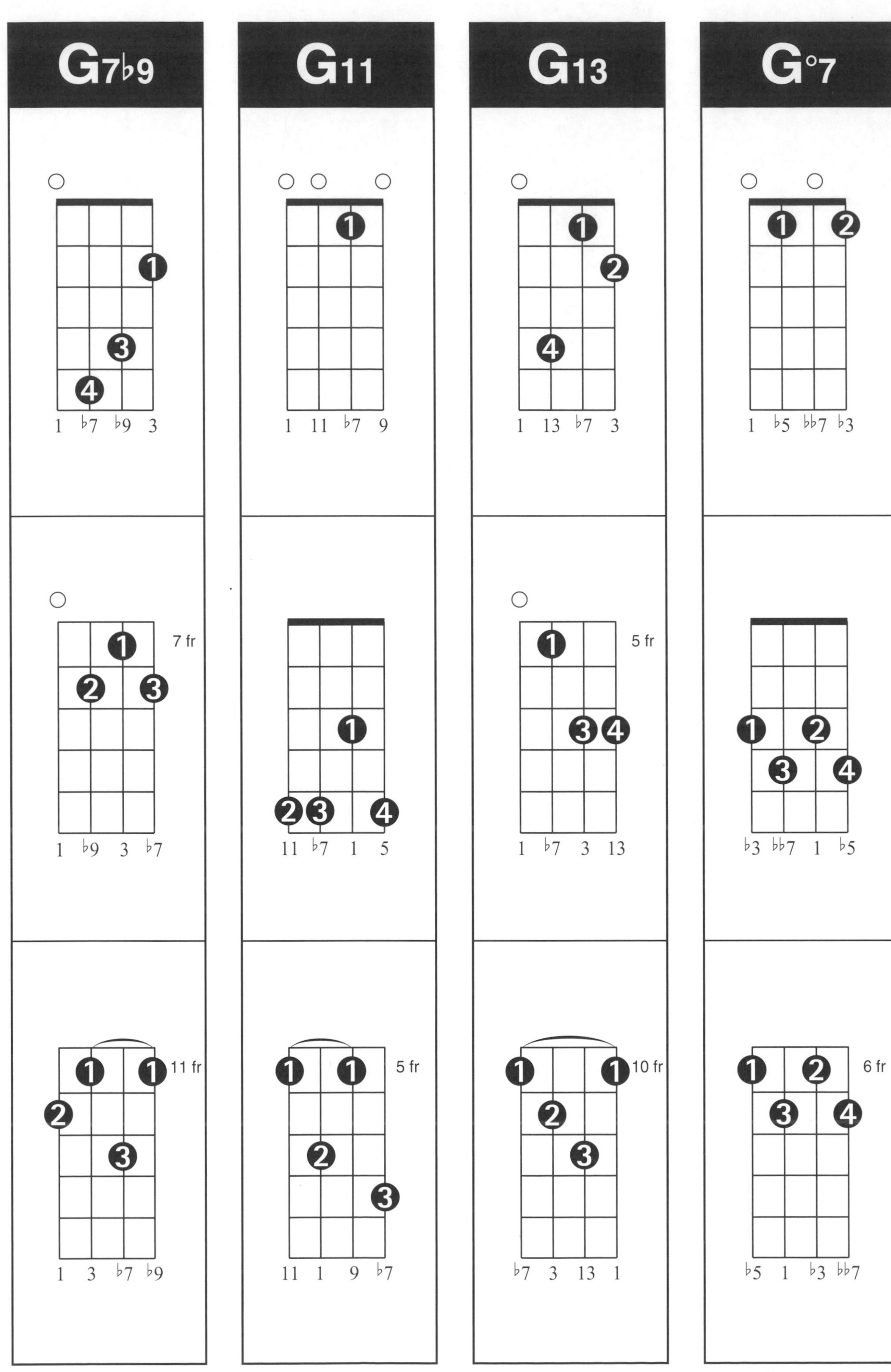
G7♭9
G11
G13
G°7
1 ♭7 ♭9 3
1 11 ♭7 9
1 13 ♭7 3
1 ♭5 ♭♭7 ♭3
7 fr
1 ♭9 3 ♭7
11 ♭7 1 5
5 fr
1 ♭7 3 13
♭3 ♭♭7 1 ♭5
11 fr
1 3 ♭7 ♭9
5 fr
11 1 9 ♭7
10 fr
♭7 3 13 1
6 fr
♭5 1 ♭3 ♭♭7

G

A♭	A♭m	A♭+	A♭°
1 5 1 3	1 5 1 ♭3	1 3 ♯5 3	1 ♭5 ♭3
3 5 1 3	♭3 5 1 ♭3	3 ♯5 1 3	5 fr ♭5 1 ♭3 ♭5
8 fr 5 1 3 1	6 fr 5 15 ♭3 5	8 fr ♯5 1 3 1	10 fr 1 ♭3 ♭5 1

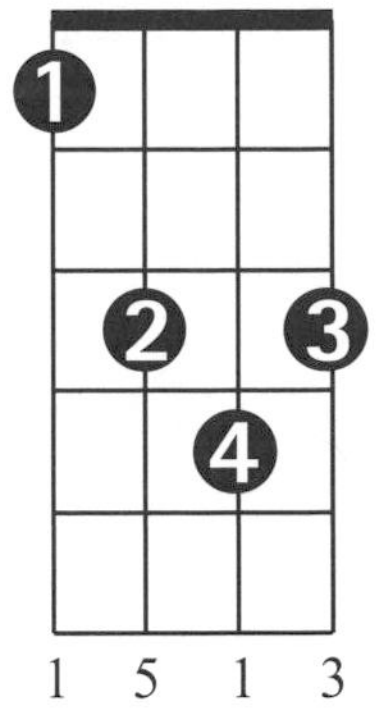

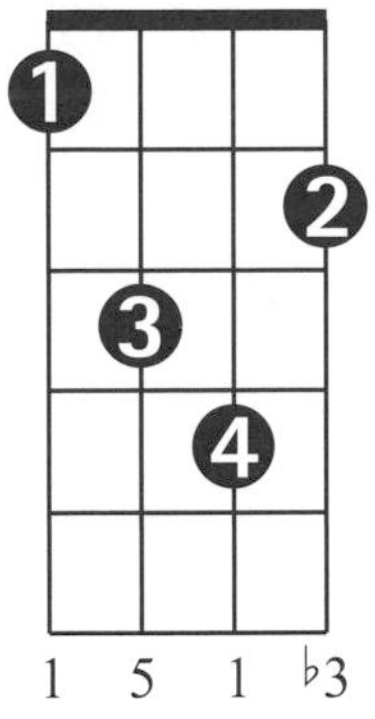

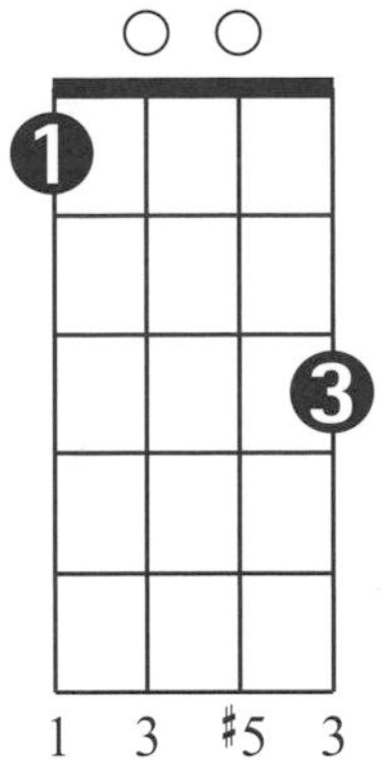

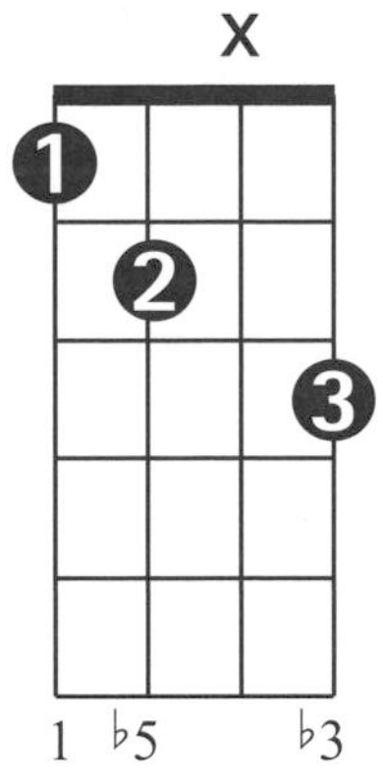

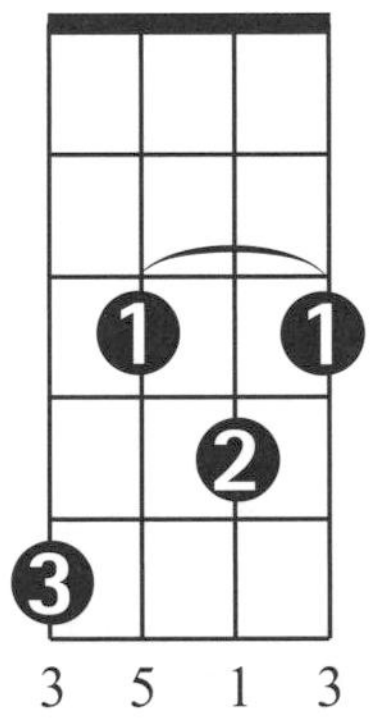

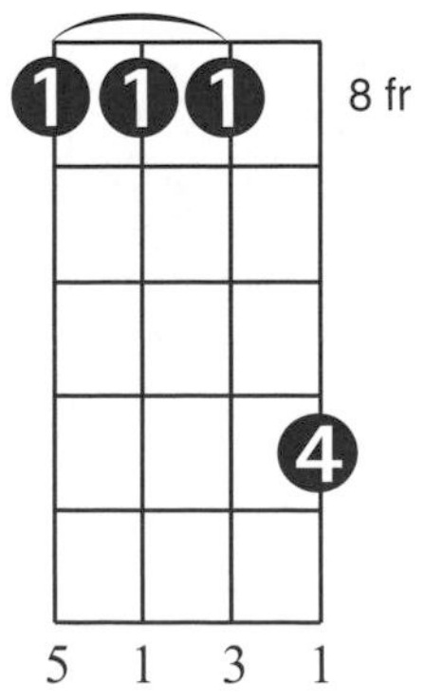

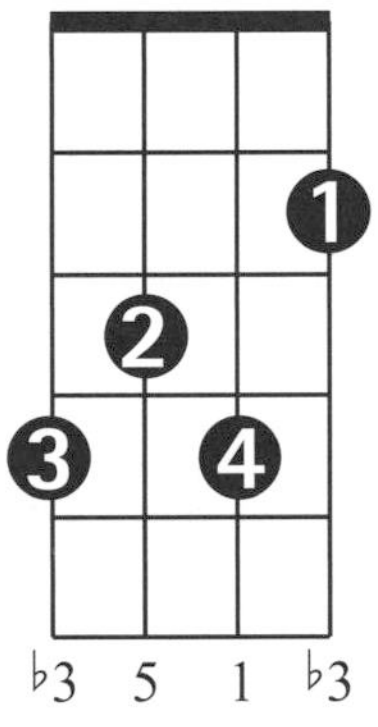

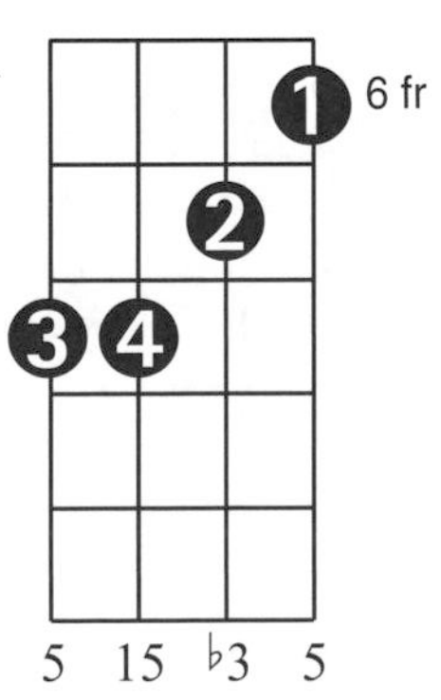

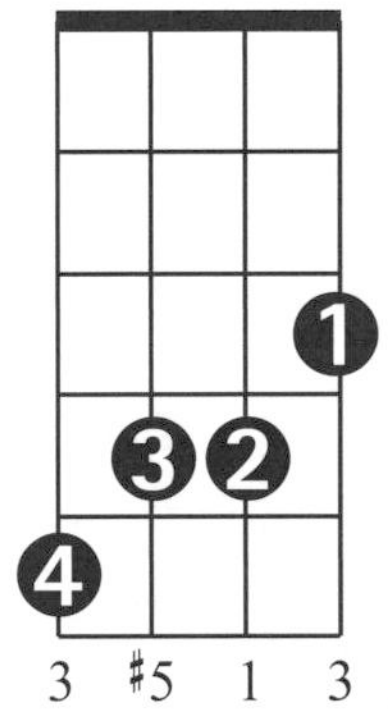

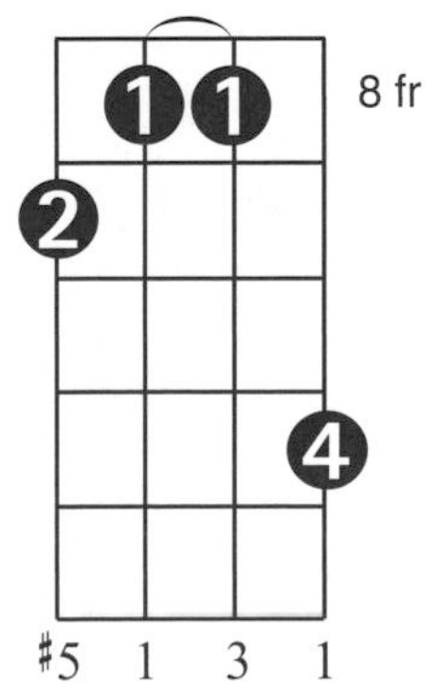

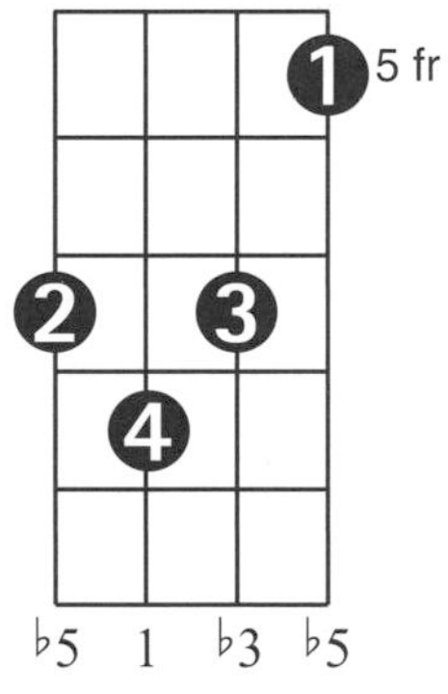

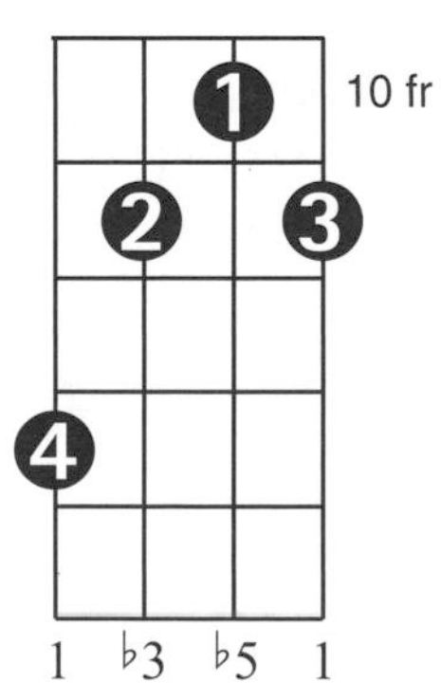

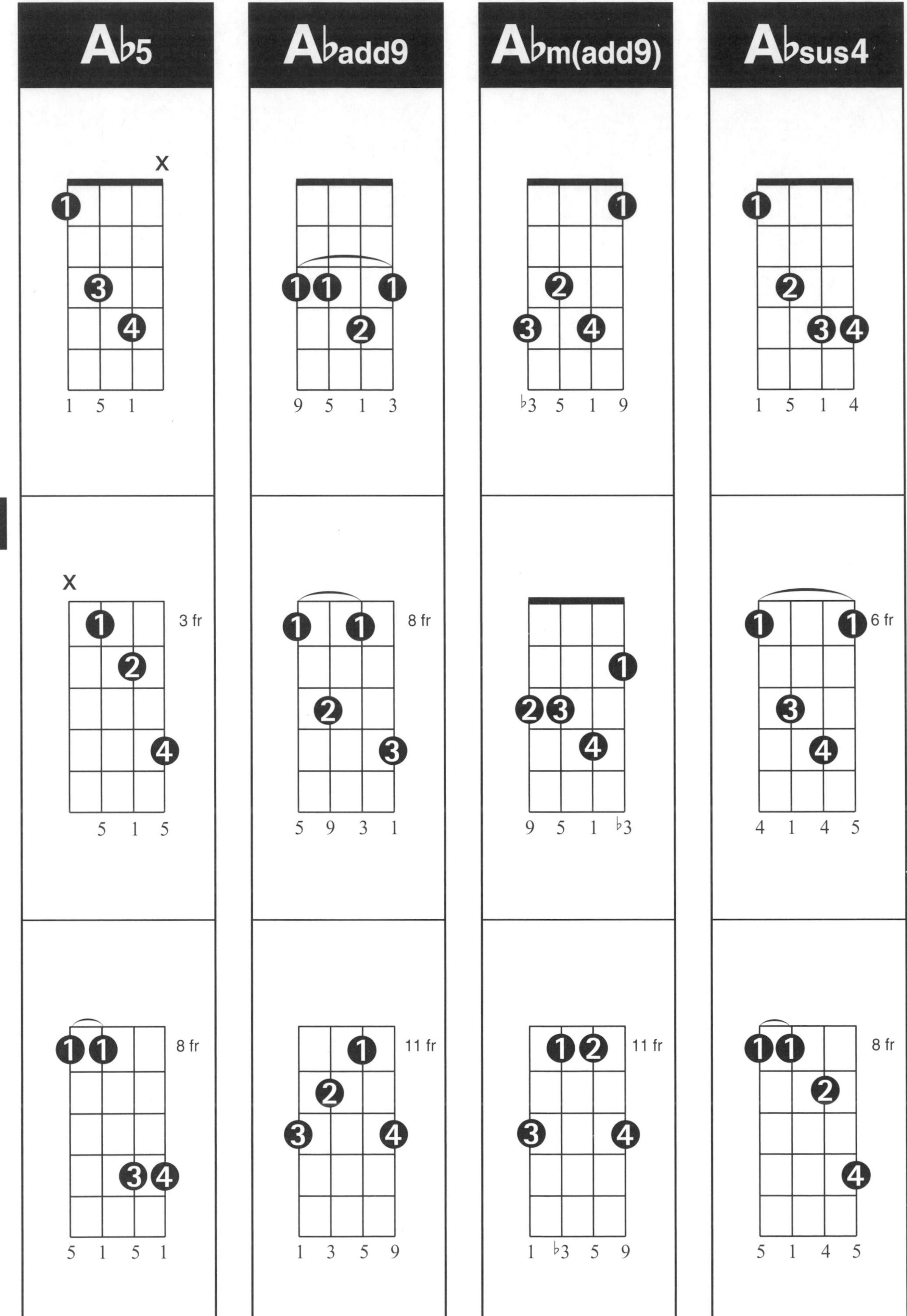

A♭5
A♭add9
A♭m(add9)
A♭sus4
A♭/G♯
x
1 5 1
9 5 1 3
♭3 5 1 9
1 5 1 4
3 fr
8 fr
6 fr
5 1 5
5 9 3 1
9 5 1 ♭3
4 1 4 5
8 fr
11 fr
11 fr
8 fr
5 1 5 1
1 3 5 9
1 ♭3 5 9
5 1 4 5

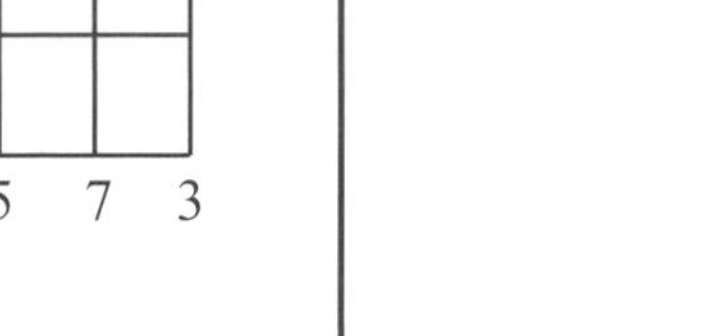
A♭/G♯

A♭sus2

A♭6

A♭m6

A♭maj7

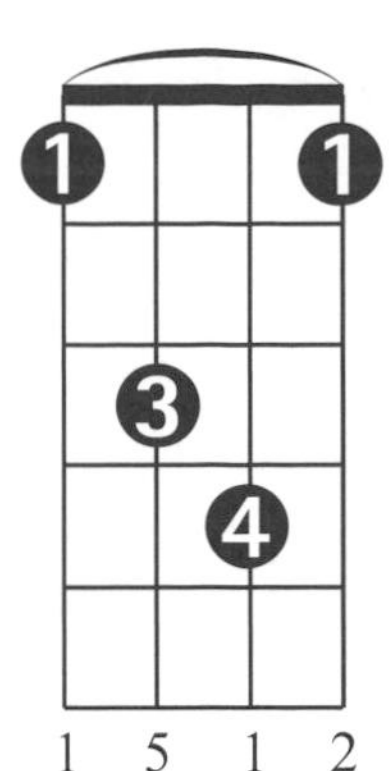
1 1
3
4
1 5 1 2

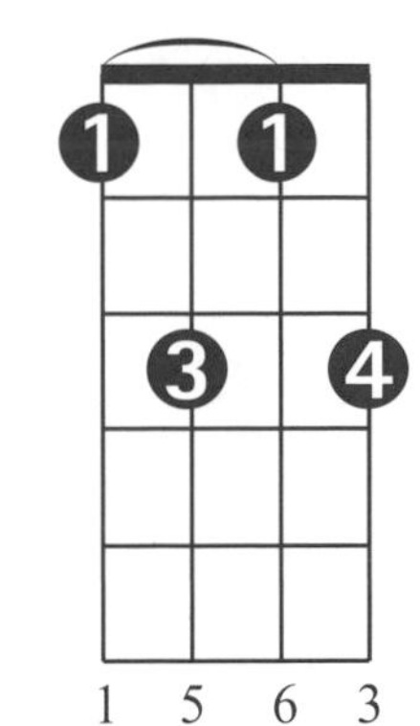
1 1
3 4
1 5 6 3

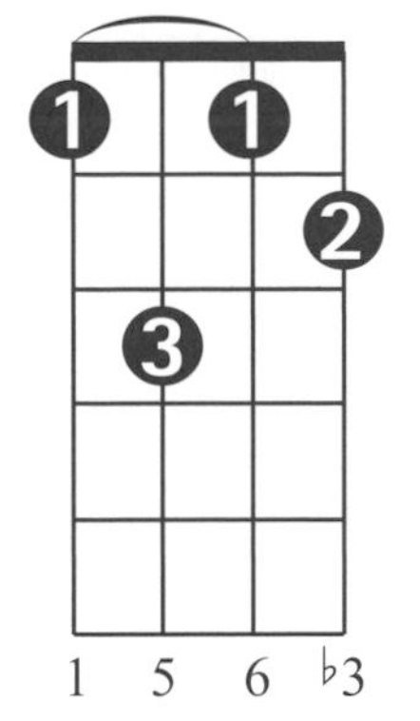
1 1
2
3
1 5 6 ♭3

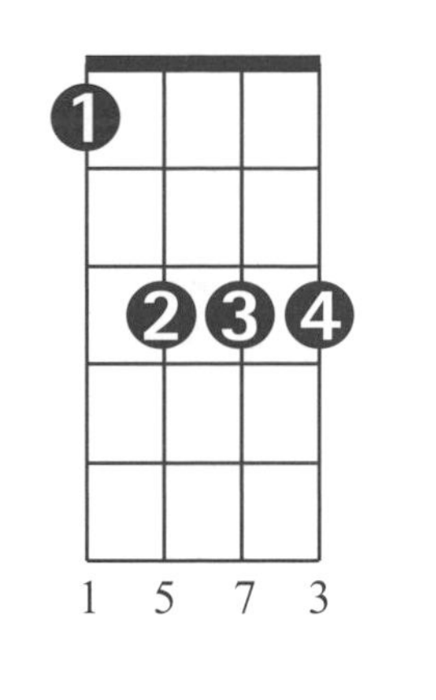
1
2 3 4
1 5 7 3

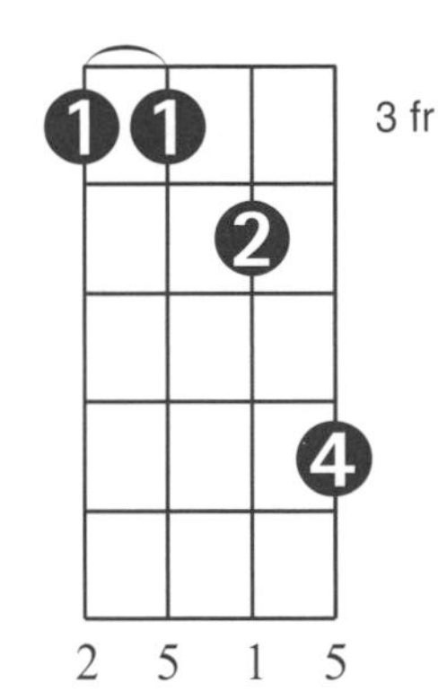
1 1
3 fr
2
4
2 5 1 5

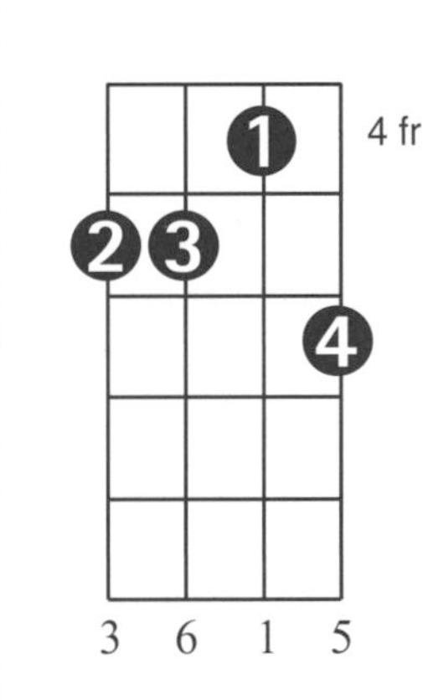
1
4 fr
2 3
4
3 6 1 5

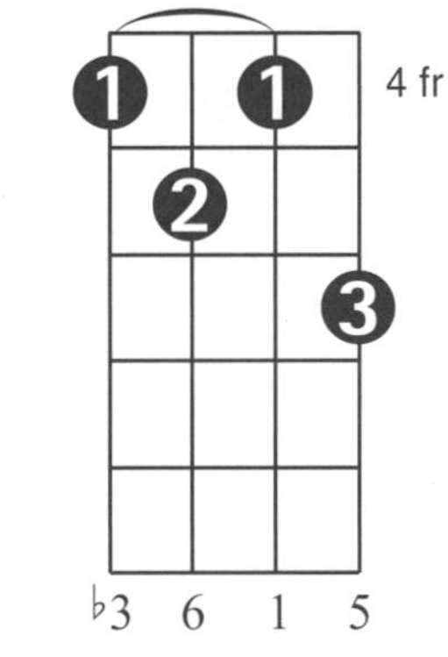
1 1
4 fr
2
3
♭3 6 1 5

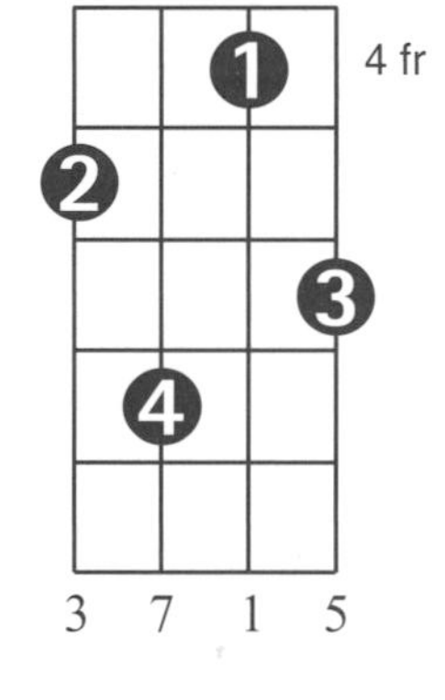
1
4 fr
2
3
4
3 7 1 5

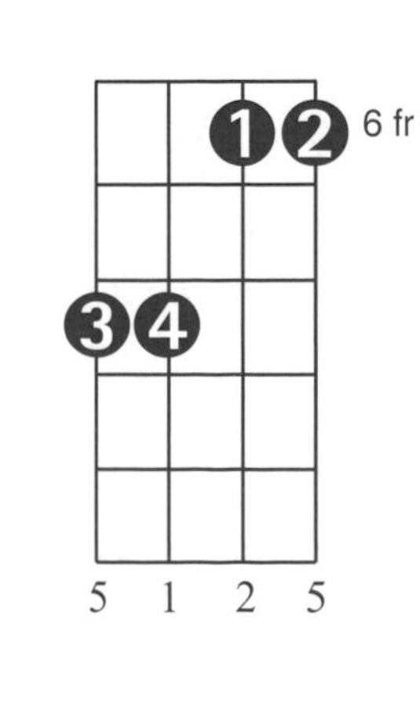
1 2
6 fr
3 4
5 1 2 5

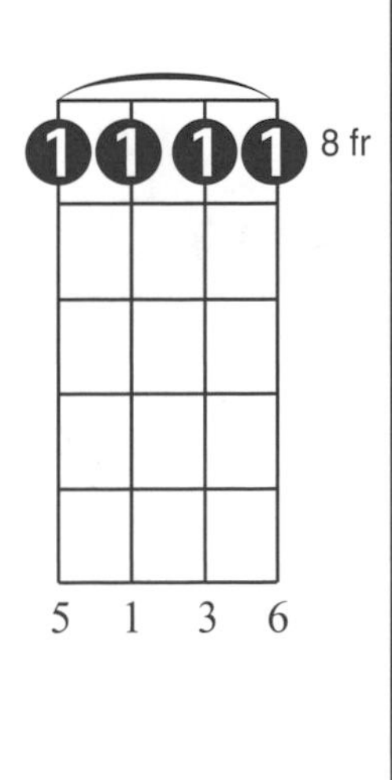
1 1 1 1
8 fr
5 1 3 6

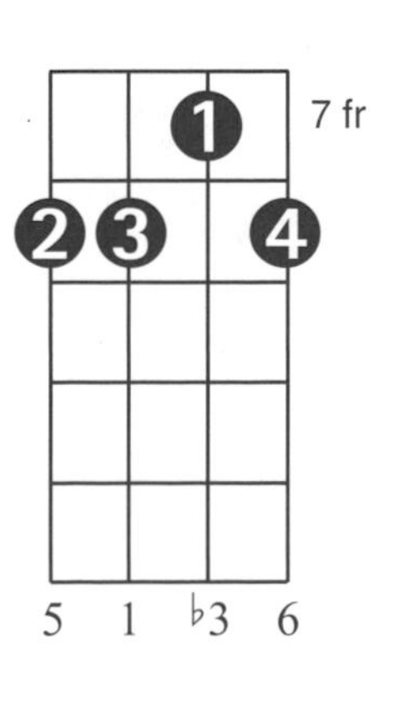
1
7 fr
2 3 4
5 1 ♭3 6

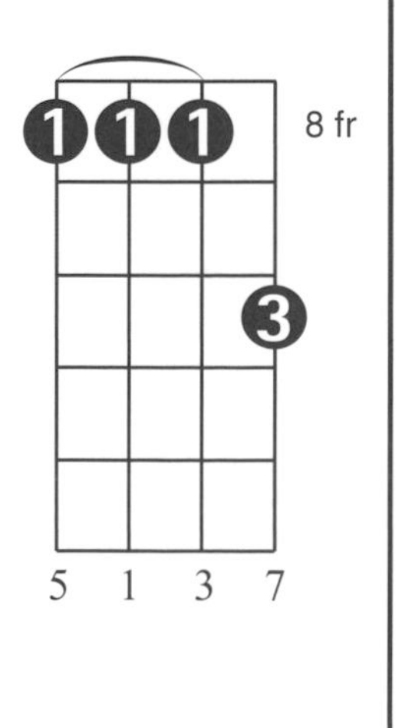
1 1 1
8 fr
3
5 1 3 7

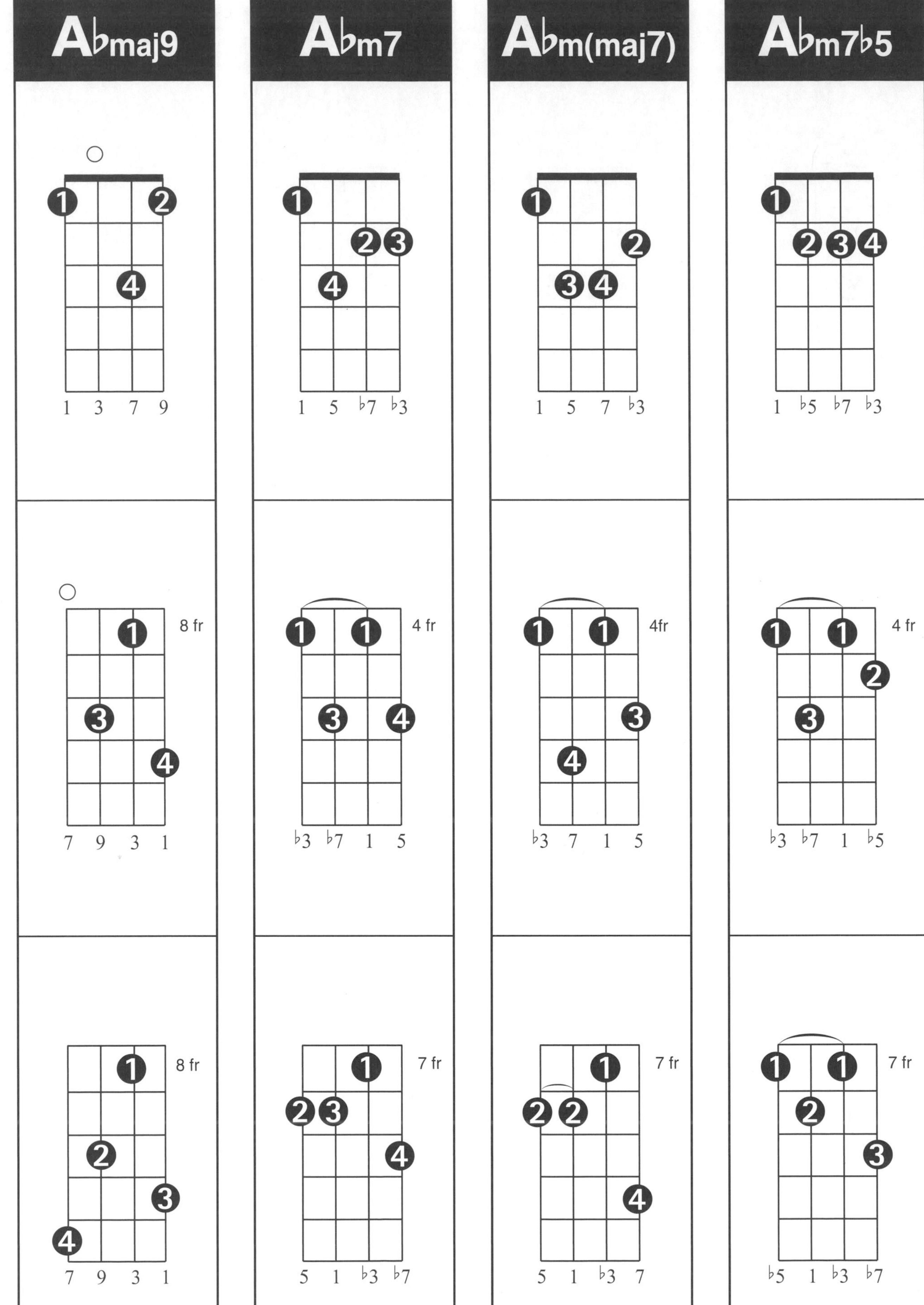
A♭maj9
A♭m7
A♭m(maj7)
A♭m7♭5
1 3 7 9
1 5 ♭7 ♭3
1 5 7 ♭3
1 ♭5 ♭7 ♭3
8 fr
4 fr
4fr
4 fr
7 9 3 1
♭3 ♭7 1 5
♭3 7 1 5
♭3 ♭7 1 ♭5
8 fr
7 fr
7 fr
7 fr
7 9 3 1
5 1 ♭3 ♭7
5 1 ♭3 7
♭5 1 ♭3 ♭7

A♭/G♯

A♭m9

A♭m11

A♭7

A♭7sus4

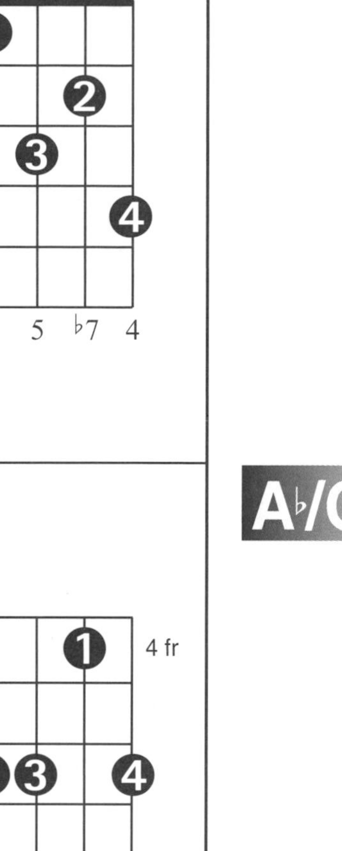

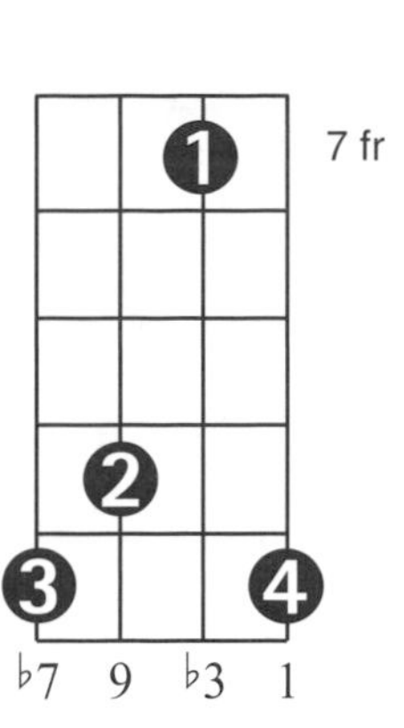

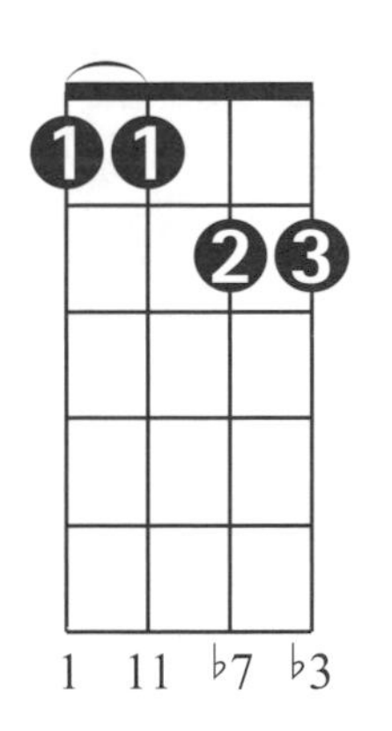

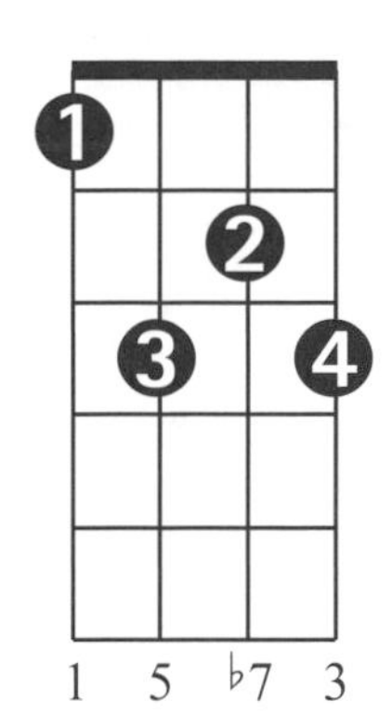

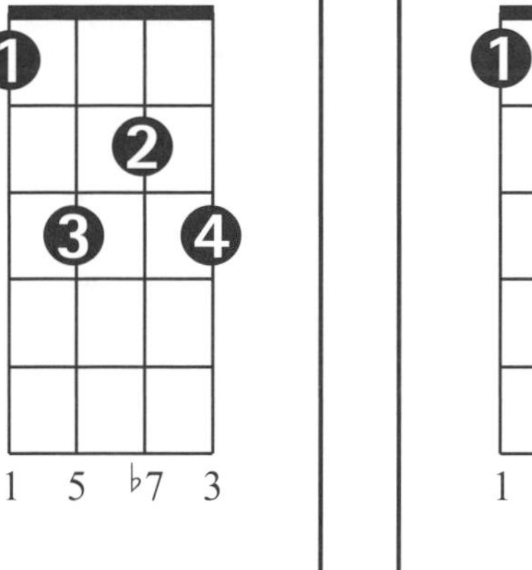

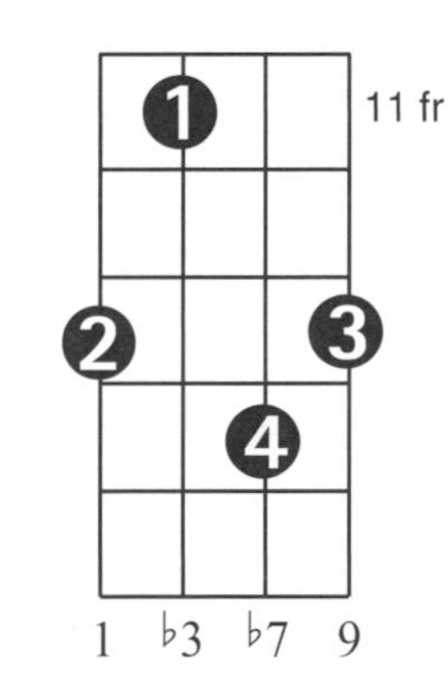

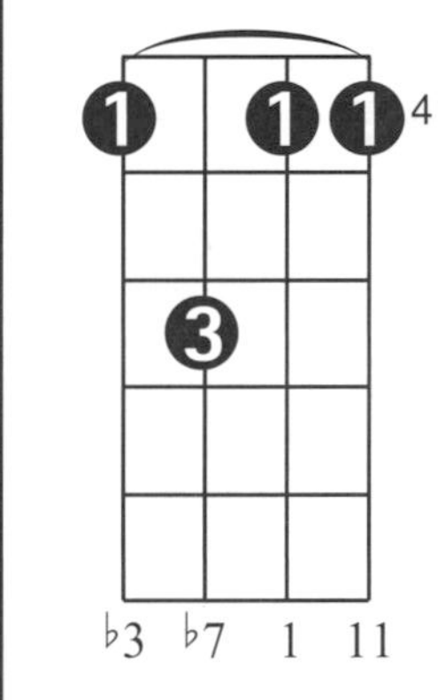

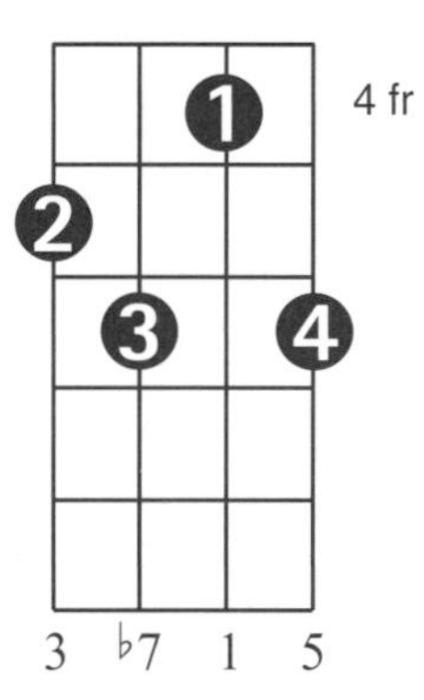

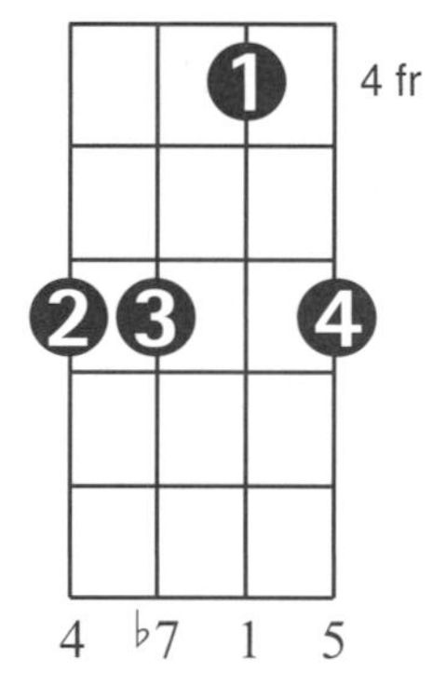

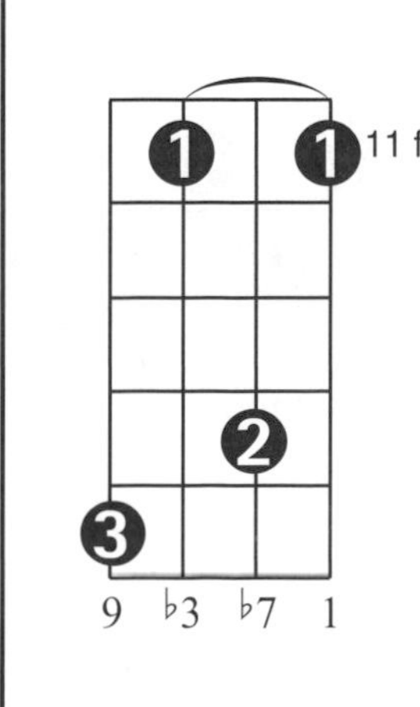

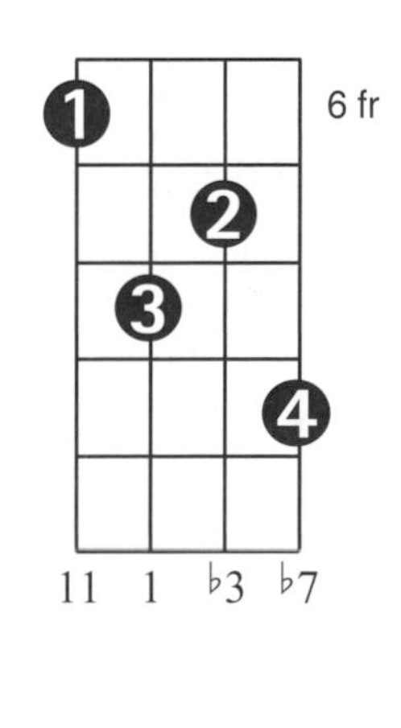

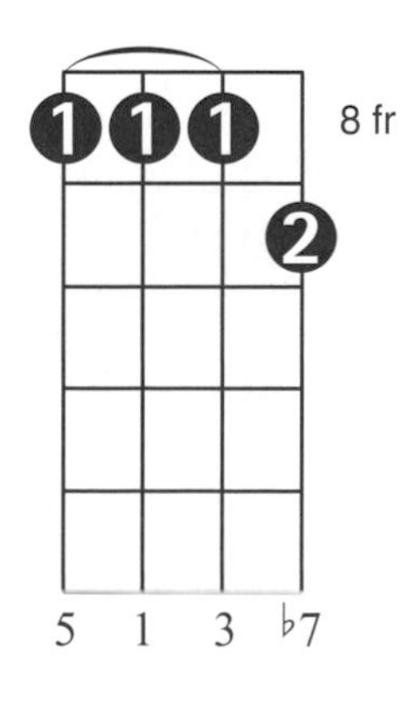

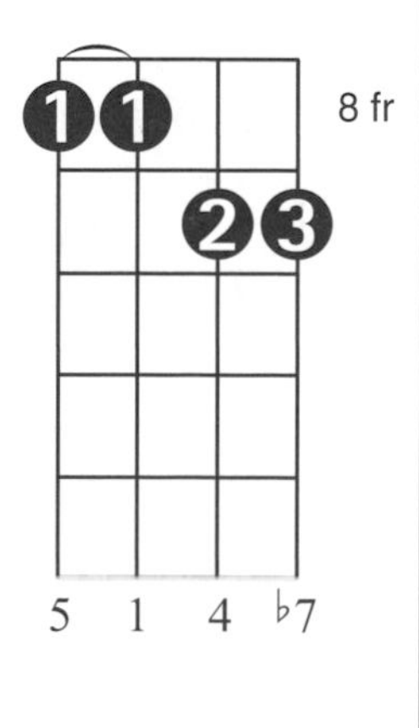

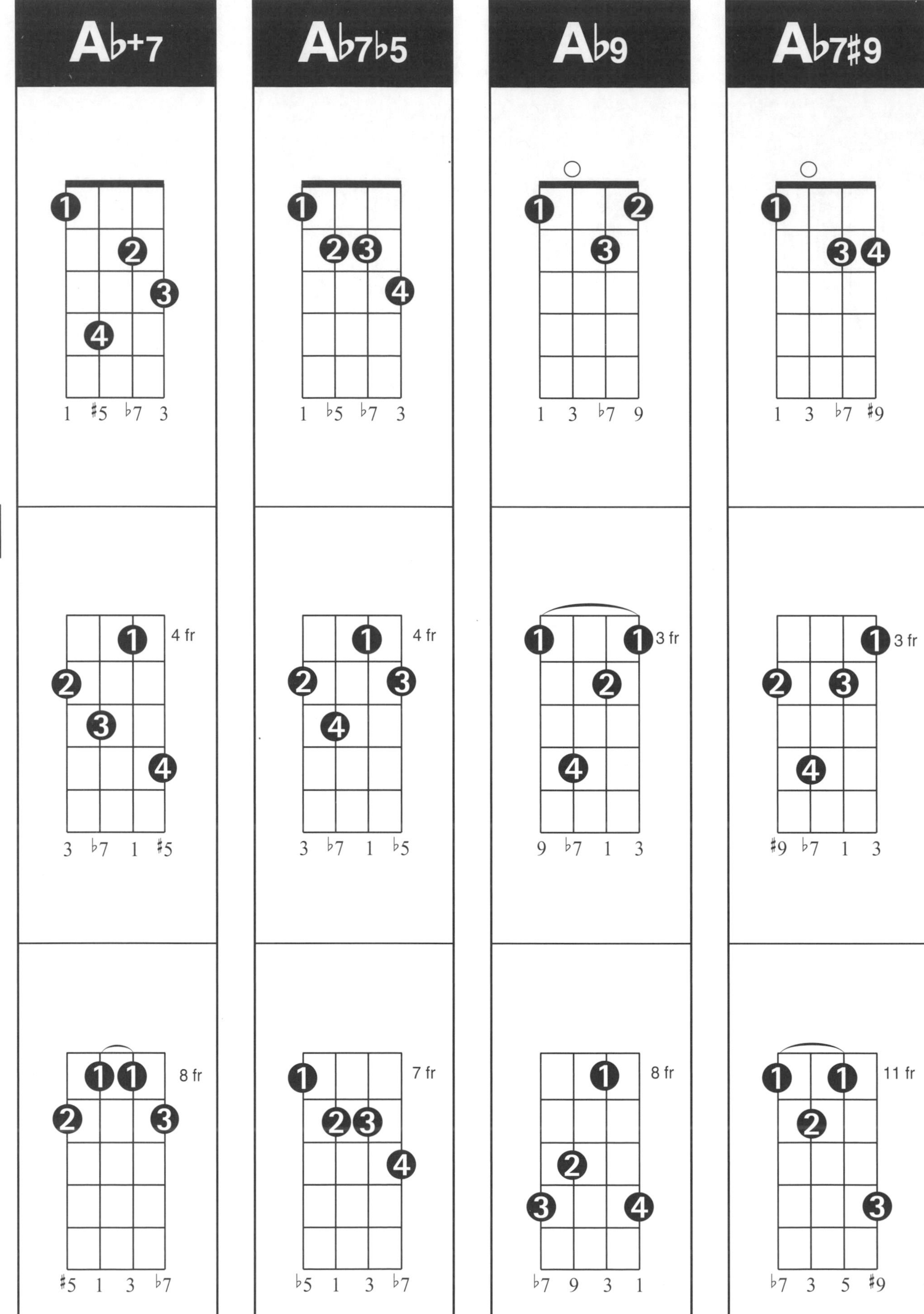

A♭+7
A♭7♭5
A♭9
A♭7♯9
1 ♯5 ♭7 3
1 ♭5 ♭7 3
1 3 ♭7 9
1 3 ♭7 ♯9
4 fr
4 fr
3 fr
3 fr
3 ♭7 1 ♯5
3 ♭7 1 ♭5
9 ♭7 1 3
♯9 ♭7 1 3
8 fr
7 fr
8 fr
11 fr
♯5 1 3 ♭7
♭5 1 3 ♭7
♭7 9 3 1
♭7 3 5 ♯9

A♭/G♯

A♭7♭9

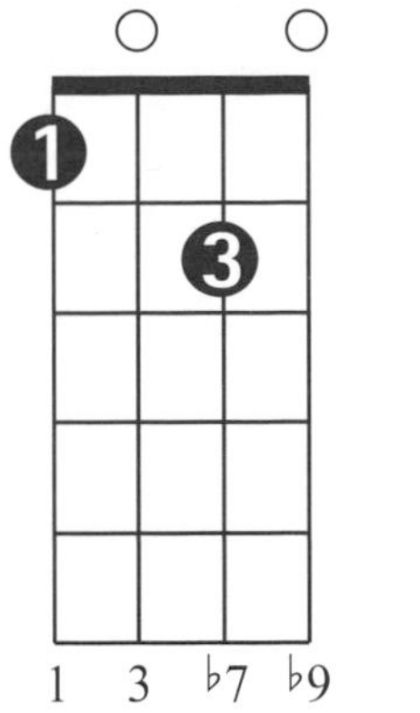

1 3 ♭7 ♭9

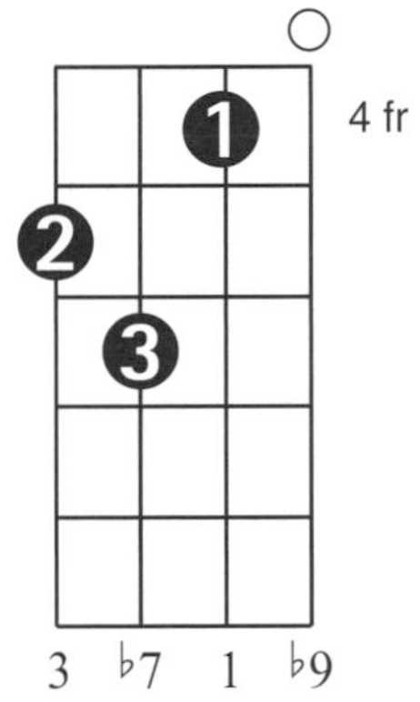

4 fr
3 ♭7 1 ♭9

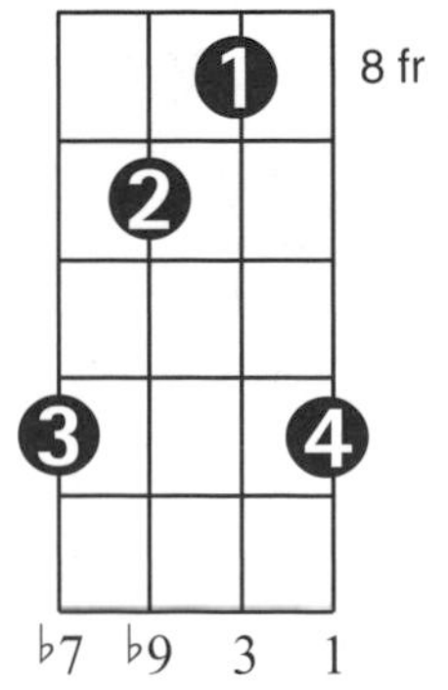

8 fr
♭7 ♭9 3 1

A♭11

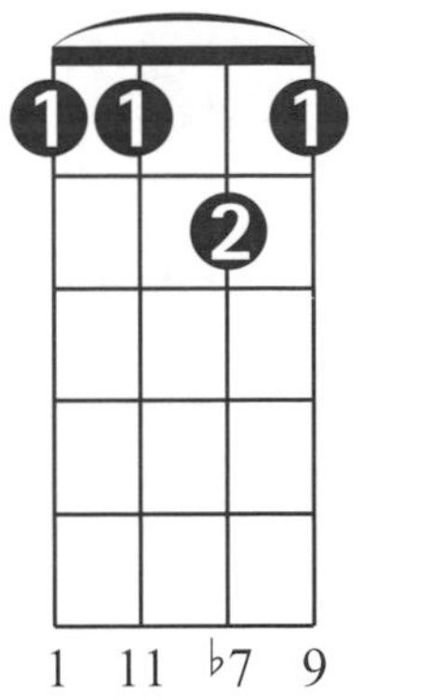

1 11 ♭7 9

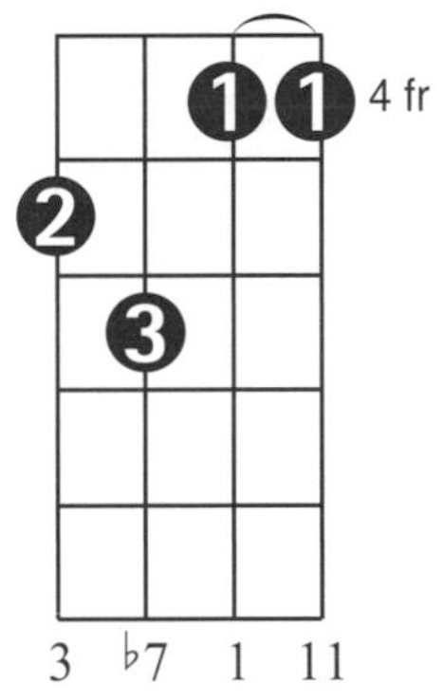

4 fr
3 ♭7 1 11

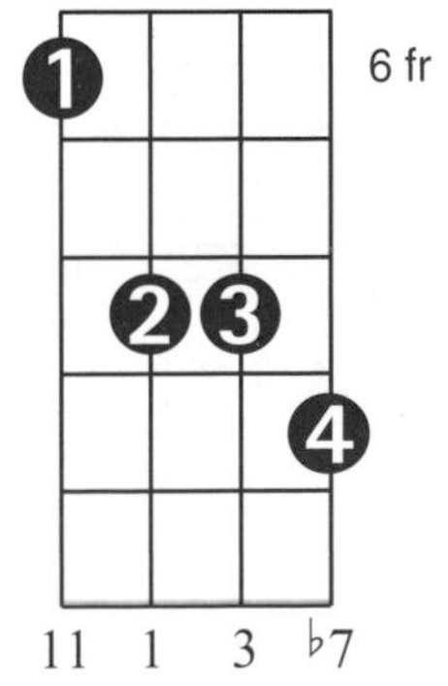

6 fr
11 1 3 ♭7

A♭13

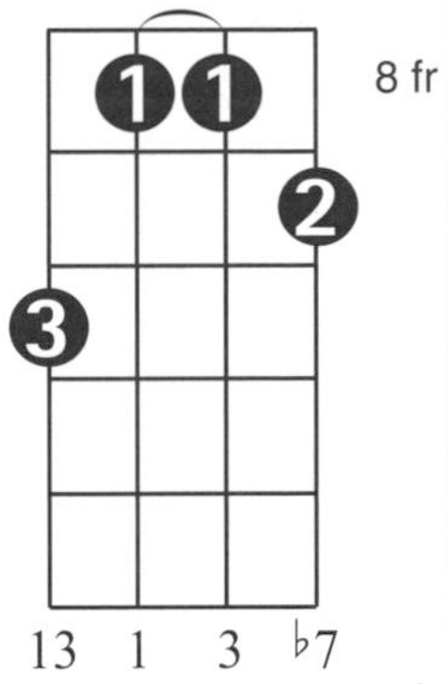

8 fr
13 1 3 ♭7

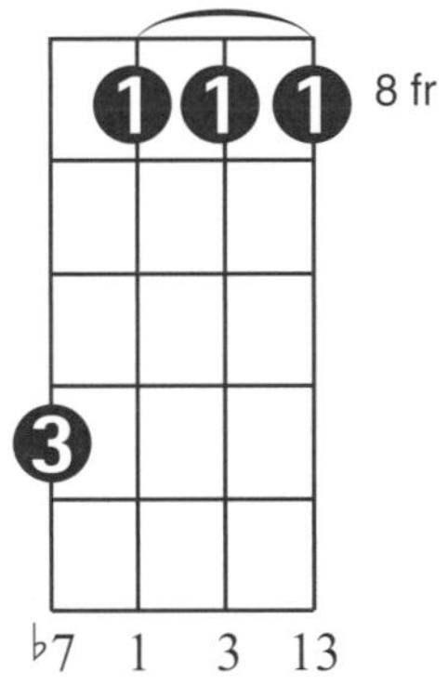

8 fr
♭7 1 3 13

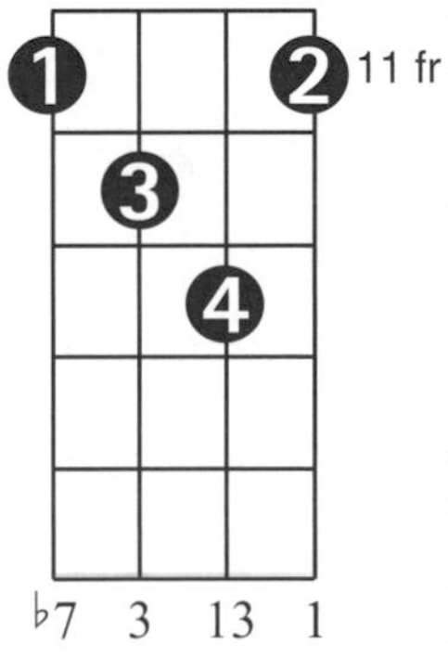

11 fr
♭7 3 13 1

A♭°7

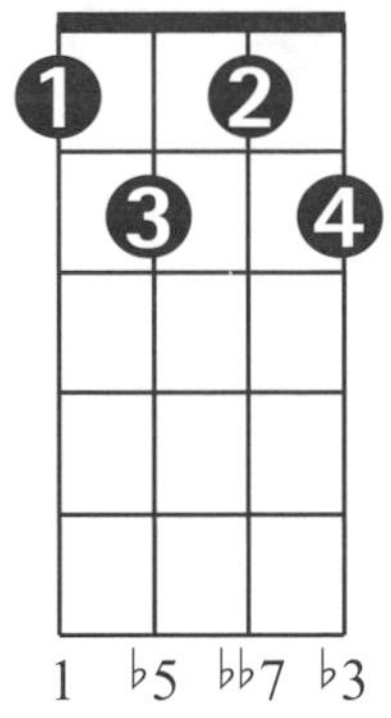

1 ♭5 ♭♭7 ♭3

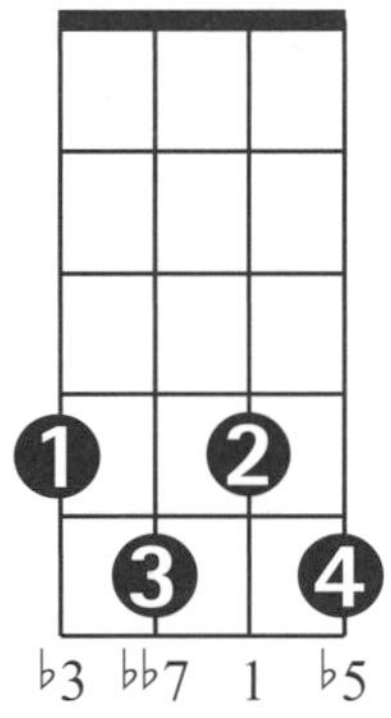

♭3 ♭♭7 1 ♭5

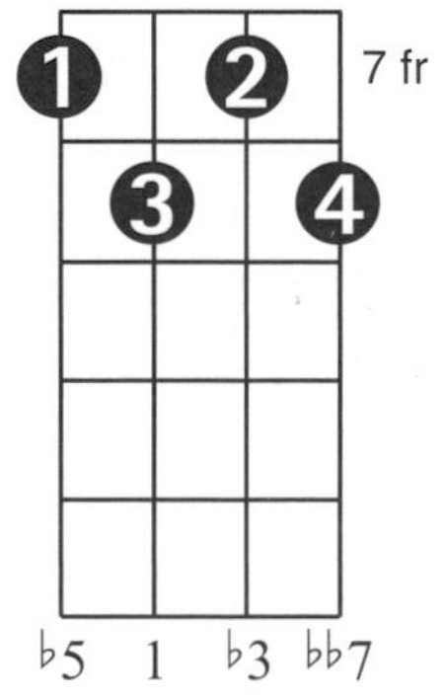

7 fr
♭5 1 ♭3 ♭♭7

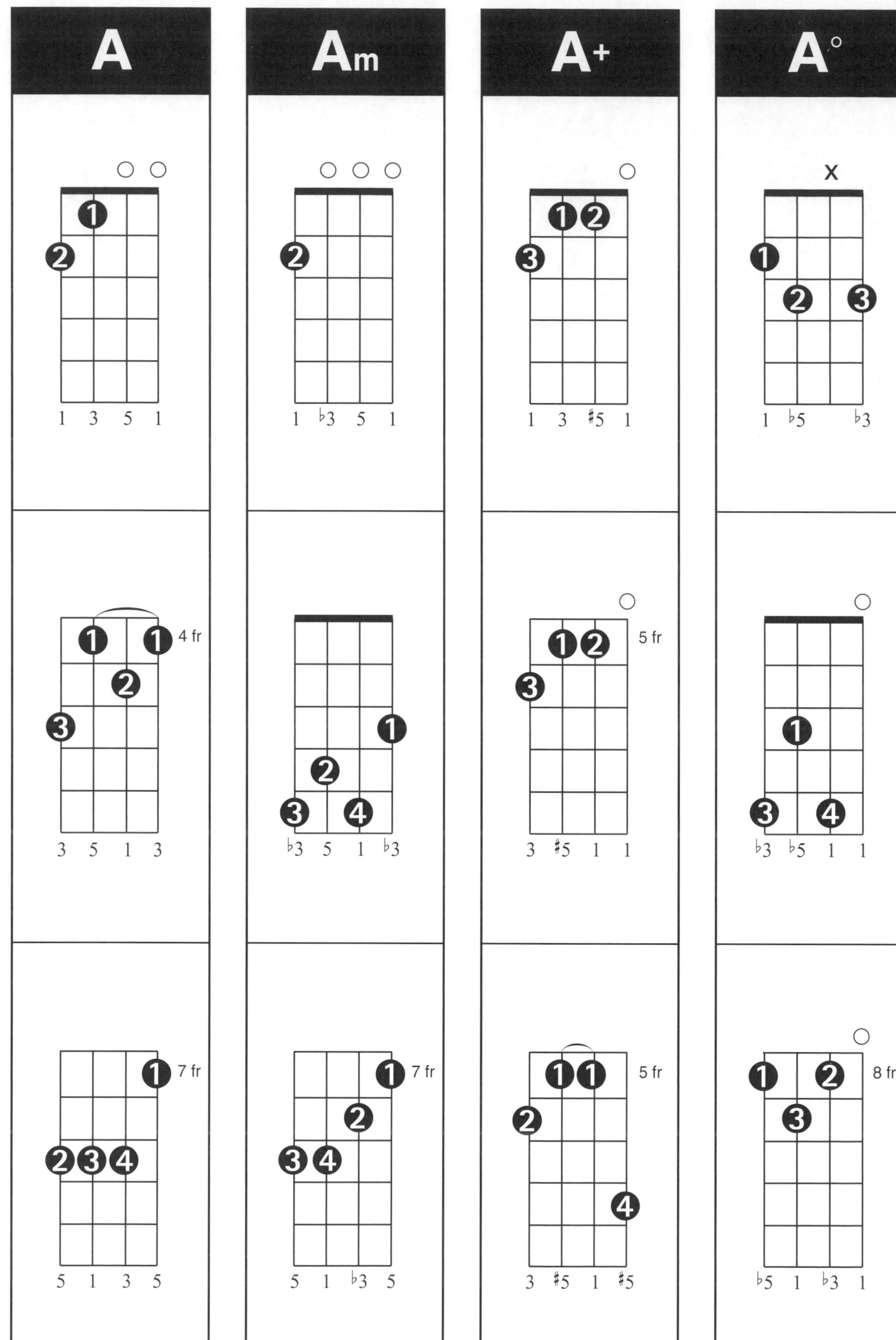
A
Am
A+
A°
1 3 5 1
1 ♭3 5 1
1 3 ♯5 1
1 ♭5 ♭3
4 fr
3 5 1 3
♭3 5 1 ♭3
5 fr
3 ♯5 1 1
♭3 ♭5 1 1
7 fr
5 1 3 5
7 fr
5 1 ♭3 5
5 fr
3 ♯5 1 ♯5
8 fr
♭5 1 ♭3 1

A

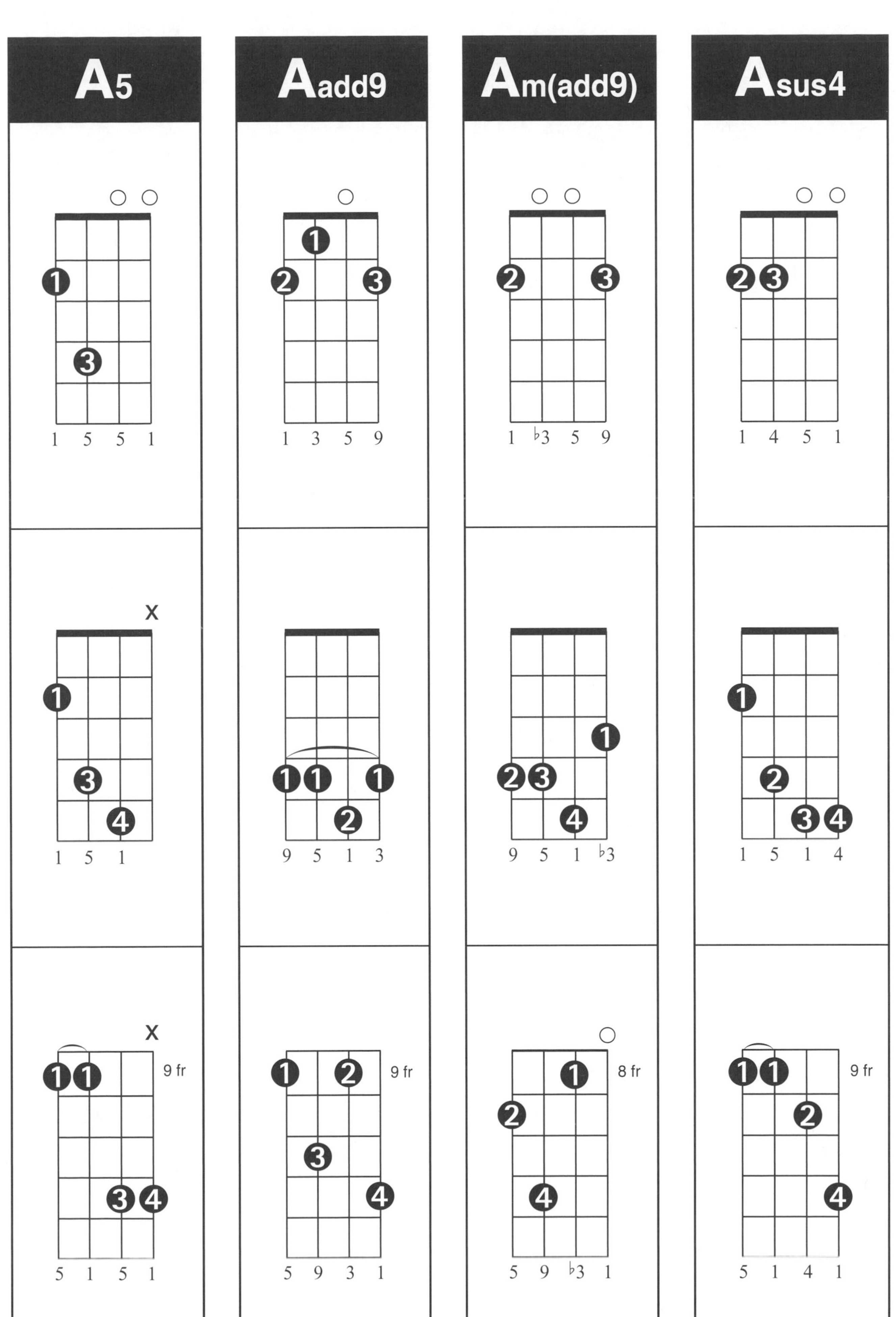

A5
Aadd9
Am(add9)
Asus4
1 5 5 1
1 3 5 9
1 ♭3 5 9
1 4 5 1
1 5 1
9 5 1 3
9 5 1 ♭3
1 5 1 4
9 fr
5 1 5 1
9 fr
5 9 3 1
8 fr
5 9 ♭3 1
9 fr
5 1 4 1

A

Asus2

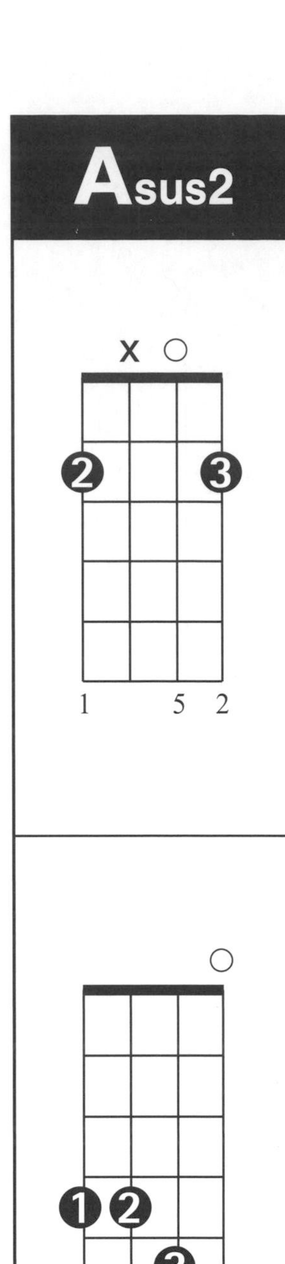

7 fr

5 1 2 5

A6

1 5 6 3

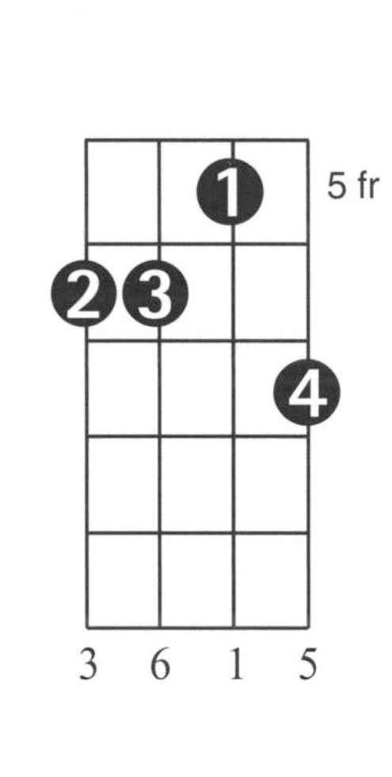

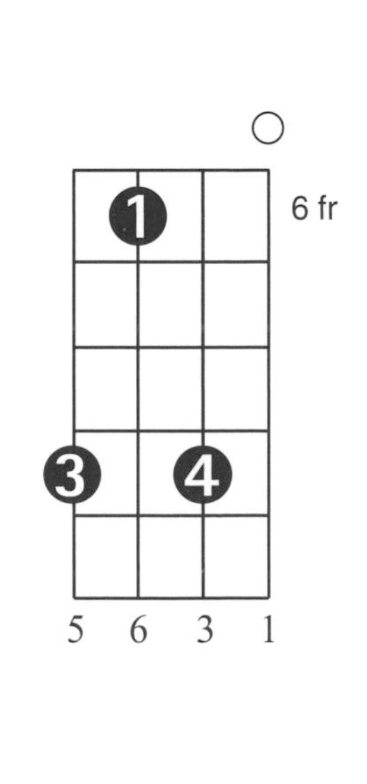

Am6

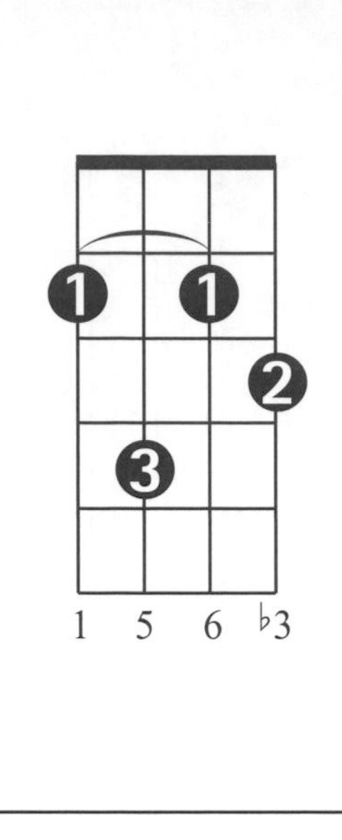

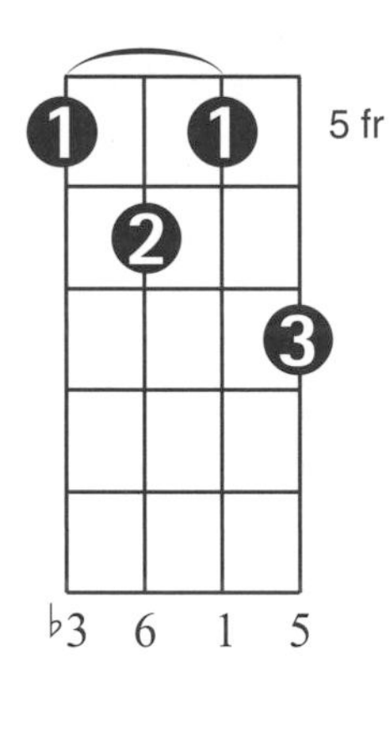

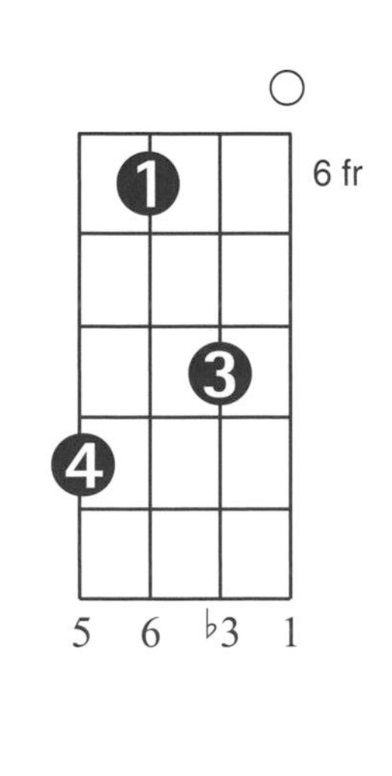

Amaj7

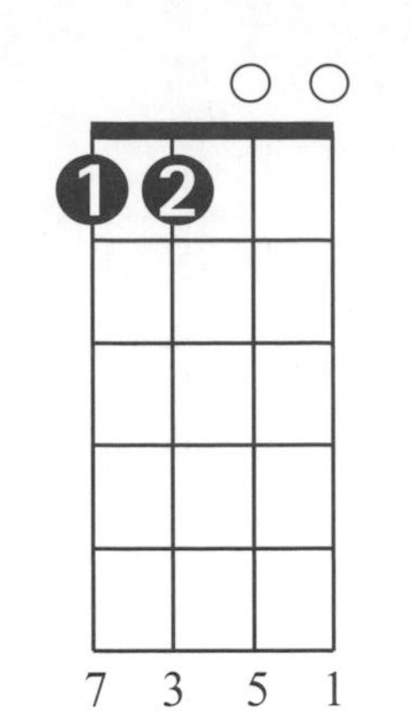

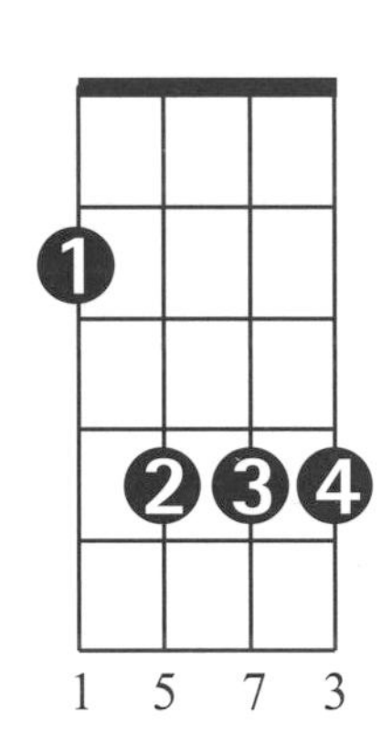

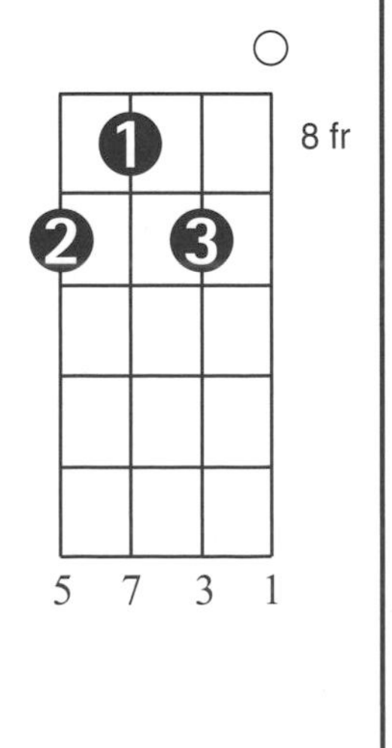

A

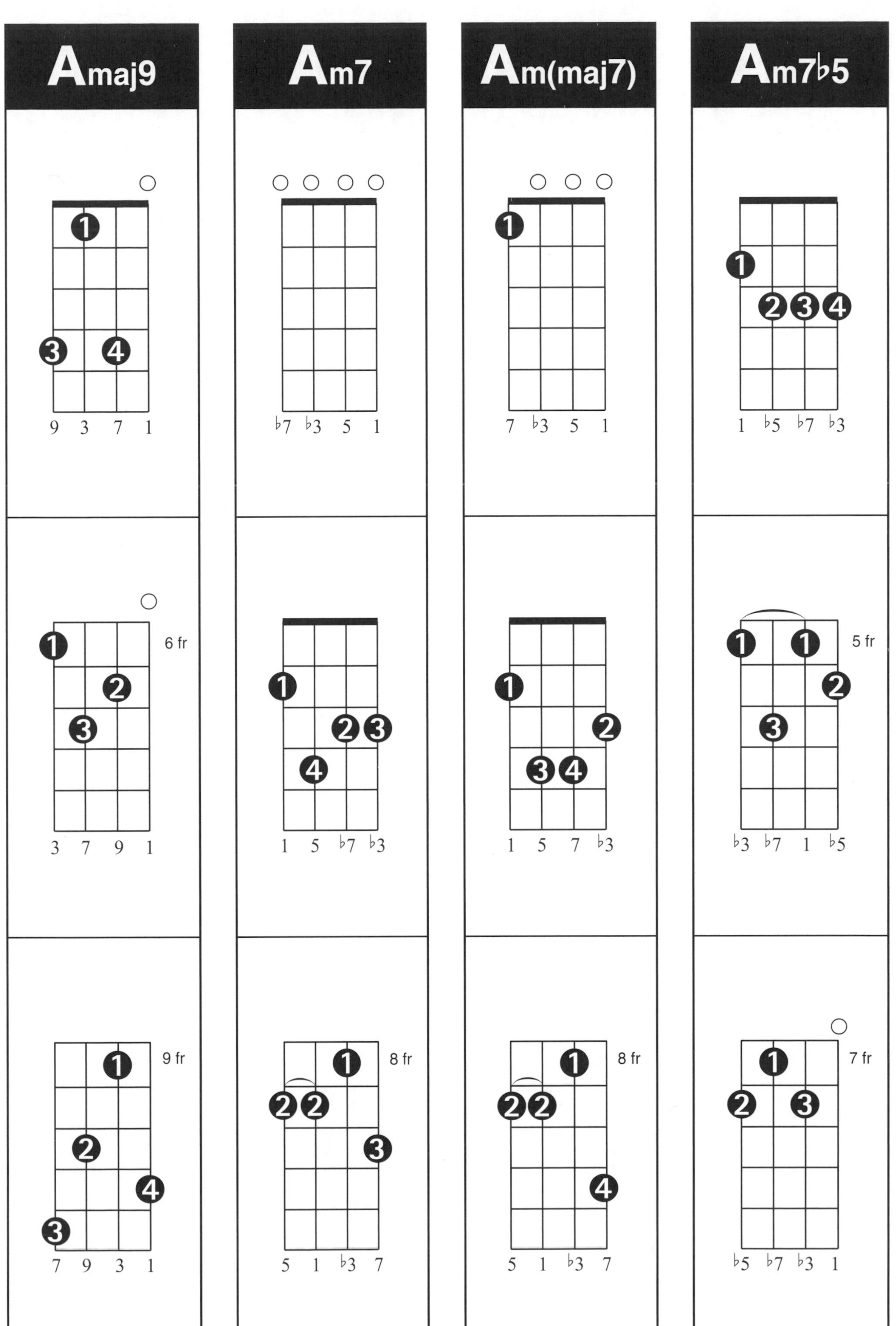
Amaj9
Am7
Am(maj7)
Am7♭5
9 3 7 1
♭7 ♭3 5 1
7 ♭3 5 1
1 ♭5 ♭7 ♭3
6 fr
5 fr
3 7 9 1
1 5 ♭7 ♭3
1 5 7 ♭3
♭3 ♭7 1 ♭5
9 fr
8 fr
8 fr
7 fr
7 9 3 1
5 1 ♭3 7
5 1 ♭3 7
♭5 ♭7 ♭3 1

A

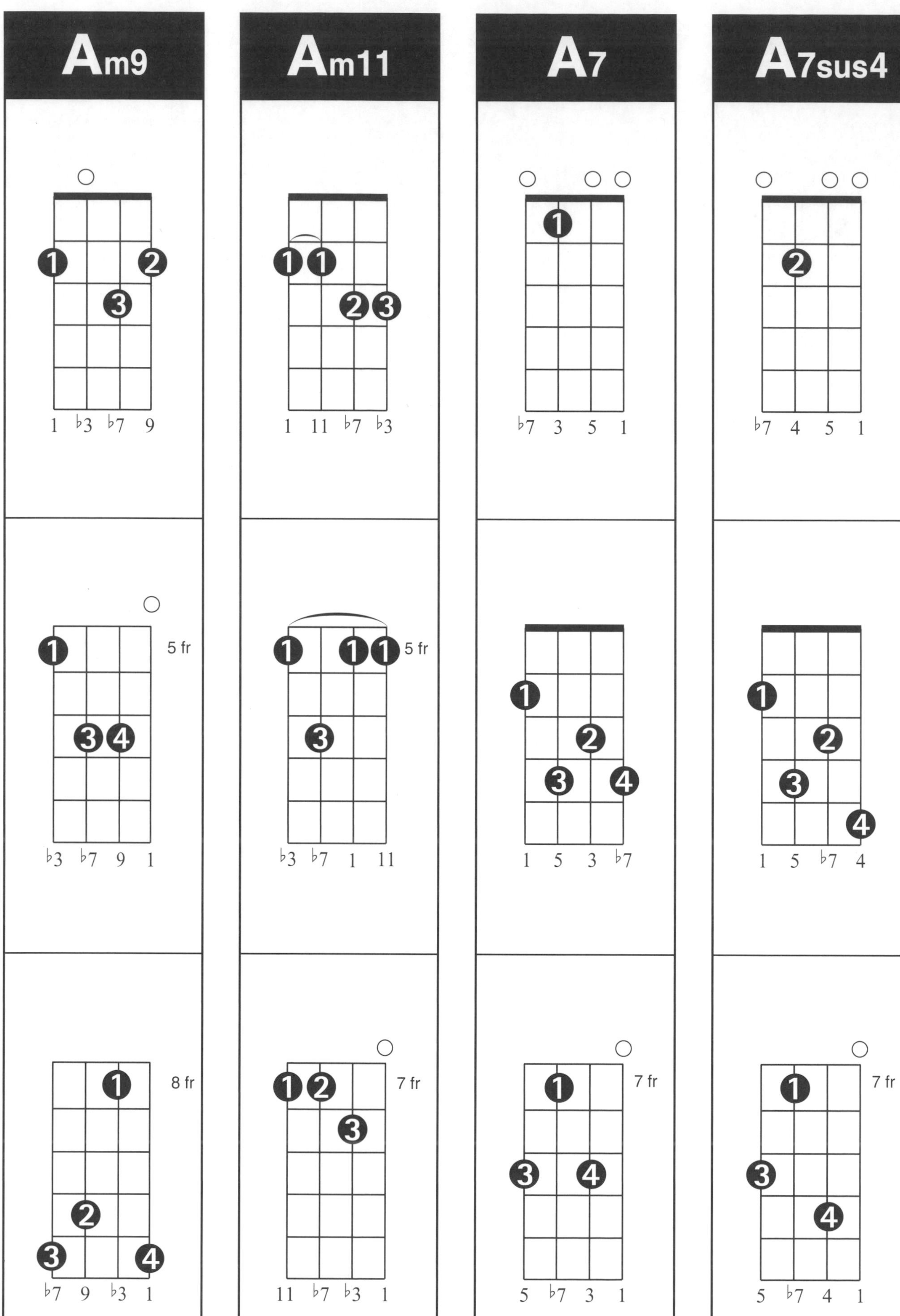

Am9
Am11
A7
A7sus4
1 ♭3 ♭7 9
1 11 ♭7 ♭3
♭7 3 5 1
♭7 4 5 1
5 fr
♭3 ♭7 9 1
5 fr
♭3 ♭7 1 11
1 5 3 ♭7
1 5 ♭7 4
8 fr
♭7 9 ♭3 1
7 fr
11 ♭7 ♭3 1
7 fr
5 ♭7 3 1
7 fr
5 ♭7 4 1

A

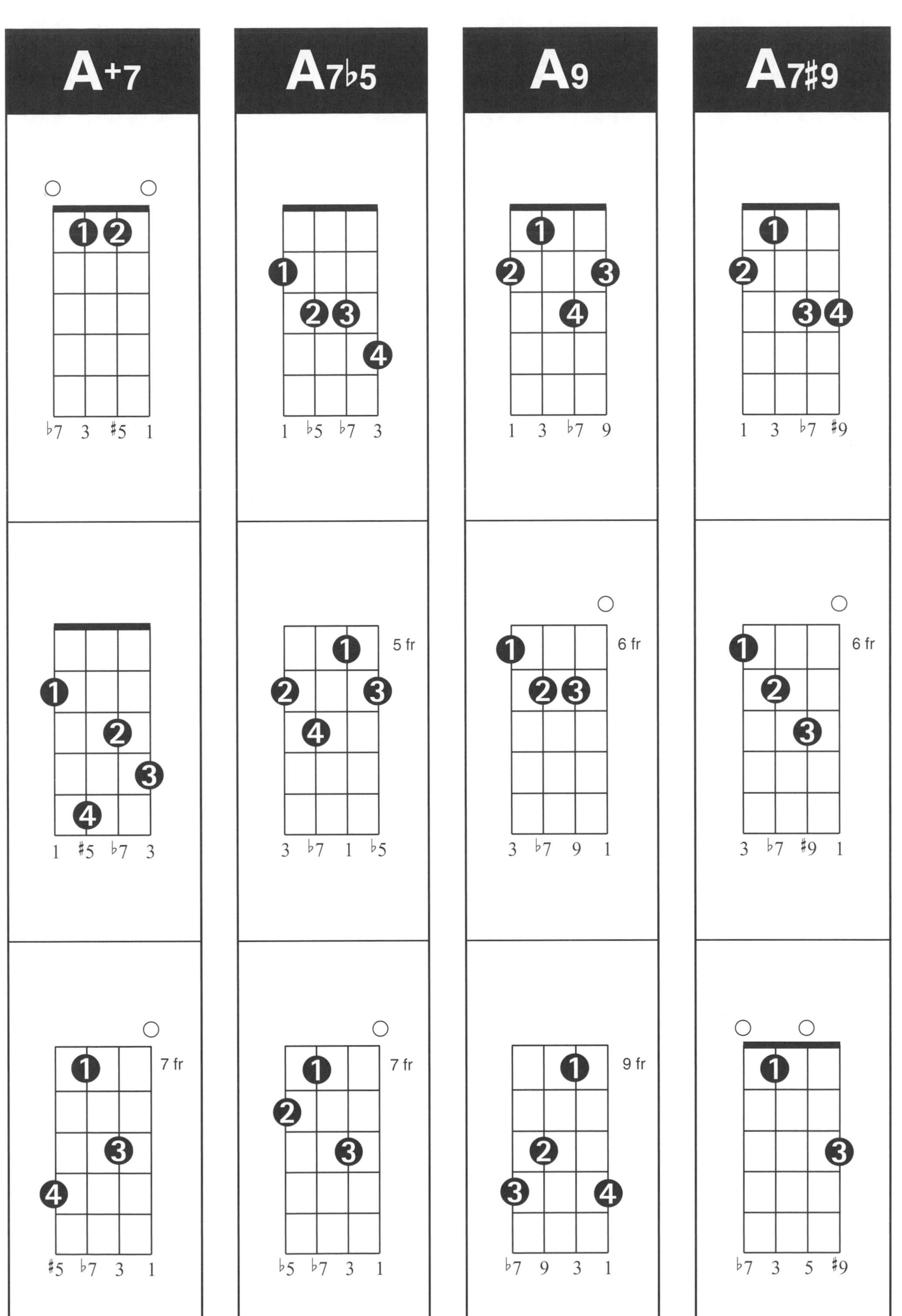
A+7
A7♭5
A9
A7♯9
♭7 3 ♯5 1
1 ♭5 ♭7 3
1 3 ♭7 9
1 3 ♭7 ♯9
5 fr
6 fr
6 fr
1 ♯5 ♭7 3
3 ♭7 1 ♭5
3 ♭7 9 1
3 ♭7 ♯9 1
7 fr
7 fr
9 fr
♯5 ♭7 3 1
♭5 ♭7 3 1
♭7 9 3 1
♭7 3 5 ♯9

A

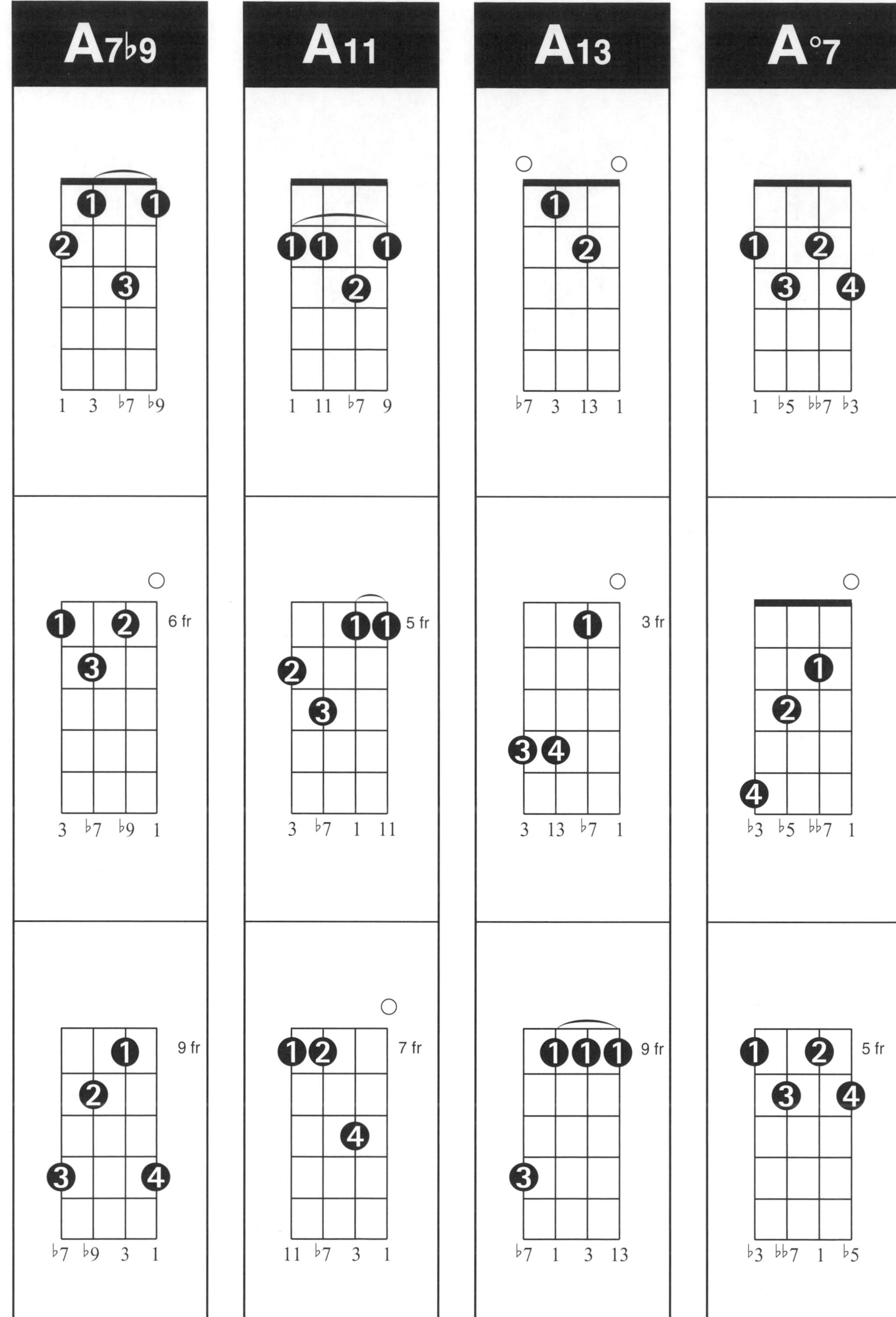
A7♭9
A11
A13
A°7
1 3 ♭7 ♭9
1 11 ♭7 9
♭7 3 13 1
1 ♭5 ♭♭7 ♭3
6 fr
5 fr
3 fr
3 ♭7 ♭9 1
3 ♭7 1 11
3 13 ♭7 1
♭3 ♭5 ♭♭7 1
9 fr
7 fr
9 fr
5 fr
♭7 ♭9 3 1
11 ♭7 3 1
♭7 1 3 13
♭3 ♭♭7 1 ♭5

A

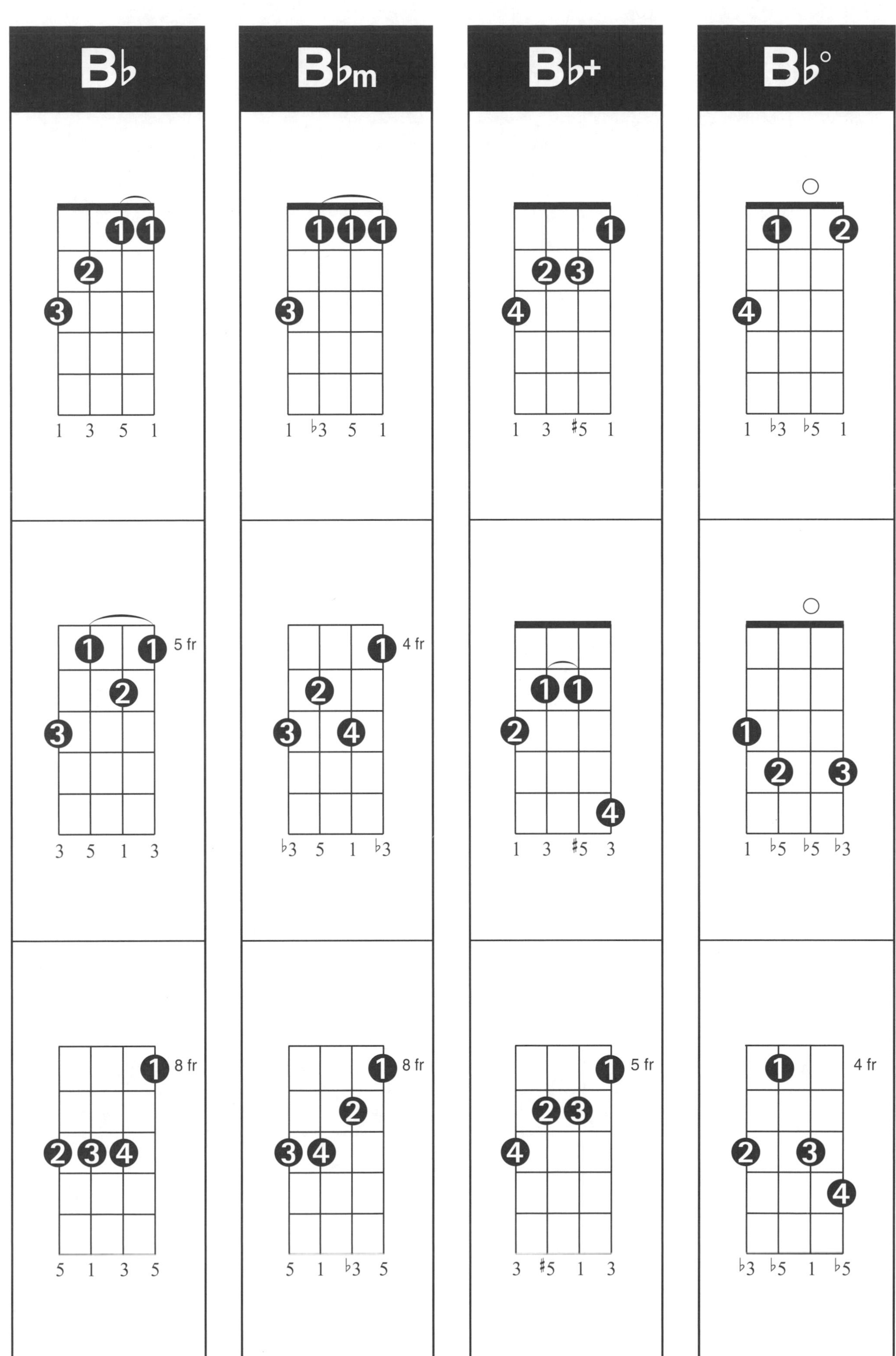

B♭
B♭m
B♭+
B♭°
1 3 5 1
1 ♭3 5 1
1 3 ♯5 1
1 ♭3 ♭5 1
5 fr
3 5 1 3
4 fr
♭3 5 1 ♭3
1 3 ♯5 3
1 ♭5 ♭5 ♭3
8 fr
5 1 3 5
8 fr
5 1 ♭3 5
5 fr
3 ♯5 1 3
4 fr
♭3 ♭5 1 ♭5

B♭/A♯

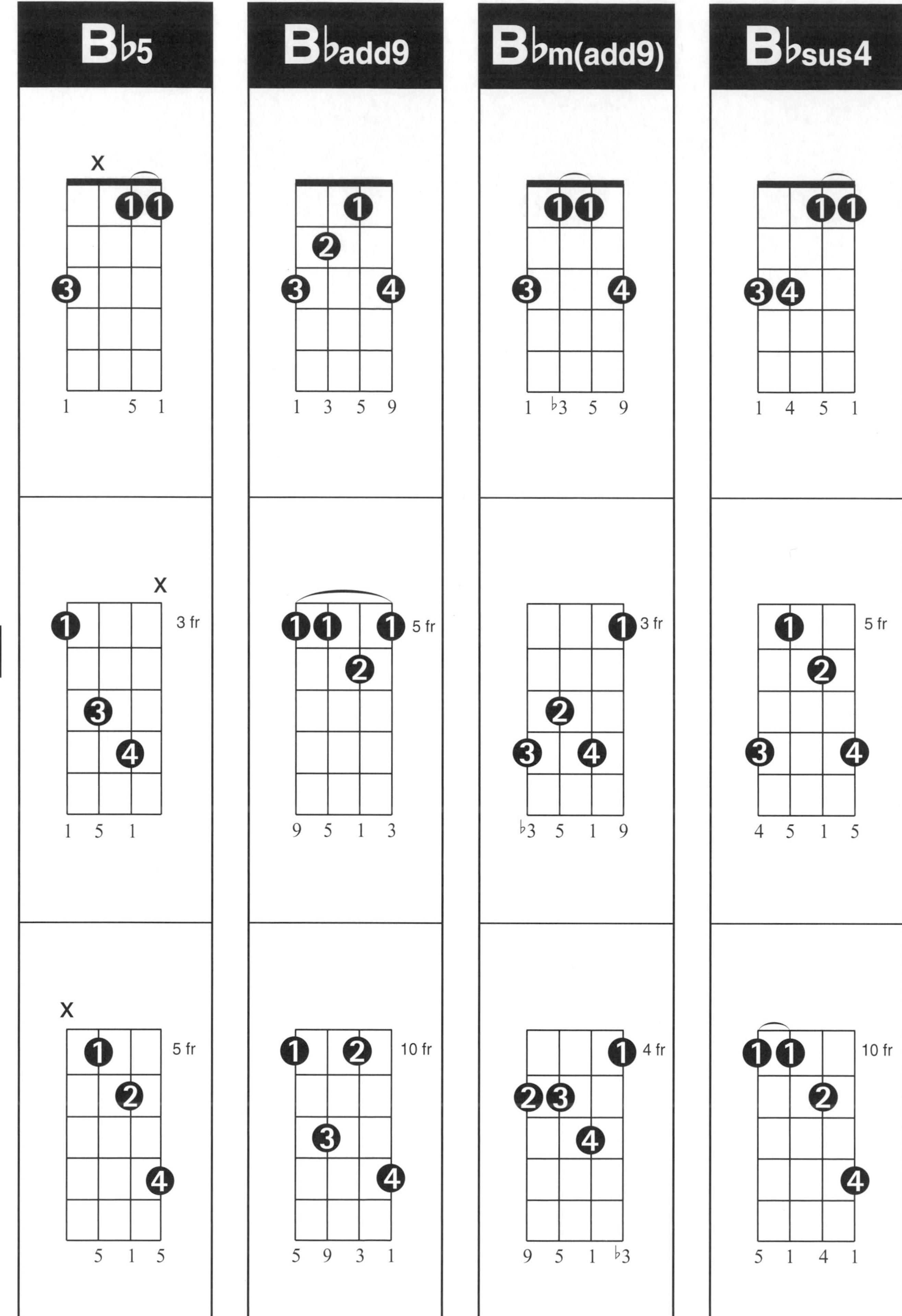
B♭5
B♭add9
B♭m(add9)
B♭sus4
X
1 5 1
1 3 5 9
1 ♭3 5 9
1 4 5 1
X
3 fr
5 fr
3 fr
5 fr
1 5 1
9 5 1 3
♭3 5 1 9
4 5 1 5
X
5 fr
10 fr
4 fr
10 fr
5 1 5
5 9 3 1
9 5 1 ♭3
5 1 4 1

B♭/A♯

B♭sus2

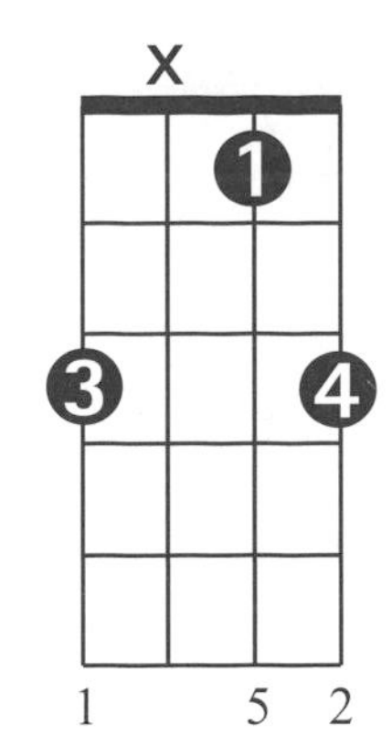
X
1
3 4
1 5 2

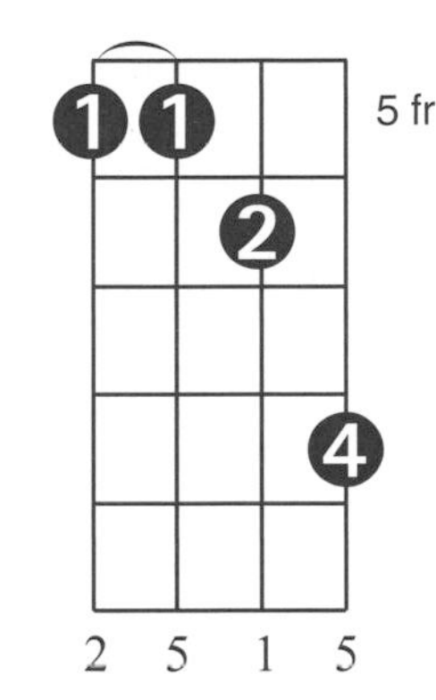
5 fr
1 1
2
4
2 5 1 5

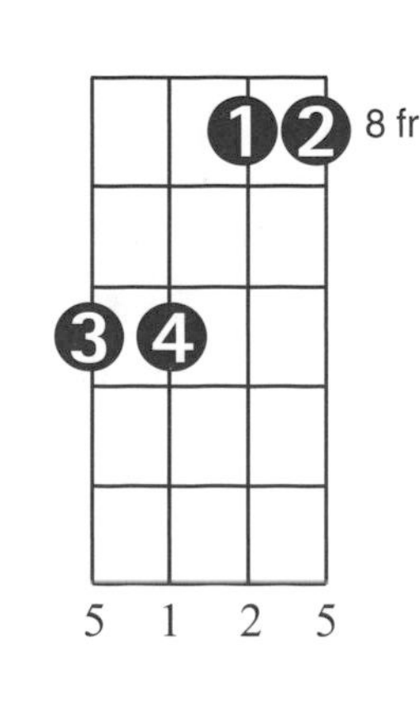
8 fr
1 2
3 4
5 1 2 5

B♭6

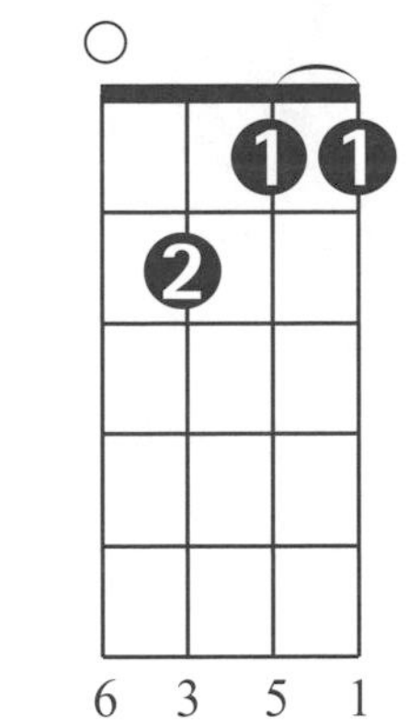
1 1
2
6 3 5 1

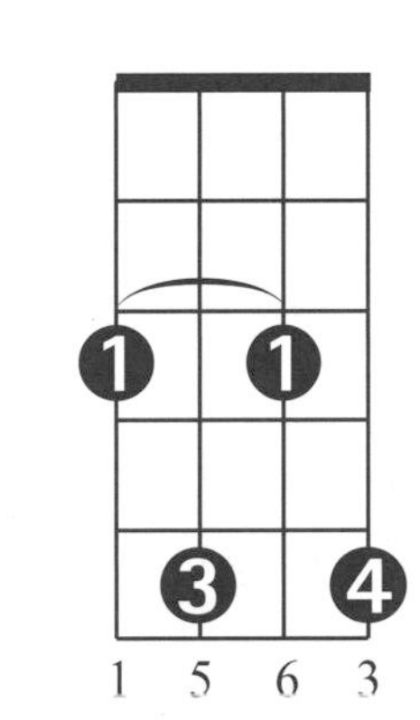
1 1
3 4
1 5 6 3

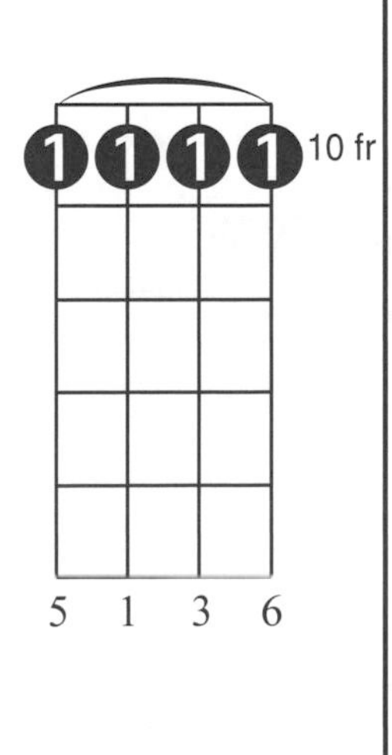
10 fr
1 1 1 1
5 1 3 6

B♭m6

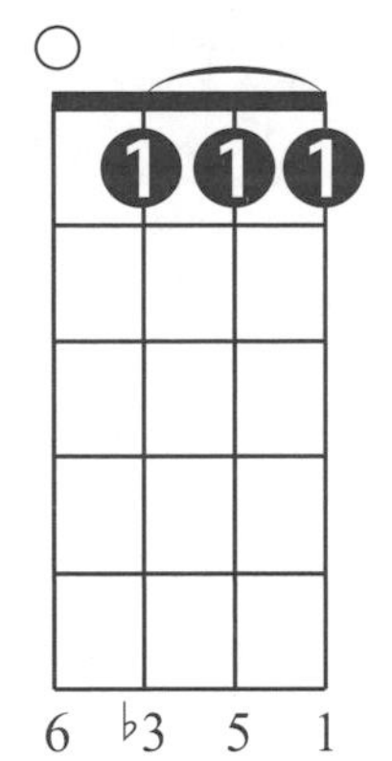
1 1 1
6 ♭3 5 1

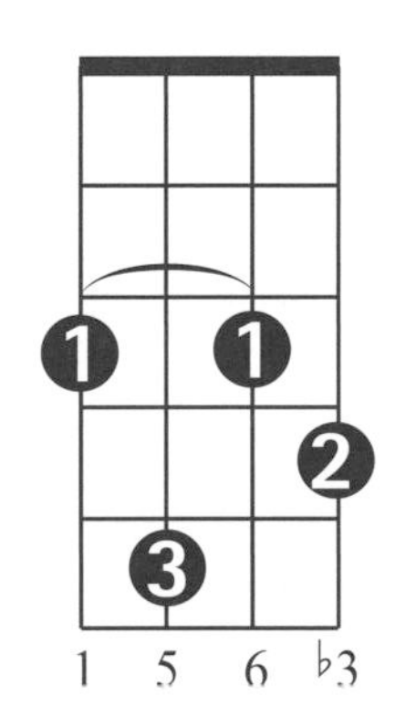
1 1
2
3
1 5 6 ♭3

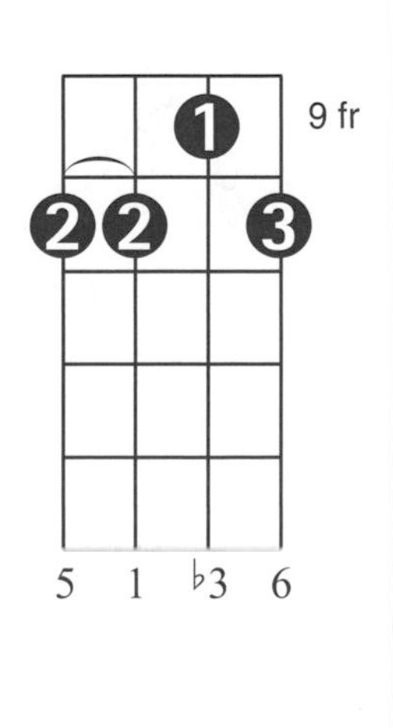
9 fr
1
2 2 3
5 1 ♭3 6

B♭maj7

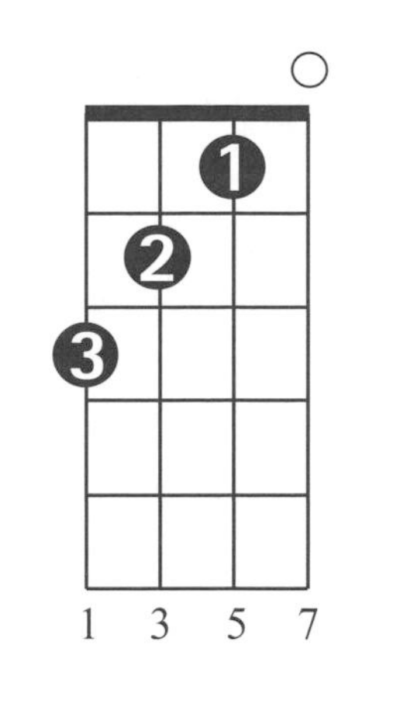
1
2
3
1 3 5 7

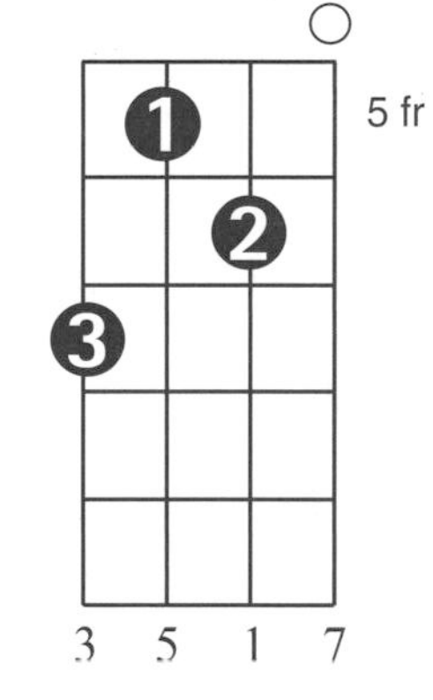
5 fr
1
2
3
3 5 1 7

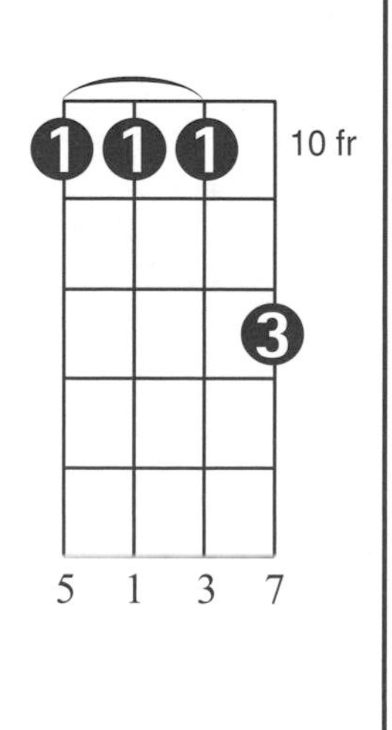
10 fr
1 1 1
3
5 1 3 7

B♭/A♯

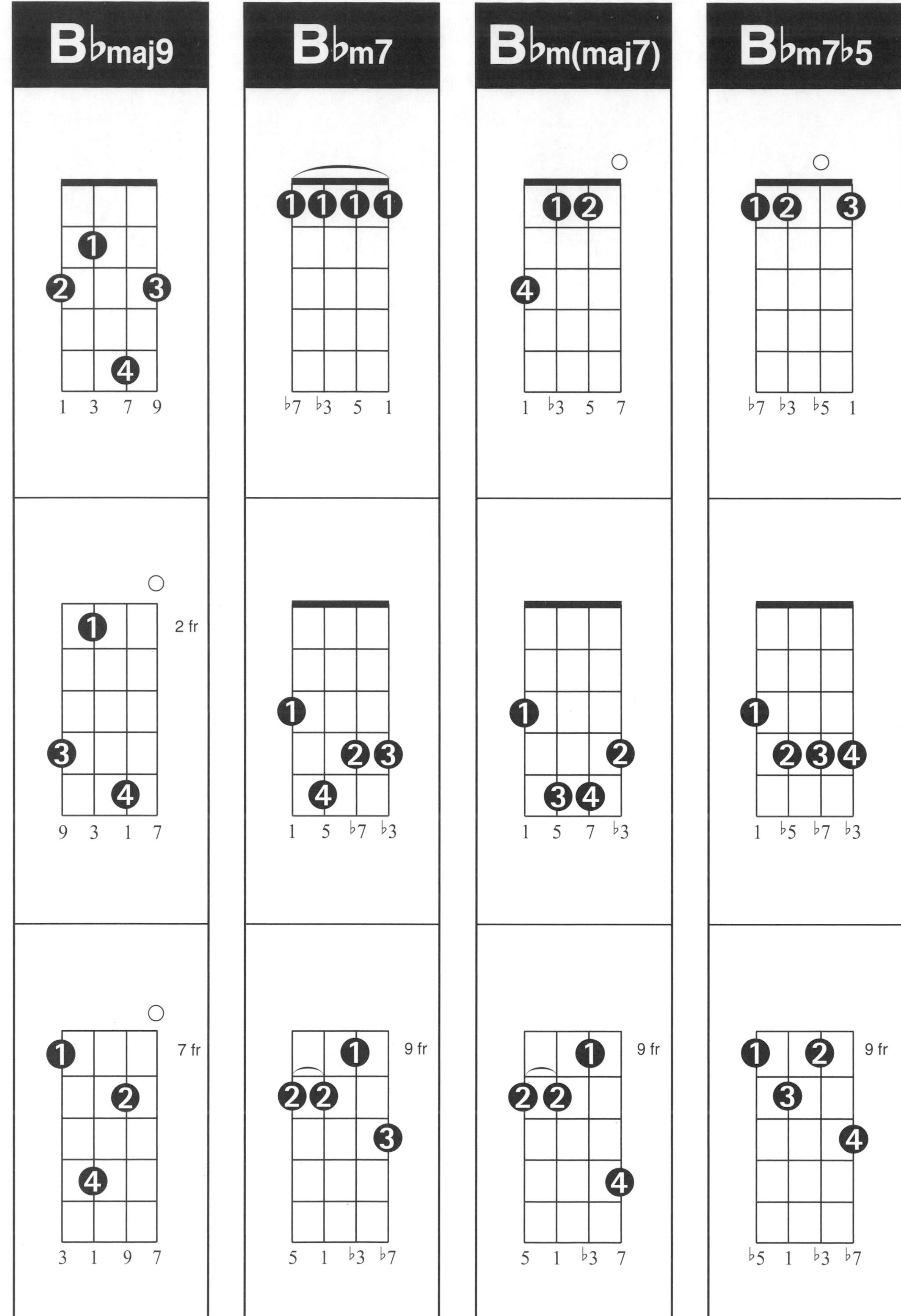

B♭maj9
B♭m7
B♭m(maj7)
B♭m7♭5
1 3 7 9
♭7 ♭3 5 1
1 ♭3 5 7
♭7 ♭3 ♭5 1
2 fr
9 3 1 7
1 5 ♭7 ♭3
1 5 7 ♭3
1 ♭5 ♭7 ♭3
7 fr
9 fr
9 fr
9 fr
3 1 9 7
5 1 ♭3 ♭7
5 1 ♭3 7
♭5 1 ♭3 ♭7

B♭/A♯

B♭m9	B♭m11	B♭7	B♭7sus4
1 ♭3 ♭7 9	1 11 ♭7 ♭3	♭7 3 5 1	♭7 4 5 1
6 fr ♭3 1 9 ♭7	6 fr ♭3 ♭7 1 11	1 5 ♭7 3	3 fr 1 5 ♭7 4
9 fr ♭7 9 ♭3 1	8 fr 11 1 ♭3 ♭7	10 fr 5 1 3 ♭7	10 fr 5 1 4 ♭7

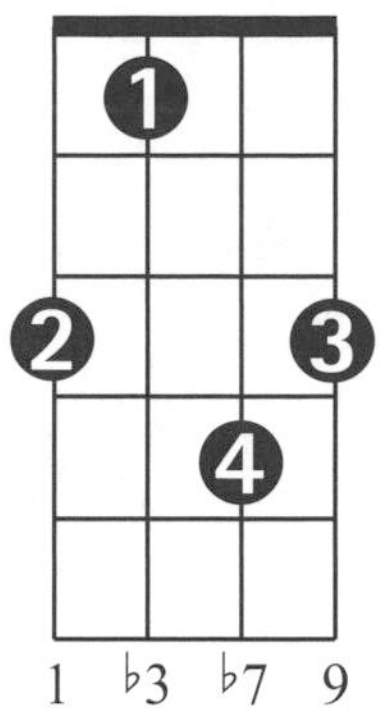

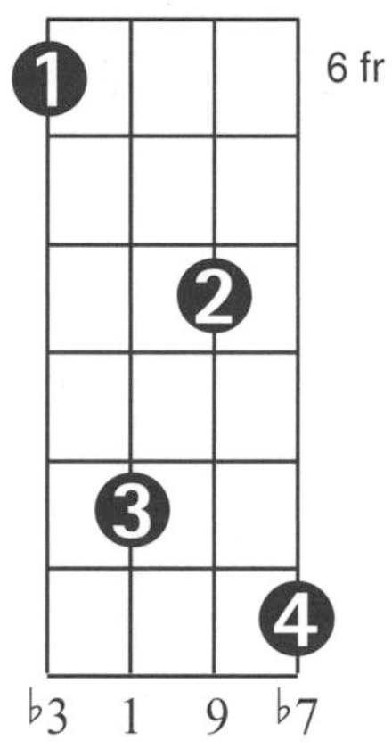

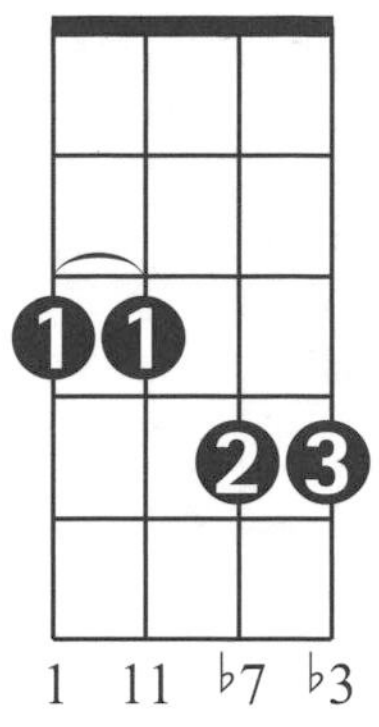

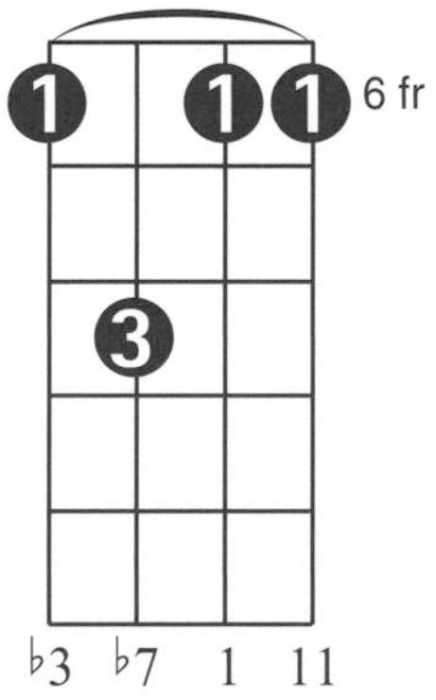

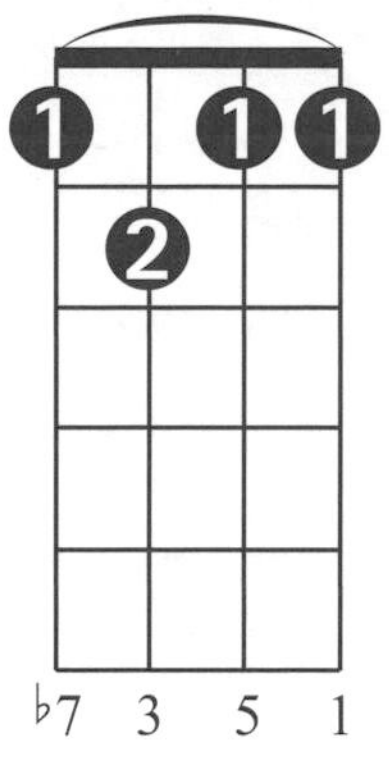

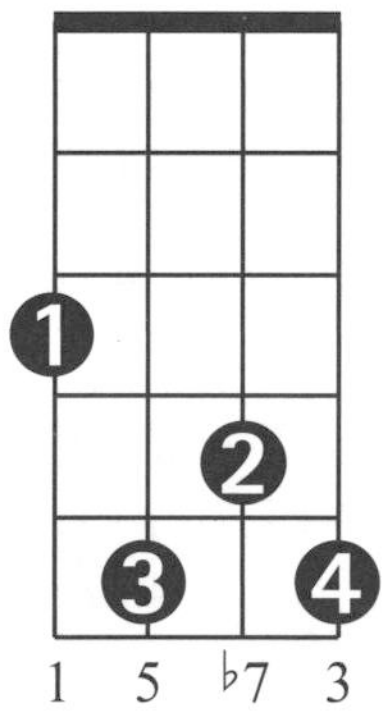

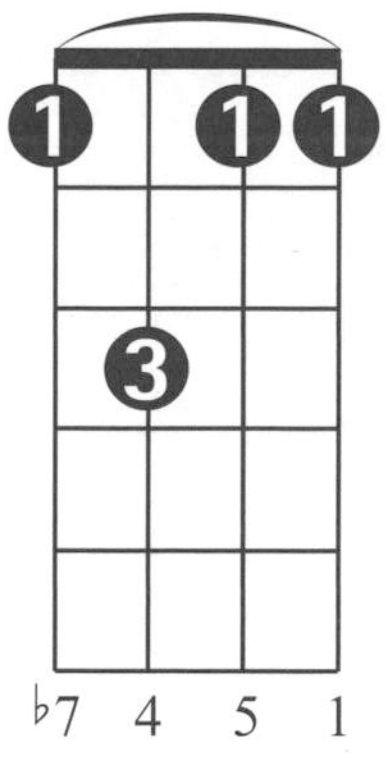

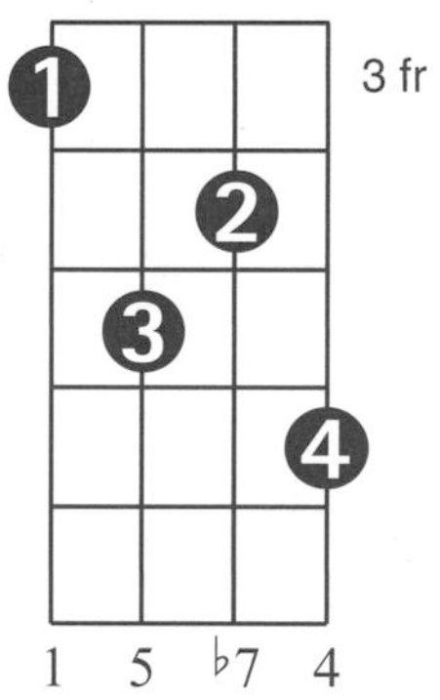

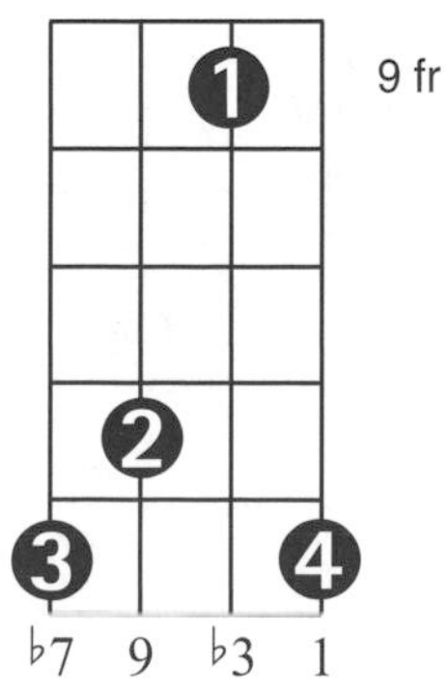

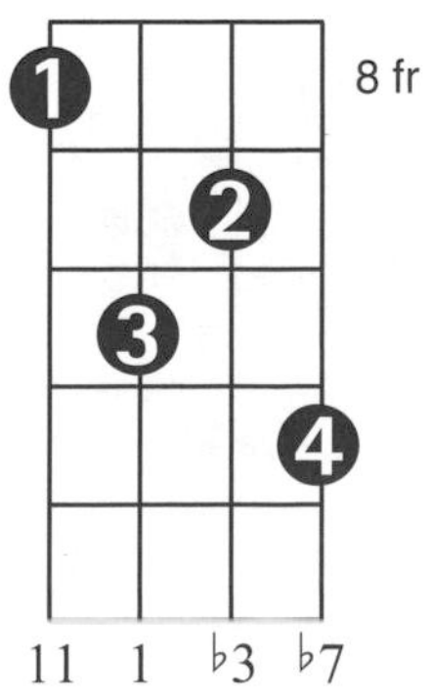

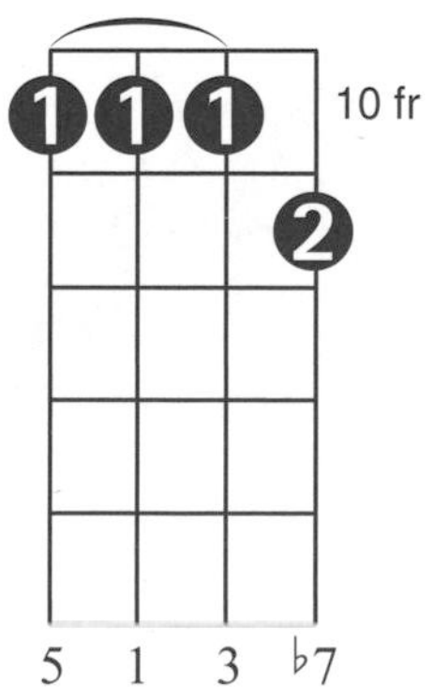

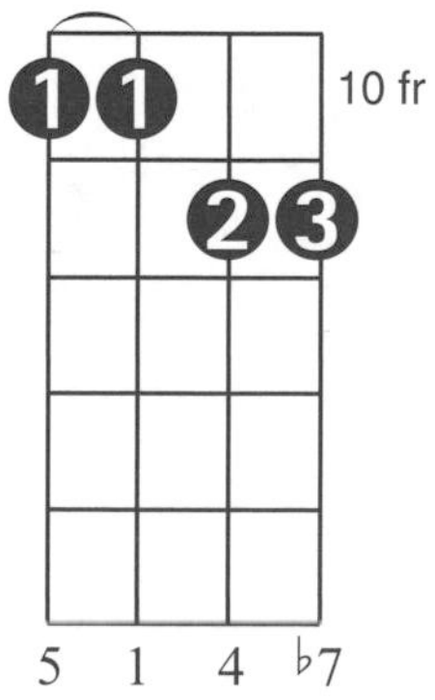

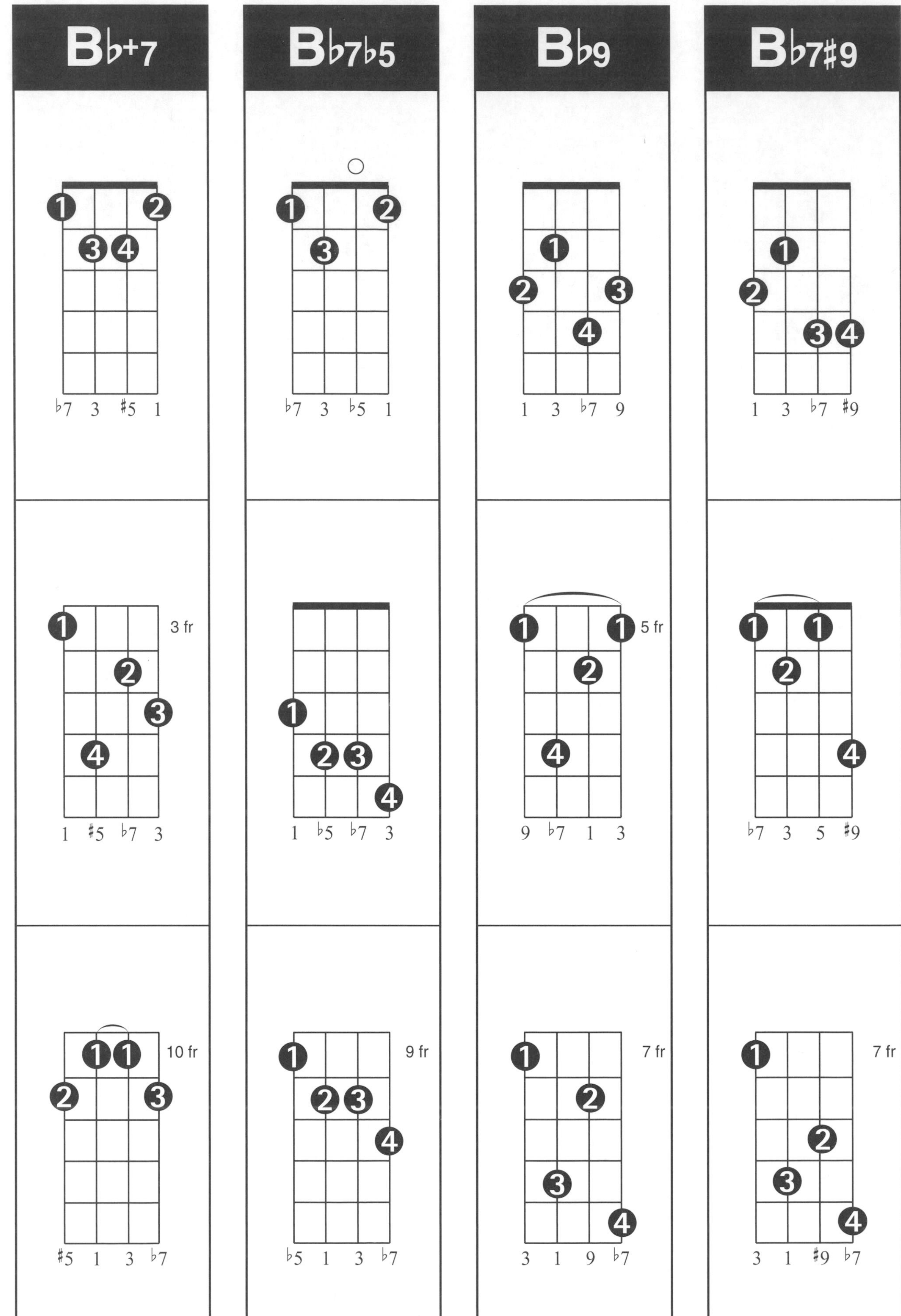
B♭+7
B♭7♭5
B♭9
B♭7♯9
♭7 3 ♯5 1
♭7 3 ♭5 1
1 3 ♭7 9
1 3 ♭7 ♯9
3 fr
1 ♯5 ♭7 3
1 ♭5 ♭7 3
5 fr
9 ♭7 1 3
♭7 3 5 ♯9
10 fr
♯5 1 3 ♭7
9 fr
♭5 1 3 ♭7
7 fr
3 1 9 ♭7
7 fr
3 1 ♯9 ♭7
B♭/A♯

B♭7♭9

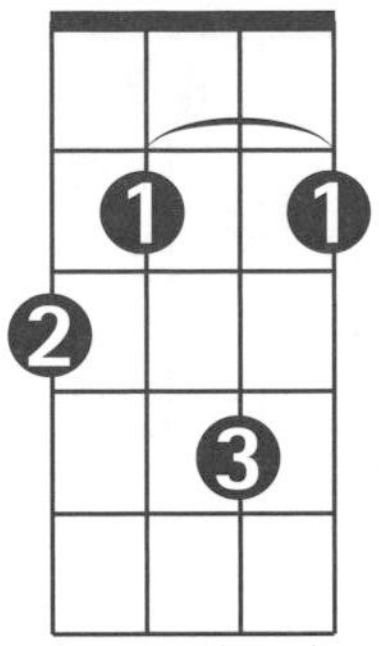

1 3 ♭7 ♭9

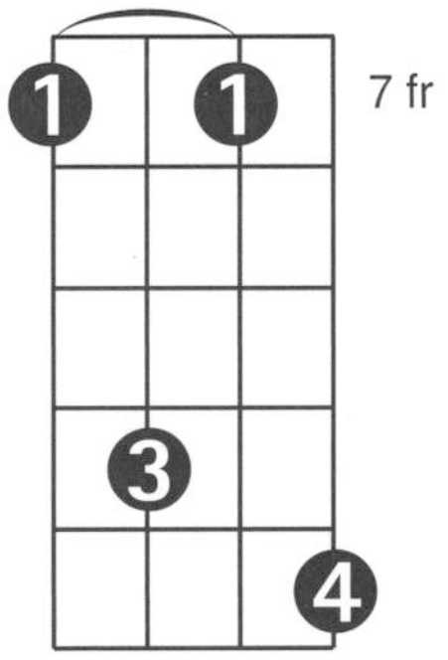

7 fr

3 1 ♭9 ♭7

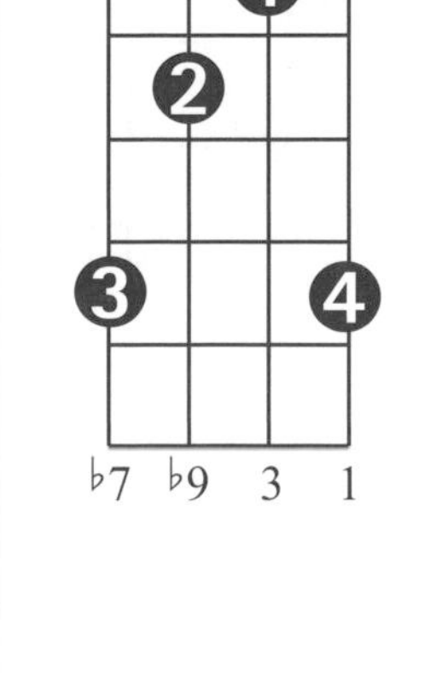

B♭11

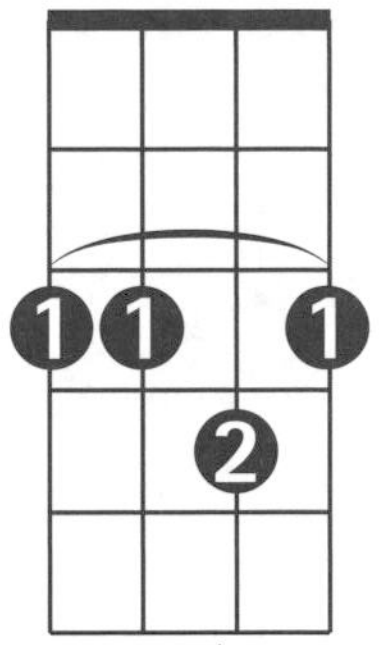

1 11 ♭7 9

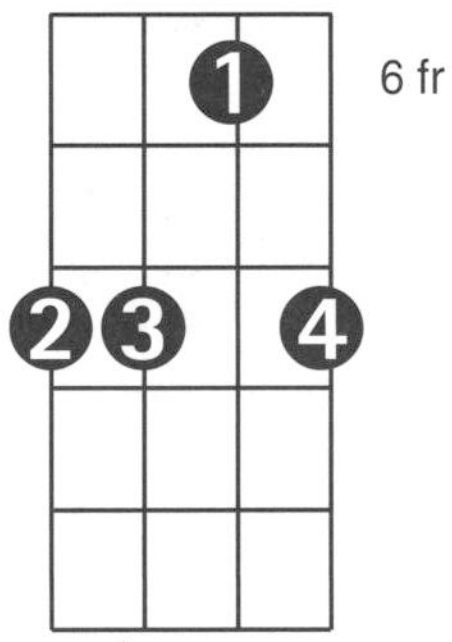

6 fr

11 ♭7 1 5

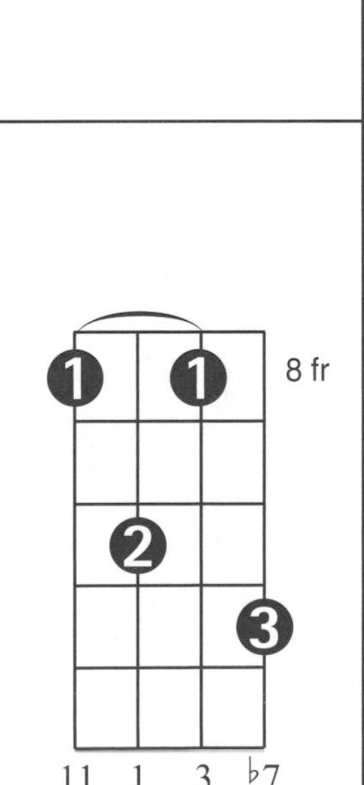

B♭13

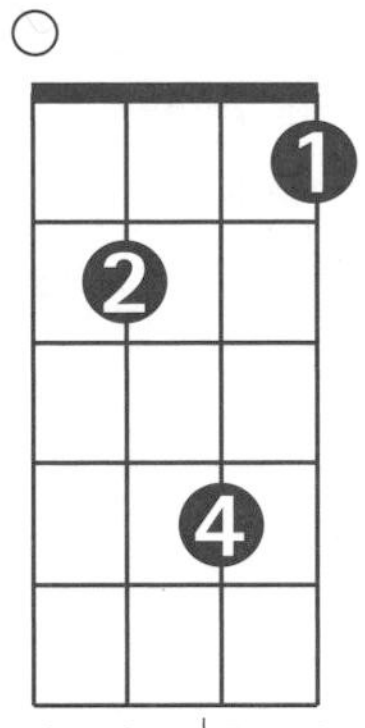

13 3 ♭7 1

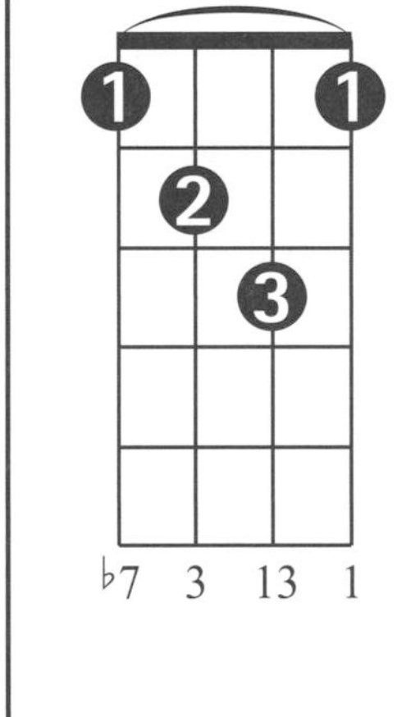

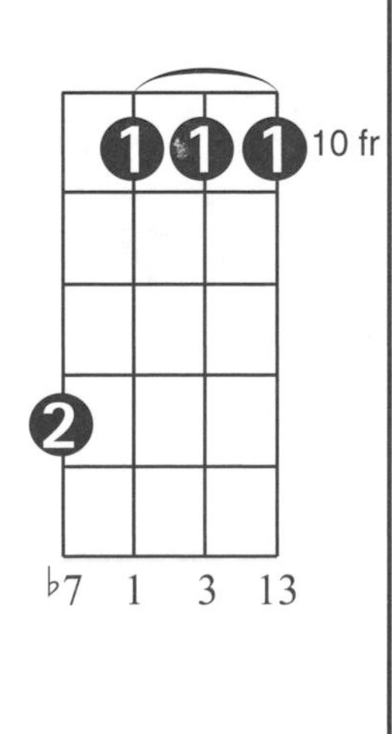

B♭°7

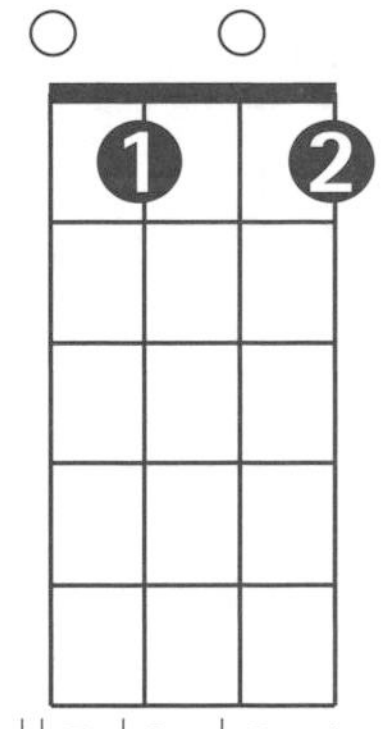

♭♭7 ♭3 ♭5 1

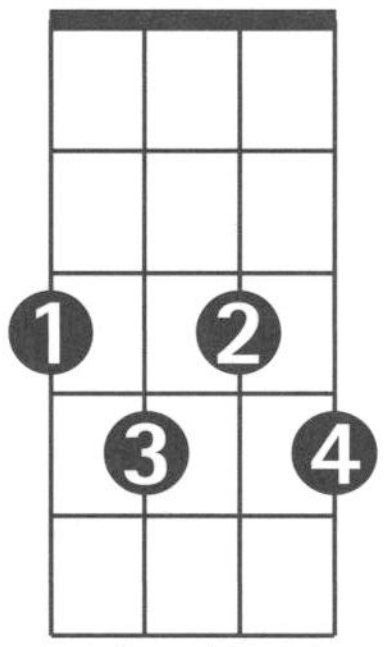

1 ♭5 ♭♭7 ♭3

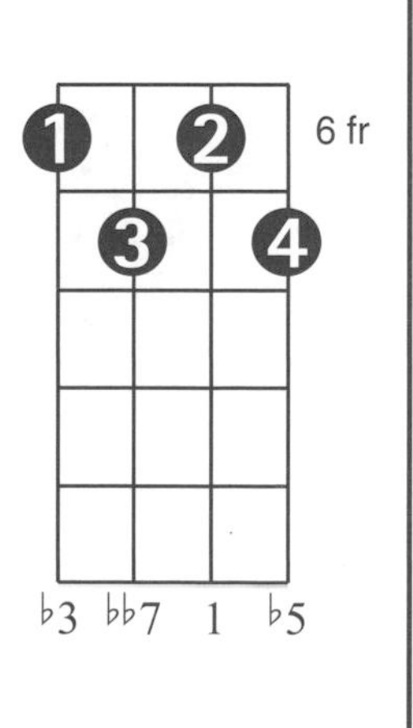

B

1 3 5 1

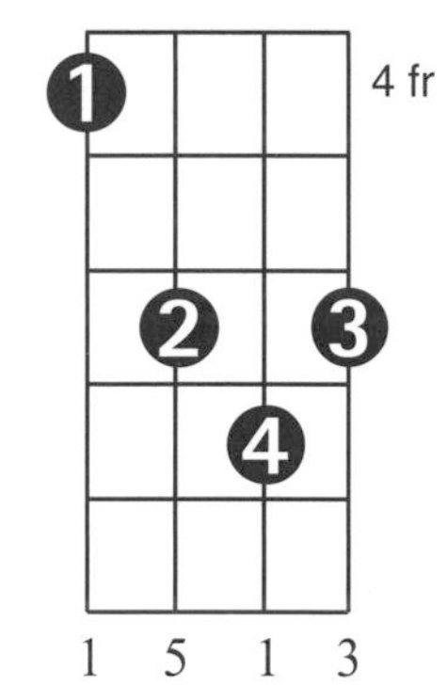

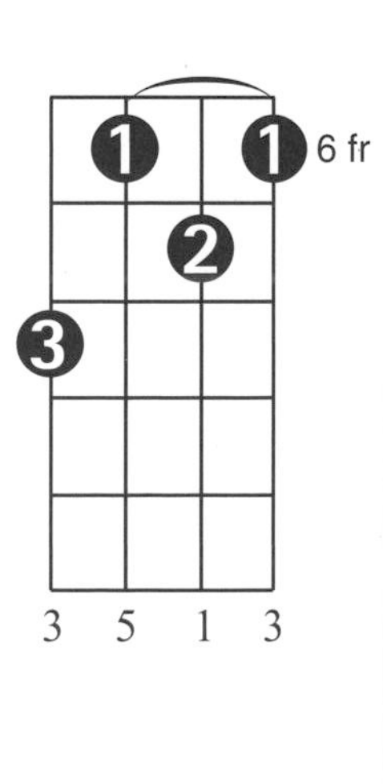

Bm

1 ♭3 5 1

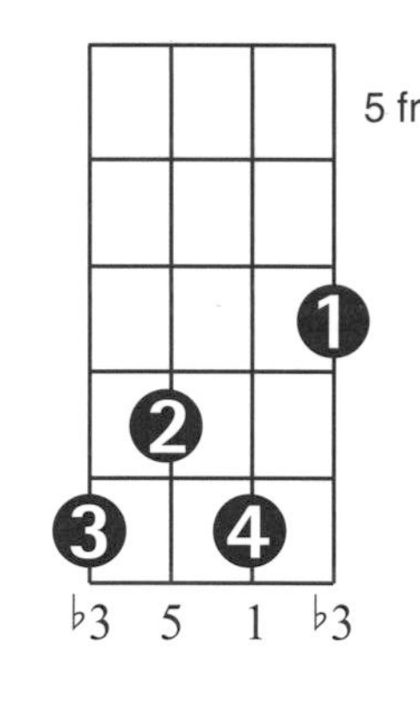

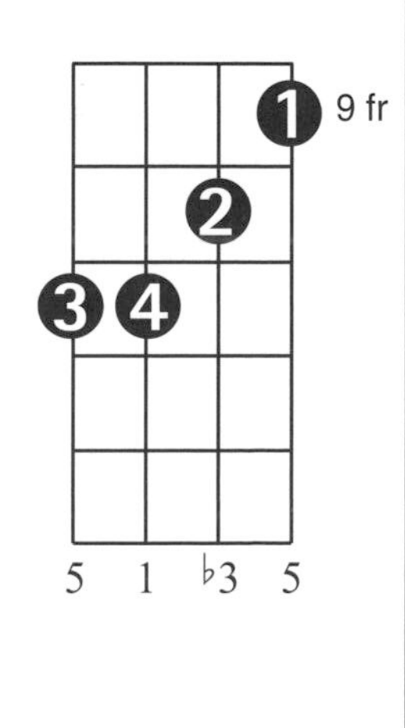

B+

○

♯5 3 ♯5 1

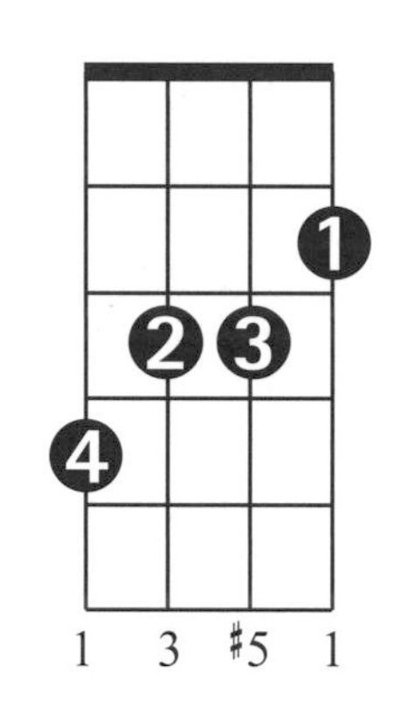

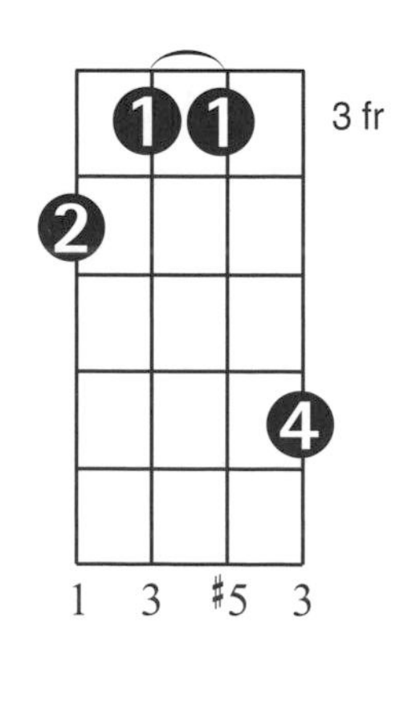

B°

X

1 ♭3 ♭5

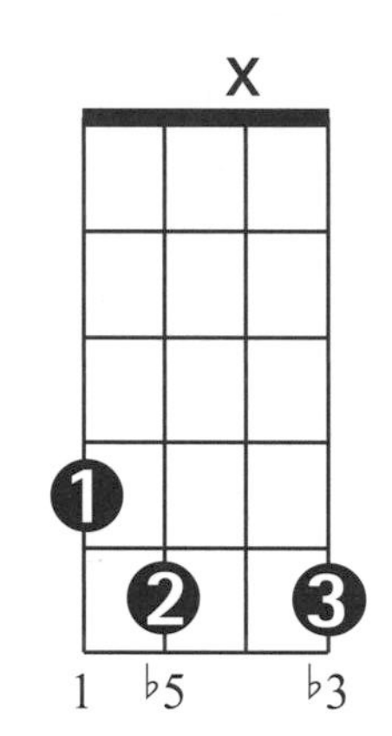

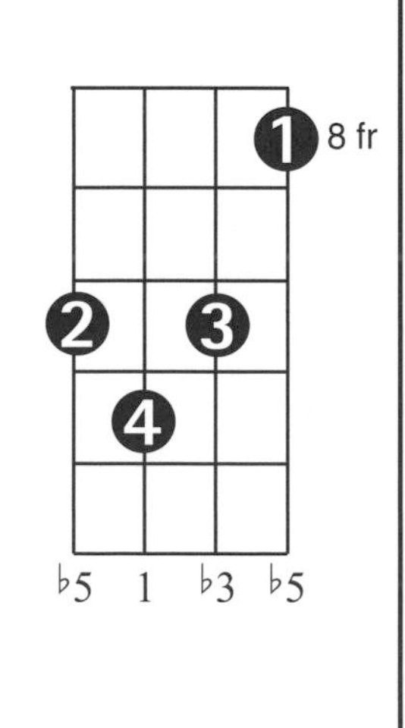

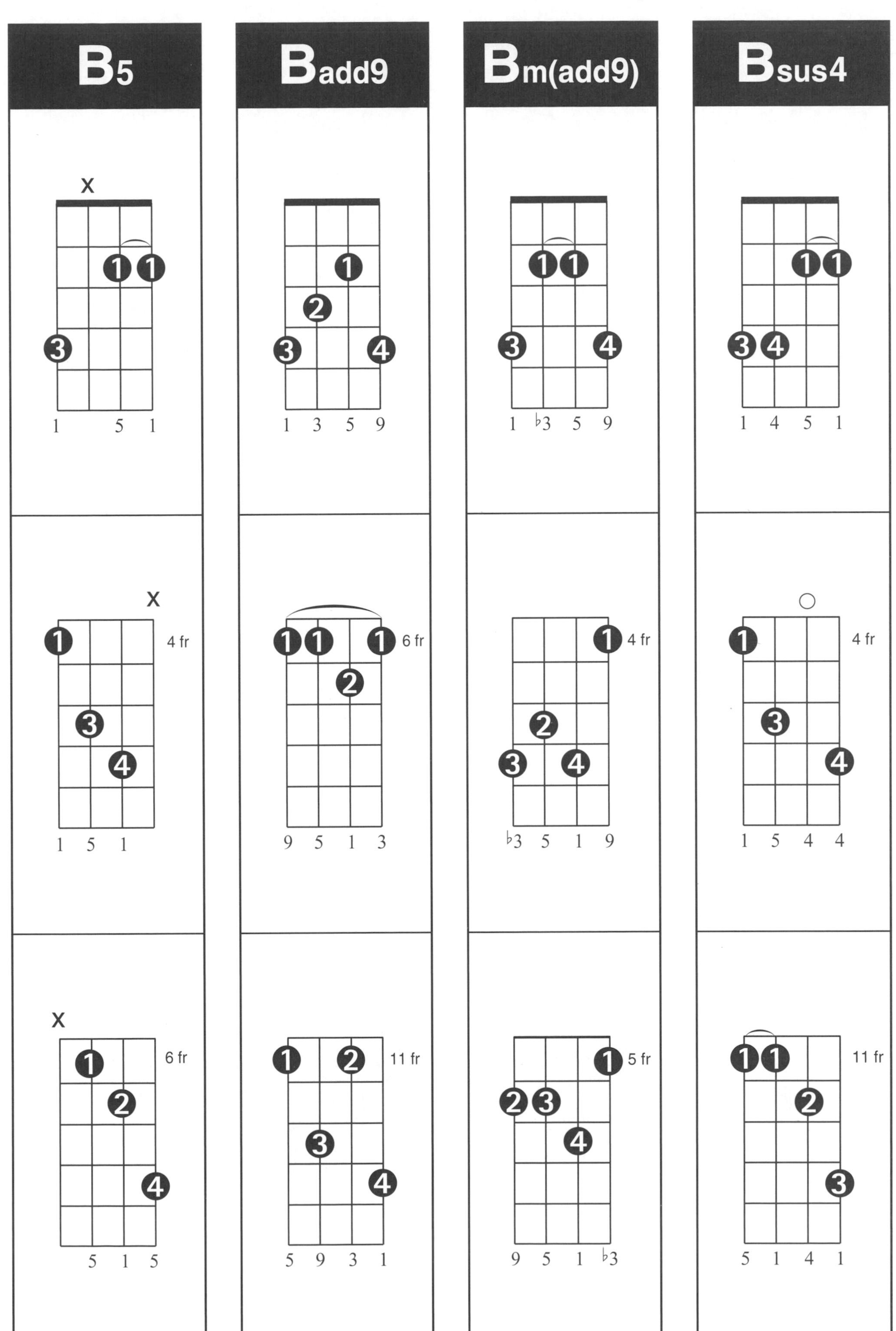
B5
x
1 5 1
x
4 fr
1 5 1
x
6 fr
5 1 5
Badd9
1 3 5 9
6 fr
9 5 1 3
11 fr
5 9 3 1
Bm(add9)
1 ♭3 5 9
4 fr
♭3 5 1 9
5 fr
9 5 1 ♭3
Bsus4
1 4 5 1
4 fr
1 5 4 4
11 fr
5 1 4 1

B

Bsus2	B6	Bm6	Bmaj7
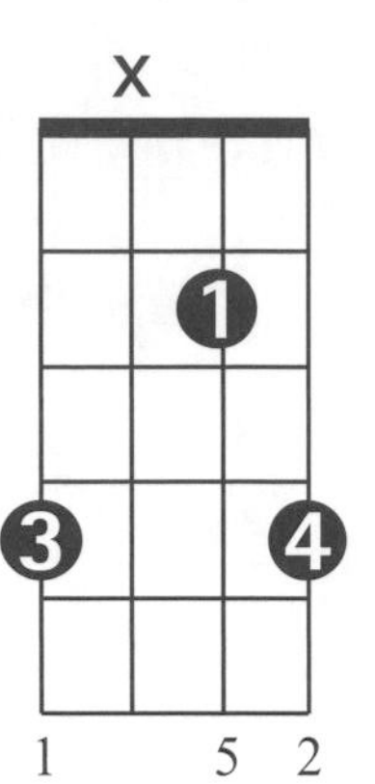	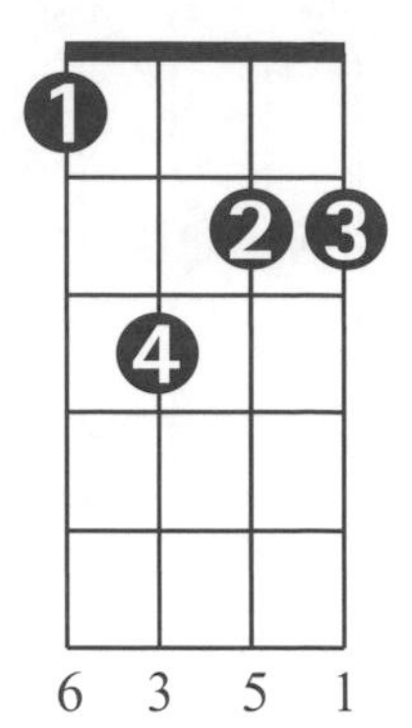	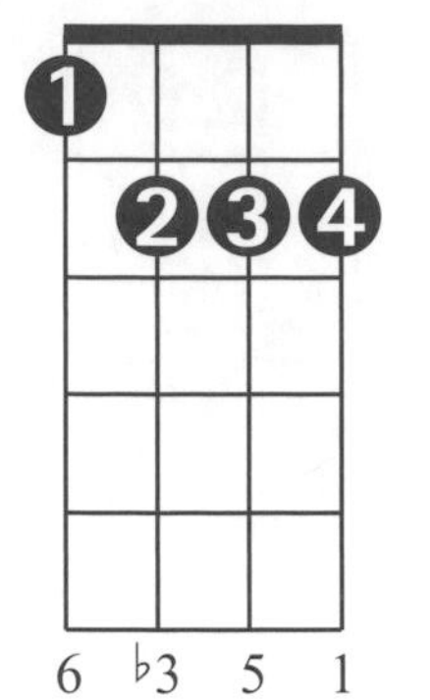	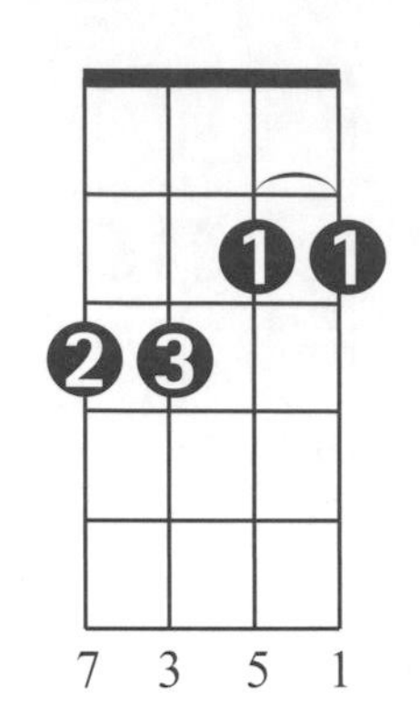
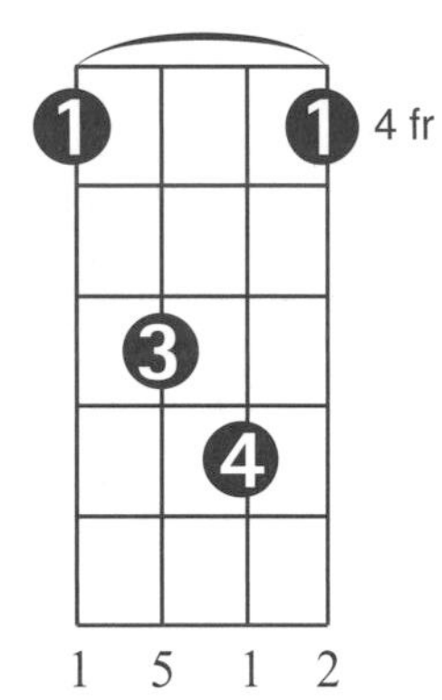	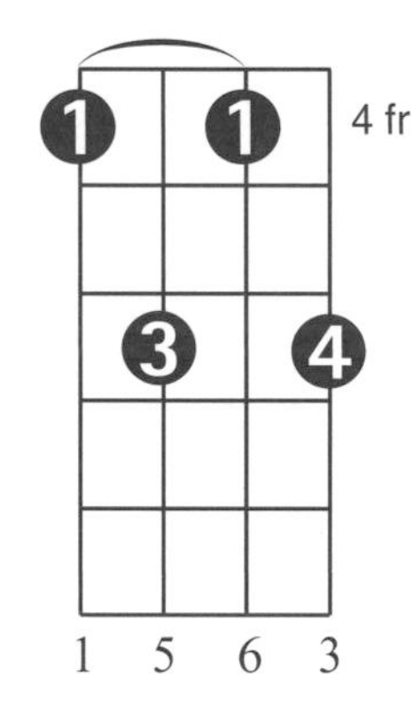	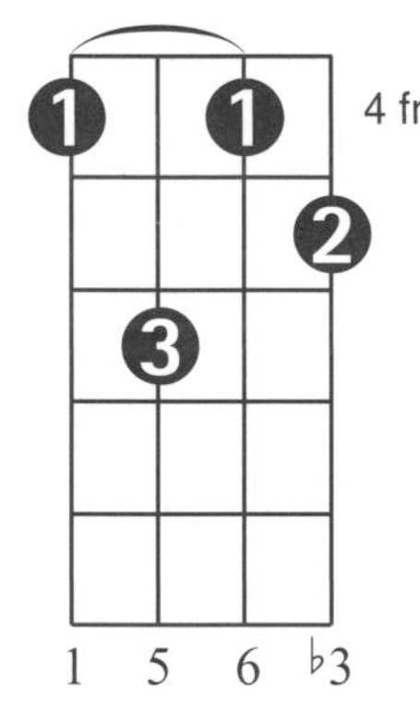	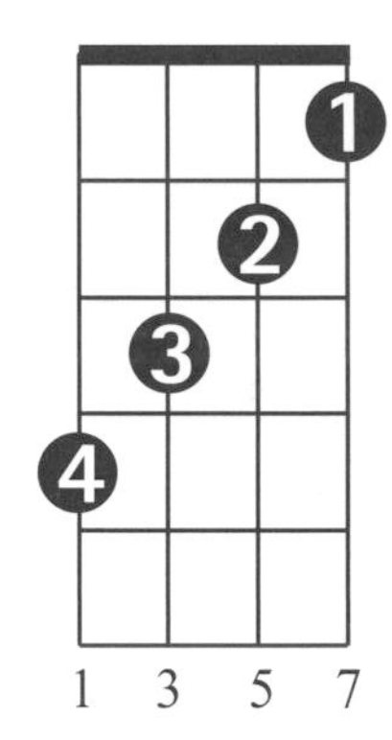
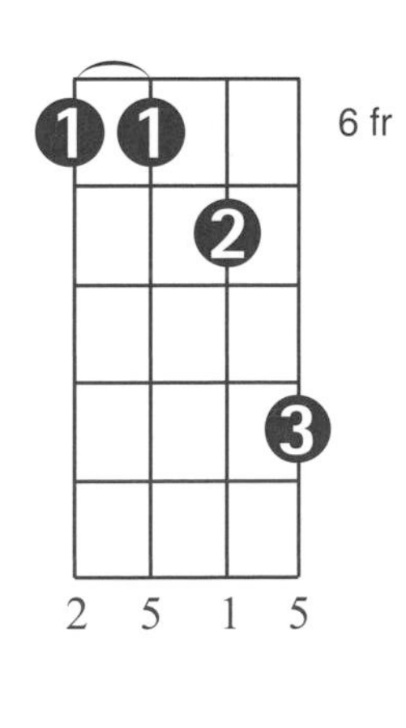	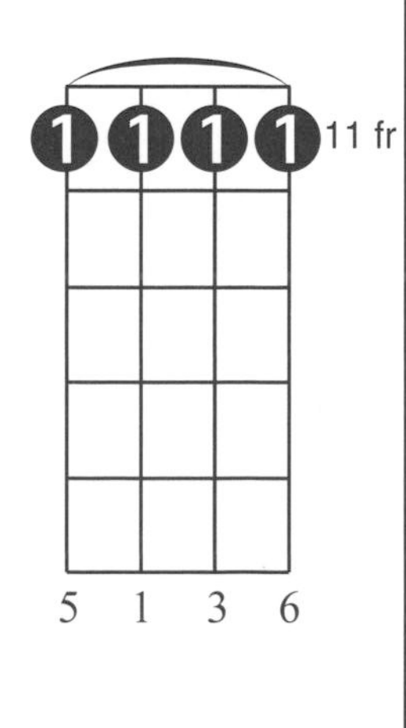	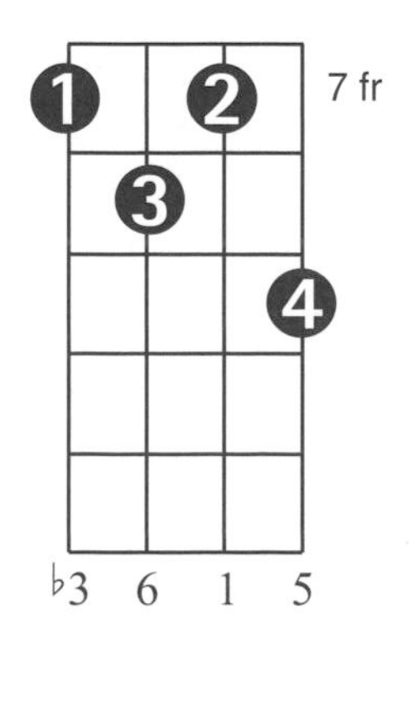	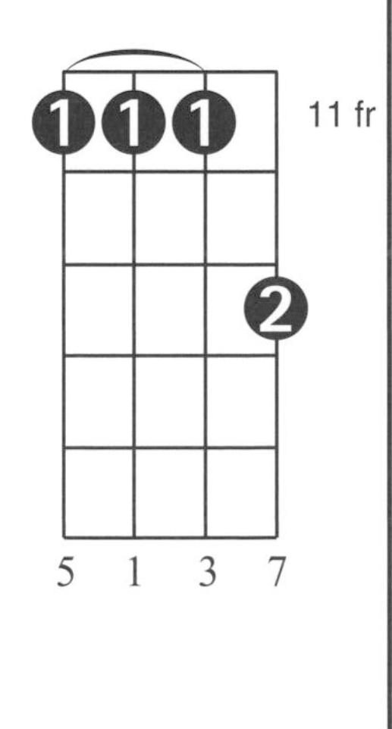

B

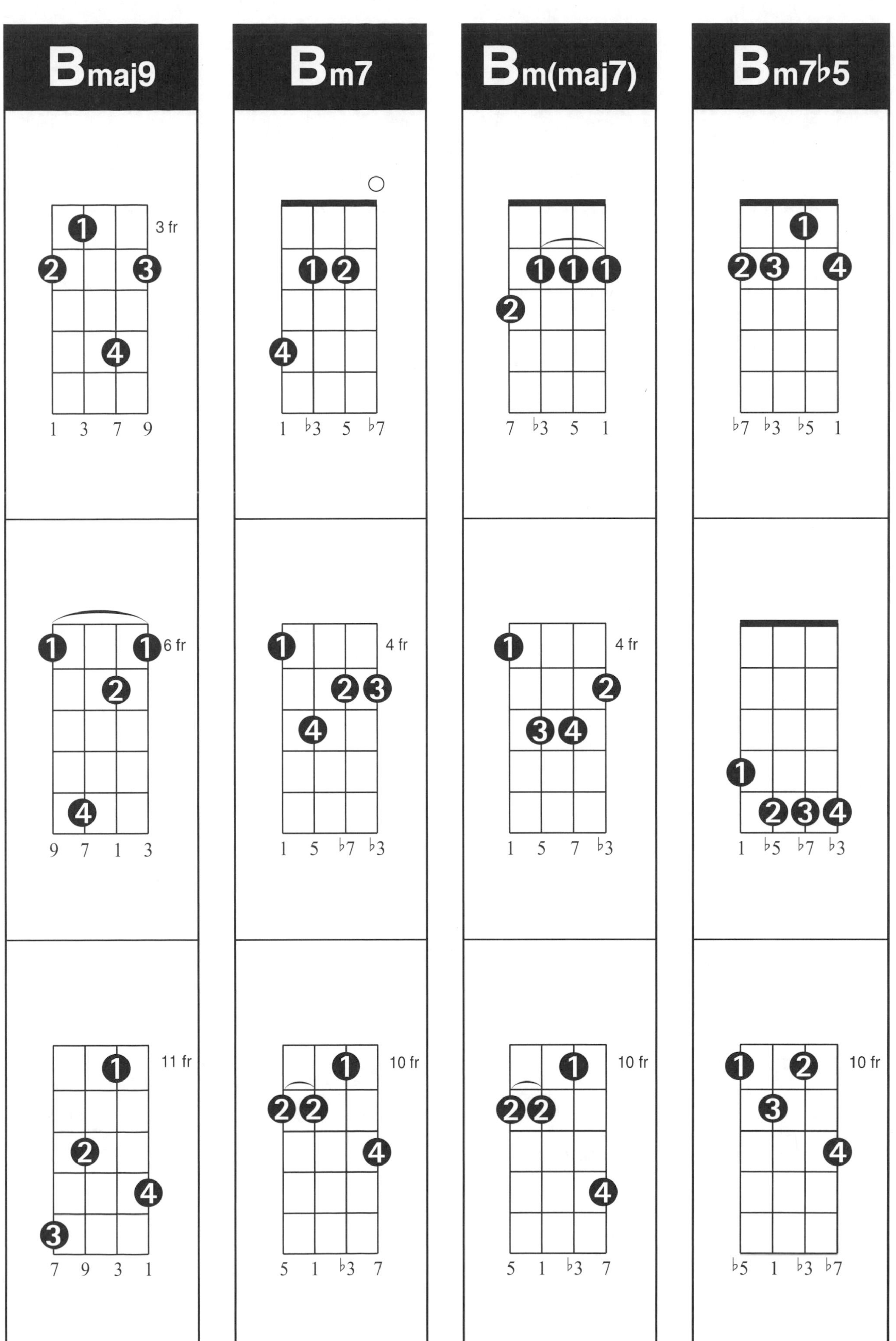
Bmaj9
Bm7
Bm(maj7)
Bm7♭5
3 fr
1 3 7 9
1 ♭3 5 ♭7
7 ♭3 5 1
♭7 ♭3 ♭5 1
6 fr
4 fr
4 fr
9 7 1 3
1 5 ♭7 ♭3
1 5 7 ♭3
1 ♭5 ♭7 ♭3
11 fr
10 fr
10 fr
10 fr
7 9 3 1
5 1 ♭3 7
5 1 ♭3 7
♭5 1 ♭3 ♭7
B

B

Bm9

1 ♭3 ♭7 9

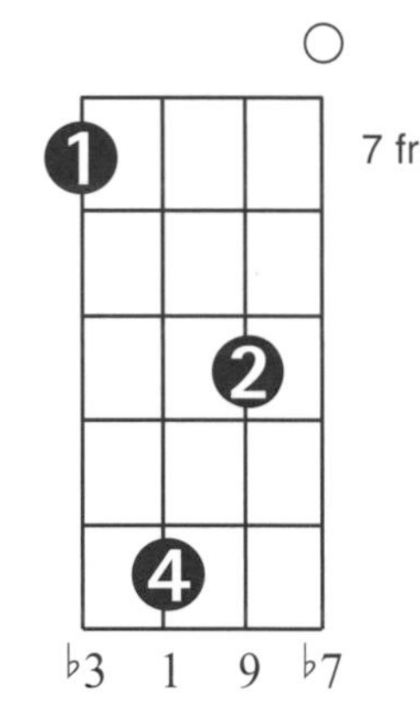

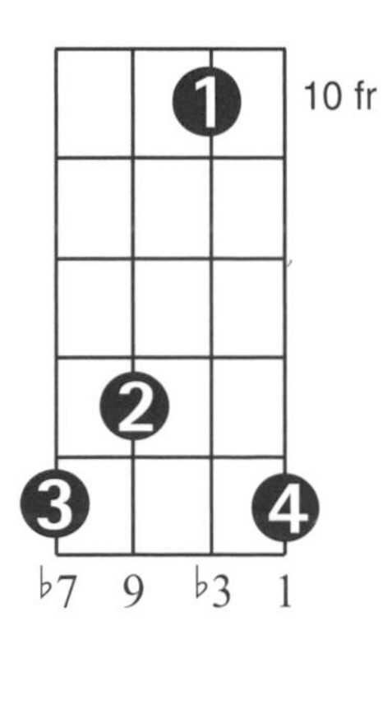

Bm11

1 11 ♭7 ♭3

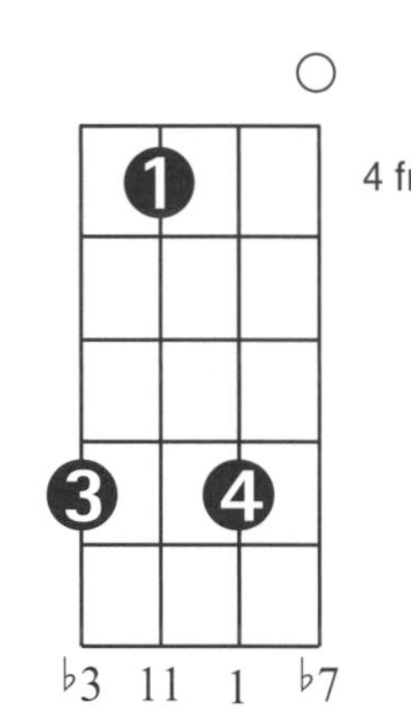

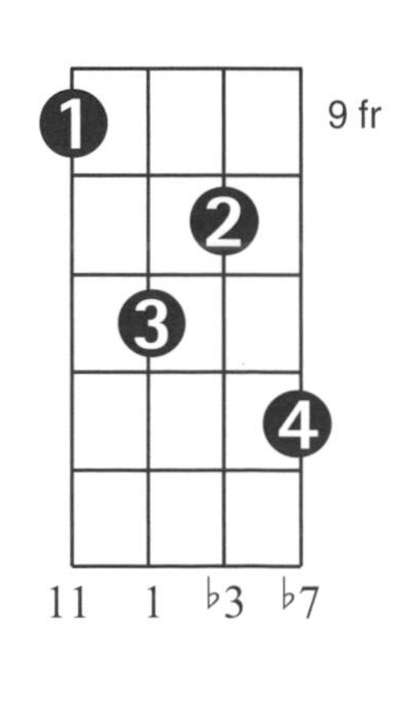

B7

♭7 3 5 1

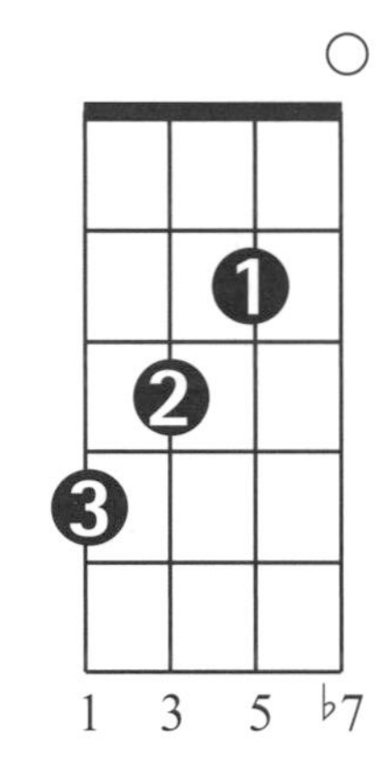

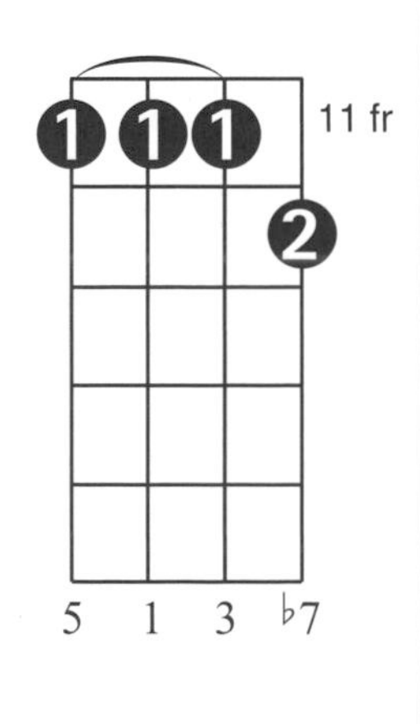

B7sus4

♭7 4 5 1

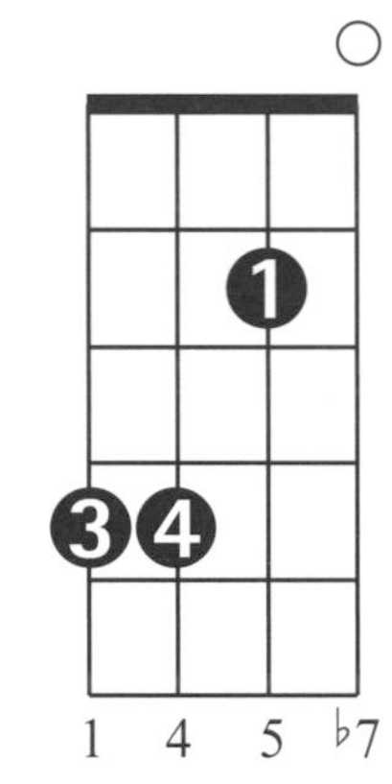

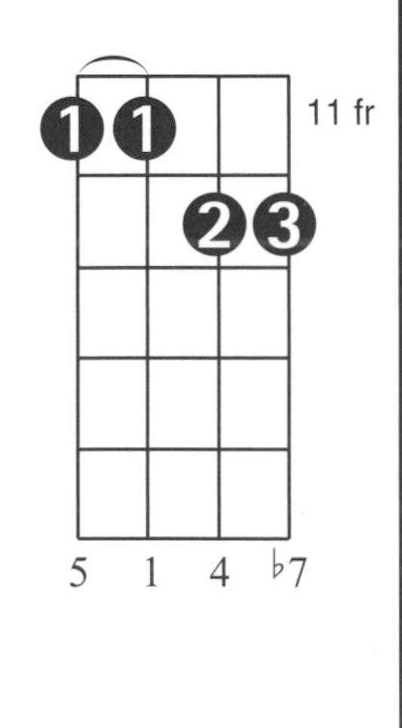

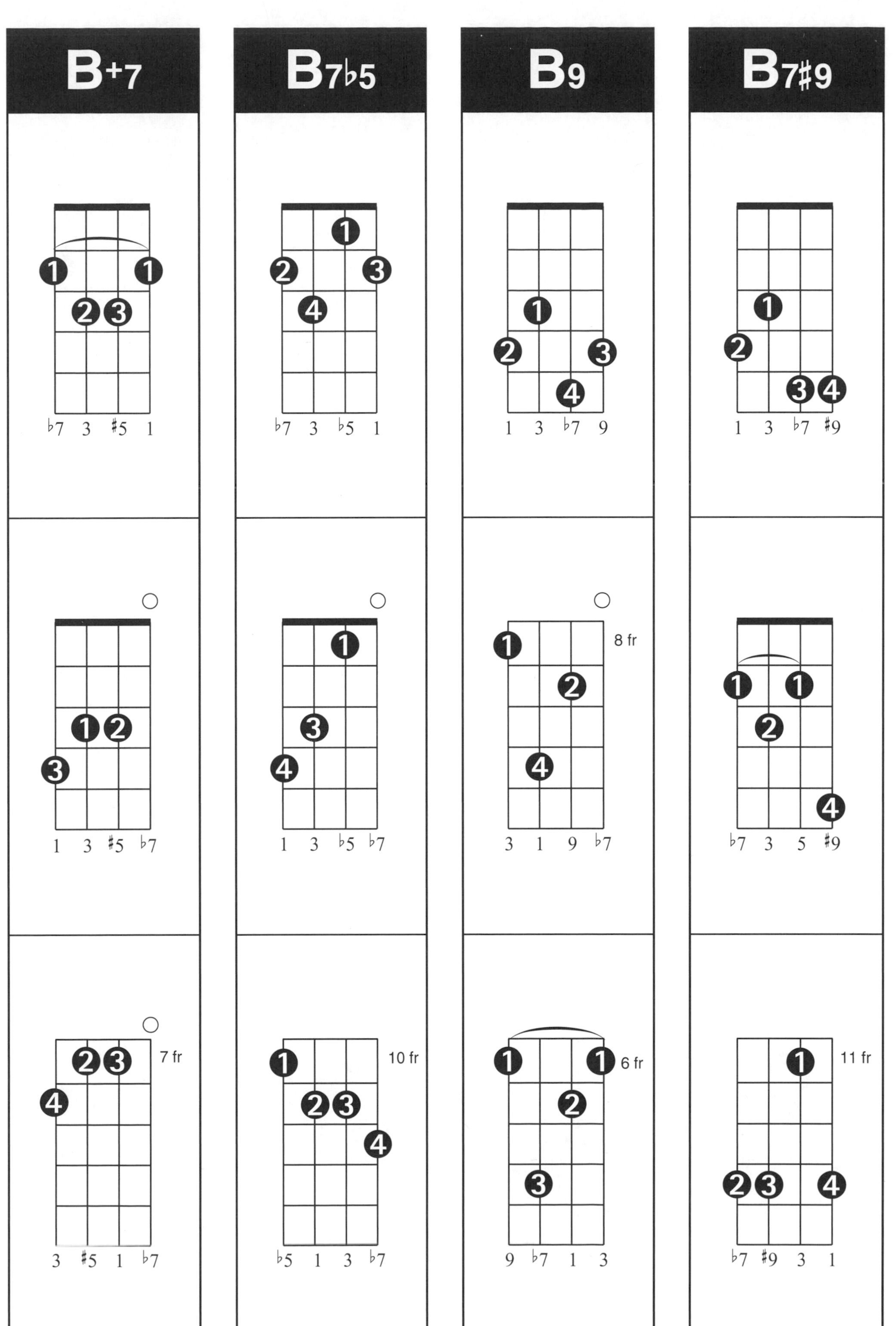

B+7
B7♭5
B9
B7♯9
♭7 3 ♯5 1
♭7 3 ♭5 1
1 3 ♭7 9
1 3 ♭7 ♯9
1 3 ♯5 ♭7
1 3 ♭5 ♭7
8 fr
3 1 9 ♭7
♭7 3 5 ♯9
7 fr
3 ♯5 1 ♭7
10 fr
♭5 1 3 ♭7
6 fr
9 ♭7 1 3
11 fr
♭7 ♯9 3 1

B

B7♭9

1 3 ♭7 ♭9

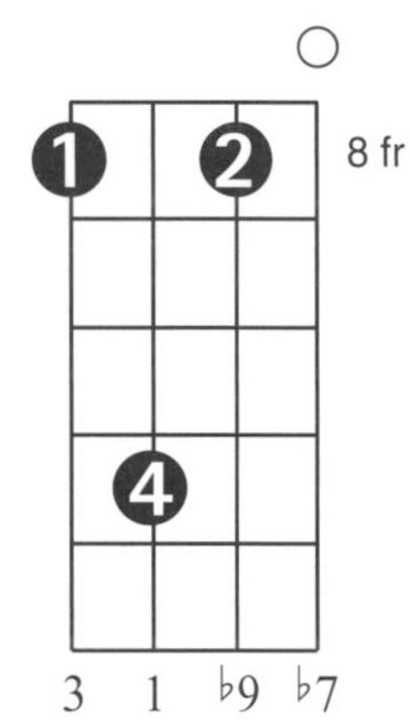

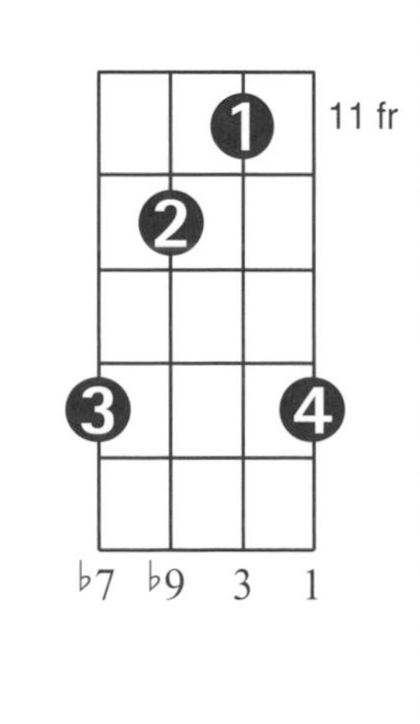

B11

1 3 11 ♭7

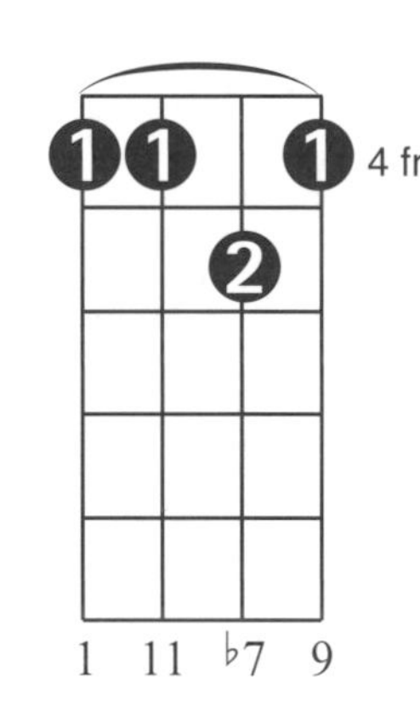

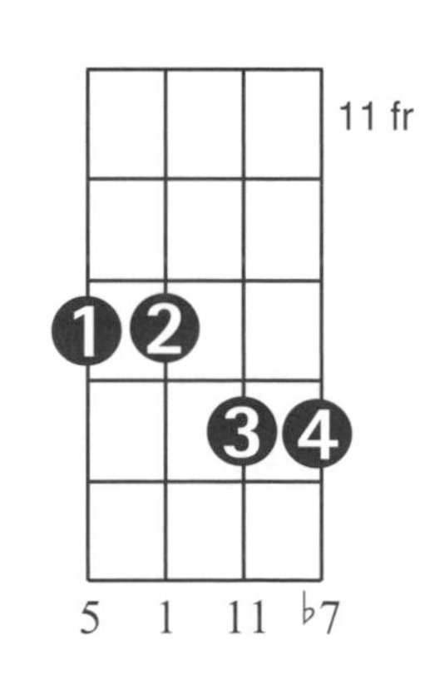

B13

♭7 3 13 1

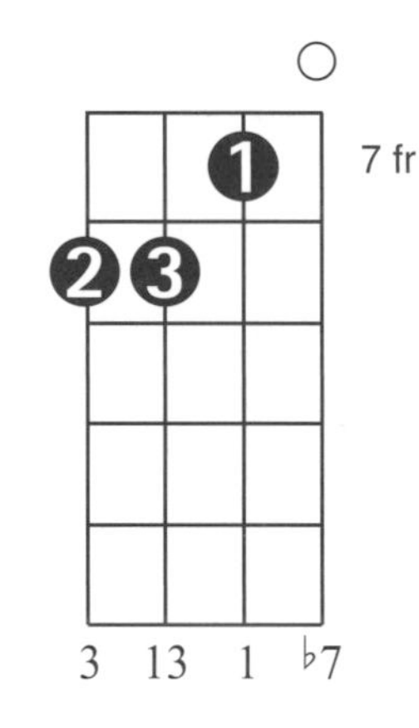

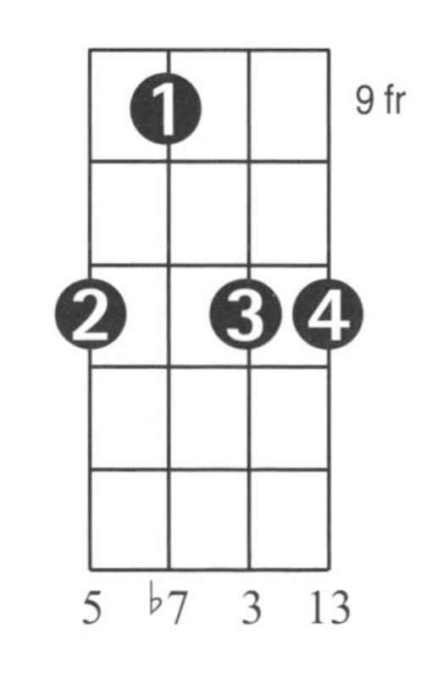

B°7

♭♭7 ♭3 1 ♭5

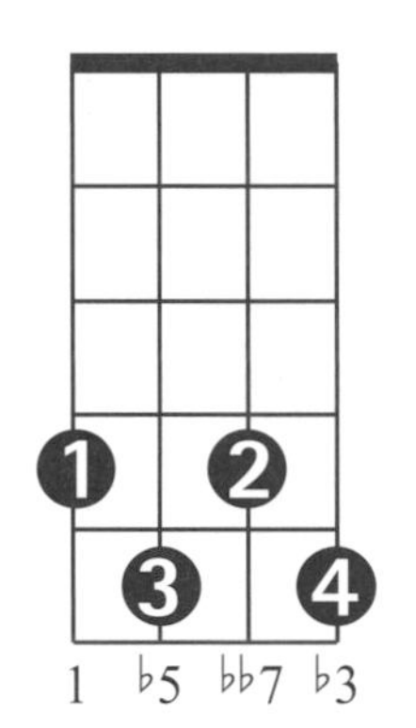

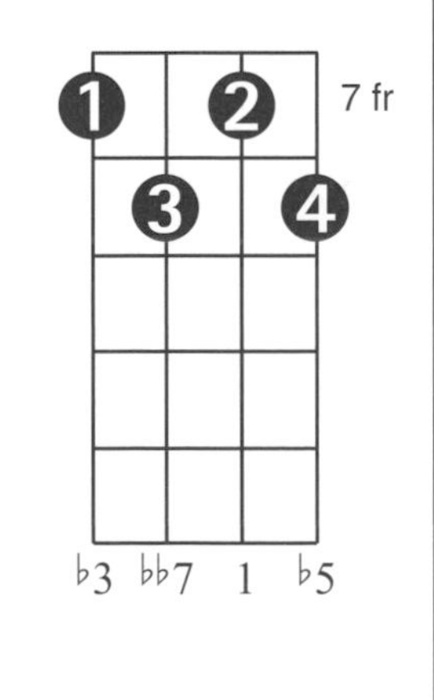

B

T
A
B

T
A
B

T
A
B

T
A
B

T
A
B

TAB
TAB
TAB
TAB
TAB